Also by John Barclay

The Blood of Others (book of poems)

In Preparation

Dinners, Dogs & Derrières

Amazing Mini-dramas

Diary of an Incomer (1989 – 1996)

SURFACE MALE

Round the World Without Flying

John Barclay

Matador
9 Priory Business Park,
Wistow Road, Kibworth Beauchamp,
Leicestershire. LE8 0RX
Tel: (+44) 116 279 2299
Fax: (+44) 116 279 2277
Email: books@troubador.co.uk
Web: www.troubador.co.uk/matador

ISBN 978 1848767 928

British Library Cataloguing in Publication Data.
A catalogue record for this book is available from the British Library.

Typeset in 11pt Adobe Garamond Pro by Troubador Publishing Ltd, Leicester, UK
Printed and bound in the UK by TJ International, Padstow, Cornwall

Matador is an imprint of Troubador Publishing Ltd

To my grandchildren, Oliver, Felix, Sam and Miranda – in the hope that during their lives the peoples of the world I travelled will learn to care for it as the home of all life, respecting its resources and sharing them peaceably.

Acknowledgements

My thanks to the small group of individuals who supported me while I was travelling and encouraged me to write this book. At the same time I should like to express my warmest gratitude to all those friendly and generous people I met in far-off places, who put themselves out to help me on my way.

I am greatly indebted to my daughter-in-law Mo Pickering-Symes for her painstaking editing and constructive advice, to Stephen Attridge for a check at a later stage and to Anne Attridge for proofreading and advice on linguistic matters. I'd also like to thank my son Edward Pickering-Symes for his input and considerable technical support throughout the project.

John Barclay

All photographs by the author

Front cover: The view from the owner's room on Theodor Storm, bound for Klang, Malaysia

Back cover: Enjoying a beer with some new friends in Vinh, Vietnam

'I'll put a girdle round about the earth . . .'
Shakespeare – A Midsummer Night's Dream

'Aircraft are the fastest-growing source of carbon dioxide worldwide and, although not yet at the same total level as power production or cars, are making an increasing impact. And not only are emissions from planes going up, they are also particularly damaging: carbon dioxide and other emissions released at high altitude cause between two-and-a-half and four times as much global warming as the equivalent pollution released at the earth's surface.'
Tony Juniper – Saving Planet Earth, Harper November 2007

'I believe that to be flipped through the air from one continent to another diminishes them both, in a way that is contemptuous of space. But contempt for space and time characterises the age we live in, and it would be foolish to deny it.'
Ted Simon – Dreaming of Jupiter, Little, Brown Book Group

'Experimental travel is travel with constraints, but at the same time you feel liberated from the limitations and expectations of classic tourism. By travelling with the constraints of experimental travel, you conversely have more freedom.'
Jöel Henry, co-author, The Lonely Planet Guide to Experimental Travel

'If you travel on your own, you need to be extra vigilant – there is no one else to look out for you.'
Mark Hodson – Independent Travellers Passport to Safer Travel, Thomas Cook Publishing

'By nature men are alike. Through practice they have become apart.'
Confucius

Contents

STEELING MYSELF

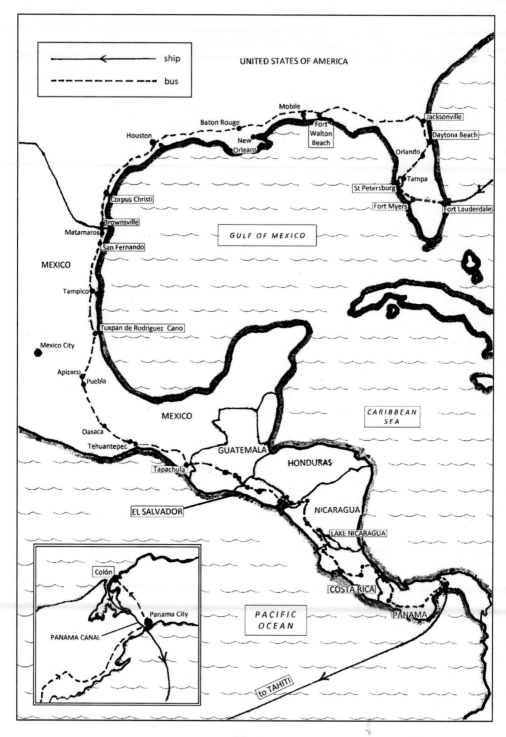

Map 1
Central America

1. The Atlantic

March 26 – April 2

My elder brother and I were building a car out of sand. I wandered off looking for sticks to make the gear lever and handbrake. I hadn't told anyone I was going and no one saw me set off so when my parents woke up to the fact that I was missing they became frantic – I was only five. My father contacted the police. Yes, they said, they did have a boy at the police station. But when my father turned up to collect me he could see it was someone else's child, so he went back to join my mother and my brother in a nightmare, the horror of which I only really understood when years later I became a parent myself. I, meanwhile, walked right to the end of the beach but found no stick, so I walked back again and carried on playing, unaware of the drama I'd caused.

From an early age, you see, I possessed the doggedness to pursue a simple challenge to the end and my taste for such ordinary adventures never left me. In my lifetime, with the growth of air travel and the revolution in international communications, our horizons have broadened, while the big issues of the planet have become the concern of people everywhere. Hardly surprising then that by the time I reached a stage in life when I had the freedom, the means and the time to go round the world, this had become an adventure I couldn't resist. But, in today's climate, to make even a segment of such a voluntary journey by aeroplane seemed to me out of the question. This turned the project into a challenge – to go round the full circumference of the globe without flying and, to make it more interesting, to do as much as possible by land.

I decided to start by crossing the Atlantic. That way I would leave the hardest part, traversing Asia, to near the end. While a complex and comprehensive worldwide network existed for those wishing to fly, passenger travel by sea was severely restricted. In planning my route I started by looking for vessels to take me across the Atlantic and Pacific Oceans. I discovered that the Queen Mary 2, which had already embarked on a round-the-world cruise, was taking bookings at a reduced rate for the final leg from Southampton to

Fort Lauderdale in Florida. I wanted to include Australia and New Zealand and I found that, circling the world, a British freight ship called M V Tikeibank, which accepted passengers for part voyages, would take me from Panama to Auckland. So I took a deep breath and booked both crossings. This took care of the two longest sea voyages. All other transport I would arrange as I went along.

My preparations consisted mainly of psyching myself up to the challenge. I arranged to have a private medical check. I got myself inoculated against tetanus, hepatitis, typhoid, yellow fever and rabies. I bought water-purifying and anti-malarial tablets. I persuaded my doctor to prescribe my blood-pressure tablets four months ahead. I obtained a traveller's cheque card and ordered a new PIN number for my credit card because I'd forgotten the old one. Unfortunately the new number didn't arrive in time so I couldn't use the card for drawing money, but I had a debit card so I thought I could manage. I arranged for a friend to keep an eye on my house. I bought a digital camera, a map of China and a pair of lightweight trousers with five zip pockets. I tried to learn a little Mandarin Chinese. I wrote an information sheet about myself and my travel plans, to show to anyone who questioned me. I had this translated into Spanish, Chinese, Kazakh, Russian, Ukrainian and Polish. I told people I would be away for six or seven months and just before I set out I made a last visit to my two sons and their families. I was as ready as I could be.

I took a train from London Waterloo to Southampton, where I had lunch in a pub with my friend Toby, before he drove me to Immigration. Feeling anxious, I entered the building carrying a rucksack and a small suitcase of clothes suitable for a luxury cruise. Weirdly, at no time could I see the ship I was joining. The passage from the embarkation hall through a great opening in the vessel's side was so smooth and well ordered that I'd no idea at what moment I actually did so. But I presumed I was aboard when I saw the red carpet, the two-metre-high flower arrangement, the photographer and the uniformed team waiting to greet passengers. A harpist was playing to calm our nerves.

The ship was spotless, the décor elegant – sumptuous but tasteful, recalling the grand days of passenger shipping. The main lifts had mirror-glass doors engraved in an art-nouveau design. My cabin was at the end of the longest, straightest corridor I had ever seen. My bed was 'super king' size. Half a bottle of sparkling wine reclined in a bucket of ice with two glasses beside it so I could enjoy a drink with myself. A notice said, 'Please retard your clocks and watches by one hour tonight.' As we steamed west we'd have to make the same adjustment most nights. Thus our days would average some 25 hours, reinforcing the leisurely tempo of the voyage. Another notice told me that in an emergency I should go to my cabin and fetch my lifejacket, something warm to wear, head covering and any medicines I was taking. The cabin had a screen to view the ship's own television programmes, including news of the liner's progress and the activities on offer.

I went up to the viewing deck above the bridge, where I could look along a line of staterooms with balconies, which resembled an endless seaside hotel. From this height a ferry crossing Southampton Water looked like a toy. I watched a pair of tugs slowly turn a freight ship. Three long blasts and a puff of smoke signalled that we were about to sail. I was on my way.

My ticket entitled me to eat in the main restaurant, which was vast and on two floors. I found myself sitting down to dinner with a retired civil engineer, his wife, an elderly Scots couple and their youngest son, whose role was to stop his somewhat senile father from driving his mother round the bend. I ordered cream-of-butternut-squash soup, followed by pan-fried loin of cod, under 'a green sauce' and augmented with sautéed spinach and mushrooms, followed by *crème brûlée* with ginger cream. Our waiter picked up a segment of lemon with one fork and with another squeezed a large quantity of juice straight onto my fish. The meal, presided over by this conscientious professional, was genteel, meticulous and drawn out. I slept well.

At breakfast I was greeted by a senior waiter, who detailed one of a line of junior waiters to conduct me to a large round table with a vase of fresh alstroemerias. The table filled up quickly. Immediately a well-drilled team sprang into action. I had never before accepted so many apparently sincere smiles.

Each waiter had his allotted task. The 'chair waiter' drew my chair back and slid it forward again as I sat down. In case I had arthritic wrists, he opened my artistically folded linen napkin and dropped it decorously on my lap. I'm sure if I'd neglected to do up my flies he would have leant forward and discreetly dealt with the matter. A glass tumbler had been placed upside-down in front of me but a 'glass-tumbler waiter' appeared from nowhere to turn it the right way up. A moment later the 'iced-water waiter' poured iced water into the glass tumbler, entirely unsolicited. I learned another day that if you declined the iced water, the iced-water waiter would turn the glass tumbler upside-down again for the glass-tumbler waiter to remove. The 'fruit-juice waiter' brought fruit juice. The 'coffee waiter' brought coffee and returned to top up my cup every time I had drunk to the halfway mark. Thus the pleasure of sipping really hot coffee came only once, at the beginning of the meal. A pastry waiter approached with a platter of pastries from which I chose a croissant, which turned out to be cold.

When I had finished my muesli someone I hadn't seen before, the 'empty-bowl waiter', took the empty bowl away. Then I had scrambled egg, American bacon, mushrooms and whole-wheat toast. I'd been allocated four mini-pots of conserves – honey, black cherry and two of sweet orange marmalade. The 'conserve waiter' caught me starting to open one of the mini-pots and hurried forward to do it for me, in case with all the attention I was getting my muscles had atrophied to such an extent that I couldn't manage the task myself.

The next day I had breakfast on another deck, where mercifully we were expected to help ourselves, although a disinfectant waitress stood at the queue with one duty – to squirt disinfectant onto the passengers' hands before they could get at the serving spoons. The food was superb.

You could easily get fat on the QM2, but there was plenty to do apart from eating. In the two months before I'd left England I'd tried to exercise every day to get fit for my odyssey. I tried to keep this up during my seven days on the ship. I never took the lift and sometimes climbed 12 flights of stairs just for the exercise. I saw an unfortunate woman so obese that she took the lift to go down a single flight. Walking twice round the ship was a kilometre, but I preferred swimming. The Pavilion Bar and Pool had been designed to create a holiday atmosphere. A glass roof kept the wind off and the greenhouse effect warmed the air. At certain times a five-piece West-Indian band played at the poolside. I saw an elderly couple dancing in the water. But once, when it wasn't busy, I managed to swim 125 lengths. That's only a kilometre because the pool was no more than 8m long.

I needed to unwind. Watching the grey sea speeding by and the ever-changing pattern of the wash brought a feeling of calm but relentless progress. However, I was still anxious. I wasn't afraid that I would fall in, but I often thought about what would happen if I did. I was alarmed to see a child near the rail, so I turned away. When I looked back the child had gone. It was all I could do to stop myself running to the rail and looking over the side.

The ship was a moving holiday resort. There was an attractive library with a large section on travel and travel writing, five copies of the 'Da Vinci Code', even a tiny section on poetry. There were computers with hand-sanitising wipes known as 'Sani-hands'. At a cost I sent a short e-mail message to my family and other supporters who would follow my progress around the world.

The entertainment programme was extensive. One evening I found myself standing on the balcony of the Grand Lobby listening to a string quartet. I'd a splendid view of the viola player, the only female in the ensemble, an animated woman with a sensuous mouth, dyed blond hair and a cleavage that caught my eye and could surely have caught a tennis ball. They played a jumble of arrangements drawn from the popular classical repertoire and 'songs from the shows'. Passengers on their way to the main restaurant stared like tourists. A woman stood behind the players while her friend photographed her from in front of them, the camera flashing in the musicians' faces as they played. A small glass lift kept arriving from the upper decks and announcing itself with a loud ping, irrespective of whether the quartet were offering an arrangement of Leroy Anderson's 'Concerto for Typewriter and Orchestra' or the 'Meditation' from Massenet's opera 'Thaïs'. But the four had been booked to play and play they did, with as much determination as the orchestra that went down with the Titanic.

During their break the cellist told me they were from Ukraine and known as the 'Paradiso Quartet'. Like the two violinists he wore very pointed shoes, a fashion I was to see again when eventually I travelled through their country. When I told him I hoped to visit Ukraine, he said I should go to Kiev, which had 'beautiful buildings'.

An English pianist appeared three afternoons during the week in the nightclub, garish with its blue lighting and points of red light along the edges of the steps. I expected a magician to appear in a flashy suit with an assistant in a sequinned leotard. Instead, a small man in a lounge suit introduced a middlebrow programme with some homely chat, getting off his stool and coming down to the front of the stage to talk to us. He referred to Mozart as 'moo's art' and joked about the austere accommodation suffered by the artists in the lower decks. His actual playing was expressive and polished, marred only by the rumble of the engines and the hum of the air conditioning. A woman sat near the front doing a crossword. The trouble with onboard entertainment is that none of the audience has paid for it. We had, of course, but not item by item. There were a few of us like me who really enjoyed piano music; the rest were there because they had nothing better to do.

Other pianists provided background music around the ship and the harpist, who had plucked us aboard, sometimes took the place of the Paradiso Quartet. I once saw her harp being wheeled into position, still in its cover, which resembled a giant black mitten. Like the Ukrainians the harpist had a repertoire of pieces we know in other contexts – 'The Girl I Left Behind Me', 'Moon River', Beethoven's *Für Elise*. She rocked with the harp as she played. But it's a gentle instrument that cannot compete with background noise. She was a serious, shy performer, who didn't make eye contact with her audience. I hoped the ping of the lift didn't drive the poor girl mad.

One night a Liverpudlian comedian was top of the bill – after a brilliant comedy juggler from the States.

'It's lovely to see such a young audience!' said the comedian.

This went down well with us oldies. But then he ran through all his jokes about the problems of old age. Considering that some of his audience had chosen a luxury cruise because it was the only sort of holiday they could physically manage, this was too near the bone. Another night a feisty young woman gave a recital of songs from operas and the shows. She looked good in a little black number but she had more nerve than talent and waved her arms about like Shirley Bassey.

Two of the best items were morning talks in the theatre by Rita Moreno, the Puerto Rican star, who had played Anita in the film of *West Side Story*. Now 75, she was a trim, charming and vivacious woman with an engaging sense of humour. Like most dancers she moved beautifully. Her prepared talk was a bit pedestrian but once she began taking questions the audience hung on her every word.

These events were included in the price of the cruise but if you wanted to spend more money there were plenty of ways of doing so. The ship issued smart cards so that passengers only had to pay one bill when they left the ship. There were bars, a casino, an art gallery with art auctions, permanent shops selling gifts and prestigious brands of clothing, and a high-class market with a different theme every day, such as jewellery or gifts. For a fee, professional photographers would immortalise you in front of large photographic backgrounds of the ship.

The passengers had clothes for every occasion – outfits for walking round the ship for exercise and outfits for merely sauntering. The dress code on the QM2 was precise. Some evenings the main restaurant was 'black tie' or 'business suit', neither of which I had with me, but I managed to get in wearing a navy blazer and charcoal trousers. Once I'd tucked my legs under the table no one could tell.

Passengers ranged from those who could easily afford a five-figure sum (excursions extra) for a suite with a balcony and admission to the top class of restaurant – down to me on a cut-price standard cabin for one week only. The richest people seemed the glummest, as if life had dealt them a mean hand, when clearly it hadn't. Some people looked happy and I saw couples walking on the deck hand in hand, but I felt uncomfortable among so many people for whom money seemed to be the most important factor in their lives. Meanwhile, the Filipina maid who cleaned my cabin told me she worked 10 hours a day and seven days a week – and would do so until December when her contract ended.

Along one corridor there were seats in pairs. A couple appeared, hoping to find somewhere to sit. The only free seats were two separate single seats. I offered to move to let the couple sit together. They thanked me profusely.

'That was kind of you,' said the woman I then joined.

'It was the obvious thing to do,' I said.

'People are surprised by kindness,' she said, which suggested to me that in her world kindness must have been in short supply.

At lunch one day I got into conversation with a Yorkshire couple. The man was called Gordon. He ran a pub with his wife, built houses and had a sign-writing business. The pair's down-to-earth attitude and direct way of speaking was in contrast to the arms-length manner of most of the passengers. In the evening, I found myself drawn to a karaoke session at a mock-English pub next to the casino, called the 'Golden Lion Bar'. I was wondering where to sit when I spotted Gordon and his wife. He beckoned me over to join them. A barwoman came along. I produced my smart card, but Gordon insisted on paying so I put my card away. A minute later I absent-mindedly put his card in my pocket as well.

'That's my card!' said Gordon, rather bluntly but without a trace of indignation.

'I'm sorry,' I said, 'I don't know what made me do that.'

Gordon asked me if I was going to enter the Karaoke competition and passed me a long list of songs to choose from, but there wasn't one I felt confident to tackle. Another couple joined us, also from Yorkshire, also in the pub business. He was called Roger; I can't remember the wives' names. I never saw two women so utterly contented, at ease with themselves and full of fun. Gordon's wife said she was bored on the ship, but did so cheerfully, as if she didn't take it personally.

The barwoman came round again. I got out my card, but this time it was Roger who insisted on paying. The karaoke became a contest between the American passengers and the British, who far outnumbered them. Gordon had put his name down to sing, so although I hadn't much in common with the forthright foursome I felt I had to stay and support him.

'Everyone in the north of England is friendly,' I said carelessly.

'That's not friendly,' said Gordon, 'it's normal!'

When his turn came, he stood up in his dark suit, held the microphone as if he'd done it a few times before and paced himself nicely with the machine. 'I Did it My Way' was just the song for such a self-made man.

'I don't want to retire,' he told me. 'I'm scared of not having to go to work in the morning.'

Roger sang 'That's Life', a song I'd never heard before. I drank more beer than I had for a long time, although far less than the publicans, and I only paid for one round. I got to bed well after 1am.

In all, I sampled a mere handful of the delights offered on the ship. I blundered into the spa but came out straight away. I never found the gym, but then I wasn't looking for it. I didn't play chess or bingo, enter the paddle-tennis tournament or the golf competition, or take a refresher course in contract bridge. I didn't visit the planetarium. I watched no film. I declined to attend Mass, the cognac-and-armagnac-tasting session and the lectures on carriage driving and avian flu. I kept out of the needlework-and-knitting circle and I let the 'pirate party' walk the plank without me.

I did, however, sign up for a 'singles lunch', which was just that – a lunch. No member of the staff was there to greet us, no 'welcome drink' and no chance to mingle before we sat down. I found myself on a table with nine women. One was a friendly German called Ursula, very striking with her hair dyed a bright auburn. Another woman told me she loved dancing. She said the ship provided 'dance hosts', men available to partner single women on the dance floor. Her knee was 'a mess', she told me, but she managed to go to the evening dances and the tea dances as well. She spent the morning recovering with rest and ice packs, before going through it all again. I learned that there was another category known as 'gentleman hosts'. I wasn't clear what their role was but I spoke to one on another occasion, a sullen American.

'Two more days!' he said.

'You sound as though you've had enough,' I suggested.

'I have.'

'You've done the whole world cruise?'

'All eighty days. It's too long. I won't do this again.'

I told him of my plan to cross the States and, when I met him later in the library, he found an atlas and showed me different routes I could take from Florida to Mexico.

'Trains are not a good bet in the States' he said. 'It's not like Europe – freight gets priority. And keep away from Mexico City!'

Not the first warning I'd had about Central America!

I went to investigate the 'Queen's Room', a small ballroom with chandeliers steadied with horizontal wires so that they wouldn't go mad when the ship rolled. This was the venue of a talent show to be held the next day. I thought I'd enter and perform one of my monologues. That evening I decided to have one drink before an early night. I thought that if I went to the casino bar I'd have less chance of bumping into Gordon and Roger. It would be difficult to have only one drink with them. But the casino bar did not have the beer I wanted, so I returned to the Golden Lion. Gordon wasn't in his usual place, but in case he came in I went round the other side of the island bar. I bought myself half a pint of beer and stood watching a silly game in which three men on a platform were being questioned about their other halves.

'What is your partner's bra size?' the organiser was asking.

I thought this to be in poor taste so I finished my beer and walked out – straight into Roger and his wife.

'Have you seen our friends?' he asked me.

'No, I haven't. I've been watching this silly game. Can I get you a drink?'

'No, no,' said Roger, 'it's all right.'

And he and his wife marched towards the bar. For some reason I followed the pair. I was still a couple of paces behind them when they spotted Gordon and his wife in their usual place. They must have come in while I was on the other side of the island bar. Now it looked as though I'd been lying to Roger or hopelessly unaware of people around me. I panicked, did an about turn and walked away down the corridor, hoping desperately that Gordon and his wife hadn't seen me. I kept on walking until I got to my cabin, where I shut myself in.

They were decent, kind people, a breath of fresh northern air, but I wasn't on their wavelength. They were so straightforward – I couldn't expect them to understand my neurotic behaviour. I decided to lie low for the rest of the voyage. Now I didn't dare enter the talent competition, because with their liking for karaoke Gordon and Roger could well be there. I felt safe in the library. I took my meals at one of the buffets, choosing a seat tucked away in a corner. How was I going to get round the world if I were scared of two harmless publicans?

On the last night I went onto the Observation Deck. We were passing between two islands of the Bahamas. There was a full moon and a warm wind. A man with binoculars gave a commentary. He agreed with me that we could see 'Orion's Belt' but an American, who'd appeared with his two sons of about 13 and 11, told them it was 'Andromeda'. An American woman was taken in by this and the father began to show off to her in front of the boys. Then, to anyone who'd listen, he held forth on the pronunciation of the name of the British port where many of us had joined the ship.

'It's *Sou – thampton* he declared, 'not *South Hampton!*'

The next day I woke at 5.30am. I heard the engine go quiet after almost a week of steady throbbing. Then I heard the noise of the engines return and keep altering and I guessed that the QM2 was being manoeuvred into the vast berth reserved for her. At 5.50 the engines went quiet for good. Then I heard a sound like someone tapping on an empty lorry, followed by a deep, metallic rattle like chains being unwound. At 6.15 I pulled up my blind. It was dark but bit by bit I made out blocks of flats, other buildings, cranes, palm trees and eventually coaches lined up on the quay. The spookiest thing was seeing the lights of the QM2, including the flashes of passengers' cameras, reflected in the portholes of a container ship. After nothing but sea for a week, it seemed a hectic scene. The sun was rising over the ocean. The ship's TV announced that we had gone 3,926 miles in 6 days 13 hours, at an average speed of 25 knots. I calculated that I had completed one-fifth of the way round the world – the quickest and easiest segment of my journey. I was anxious about entering the unknown, particularly Central America, but after a week of hyper-luxury I couldn't wait to get onto land.

2. The United States

April 2 – 17

The passenger-liner company had required me to book my first night in Florida before I left England. By the time I'd found my way to the Sea Club Resort Hotel I was very hot, so after checking in I decided to take a dip in the Atlantic. I had no one to guard my clothes while I was in the water so I put on my swimming trunks in my room, slipped the door key in the pocket and walked across the road to the beach like that. The sea was too boisterous for swimming but I had an excellent buffeting.

From the hotel you could see ships approaching and leaving the harbour. I spotted the QM2, off on its next voyage. I had dinner at a restaurant enjoying a splendid position on a street corner, across the road from the beach – very lively for a Monday. There was a warm breeze and the moon was a pink disk balanced on the horizon. It rose obliquely, passing behind a lamppost. Wonderful to be sitting outside at 8.30pm in the first week in April!

I was due to visit relations of a friend of mine, religious people who lived in Jacksonville, 300 miles up the coast. I had time first to see a little of Florida and decided to cross to the west coast. At the bus station I saw other travellers go straight up to the ticket desk and lean against it, so I did the same.

'I ain't servin' no body,' the woman behind the counter announced over the public address system, 'until you wait in lahn. Wait behind the mark until a hagent colls you!'

I was the only person to move behind the line. Nobody got served, but as a fearless Brit, with centuries of empire building behind me, I found myself taking charge.

'She wants us to wait in line,' I pointed out. 'We won't get served otherwise.'

Someone moved behind me. The others followed. The woman served me first. The seats on the Greyhound bus were comfortable, the vehicle had air conditioning and the windows were big. Once out of the town it wasn't long before we entered a flat, marshy region with dense vegetation. I took this to be one of the Everglades.

American birds are different from European. I kept seeing a white chap like a small heron and a black fellow with a neck like a cormorant's. There were numerous water lilies. Glossy black cows stood in the water, drinking it. People were fishing from flat-bottomed boats. There were little car parks with slipways for launching boats from trailers.

A white American joined the bus and sat next to me. He saw that I'd put my hat in the pocket on the back of the seat in front.

'Don't put it there,' he said. 'You'll forget it. I've done it myself.'

'Thanks,' I said.

'I'm on my way to Lakeland – see my sister. Haven't seen her for four years,' he told me. 'I'm 51. My wife is 15 years older than me. She encourages me. I'm gonna water the garden, feed the fish. I've got the time, you see. I'm a glazier, but I've been laid off.'

'There seems to be plenty of building going on around here,' I pointed out. 'I'm sure you'll get some more work.'

'Mebbe. I'm Michael, by the way.'

'My name's John.'

We shook hands.

'What do you do?' he inquired.

'I was a company speechwriter, but I'm retired. I've got the time now for travel.'

'Do you like American music?' he asked, untangling the leads of his personal stereo. 'If this works I'll let you have a listen for a bit.'

'Thank you,' I said, eyeing the apparatus. 'I'm not used to these things.'

'It's easy. They just clip on your ears like this.'

It wasn't my kind of music, but I listened to a whole number before handing the earpieces back.

'Thank you very much. In England we are familiar with a lot of American music,' I said tactfully. 'So much of your culture comes to us.'

He put the ear pieces in his own ears and opened a book called 'Why Do I Fall Asleep After Sex?'

Maybe his sixty-six-year-old wife had given it to him. The bus station in Fort Myers, like most I passed through, had no town plan and no map of the bus network, but I found a cool public library, where I discovered that we were on the delightfully named River Caloosahatchee. When I came out of the building it was still very hot and I was glad to find the well-named 'Oasis restaurant'. The day's special was 'goulash with side salad and garlic toast'. It was more like a spaghetti Bolognaise made with macaroni and sugar. The garlic toast was soggy with oil.

I was carrying some of my things in a carrier bag with a hole in the bottom. In a little general store, the guy serving gave me two new bags, and I bought a better map of Florida. I pressed on in the direction of the Caloosahatchee, hoping to find a cool place under a tree, but I ended up in the grounds of the Royal Palms Yacht Club. I sat in a shady porch. A doorman came out.

'How ya doin', sir?' he asked gently.

'I'm just repacking my bag,' I explained. 'Could you tell me where I would find a hotel?'

From now on I would be finding accommodation as I went along. He gave me detailed instructions, consisting mainly of street names. In the States these are difficult for a pedestrian to find because the signs are placed high up and with motorists in mind. I was soon reduced to following my nose. The local industry seemed to be litigation, so densely populated was the area with attorneys-at-law.

I didn't see a single hotel so I decided to cut my losses and take a bus on to St Petersburg – not the one in Russia, although that would have had more to offer in the way of culture. The Florida version is on the coast and, lying as it does between the Gulf of Mexico and Tampa Bay, has water on three sides. The bus approached it from the south on a raised road known as 'The Skyway', which soared above the Bay on a great hump-backed suspension bridge, which allowed ships to enter from the Gulf. I walked from the bus station into the centre of St Petersburg. The cheapest hotel I could find was $167. For this I had two double beds. I sorted my kit on one and slept very well on the other.

In the morning I saw a skyscraper so high that, when I'd counted six stories from the bottom, my old fear of heights returned and although I was standing securely on a very flat sidewalk, I had to give up the exercise.

In downtown St Petersburg there was an upmarket shopping mall. I needed something more durable to replace my new carrier bag. I went in to a classy luggage shop in my floppy white sun hat, travelling trousers and walking boots.

'You lookin' for anythin' particular?' a woman asked graciously.

'Yes. I'm looking for … a bag,' I said.

'We have this on special offer.'

It was a lady's bag, bigger than a handbag – very practical with an adjustable carrying strap, zips, visible pockets, hidden pockets and a purse secured to the inside of the bottom by 23 cm of thick thong. The bag was well made, of leather. The only thing wrong with it was that it looked worth stealing, but I could soon fix that. I bought it and as soon as I got a chance I scratched it, marked it with biro and dragged it through some wet mud. The bag did good service for the rest of the trip.

I took a bus to Tampa, on the other side of Tampa Bay. At Tampa bus station I went up to the counter.

'Do you have a map showing the Greyhound services throughout Florida?' I asked.

'No, sir. We just go city to city.'

'Do you have a local map of Tampa?'

'No, sir.'

So I set out blindly. A woman in a uniform labelled 'Security' saw me looking around.

'How you doin', sir?'

'I'm looking for somewhere to stay.'

'Well, there's the Salvation Army Church,' she said. 'Go that way, two blocks down, turn left and it's on your right.'

It wasn't – as far as I could see. But I was thrilled that she had taken me for a hobo. If I were an object of pity, I would be less likely to be robbed. I might be kicked to death, but I wouldn't be robbed. I was looking ahead to Central America. Whenever I did this I got a tight feeling in my chest, for me a sure sign of anxiety.

After twenty minutes I found and bought a map of the City. I wandered all over before stumbling on the '(Marriott) Embassy Suites'.

'Have you a room for one person?' I asked, 'for one night?'

'Sure.'

'How much is it?'

'$219,' the receptionist said.

'That's a lot for one person,' I protested. 'Do you know anywhere cheaper?'

'You could try the Tampa (Marriott) Waterside – over there.'

'Thank you very much.'

The cheapest room in the Tampa (Marriott) Waterside was $240.

'That's too much,' I said.

'You could try a couple of *standard* hotels,' the second receptionist suggested. 'I'll write down the details.'

She sent me a good half-mile – a bad half mile, more like – back to where I'd started my hunt. There were two hotels in the same block: the Residence

(Marriott) Hotel and the Courtyard (Marriott) Hotel. Both charged $219. According to my map there were no more hotels to try. The (Marriott) empire seemed to control all the hotels in the area; they could charge what they liked. What made me angry was the fact that the receptionists were quite happy to pass me round the chain, when I might just as well have settled for the first one.

I checked into the Courtyard (Mariott) Hotel, went up to my room, only to find that it wasn't a room – it was an apartment! The living room had a desk, telephone, table lamp and socket for a laptop. There was an L-shaped sofa to seat three, a television and a standard lamp – in Marriott hotels, I guess, standard lamps are standard. There was a small dining table, a fitted kitchen area, an empty refrigerator big enough to hold the carcass of a sea lion, a freezer, a dishwasher, a sink, two cooking rings, cupboards with no food and a coffee maker with no coffee. The double bedroom had a dressing area with a built-in basin. There was an entire separate bathroom.

Somebody slid a receipt under the door:

Room charge – studio	*$219.00*
State Occupancy Tax	*$15.33*
Convention and Tour (local tax)	*$10.93*
Total	*$245.26*

At breakfast the next morning a family on a nearby table had their strawberries and yoghurt on toast – with a side serving of scrambled egg. Half the guests looked well fed; the other half looked overfed.

I decided to proceed via Orlando but not to try to stay there as it was the Easter break and the place would be swarming with families doing Disney World. At Orlando bus station everyone had to vacate the bus while the driver took it for servicing. As I queued for refreshments, I spotted Ursula, the German redhead I'd met at the singles lunch on the QM2.

'Zis ees amasing!' she exclaimed. 'You vair on ze sheep – and now you are heeah! I can't get over eet!'

I didn't find it amazing. Everybody on the ship was going to Florida. Here was I in Florida and – blow me down – if one of the people, who had been going to Florida with me, happened to be at one of the State's larger bus stations. But it was nice to see her again. We exchanged details and went our separate ways – she to New York, I to Daytona Beach.

This resort boasted greyhound racing and a speedway. It also offered budget hotels and I soon found The 'Raintree Motel'. The nearest I'd ever got to staying in a motel had been watching Alfred Hitchcock's thriller 'Psycho' – you know, with the shower scene, where Janet Leigh's blood runs across the floor. The room was $45 – a refreshing change after Tampa prices, and the shower had no blood at all.

In the morning I was washing my hands after using the loo. I turned round and was alarmed to see, through a window in the bathroom door, a strange man looking at me, with his trousers around his ankles. Then I realised that the 'window' was actually a mirror and the strange man was me. When I was dressed I threw open the curtains. They came right off the rail and fell on the floor. I opened the window letting a pleasant breeze in through the mosquito mesh. Because I had avoided staying in Orlando I was ahead of schedule so I paid for a second night.

I spent a long time in a second-hand bookshop on the sea front. In the same street a woman was trying on wigs with the help of a hand mirror and a friend, bringing both out into the daylight each time she tried a new style. I had lunch at the *'Dancing Avocado Kitchen'*. The Floridians are good at names: *'Pumpernickel Pop's Smoke Shop'* and *'CLUB TOPIC Gentlemen's Club – Best Girls in Town'*. A sign outside an eaterie said, 'Name this restaurant'. I thought of suggesting, *'CLUB TROPIC – Gentleman's Grub – Best Grills in Town'*.

Eventually I came to the 'Jackie Robinson Ballpark & Museum', named after the first Afro-American to break the colour barrier in baseball (in 1946). Robinson became a celebrated and highly successful player in major-league baseball, paving the way for racial integration in this and other sports.

When I got back to the Raintree the landlord and his wife told me they were Ugandan Asians who had fled to England in the 70s.

'Leicester, Brighton, Wembley, Croydon, Thornton Heath,' he listed. 'Do you know any of these places?'

'I know them all,' I assured him.

'It was too cold,' he went on. 'I got chilblains, even though I wore gloves. I went to the doctor, "It's no good," the doctor said. "The only thing to do is to move to a warmer country." So we came to Florida. We've been here twenty-five years.'

'You're in a good position here,' I said, 'You're the first motel from the bus station.'

'And if they have to appear at the court house,' the wife added with satisfaction, 'they come and stay here.'

I decided to check the time of my bus the next morning. I couldn't find the bus station because, as I found out later, the sign had been knocked down.

'How ya doin'?' a white man asked. 'What's your name?'

'John,' I said.

'I'm Vernon,' he shook my hand.

'I'm looking for the bus station,' I told him.

'You don't want to go that way. I'll show you where the bus station is.'

He shook my hand again.

'You from England?' he asked. 'My mother is in England. I wanna get there.'

He shook my hand a third time. Then he led me into a grey, featureless area. Any moment, I thought, he'll grab my hand again, pull me into a dark corner and relieve me of my valuables. He shook my hand yet again.

'We've done that bit,' I said, trying to keep the conversation light.

'Would you give me two dollars for the bus?' he asked, when we reached the bus station.

I had to pull out a wad of higher notes.

'Just give me what you've got,' I thought he would say and take the wad, but he waited patiently until I found two single dollars. He took these in one hand and put out the other to shake mine a fifth time.

'Do you like Sussex?' he asked apropos of nothing.

'Yes,' I said, not quite sure where this was leading.

'What about the tax?' he asked.

'Well,' I said, 'most tax in Britain is income tax, so they don't tax you unless you can afford to pay.'

'Are there strippers?'

'There are in London, … and maybe in Brighton.'

He shook my hand one final time and we parted the best of acquaintances. The next morning Uganda man came to my room just as I was moving out.

'Everything all right?' he enquired.

'Well, the curtain needs fixing,' I said, 'and the hot tap drips.'

'Are you going to the bus station?'

'Yes, I am.'

'Would you like me to run you round there?'

As we got into the car I saw that a man had started cleaning my room. He was putting chairs outside.

'He's doing it properly,' I observed.

'I'm teaching him,' said Uganda man. 'Difficult to get the staff, people you can trust. They steal things, you know. My mother was Indian. I was born a British subject. I could go back to England and work there if I wanted to.'

'You seem to be quite happy here,' I said.

'I used to advertise,' he told me. 'I don't need to now – only the "Yellow Pages" – just a token. A lot of my customers come back.'

He'd a kindly face and a gentle manner. He gave me the warmest of old-world smiles. We shook hands. He had a faint Indian accent, although he had never lived in that country. We had a fellow feeling because we had both come from England – although he had done so twenty-five years ahead of me.

The bus had what was euphemistically called a 'restroom'. There was no washbasin and when you lifted the toilet seat you could see through a hole in the floor to a tank whose contents swirled with the motion of the vehicle.

My host Alan met me at St Augustine and took me on to the family's house on the edge of Jacksonville. He was a quiet man with a gentle manner and an unshakeable faith. His wife Rochelle shared his religious conviction. I presented her with flowers and him with some lime cookies. These helped to 'break the ice', although there was no coolness in their welcome – just my own awkwardness on arriving in such a religious household.

'We're not Catholics,' Alan explained. 'We don't believe in Lent as such, but we've encouraged the children to give up something and Skylar's given up chocolate milk. About drinks with the meal: we would normally have wine, but as it's Holy Week, Rochelle and I won't, but you can have some if you like.'

'Thank you,' I said. 'I'll have the same as you.'

We sat at the dining table to drink tea and eat some of the lime cookies. Rochelle brought a globe so that I could take them through my intended route.

'I'm going to make my way across the southern states to Texas,' I explained, 'then head down through Mexico, Guatemala and so on to Panama, where I take a freight ship to New Zealand. Then Australia, Hong Kong and across Asia back to Europe. This is the easy bit.'

On the wall were two religious texts: 'I can do all things through Christ' – *Philippians 4:13* and 'As for me and my house, we will serve the Lord' – *Joshua 24:15*.

I felt a little suffocated so after tea I got Alan to show me round 'the yard'. The house was part of an attractive development with plenty of trees and grass. The front gardens were not partitioned.

'We thank You for this food, Lord,' said Alan at dinner, 'and for all Your blessings. Thank You for bringing John to us, and we pray that he may come to know You.'

'Rochelle is a lapsed Catholic,' Alan confided. 'I was a lapsed Episcopalian – that's like Church of England. We wanted to get married in church but the question was – which church? Having three boys, we wanted a church with a strong male leader and role model.'

'Boys need that,' added Rochelle.

'We went to the Christian Family Chapel,' Alan explained. 'I was born again. I made Jesus my Lord – amazing experience being born again in my forties.'

I felt I'd better reveal that I was a non-believer.

'Do you know anything of the Bible?' Alan asked.

'I've got a reasonable knowledge of it, yes,' I said.

He pursued the matter no further at this stage, instead announcing that they usually watched the ten o'clock news. This was frequently broken up by advertisements, the most tiresome being the network's own, repeatedly asserting how wonderful it was.

The next day being Easter Sunday, the family went to church and I felt I should go with them. The Christian Family Chapel was a chapel in name only, being two large buildings with a vast car park. A welcome party stood outside. I collected some literature.

'We are delighted that God has brought you to Christian Family Chapel,' a leaflet said. 'We trust that, as our guest, you will experience a "stirring up" of your desire to know and worship Jesus Christ in a deeper way.'

The organisation was impressive and included the following: 'Pastor of Discipleship, Communications Director, Director of Missions, Pastor of Worship, Minister to Women, Minister of Shepherding, Director of Ministry Development, Executive Pastor, Pastor-Teacher, Minister to Children, Minister to Junior High & College and Minister to Senior High'.

There was none of the reverent hush you get in the Church of England. The congregation was relaxed, its members speaking loudly to be heard in a crowd of 600. When we arrived there was nowhere to sit, but an army of helpers quickly brought out extra chairs and put them wherever there was room, until we were all seated. The family and I sat in one of two columns stretching the length of the wide central aisle. The sense of anticipation was taken up a notch or two by a well-amplified seven-piece band on the platform, including keyboard, drums, a number of guitars and two singers. The eldest son, who couldn't bear noise, sat with his head bowed and a finger in each ear throughout the service. During some of the songs the congregation stood and clapped on the offbeat or swayed side to side. The term 'happy-clappy' would be just right here.

The pastor-teacher was driven by an undeniable zeal. He had compelling blue eyes and a shining, fearless countenance, which seemed to gleam with the glory of Heaven. We sang the hymn 'Christ the Lord is risen today' and we sang it lustily. Then the pastor-teacher introduced a film on a big screen of a presentation in Houston by an evangelical preacher, showing images of some of the most distant objects known, including a few a million light-years away.

'I'm not trying to make you feel small,' the preacher declared, 'I'm telling you, you *are* small!'

We saw that at the centre of a certain 'whirlpool galaxy' there is the apparent form of a cross. This image was immediately followed on the screen by a harsh and piteous artist's vision of Christ, scourged and bloody on the Cross. The message was that within this mighty 'creation' we were very small indeed – and yet Jesus loved us and knew each of us by name. The sound level of the presentation, even to my poor ears, was deafening.

Three individuals, who had elected to be baptised on Easter day, had to tell the enormous congregation of their own personal journeys to Christ. They were then led to a tub of heated water where another man spoke some prepared words into a microphone. Then, still clothed, the candidate was fully immersed, emerging dripping wet to be wrapped in a towel. After two people had been baptised, someone considerably lowered the height of the main microphone. I was expecting the next candidate to be a wheelchair-user or an adult of restricted growth, but it turned out to be a boy of six, who was led to the microphone, where he stood fearful, tearful and shaking his head. Everyone waited patiently until he got his little self together and in a high and tiny voice made his testimony. He had to be lifted into the tub, dunked and lifted out. Thinking of Felix and Sam, two of my grandchildren, who were the boy's age, I felt bewildered and alarmed.

The 'on-stage' musicians began a song, giving it a thumping beat impossible to ignore. After a while a woman stood up, her arms outstretched, her hands and forearms upright. Others joined her, then more and more, in affirmation of their belief, like a standing ovation for Jesus. The words of the song were shown on a big screen. I couldn't read them because the people in front of me were standing up. Everyone I could see was on their feet, except for the eldest son, for whom the noise must have been horrific, and me. I was aware of my heartbeat and had to breathe deeply to stay calm. If I'd been on my own I would have walked out.

In the afternoon we went for a walk by a river. Then I played Monopoly with two of the boys. I kept saying 'pounds' instead of 'dollars'. I won and felt bad about it. I had dinner with the whole family.

'We thank You for Your sacrifice,' Alan prayed, 'and for this food. And we pray for John as he journeys on ...'

This time we had a soft red wine in capacious glasses. When we'd finished eating, the boys disappeared and Rochelle and Alan, their tongues loosened by the alcohol, told of fostering children from dysfunctional families and of adopting the children they had now. The three boys were very different. They'd all joined my hosts as children rather than babies. This implies not only that they had come from difficult family situations but also that the change of family would itself have been unsettling for all concerned. I felt respect and admiration for Alan and Rochelle for taking on this challenge and for seeing it through, giving three damaged children a secure home as well as a calm and loving family life. Particularly moving was the story, before the arrival of the boys, of a baby girl, brain-damaged by her stepfather and nursed by Rochelle until the child was too ill to be at home anymore and had to spend her final days in a children's hospital. In all these experiences they could see the hand of God.

'You said you were familiar with the Bible?' Alan reminded me.

'Yes,' I said, 'I was a believer.'

'If you were a believer then,' he said, 'you'd be a believer now.'

'How do you know what it was like for me?' I argued. 'I *was* a believer in my teens. I wanted to be a missionary. I decided that I could be more effective as a medical missionary, so I switched from arts to sciences and applied for a place at a medical school. But after I'd made that decision I lost my faith.'

Alan and Rochelle seemed finally to accept that I held my view with a conviction equal to theirs.

The next morning Alan took me to the bus station on his way to work. In the Christian Family Chapel almost everyone had been white, but here most were black or Hispanic. I boarded a bus that headed west along a straight road with generous verges and a wide central reservation. Our progress was steady and relentless. At the back of the vehicle, on three seats, a man was stretched out with a blanket over his head.

At Tallahassee a man joined the bus, so obese that he walked with his feet well apart and edged sideways down the aisle, looking for a seat. I hoped he wouldn't sit next to me – or, worse still, on top of me.

'Remember what Ah said about radios,' the driver said. 'You can listen to your music but don't have it loud enough for other folks to hear it. If you wanna do that, I'll give you your cases and you can get off the bus straight away!'

At Panama City (Florida, that is, not Panama), Mr Huge squeezed between the seats, got off the bus and stretched himself. He put his hands inside his tracksuit bottoms and took hold of the elasticated waistband of his voluminous underpants and pulled them up to cover a greater extent of his voluminous buttocks. He took hold of the elasticated waistband of his voluminous tracksuit bottoms and pulled them up to cover a greater extent of his voluminous underpants. Then he lumbered off.

At Fort Walton Beach I booked in to an economy motel near the waterfront and went out to explore. Grassy terraces led to a beach of white sand with the musical sound of the sea lapping against the concrete skeletons of derelict jetties. One still in use had a lamp on the post furthest out and this threw something like moonlight onto the water.

In a Thai restaurant the waitresses were charming and their daintiness contrasted with the bulk of the Americans. My meal was classed as 'medium spicy'. I thought it would set fire to my tonsils. I wondered what 'very spicy' would have done.

Back in the motel, a notice warned, 'No children allowed in the ice box.' Who would put a child in an ice box? I'd a king-size bed, which gave me a large surface on which to sort out my kit. I re-packed my suitcase to send it home with my blazer, trousers, patent-leather shoes, dark socks and everything else I no longer needed.

The next day I booked a second night in the motel. As I walked to the post office with my full suitcase, it began to rain but I felt cheerful at the thought of getting rid of so much encumbrance. The post office was a light-hearted place. A young man went down the line.

'Anyone need help?' he asked.

'Yes,' I said, showing him the suitcase, 'I want to send this.'

He found me a collapsed box, a roll of strong adhesive tape, sheets of 'bubble' as they call it, a sticky label and a form to fill in.

'Are you gonna take it home and do it?' he asked.

'Home is England,' I said. 'That's where I'm sending this stuff. I don't want to have to walk back to my hotel.'

'While we're not busy you could do it over there.'

In a space on the floor I set to with a will. Having re-constructed the box, I wedged the suitcase in it, turned the thing over and taped the cracks. By then an older man was on duty.

'Have you got a knife,' I asked him, 'to cut this box down?'

'They don't trust us with knives,' he said, 'but I've got scissors you can have.'

I struggled with the scissors, now kneeling on the floor.

'I'm not in your way, am I?' I asked a middle-aged woman.

'Do you want to use this knife?' she asked me.

'Thank you!'

Everyone smiled to see me struggling with my parcel. It was a strange shape and needed metres of sticky tape. I returned the knife to the woman and the scissors to the man.

'You wouldn't give *me* a job in the packing department!' I suggested.

'You're better than him!' he said, indicating a colleague.

I handed my parcel in to a woman at the counter, together with my completed form.

'Is that all right?' I asked.

'I've put "personal belongings",' she said, 'might help to stop them opening it up.'

It was heartening, far from home, to be surrounded by so many helpful people. In a flea market I bought a two-blade penknife and a second-hand copy of 'Elephant Bill'.

That evening I found a restaurant with a professional air. On my table there was a real pink rose in a froth of Gypsophila. The locals seemed to dress down to go out. One guy looked like Dennis the Menace in jeans and a jumper with horizontal red-and-black stripes. Another wore a baseball cap. None was obese.

I started with a creamy crab bisque with corn – sophisticated comfort food. It came with 'French-style' bread served hot between napkins in a basket and with a bowl of the restaurant's own balsamic-vinegar dressing. This was wonderfully garlicky so I dipped the hot bread in it, making my own delicious 'garlic bread', which remained surprisingly crisp. A fish called 'grouper' came in lemon-butter sauce, accompanied by a dollop of sour cream the size of a Ping-Pong ball and a large salad with no onion. I was wearing out my pencil, writing notes. Without being asked, a waitress whisked the pencil away and brought it back sharpened.

'I'm writing a book,' I explained to a man on the next table.

'Or a blog?' he suggested.

'No, a printed book.'

'How did you smell this place out?'

'When I'm looking for somewhere to eat,' I said, 'I look through the window to see if the restaurant is busy. And this place had bottles of wine in a rack at the door.'

'We've driven seven miles to come back here. Where have you come from?'

'I'm staying in Fort Walton Beach tonight, but I'm from England.'

'England!'

'Yes, I'm going round the world.'

'Where are you going next?'

'I'd like to see New Orleans.'

'Why d'ya wanna go there?'

'Well,' I said, 'the hurricane was widely reported in Britain – the flooding, the damage, the initial response and the subsequent recovery programme. It would be interesting to see how it was getting along. But I've heard that as well as petty crime, there's also organised crime … '

'I used to live there. We're going to the jazz festival.'

Two other men nodded.

'I wouldn't go,' the first advised. 'People don't know what's going on. I suppose you could go for a couple of hours in the morning but you wouldn't see much. If you wanna see something of Mississippi, go to Natchez.'

That was miles inland. A waiter brought me more coffee without being asked.

'Where are you from?' I asked him.

'Czechoslovakia,' he said in a southern drawl, 'I've been here eight years.'

The coffee was so hot I burned my tongue, but in a second I'd cooled my mouth with the iced water. The restaurant was run by the chef, who was originally from South Vietnam but grew up in Florida and graduated from the local high school, with his wife, who came from Thailand. The meal was $39 including two glasses of Californian Chardonnay and a tip. If you're ever in Fort Walton Beach, look out for the Sealand Restaurant on Miracle Strip Parkway.

Next day I was off again by Greyhound bus, along the coast in the direction of Texas. The vehicle was a 54-seater and noisy in the lower gears. A bridge three miles long over water brought us into the next resort, Pensacola, where we had a 15-minute break. I checked that my rucksack was still in the hold. We crossed the border into Alabama.

The next big place was Mobile. In a large harbour used for shipbuilding I saw a battleship bristling with guns. There were grand houses with pleasing gardens and the long branches of oak trees snaked across the roads above the traffic.

I needed to post some cards home and a jigsaw puzzle of the QM2 as a birthday present to one of my grandchildren. I also wanted to send home some more kit. The less you have the more flexible you are and the less there is to look after. They told me at the bus station that the post office was five blocks away. It seemed more like ten. It was the middle of the day and rather hot for walking. The round trip took me over an hour. I got back just in time to hear my bus called. I grabbed a sandwich and a blueberry muffin.

'Do you want chips?' someone called out.

No wonder the locals were so big! On the bus a black man, nearly two metres tall, settled his small daughter on the seat next to him, her head resting on his thigh. He spread a small rug over her and put his own hand over that to stop her rolling off.

Alabama has very little coastline. In no time we had crossed the narrow tongue of land that reaches to the Gulf of Mexico and entered Mississippi, another state that's narrow near the sea. We crossed the Pascagoula River. The highway was raised four metres above the ground. I realised I hadn't seen a hill since I'd left England. The road rose high again over another river. I saw the driver of a tanker take his shirt off as he drove. A sign said we were 60 miles from New Orleans. Next we entered Louisiana. The wide verges continued, but bright green. We passed through swampy woods with glades, but missed out New Orleans altogether. We seemed to be hurtling across America, like in a road movie. I saw four states in a single day. The little girl slept all the way to the capital, Baton Rouge.

As we came into the state capital, an advertisement said, *'Laissez les profits rouler.'* I took a bus along Florida Boulevard and got off when I spotted the Alamo Plaza Motel. I paid $50, which included a $5 deposit for the key. The walls were dirty, the décor neglected. No one had hoovered under the bed for months. The under-sheet had numerous holes from cigarette burns. The room had a filthy armchair, a free-standing wardrobe and a large, six-drawer chest. There was also a walk-in hanging space, where only a vertically challenged suicide could have hanged himself. The basin was scratched and dirty, the hot-water tap dripping. There was no plug but I'd a complimentary bottle of shampoo from another hotel and this fitted the hole well enough. A black soap dish had been painted cream for some reason although most of the paint had since come off. A single fitting on the wall indicated that there'd once been a towel rail. There were the remains of something like a thermostat. The air conditioning worked although the dials had been removed. There were two naked bulbs above the mark on the wall where a bathroom cabinet had been. The effect was garish but luckily only one of the bulbs worked. A fluorescent light on the ceiling did nothing to mitigate the general impression of in-your-face squalor. It was good preparation for the poorer countries I would come to.

I never feel particularly safe staying on the ground floor but I was able to lock the back window. There was a lot of noise during the night, but I managed to get to sleep. I woke at three and checked my belly-bag, which I'd got in the bed with me. I was alarmed to see that the zip of the bag was undone and my passport gone. When I calmed down I found it lying on the bedclothes for any intruder to lift. I must have taken it out for some reason and forgotten to put it back. I would need to sharpen up my act if I was to reach the Panama Canal. At 3.30am people were still hanging about outside, talking loudly. Two guys seemed to be watching my room. I was careful not to put my light on.

In the morning I bought some banana bread and sat down to eat it on the grass at the side of the road. It was after nine o'clock but a number of young black men were smoking, staring into space or shifting restlessly. I felt self-conscious and a bit insecure. At first I couldn't think why they were there. Then it dawned on me that they were unemployed. They were doing nothing because they had nothing to do.

On the bus, we crossed rivers the colour of white coffee. I saw crawfish beds, the location of the crawfish pots indicated by red markers. For miles through swampy forests the road was raised on columns, often as high as the tops of the trees. Eventually we came into farmland, the farms becoming larger and more organised as we entered Texas, with more livestock than I'd seen in the other states.

We came into Houston early evening. The Greyhound Bus Station, the biggest I'd encountered so far, was in the downtown, business area of the city. With my experience in St Petersburg still fresh in my memory I was determined to find something other than a business hotel. A map showed the location of the tourist information centre as part of the City Hall. When I got there, a good-looking young black man, well groomed and wearing a smart suit, was sitting at a table outside reading a financial newspaper.

'Excuse me, sir,' I said, 'I'm trying to get to Tourist Information. Do you know where the entrance is?'

'I'm afraid I don't,' he said, 'but it's probably closed now. What are you looking for?'

'I want to find out where the ordinary hotels are – not the big business hotels.'

'There's none round here. I know a hotel you could reach by tram. Where are you from?'

'From England.'

'England!'

'Yes, I'm going round the world.'

'Where are you heading?'

'Mexico. Are you in business?'

'I'm in the contract chauffeur business. That's my limo there.'

A black car was parked in the road, spotless and gleaming. I think the man was contracted to companies to provide a high-class private taxi service for business purposes. He took me to a smart motel on the edge of town. He said he was going that way anyway and wouldn't accept a dollar. He gave me his card and I promised to send him a postcard from Mexico.

Once I'd checked in I walked back towards the centre of the city to find somewhere to eat. The first restaurant I came to was a big Mexican establishment with a friendly atmosphere and Mexican music, easy on the ear. Although the menu was in English my waitress spoke only Spanish, like everyone else in the restaurant. I talked slowly in English and, pointing to the words on the menu, ordered the snapper. When it arrived it looked a lot to eat. There was a lemon sauce, as well as rice, French fries, fried bread and a good mixed salad. I had two glasses of white wine. At eight o'clock a band started up. An enjoyable meal and a foretaste of the real Mexico, I thought, but when I got my bill I realised that, because of the language difficulty, I had ordered – and eaten – a dish intended for two people and thus had to pay twice as much as I'd expected.

The next day I walked towards the city to get a bus into the centre. The skyscrapers huddled like mighty monoliths, the tallest disappearing into a cloud, presumably of moisture and pollutants. In a square near the centre, I stumbled on 'Fresh Air Friday'. On a platform a band was playing. There were stalls under canopies, which protected them from the fine rain. These were labelled 'Mothers for Clean Air', 'The Air we Breathe' and so on.

At Houston's Greyhound Bus Station the security was tighter than at many airports. You had to negotiate a deliberate bottleneck with guards either side before you were allowed near a bus. As I boarded the bus to head south towards Mexico, I noticed that the windows were reinforced with perforated black sheets, which spoiled the view. After an hour there was a police check. A sign said, 'Slow! Be Prepared to Stop!' Later a man got off to be greeted by his daughter. The two hugged enthusiastically – a relaxed and happy scene, the like of which I never saw in Houston.

I noticed a tanker on the road labelled 'drilling fluids' and we passed what I took to be an oil refinery. As we got nearer to the national border the roads became narrower and there was less traffic. After some time I saw a winding, brown river; finally, the sea, which also looked brown, but only because I was looking through the grille over the window. We passed another huge refinery.

It had been overcast in Houston; now there was blue sky with little white clouds. As we approached Corpus Christi the land became very flat. We were close again to the Gulf of Mexico. A warship with aircraft on it was a reminder of America's enormous budget on so-called 'defense'. A notice advertising the 'South Texas Gear Tactical Division' offered, 'World-class Snody knives', pepper spray and tactical knives 'custom-made here'.

I bought a map of Corpus Christi in a shop run by a North Korean, who told me he'd been in Texas ten years. During my trip I found immigrants particularly friendly, presumably because they knew what it was like to be alone in a strange place. He suggested the Bay Hotel. I stayed on the eighth floor, where I enjoyed a dizzy view of both bay and city. The skyscrapers here were brutal, representing America's 'Up Yours' school of architecture – mission statement 'Two Fingers to the World!' They made Houston's giants seem mellow and restrained.

It was a luxury to be settled in my room by 4pm and I made myself a cup of coffee. Then I went out without my rucksack and walked north along the sea front, where I saw a pelican. On a circular lawn teenage girls were running, stretching and doing handstands, coached by an older boy. They practised a stunt in which three of them lifted a fourth girl in a standing position as high as they could by one ankle while she held the other leg up with a hand. She balanced for a moment; then they threw her even higher and caught her when she fell.

'Excuse me,' I said to one of them at a suitable moment, 'I'm a visitor from England. Do you mind telling me – are you gymnasts, or dancers?'

'Cheerleaders,' she replied.

I should have guessed. Nearby was a baseball ground. A game was in progress – the Corpus Christi Hooks at home to the Wichita Wranglers on the Whataburger field. (You couldn't make it up!) The place was laid-back and informal. Even the girls on the gate, who couldn't watch the game from their kiosk, seemed to be having a good time. They sold me a ticket for the paltry sum of five dollars and explained the procedure – or lack of it. Once inside you could sit or stand where you wanted, wander about, watch the game from any angle, buy beer or coke from the ambulant vendors or visit various stalls. If you sat in the main stand, you found a recess in front of you to hold your drink. Or you could loll on a grass slope some distance from the game. You could climb an artificial rock face. You could throw a private party around a pool. You could even organise your own private game of baseball.

I'm sure cricket is as strange to Americans as this baseball seemed to me. As far as I could make out, it's a cross between rounders and a coconut shy. The guy who starts off with the ball stands on a specially prepared mound dangerously close to the striker. He hurls the ball in the way he judges most awkward for his opponent to hit with his bat, a weapon as narrow as a beer can and therefore more suited to brawling and rioting than hitting an object little wider than itself.

The crowd treated the whole thing as a jolly Saturday evening out for the family, occasionally exciting but always fun. Any impressive play was greeted with rhythmic clapping. Every stray ball was retrieved by a ball boy. Every natural break in the play was immediately covered by a burst of canned music, a live announcement or a clown disguised as an outsize seagull running round the ground, pursued by a dozen little children. For good measure real seagulls swooped, whooped and, for all I knew, pooped. I didn't understand the game – but, boy, did I enjoy it!

I was pacing myself, in order to reach the Panama Canal in good time to board my ship but not so early that I'd be hanging around too long in an unsavoury port. I'd moved fast through the southern states and now felt I should take a day off before leaving the country and plunging nervously into darkest Mexico. I hoped too to buy a map of that country, a can of fly spray, a litre bottle for water and a tiny screwdriver to tighten the screws on my glasses. In the event I never came upon a single ordinary shop. The next day, however, I enjoyed a salad of cultural activities.

In the Texas Surfing Museum you could study the history of surfboard design, while admiring the sleek and colourful boards of famous surfers. Films of surfing were continuously shown on three screens, which you could watch from a seat made out of a surfboard, smooth, polished and good to sit on.

In the afternoon I went to a free concert at the Del Mar College Department of Music. The young players sauntered in and took four minutes to tune up, guided by the adult leader, who indicated with a finger whether their instruments were sharp or flat. One of the bassoonists wore a sleeveless dress, which revealed what I took to be tussocks of black hair sprouting from her armpits, but I think this may have been a spiteful trick of the overhead lighting.

When it came to Beethoven's Pastoral Symphony I was worried that there was not one kettledrum on the stage. But I'd no right to expect a complete orchestra as they didn't perform the complete work. The woodwind players were experienced and produced a lovely sound together, so I was looking forward to the bird calls in the second movement but they missed it out. They also missed out the fourth ('Thunder and Storm'). So, no thunderclaps. The only claps came between movements, from anxious parents urging on their variously talented progeny. It wasn't clear whether the omission of the storm was the reason for the absence of tympani or the result of it. The orchestra played the fifth movement rather sweetly but as this represents 'Thanksgiving after the Storm' there didn't seem to be much point. They might have been better advised to rename the movement 'Thanksgiving for the Fact that the Storm Forecast Earlier Didn't Arrive After All.'

That evening the tower and spire of Corpus Christi's First United Methodist Church cast a shadow 150m long – across the road, down the beach and onto the sea itself. I caught the tail end of a cultural festival. A group of women of all ages wearing coloured bras – and skirts fastened low enough to display generous bellies with deep, deep navels – performed a rather Texan belly dance. The star of the troupe could send ripples across her brown tummy, her flesh moving like liquid mud from right hippy to left titty.

The next day I got on a bus waiting to take people on towards the Mexican border. The engine was kept running to power the air conditioning. A man in the driver's seat stopped reading a newspaper and taped it to the window beside him to keep off the sun. I thought we were starting because I felt the bus move, but it was only a heavy man getting on. He turned out to be the driver. The man who'd taped the newspaper was his co-driver.

The countryside was flat as an airfield. I had just finished a chapter of 'Elephant Bill', one man's account of 25 years in Burma, living and working with elephants. The book revealed its English author as cool but humane, with a love of animals, a belief in fair play and a strong sense of irony. I looked up to see that the bus was cruising at about 60 mph, quite happily on its own without a driver! Then I realised that, possibly under the influence of the very British book I'd been reading, I'd looked for the driver on the right side of the bus, instead of the left.

We'd a half-hour wait at the bus station in Harlingen. In the hall there was a fan but no air-conditioning so I moved to a covered way for the buses, which as well as protecting people from the sun acted as a wind tunnel, blowing my floppy white hat off. When our bus arrived the driver stayed in his seat.

'Are you a bird watcher?' he asked me in his Tex-Mex accent.

'No,' I replied.

'You look like a bird watcher,' he insisted.

'I'm British,' I said, 'but not a bird watcher.'

'Oh!'

Apart from Hawaii and the toe of Florida, Brownsville is the southernmost part of the United States, the same latitude as Luxor on the Nile or Jaipur in India. No wonder it was hot. I booked in to the Colonial Hotel and went out to explore.

Brownsville had something I hadn't encountered before in the southern states, a high street – an unbroken line of shops on each side of the street, and only metres from the Greyhound bus station and my hotel. It was like arriving in an old-fashioned European town, except that the place was run down and everything was incredibly cheap. You've heard of 'downmarket', well this was 'rock-bottom market'. A large notice on The Nuevo York Trading Company read 'TOTAL LIQUIDATION'.

I bought a map that showed Brownsville and Matamoros, the Mexican town the other side of the Río Grande, which marked the frontier. The river was only a few blocks from the Colonial Hotel and I decided that when I crossed the border I'd do so by walking over the bridge.

Back in the hotel a large woman was sitting at a computer, eating a very late lunch, possibly a second lunch. She had the biggest girth of any black person I'd ever seen.

'Excuse me,' I said, 'please may I use the computer to check my e-mails?'

'Okay.'

'I didn't want to disturb you.'

'I'm only playing a game.'

She got up – which can't have been easy – and waddled away. I hadn't been at the screen long when a rhythmic noise started up like an automated suction device.

'Everything is going according to schedule,' I told my support base. 'The freight ship from Panama is still due to leave the first week in June. I've six weeks to pass through Central America. As I've got nearer the border, everything including the people has become more Mexican. The culture shock when I enter the real Mexico will not be so great. It's been good training – now to put it to the test!'

When I got up I discovered the source of the pumping noise. It was Madam herself, snoring on the sofa, not sitting or lying but resting obliquely and unbent against two firm edges, the top of the back of the sofa and the front of the seat, while filling most of the space between.

I did a recce of the border crossing. Climbing a bank, I could see the Río Grande, green and not very wide. It looked an easy swim and I was sure that many a Mexican had tried it in the direction of Texas. I walked along a rough track close to the water. This brought me up to the Brownsville and Matamoros International Bridge. A line of cars was crawling along it from the Mexican side. A police car appeared on the track and stopped beside me. The driver wound down the window.

'How ya doin'?' a cop asked. 'You all right?'

'Yes, thank you. I just thought I'd have a look at the river, the bridge – it's very interesting,' I said, trying to sound innocent. 'I'm staying at the ...' I tried to remember the name of my hotel. 'It's called the ...' (what's that word, I wondered, for describing one country governed by another) '... the Colonial Hotel,' I managed in the end.

I wouldn't make a very good secret agent.

'Nice to talk to you,' the policeman said, and drove off.

When I got back to the town, I came upon several people sleeping rough, although it was early in the evening. A feral kitten with beautiful grey fur was trying to lick the inside of a discarded food can. Numerous restaurants were closed and I couldn't find a single bar, although I was thirsty enough to have a good look for one. I did, however, discover a row of currency changers and planned to exchange some of my dollars there the next day. I also found a second bridge over the river, the Gateway International Bridge, which looked more convenient for my purposes.

The next morning I noticed a cockroach on its back in the shower. While I was thinking what to do about it, it died, so I had the easier problem of arranging the funeral. I would soon be in Matamoros, the gateway to Mexico, to Central America and, for me, wholly uncharted territory, where I couldn't speak the language. People who'd talked to me before I left home and books I'd read about travelling in Central America had warned me to beware of mosquitoes, rabid dogs, beggars, pickpockets, muggers, burglars, drug traffickers, gangsters, terrorists, travelling on my own, revealing that I was travelling on my own, buses, taxis, going out after dark, the sun, the water, the food and the language difficulties. And in films I'd seen Mexican bandits. I had every right to be nervous – and I was. As I packed and checked out of the hotel, the tight feeling in my chest returned. I went to a café for a cup of coffee, but after that I knew I couldn't put my departure off any longer. I went back to the moneychangers.

'May I speak English?' I asked.

'No,' she said sweetly.

I produced my bank cards. She shook her head. I handed her $70 in cash and she changed this into Mexican pesos. I walked to the border and let the security guards check my passport. I stepped onto the bridge and advanced until I was above the river. I felt scared and rather lonely, but there was no going back.

3. Mexico

April 17 – May 1

While Brownsville was down in the dumps, Matamoros was vibrant and fun. To get to the main bus station I took a small bus, whose seating consisted of two benches inside running the length of it. There was a large area between them for standing passengers, with rails above to hold onto. The town was crowded with traders and shoppers. The streets were so narrow I could have leaned out of the window and raided the displays. The driver shouted at pedestrians to get out of the way.

The main bus station was organised like an airport with each bus company having its own ticket counter and check-in. I dealt with Autobuses de Oriente (ADO) and bought a ticket to San Fernando, 137 km to the south. From a stall I bought some chilli-spiced dried strawberries, which made rather good savoury 'sweets' to eat on the bus.

Seat tickets were numbered and you could choose where to sit. There was a proper bag check. For each item going into the hold they issued three luggage tags marked with your name and destination – one attached to the bag, one for the passenger to hold and one for the driver. The seats of the bus were superior and comfortable. A Canadian man on the bus said Mexican buses were much better than those in the States.

Mexico seemed unpretentious. There was no attempt to keep the place clean and tidy. Broken-down cars and other rubbish cluttered the side of the road. A dustcart open at the back discharged dust and rubbish into the air as it went. I saw a van loaded with clear plastic bags of prawns and a live man lying on top. There were some smart new cars on the road but the overall impression was of a people struggling to make ends meet.

The countryside was wild and coarse, a minimalist landscape. We crossed a green and grubby river. Instead of the large organised farms of Texas there were numerous smallholdings and irregular scraps of land had been planted. I saw a horse grazing on the verge tethered to a fence. There were goats on the verge and a single tethered cow. A lemon tree was laden with fruit. Tombstones and crosses appeared in the middle of nowhere; there were half a dozen shrines beside the road. The terrain became hillier and we got a splendid view with hills all shades from greens and browns in the foreground to pale blue-grey in the distance. I was excited to be going deeper into a country completely new to me and my anxieties gave way to enjoyment. The vehicle had 'in-flight' entertainment on a number of screens. This consisted of a safety film followed by two full-length feature films.

A minute's walk from San Fernando bus station I took a room in a hotel for 200 pesos (about £10). I went out and soon came across an attractive restaurant, whose roof was made of a mesh of bamboo visible inside and out. I had *'fajitas a la Mexicana'* (pieces of beef with tomatoes, onions and hot peppers). A good-looking woman with black hair, blue eyes and a cuddly figure came in with a young boy. At the end of the meal she saw me looking at my phrase book.

'Do you need any help?' she asked with a mild Texan accent, although she didn't seem a bit American.

'Oh, thank you,' I said, 'I'm trying to learn some Spanish. You sound as though you speak good English.'

'I learnt it in Texas.'

I was immediately attracted to her, obviously because of her looks but also because she seemed genuinely interested in my travels. I sensed we were on the same wavelength, but I felt inhibited by the presence of the boy. She asked me about my children.

'What do you have?' I asked, meaning 'what family?'

'We're in the trucking business,' she replied, misunderstanding my question.

Back in my room I washed some clothes in the basin. There was no plug, only something like a pepper pot, which didn't fit, so I literally put a sock in it. I wasn't sure if the lock in my room worked. One of my friends had advised me to take a wedge to use in strange places. I pushed the thing under the door as far as it would go. Then I gave it a kick for good measure. But when I tried the door it opened easily dragging the wedge with it. In the night I woke, alarmed to see that the door was wide open. Then I realised it was the bathroom door. I woke again at about 5.45. I was settling down to have a bit more sleep when I was scared to hear a man's voice and to see a light come on in the room. It was the television starting up on its own. At 6.40 there were cats screaming. When I got up I was surprised to find that the clothes I'd washed hadn't dried. In Texas I could dry clothes over night. In San Fernando even my notebook was damp – and I hadn't washed that! Clearly, I'd entered a more humid environment. The shower had no nozzle and played on my back with all the finesse of a urinating cow. The jet had some force so I used it to massage a painful shoulder. When I was dressed I realised that the 'pepper pot' was actually the missing nozzle.

I breakfasted on snacks left over from the day before, careful to throw some frankfurters away in case they had gone off. I resisted the temptation to confuse the chambermaid by dropping them in the toilet. I couldn't find my Latin-American-Spanish phrase book so I went back to the restaurant to see if I'd left it there.

'Is there anyone who speaks English?' I asked a waiter.

'No.'

I could have done with the help of a Latin-American-Spanish phrase book to describe the Latin-American-Spanish phrase book I was looking for. I'd forgotten that I still had a dictionary of European Spanish, which was good enough at my level. When I drew a picture of the book, the waiter showed me one of the folders used to present customers with their bills. I decided to try a mime. I sat in the seat where I'd sat the night before. I ate an imaginary meal. I dropped an imaginary book on the floor. I walked to the door. I patted my pockets, threw up my hands in horror, hunted around the restaurant and peered behind the counter. But the waiter looked at me as if I were a Martian.

'I'm most grateful to you. Good-bye!' I mimed and walked out.

I had to pass through seven Spanish-speaking countries. I wondered if it would get any easier. I took another bus to continue south. Travelling this way, instead of building up an overall picture of the landscape I seemed to collect a series of snapshots. Butterflies sporting beside the road. A hawk hovering high above. Palm trees. Further on, hills in the distance. The land seemed barren, the arrangement of the landscape haphazard. I saw the first garden since I'd been in Mexico, charmingly simple with cacti in flower. A thatched roof, donkeys and a horse tethered beside the road, cattle in enclosures on bare soil – I think they were calves waiting to be slaughtered for veal. I saw someone bathing in a green river. Now there were mountains in the distance.

I'd purchased some biscuits before boarding. I should have bought popcorn as the bus was a moving cinema. For a while there was a nature programme about wildlife in Australia. The next film starred Bob Hoskins. The dialogue was in English, with Spanish subtitles. I tried not to watch the film as I wanted to look out of the window, but I found the English words and Hoskins' familiar voice very distracting. So was the violence. The third film I'd also seen before, the French '*Les Choristes*', a pleasant contrast. We were five hours on the road, moving at about 50 mph. We had to stop for some women to cross holding up parasols. To shield himself from the sun the driver pulled down a blind with a rosary dangling from it. We had entered the tropics.

I got a room in Tampico for 250 pesos (about £13), with a shower, loo, basin, air-conditioning and a fan. I went on a hunt for a map of the town. As I got hungry the map hunt turned into a meal hunt. But I found not a single map, nor a single restaurant. There were open-fronted bars, where lone men sat dolefully at high counters. I couldn't face joining them.

By eight o'clock it was dark. I'd had some tortillas with spicy meat for lunch so although it meant doing without the high spot of the day (a civilised dinner in a civilised restaurant) I decided to eat in. Once I was back in my room, I put on the fan and pulled the chair up to the table. For my starter I chose a dried chilli-spiced strawberry. I had some plain biscuits for my main course and sweet biscuits for my dessert, all washed down with half a bottle of tap water treated by me with purifying tablets.

After 'dinner' I went back to the lobby to study two maps I'd noticed earlier. One was framed and hung on the wall. I took it down and tried to find where we were on the map but I could see marked neither the hotel nor the bus station opposite it. I asked the receptionist. I don't think she'd looked at the map before. Nor do I think she understood why I wanted to find the hotel on the map when I'd obviously found the actual hotel and was standing in it as we spoke and, if I wanted the bus station, why, there it was, across the road! But she did ask Stefan, a young Mexican man she'd been talking to. He turned the map the other way up and struggled to make sense of it. I didn't know the Spanish for 'which street is the hotel in?' He pointed to a street on the map and sure enough there was a picture of a double-decker bus and the words '*Estación de Autobuses*'!

'Where you come from?' he asked.

'England,' I said.

That always impressed people, presumably because it was the other side of the ocean.

'Where you going?'

'Around the world – without flying.'

'Why don't you fly?'

'It's too easy. Doing it this way I see the country. I see the people. I meet people like you. You speak very good English.'

'I worked for four years in Washington.'

'Are you travelling?'

'I'm going to Mexico City to work. I've got two daughters, nine and seven.'

'That's like my grandchildren – eight, six, six and three. I'm scared of Mexico City. It's so big – I'd get lost. There are so many people. And when there are lots of people somebody will pick my pocket.'

I did an appropriate mime. He laughed. For me, it was as good as counselling. That night I pushed my wedge under the door. Then I rested a leg of the table on the wedge. I hooked a plastic stool onto the door handle and balanced as many objects as I could on the top of the stool, to make an almighty clatter when the intruder opened the door. In the morning this booby trap had not been disturbed and it looked rather silly.

When I went out there was a slight breeze and it was very pleasant if you weren't in the sun. The road was busy and there was much hooting. The parked cars were dirty, their hub caps, bumpers, radiator grilles and headlamps thick with dust. Shopkeepers were sweeping the pavement or just wetting it to keep the dust down. There was a smell of drains. I followed signs to *El Espacio Cultural Metropolitana*, a new building in a large area in the process of being landscaped, beside a lake called *la Laguna del Carpentera*. I walked up grand, wide steps into an environment in complete contrast to the streets I'd come from. It was cool, spotless and bright because the wall facing the lake was largely of glass.

I was the only visitor to *El Museo de la Cultura Huasteca*, designed to show something of the cultural heritage of the region. The text accompanying the exhibits was in Spanish only, so I couldn't get any detailed information. I did come away, however, with a vivid picture of the indigenous people, small with wide faces, dignified, peaceful and serene, who lived close to nature and respected her.

The building housed two theatres and an art gallery. There was also an up-market restaurant on the top floor, with a fine view of the lake and tables elegantly laid for lunch. Unfortunately, it was too early to eat but a waiter let me look round and take photographs. Outside there was a helipad. The whole effort represented a big investment, somewhat divorced from the town, whose inhabitants, I guessed, were preoccupied with more down-to-earth matters. On the way back I saw a man leading a bony mare, to which was tethered a skinny colt.

Determined to avoid the dangers of Mexico City, I took a bus to Tuxpan de Rodríguez Cano, 150 km further down the Gulf coast. There was another showing of the film *'Les Choristes'* – a chance for me to brush up my French, a language I wouldn't need on my travels, except possibly in Tahiti. I found the films tiresome – it's hard to cut out the sound if you want to sleep, read a book or look out of the window. At least on planes you have individual headphones. At 3.45 I had a chance to get off and stretch my legs. It was like stepping into an oven. As I was going back to my seat I banged my head on a flap hanging down from the ceiling like the lid of a locker. I was about to try to close it when I realised that it was one of the TV screens. We'd a Spiderman film next, violent and dubbed in Spanish. Alfred Molina, a fine actor, played the part of a malevolent monster, who could sprout powerful metal tentacles when he got angry. I imagined Molina was paid a lot of money for this nonsense – he had no other excuse. I tried to settle in a corner with my hat over my face to keep off the sun, but I soon found myself peeking at the screen through one of the hat's ventilation holes.

The countryside was changing. The grass became lusher. There were perky little hills, green and rounded, houses tucked in between trees. Imagine Tuscany, but hotter, dustier and scruffier. We passed two women balancing shopping on their heads.

At Tuxpan I checked into the Hotel Florida. There were five original oil paintings on the stairs. Someone had branded the carpet in my room with an iron. I went out to explore the waterfront beside the river. The trunks of the palm trees reminded me of elephants' legs, except that they'd been painted white from the ground up to a blue border at hat height. I hadn't had a good meal for 48 hours. I came to a floating restaurant called the Afracadero and went aboard. There were two decks, the upper one open to the breeze through insect-proof mesh at each end. The restaurant looked elegant with little squares of navy linen placed diagonally on full white tablecloths. Charming waitresses fell over themselves to look after me. They called the boss up from the lower deck.

'Where would you like to sit,' he asked me, 'up or down?'

'Oh, up, please,' I said.

'Which table? You could have this, or this, or this?'

The restaurant was empty.

'Er, this would be fine,' I said, choosing a table on the river side of the vessel.

He got his son, a well-presented young man of about twenty, who spoke English, to come and talk to me. I asked him for half a bottle of white wine.

'We haven't got any half bottles,' he said. 'We'll just give you half a whole bottle. Would you like Californian Chardonnay – or we've two Italian wines?' he asked.

'It must be from the New World,' I said.

He went away and asked his father. After some delay he came back.

'Don't worry, we don't keep all our wine here. We have some more in the cellar,' he said, indicating somewhere on the land.

'Okay,' I said, 'as long as it's cold.'

I was being treated as a VIP, and I behaved like one. He came back with the wine and when he'd poured me a glass he put the bottle in an electric wine cooler and plugged this in. I had noodle soup with purplish-brown beans in it, then a fish called 'robalo' – from the river, the young man said. The flesh was firm and had a subtle flavour. It was served with a herby dressing, a big boiled potato and rice. We could have done with some colour – red peppers or green beans – but it tasted delicious. The air was balmy, the atmosphere wonderful. Two loving couples arrived. We'd water on three sides and there was a slight motion from the waves. Ferries were plying across different stretches of a great curve in the river. The sky was dark. There were little lights on the other side – and fork lightning.

The son had just come back from Canada.

'What are your plans now?' I asked him.

'I want to do civil engineering,' he said.

'There's a lot of building going on in Mexico – you'd have plenty to do.'

'The country is healthy now. We've a strong president. When George Bush told him to stop the drug traffic, our man said Americans should stop consuming the drugs. An earlier president couldn't have said such a thing.'

'It's important that other countries stand up to Bush. How long has the restaurant been going?'

'It's only just opened. It's always been my father's dream. My grandfather came from Spain. He was on the wrong side in the Civil War, so he decided to come here.'

'The restaurant's in a marvellous position. It's special. It looks good; the food is good – you should do well.'

I shook hands with son and father. Then I walked as steadily as I could along the gangplank. In the morning I had breakfast in the dining room of the hotel, a clean and wholesome room. I sat by the window next to the street. The orange juice was lovely, the coffee better than I'd had in the United States. The scrambled egg with stringy bits of meat in it was far better than it sounds. The mushy purple-brown beans with splashes of something white, which I took to be cottage cheese, were equally edible, but the idea of forking these onto a disc of tortilla and sprinkling it with the usual bright green and orange sauces, chopped onion and chillies seemed strange at breakfast time.

There was a controller on every major junction directing the traffic with a series of shrill signals on whistles. People were sitting on the steps of a church or hanging out on the verandah of the Palacio Municipal. Along the side of it there were eight stands for shoe-shiners. In three of the positions, shiners sat on the customers' seats waiting for them to arrive. One of the shiners saw me compiling these statistics and thought at last he'd got a customer.

I went into the Tourism Office and picked up a free, photocopied map. In the doorway of *'Boutique Unique Sencillamente Elegante'* a pretty girl stood flicking a torso with a duster. The torso was wearing just a skimpy bikini bottom. The real girl was fully clothed. She saw me looking at them both and grinned. I needed to send some more papers home. I went into a tiny stationers, where a kindly man found just the right size of envelope and a roll of sticky tape. He had been divorced for three years and appeared lonely. He had two children but didn't see them often. He seemed delighted to have someone to talk to, as I was. He'd learned his English in the American Institute in Mexico City. They'd done a good job on him.

I liked Tuxpan and decided to stay a second night. Outside in Mexico, as the heat built up, so did the haze, which acted as a partial shield against the direct rays of the sun. I found it very hot in the library. There was no air conditioning and no fan where I was looking at atlases, but I managed to plan a route to Guatemala, to take me over the mountainous inland regions of Mexico. After a while I felt nauseous and went onto a balcony to get some air. The little schoolgirls looked sweet and neat in their white blouses, pinafore dresses or skirts and long lacy white socks. I noticed that the men often wore vests under their shirts, as if they were saying, 'I'm so cool I can wear a vest in the middle of the day, yes, even at times of high humidity.'

In the night I worked out that within a week I might be in the malarial zone, so I decided to begin my anti-malarial pills. At 7am I started walking to the bus station. The town was busy. The bus was smaller than usual. The driver checked everyone's name and we left on time. By 8am we were in the hills. The land was very green, much of it planted with orange trees. There was very little in the way of human construction. It had been raining, so for once the lorries didn't turn up the dust. A man in waders was fishing in a young river.

At the first stop everyone got off so I did the same. I spent a penny and got back on again. The driver came back and began to reverse the bus. I was the only passenger on board. I started to panic. I had to do something, so I ran down the aisle of the bus, shouting something international like, 'Ohhhhh!' The driver stopped the bus and said something in Spanish.

The only thing I could think to say was, 'Apizaco' (the town I was heading for).

The driver said something else in Spanish.

I pointed to the door, meaning, 'Should I get off?'

But I thought he thought I meant, 'May I get off?'

He said something else in Spanish, which I thought meant, 'Well, if you're going to get off, hurry up!'

So I grabbed my belongings and got off. He reversed a bit further. Then I remembered he had my rucksack in the luggage hold. I might never see it again. I waved my arms frantically and pointed to the hold. He said something else in Spanish, stuck five fingers up at me and drove off. I hoped that meant he'd gone to refuel and would be back in five minutes. I stood anxiously waiting for the bus to come back. Some passengers tried to reassure me, in Spanish of course. I hoped they were saying, 'Don't worry – the bus will be back.' So I pointed at the ground as if to say, 'back here?' They nodded. After seven minutes the bus came back. I felt bad at messing the driver about, so I looked up the Spanish for 'I'm sorry' but when I got on the bus again he had disappeared.

The bus went up into the mountains. There would have been fine views if the visibility had been better. We climbed above a cloud and could look down on it, until the windows misted up. The in-journey entertainment was Walt Disney's 'Aliens of the Deep'. Each time the bus stopped, vendors would come aboard to sell refreshments and other wares. Thus, we inhabited four worlds: the rugged landscape, the clouds, the world of an American film and the world of the locals who burst in from time to time.

The road made a snakewise ascent, past isolated shacks, some extended with awnings, all offering the same selection of fruit and vegetables. Numerous large signs warned of driving dangers ahead. We entered another cloud. A sign said (I think), 'In fog follow line at side of road'. Another, 'Diminish your velocity in fog'. In one place workers with bulldozers were widening the road by cutting into the cliff. I preferred it when we were on the side close in to the mountain. On the other side there was a precipice. Once I looked out and could see nothing but mist so I couldn't tell how deep the drop was. When we came to a gap in the mist I looked down very steeply to a little patch of green far below. I have a poor head for heights, so at times I bit my lip and closed my eyes. I hoped the driver wasn't doing the same. At one point we were crawling through the mist behind a lorry. It passed several lay-bys without pulling in to let us overtake. It was not until much later on a straight stretch of road that we could get ahead of the blighter. I was glad our driver had refuelled earlier. What a place to run out of petrol!

I saw a flat-bottomed valley, very green, with a river; a church had a big green dome. We went through a town and dropped down to the river. The sun was coming out. At last there was no mist and you could take in a whole scene, a harsh, wild, timeless landscape but picturesque and grand, with rocks, bare earth and only occasional trees and fields. A man was ploughing with a pair of horses.

In Apizaco I checked in to the Hotel Plaza. The building had external air conditioning. A shell around the main building wrapped it in a thick layer of cool night air. This was open above but because cold air sinks it was trapped. It was kept cool by air-conditioning apparatus housed in the shell. The system was bulky but surprisingly effective. The temperature in the hotel was steady and we didn't have the usual air-conditioning noise.

Suddenly there was a terrible clatter. Through the transparent roof I could see the silhouettes of men moving about. A wind was getting up. One of the men dropped a rope through an opening to the sky. I thought perhaps a hurricane was on its way and they were there to tie the roof down. I put a waterproof on and went out to eat.

It's not an adventure until something goes wrong. When I came out of the restaurant there was no hurricane but it was dark and I couldn't remember which way I'd come. Apizaco was a confusing town to find my way around using a small photocopied town plan. The streets were laid out as a grid, regular as a crossword puzzle. On the map they were labelled in tiny capitals, very hard to read, especially as the names were Spanish and confusing such as 'JESÚS BARAGANZA', 'EMILIO BARAGANZA', 'BLVD EMILIO SANCHEZ PHEDRAS'. The street signs were hard to find and difficult to make out. To look at the map I had to stop near a streetlamp, take off my glasses and hold the map close to my face. At the same time I needed to keep an eye out in case I was being watched or followed, which required putting my glasses back on. I tried to find the names of two streets at right angles so that I could look for the intersection on my map, but by the time I'd found a lamp so I could read the map I'd forgotten the names of the streets. When I wasn't looking at the map I walked very fast and I kept crossing the road to dodge any suspicious characters. Once, I fell over.

As I was rushing around in the dark, the lights in the shops were going out, so the task was getting harder by the minute. Soon I'd be lost in an unlit labyrinth. I was keeping a grip on myself but underneath I felt scared. Luckily I saw a bright light coming from a pharmacy. The women assistants offered to help me although they had started shutting up shop. They were serving their last customer and he directed me to go past something called 'the bull'. I had never seen a bull in the town. I never did see a bull, but somehow I managed to get back to my hotel, although not until 9.45pm. Remember it gets dark early in the tropics. I vowed never again to get lost at night, a vow I broke many times.

In the morning the hotel receptionist recommended a lovely restaurant for breakfast. I had a glass of real orange juice, fresh sliced melon, pineapple and banana with yoghurt on top, cornflakes with milk and raisins, *pan francés* (slices of hot buttered toast sprinkled with brown sugar) and coffee. The whole meal cost 62 pesos (about £3). The way I was travelling, I missed out most of the tourist destinations, but I caught many glimpses of the lives of local people, generally denied to those on package holidays. On the next table were two couples with a little girl and a boy toddler. The boy was being noisy and difficult but everyone else was totally relaxed. All the relationships between those six people were warm and in tune. The mother saw me watching the group and smiled. When they left the little boy waved to me. The younger couple were holding hands.

Apizaco bus station was small and situated on a busy street like a café. Indeed, it was laid out like one, with a row of seats at one end, hot and cold food counters at the other, tables and chairs in the middle. All it lacked was a couple of fans. There was a single ticket counter in a corner. The buses pulled up as they would at a bus stop. What could be more straightforward?

Puebla Bus Station on the other hand was big and well organised. It took me five minutes to get out of it, into a hot, crowded, sleazy area with lots of touting taxi-drivers. I walked between these and, trusting to instinct, hiked through the extensive 'motor quarter'. This had a thriving business in spares and repairs. Lorry tyres were piled up in the street, cracked windscreens propped up. Everywhere there were cars, hoists, wheels, car seats, silencers, 'big ends' and numerous other auto parts. In dark corners I could see the blue flames of welding torches.

At 2162 metres above sea level Puebla was the highest place I stopped at in Mexico. Determined not to get lost in this town, much bigger than Apizaco, and having no map I made my own on a double page of my notebook, adding features as I came to them. I stayed at the Hotel Valencia, pleasant, new and very cheap. There was no air conditioning but at that altitude the atmosphere was agreeable enough, especially when the rain came down. The wetted dust smelled good through the bars of my windows. A notice on the door said,

> *'It is strictly forbidden to the guest to make a noise, get into musicians or animals of any kind as to make any act that bothers or incommodes other guests... Baggage and other articles that guests get into their rooms will guarantee all debts including lodging complementary services and other consumptions that guests cause.'*

I washed a shirt and two pairs of socks. Then I took a siesta. At 5.30 I got up and had a shower. Then I set out as usual to find a map and a restaurant. For the first time since I'd been in Mexico I saw some Europeans, a German mother and daughter, both with dyed blond hair, calf-length trousers and rucksacks. I had lost my floppy white hat so I bought a baseball cap to keep off the sun. It had a peak curved like Donald Duck's bill. When I wore it next day I got funnier looks than I had with the floppy white hat.

A young man, about 18, with a handsome face, seemed to be growing out of the pavement. Where were his legs? Then I realised he didn't have any. I was so shocked I didn't give him any money. He had no hat or begging bowl, but what was he there for, if not to beg? Perhaps a bowl could have been snatched from him. He was still there, of course, when I went back so I gave him something then.

There was a sort of retail slum consisting of a continuous line of stalls connected to a maze of living quarters, which looked temporary but had probably been there many years. By the side of the road a dead dog was crawling with flies.

I decided to stay a second night in Puebla. At midday in an attempt to use the sun as a compass I found myself looking for my shadow. It turned out I was standing on it. I realised then that in the tropics you could only use the sun as a directional aid in the morning or evening. I found an Internet café with air conditioning and checked my e-mails.

'I'm rethinking the next stage,' I told my supporters. 'I'll enter Guatemala as planned, then El Salvador, where I shall investigate a ferry from La Reunión on the Pacific coast to Puntarenas in Costa Rica. This is a 24-hour trip, which will make a refreshing change from the buses. This plan means I shall miss out Honduras & Nicaragua altogether, which is a shame.'

I saw some children coming out of school. Some wore cardigans over shirts and vests at a time when I felt very hot. Street sellers were waiting for them with little polythene parcels of frozen fruit or juice. I watched a woman on her way home with her three children. The youngest, who had probably been with her all day, was happy to run on ahead. The middle child was telling her mother something (presumably what had happened at school). But the mother had her hand round the shoulders of the eldest. Thus she watched one, listened to another and held onto the third – so much love! I had a drink of *'guayabo'* juice, thick and refreshing but not too sweet, without realising until later that it was guava.

The next day I missed the bus through waiting in the wrong part of the bus station. Luckily there was another due two hours later. While I was sitting in the café, I saw a young European couple at the next table. When the girl went to the loo, her boyfriend pulled out a paperback. The design of the cover looked French. When they went to the bus I contrived to catch them up and started speaking in English.

'You're not Mexican,' I began.

He was fair. She was dark.

'Yes,' said the girl, 'but I'm not English. I'm French.'

That was all I needed. I'd been struggling for a week with Spanish. At last someone with a common language! I opened my mouth and French poured out of me like water from a burst main.

'Bonjour, je m'appelle John. Je suis anglais …'

I shook their hands – very British!

'Vous voyagez en Mexique?' one of them asked.

'Ah, oui,' I replied, *'Aujourd'hui je vais à Oaxaca.'*

The man corrected my pronunciation – not of French, but how to say the Mexican town 'Oaxaca'. If you don't sound as though you've got a fishbone stuck in your throat you're not doing it right.

'Mon espagnol est terrible,' I said.

I sensed that I might have overplayed my hand, so I let them get ahead in the queue. Then I met another young couple queuing, also French. She was from the Auvergne, studying at the University of Puebla. He was there to see her and take a holiday. I told them the other couple was French. In all this excitement I lost my new cap. I ran back to the seat in the bus station but, of course, the cap had gone. However, meeting four Europeans had put me in such good spirits that I didn't mind.

Once we'd got away from the city, we entered a wide, flat valley where people were toiling in the fields. For an hour there were mountains on one side of the valley or the other – or both. Then there were mountains directly ahead of us so we turned right and started to climb. The mountains closed in on either side until the road appeared to have been cut out of pink rock. This was barren terrain indeed. I didn't see a single wayside shack, tethered animal or heap of rubbish. This scrub of cactus, stones and not much else, with mountains on both sides, was the most attractive scenery I'd seen so far. There were curious single-stem cacti, like petrified sea serpents emerging from a solid sea. I saw later that we'd been near – and might have seen – mountains of 5,000 metres or more. The young Mexican man sleeping next to me had an unruffled brow, a white vest and the daintiest of rosaries, made entirely of black thread.

At one point there was a sheer drop to a dried river bed. Sometimes we'd pass such a drop and when I looked back I'd see that we'd gone over a spindly bridge. Sometimes the drop was so scary that I had to look away. I saw three donkeys, the middle one on its side as if dead. Another donkey was immobilised because it had wound its tether several times round one leg. Irregular, small pieces of land, not too sloping, had been worked and planted. Apart from this and the occasional grazing animal there was little sign of man. As we came down from the mountains we entered a region of wooded hills. A man was herding goats along the road. We came into Oaxaca, 1550 metres above sea level and the capital of the state with the same name.

I booked in to the Hotel Anturios. The receptionist gave me a map. She told me where 'down town' was and I headed for it. I immediately took a fancy to the city and decided to stay two nights here as well. I found a splendid restaurant around a courtyard open to the sky. I went back to the hotel to wash my face, neck and armpits. I washed the shirt I'd just taken off and put on a dry one. I set off again for the courtyard restaurant. Unsolicited they gave me a starter consisting of two soft cheeses, two sauces and a segment of a large red grapefruit, served with a leaf of lettuce and a slice of bread, soft and grey with a thin, crisp crust. Then I had a soup of Oaxacan beans with avocado and tortilla strips. I followed this with 'grouper', wrapped in leaves, possibly vine leaves, and bathed in a herby lemon sauce. It was served with sautéed potatoes and round beans.

As you are not usually offered a dessert in Mexico I took pleasure in ordering the guava tart, which came with separate pieces of guava and a water ice. I heard a rumbling and thought we were going to be treated to a thunderstorm, but it was only the retractable roof sliding into place above the courtyard. There was a very civilised, middle-aged couple on the next table. They looked European.

'I hope you enjoy the rest of your meal,' I said.

They looked a little surprised.

'I thought I heard you speaking English just now?' I said.

'No, we're from Argentina,' the man said, sounding wise and cultured.

'I'm sorry,' I said, 'I don't hear very well.'

'Where are you from?' he asked.

'I'm from England.'

'Which part?'

'The South – near Southampton.'

'We've been to Scotland – and Devon,' the man said.

'You should come to Argentina,' the woman suggested.

'I'm afraid I shan't manage it this time. I've got a ship from Panama to New Zealand.'

'Perhaps another time. And Chile too.'

'Good-bye!'

Such charming people! Notice, I was careful not to mention the Falklands! It rained a bit on my way back to the hotel. I flopped onto my bed and listened as the shower developed into a noisy thunderstorm, my first tropical storm.

In the morning I realised what a delightful hotel it was, built around an attractive courtyard garden. The dining room opened onto this garden and tables for breakfast were laid inside and out, but after the rain the air was cool and most chose to eat inside. The wall was mainly of glass, however, so we were outside in spirit. Three gardeners were busy: one deadheading pelargoniums, a second trimming a palm tree and a third sweeping the paving. The best thing for me was having a real single room with a single bed. It was half the size of the double rooms and tucked into a corner of the building. Not difficult that – but oh, so rare!

I went back to the cultural heart of Oaxaca. There was an exhibition of paintings and prints by children. A seven-year-old boy had produced a painting called *'La Muerte'* (death) showing a clothed skeleton holding flowers by a gravestone. I grew fond of the square known as the *Parque Juarez* and took several photographs. I saw a poster for a recital for violin and piano to be held at 8 o'clock that evening in the *Teatro Juarez* beside *El Parque* so I went in and bought a ticket. In an outdoor-adventure shop two assistants spoke English, one better than the other.

'Ah,' I said, 'you want to try out your English!'

'You can try out your Spanish if you want,' the better English speaker said. 'I do that all day – and your English sounds really good.'

I told them I was having trouble with my compass. They discouraged me from buying a new one and sent me out into the street with my own compass, telling me where the North was. I went to the bus station, where the woman behind the 'Information' counter suggested a route to the Guatemalan border.

In the evening I went into a cheap restaurant not far from the concert hall. The folding doors were opened the width of the establishment and I'd a pleasant view of the *Parque*. It got dark quickly and in no time an impressive thunderstorm was upon us. I was the only customer but when the rain came down – and it did so with spectacular abandon – more people came in. Others sheltered under trees in the park. A couple arrived under an umbrella, looking pleased to be caught in a storm. When not serving customers, the proprietor stood watching it. The thunder made less noise than the river that quickly formed across the front of the restaurant. I had a waterproof but the storm seemed to have taken the locals by surprise. It was chaotic; the lightning and thunder seemed independent of each other, making me think that the storm had two centres.

By the time I'd finished my meal the rain had nearly stopped. I was early at the concert and could watch the audience arrive. There were lots of young people. A man with a violin on his back came in with his girlfriend. Another young couple sat down in the row in front of me. She at once pulled out a book and started reading a chapter called 'On the Obligation of Married Couples' *(my translation)*.

On the platform there were two pots of plants with pink flowers. An overhead spotlight threw a semicircle of light in the middle of the stage, making for a dramatic concentration on the musicians when they appeared, wearing what looked like black hair shirts. The violinist, one Sócrates Luis Juarez Urbieta stood in front of the concavity of the piano. The pianist, Eliseo Martinez García closed the lid. They played a sonata by 'J F Haendel'. This must have been George Frideric Handel of 'Messiah' fame, who at one time spelled his surname 'Haendel' – it certainly sounded like his work. It felt strange to be transported back to Europe by two Mexicans playing in Mexico.

The violinist had a sweet tone and tender phrasing, although he seemed scared of the music. The pianist was not fully at home either, his left hand sounding mechanical. A photographer was filming their performance and in the middle he ran across in front of the stage and set up on the other side, which can't have helped. In the Beethoven Romance in F major, Urbieta still seemed to be warming up. It was not until the violin's third entry that he was right on top of the music. The Kreisler prelude was a triumph – I wondered if the late Romantic repertoire was more their thing.

The answer came in the second half of the recital, when they seemed to be enjoying themselves, the violinist smiling for the first time. He played a piece by the Spanish Sarasate as if it was in his blood. During the final piece he was simultaneously bowing and playing pizzicato with the pizzazz of a Paganini. While this was going on, a woman in the audience was texting someone. The audience fell into a slow handclap, which I hoped had a different meaning in Mexico.

The next day I travelled south-east to Juchitan de Zaragoza on the Pacific coast. There was something very clear about the look of the landscape. Maybe the storm had cleaned the air. For the first time we had views in which mountains, fields, trees, buildings and the usual clutter made a continuous picture – like it does in Europe. The countryside had been dramatic, awesome, severe and inhospitable; now it was beautiful. I saw a pony turning a grindstone.

By eleven o'clock we'd started climbing. The road seemed particularly winding and the driver took it very steadily. At a checkpoint an armed soldier emerged from a concrete box. I saw small plantations of what I assumed was aloe vera. Some thorny bushes had seed pods like tiny black socks. There were cacti with a number of vertical branches all with flowers like prickly eyeballs looking out in different directions. A sign on a shack advertised 'Mescal', the cactus whose tubercles, I learned later, provide the hallucinatory properties of mescaline. I wonder if these were the 'eyeballs' I'd seen. An iron cross beside a steep drop told of a roadside tragedy. A brown river, like a channel in a milk-chocolate factory, gave brown-tinted reflections of its banks. We did a loop and came back higher up, allowing me to look down on the stretch of road we had just travelled. I had to breathe deeply and slowly to hold back nausea. We seemed to be as high as the tops of the mountains, which was unlikely. It was better than flying. I saw planting on slopes so steep that they must have been cultivated by hand – no plough could have managed it. Mostly the hills were covered in pines, except where fire had cleared them, blackening the ground.

Coming down there were rocks with deep holes in them making them look like the skulls of giants. Another roadside shrine. I looked down over the edge of the road to see the evidence of an upset lorry – about a hundred red plastic crates and the bottles they had contained. A rope bridge crossed another brown river. Black birds the size of turkeys were sitting in a tree and I wondered if they were vultures. By the side of the road there were piles of fir cones some 40 cm long and shaped like pineapples. When we passed some more I realised that they weren't fir cones but stumps of aloe after the leaves had been cut off. By two o'clock we had descended to a plain. A river of clear water indicated a change of rock. The cows had horns, humps between their shoulder blades and long, drooping ears. Further on, a notice at a checkpoint said it was for drugs and firearms. In a clear river, children were bathing. Beside the road a shelter from the sun had been made of palm leaves.

We came to Tehuantepec, which I knew to be near the Pacific. I was hoping to see the Ocean but it was now too hazy. In Juchitan I found a hotel opposite the bus station. My room had a big marble floor. I could have given dancing lessons – if I'd been any good at dancing. I had my hair cut short in a unisex salon. I had dinner in a restaurant called the 'Pizza Room'. It had a courtyard open to the sky apart from various roofs, designed presumably to keep off the sun. There were trees and smaller plants in enormous pots, a water feature which dripped water, an artificial stream with a bridge over it and a cart outlined with tiny yellow lights. I chose a small table in the middle. I'd been served bread, butter, limes, sauces and so on, when I realised that I could feel the heat radiating from a vast dome-shaped oven four metres away, its flaming gas burners visible through its open door. The evening was quite hot enough without this oven and I felt sorry for the two chefs who had to work with it every day.

When I got back to my room it was still very hot. I put the air conditioning on, flopped on the bed and fell asleep. I woke still hot and feeling debilitated as well. I decided to have a shower. But first I had to sort some things out. The bedside lamp didn't work. The only light was a circular tube on the ceiling above the rotating fan. The light shone through the blades with a tiresome stroboscopic effect. The toilet wouldn't flush so I decided to investigate. I took off the lid of the cistern and foolishly leant it against the wall. Immediately it fell to the floor and broke into a dozen pieces. I decided to tell the management about the cistern in the morning, if my Spanish was up to it. The tiled floor of the bedroom felt warm under my bare feet. I took a shower. The air conditioning thundered away but at 1.30am the room was not appreciably cooler. The only way to be comfortable was to lie naked under the fan.

In the morning I went out to find what a cistern lid would cost. I got some idea by looking at the prices of other bathroom fittings in a shop. I saw a cart laden with building materials pulled through the streets by oxen. A man was sharpening knives using a bicycle adapted to drive a whetstone. When I got back to the hotel I offered to pay for the broken cistern lid. A girl was sent to ask the boss. I think she was the one cleaning my room. I was glad I'd tipped her. The answer came back that they wouldn't take any money.

I had to wait nearly two hours for my bus. It was too hot for me in the bus station, even though it was draughty, so I went to the superstore, which I knew would have air conditioning. I had to hand my luggage in, which suited me. I sat for a while on the bottom shelf of a display rack. Then I moved to a pallet. After that I rested on the sofa of a three-piece suite until a couple began to consider buying it. Finally, I found a black office chair on wheels – very comfy.

As it was, the bus was 30 minutes late so I still had to wait an hour in the heat. The air-conditioned vehicle was bliss, although I could have done without the horror movie. Why anyone would want to listen to people screaming in terror while travelling on Mexico's hair-raising roads was beyond me. I dropped my notebook, which slid forward under the seats in front of me. At the next stop, with very little Spanish and much crawling around on the floor, to the amusement of everyone, I got the message through to the woman in front of me that I was looking for something. Thus I was able to reach past her legs and pick up the book. Smiles all round.

We entered Chiapas, the southernmost state of Mexico. When we arrived in Tuxtla it was dark and I was anxious to find somewhere to stay. I walked as fast as I could, looking out all the time for anyone who might attack me. I must have gone a mile and a half. I was now in an insalubrious quarter dominated by Tuxtla's motor-repair trade.

At last I saw a hotel. I shot in anxiously and took a room for 100 pesos (about five pounds). The woman at Reception gave me the key to number 205. I went upstairs, put the key in the door and opened it. A couple, short, stocky and completely nude, were in some sort of amorous engagement, one sitting on the bed, the other kneeling between the thighs of the first, both individuals now motionless. Neither turned to look towards the door. They had frozen at the sound of the key in the lock. I didn't see their faces and I shut the door so quickly that I couldn't tell the gender of either.

I went downstairs and managed to convey the interesting news that my room already had two people in it and handed back the key. She sent me to room 204. I locked myself in and pushed a wedge under the door.

The room was hot and there was no air conditioning, although there was a fan with five speeds. There were two cast-iron beds. Headboards were suggested by a break in the pebbledash so that if you sat up in bed you didn't have to lean against a rough hard surface but could enjoy a smooth hard surface instead. A signed, numbered and framed print had been rumpled by damp.

A tiny television sat in a metal frame on which I hung my socks to air. The insect mesh in the window was so badly torn it would have let in an alligator. Instead of fixing notices to the wall, they had been hand-painted directly onto it. On the door, hand-written in Spanish, was a twelve-point plan for tackling erectile dysfunction.

ADVERTENCIA
Estimado Huésped este Anuncio Puede Salvarle la Vida

Si pasa de los 45 años y tomo medicamento para lo disfuncion erectil le sugerimos:

1. No lo combine con alcohol y tabaco.
2. Si sufre de hipertensión arterial tenga a mano el medicamento correcto para evitartia.
3. Trate de que sea su chica la que se mueva casi todo el tiempo que dure la relación intima.
4. Ud. muevase lo minimo durante la relación intima.
5. No dilate mas de media hora cuando mucho con reloj ?en mano.
6. No eyacule, aprenda a no eyacular aunque tenga puesto el condón.
7. Cuando termine su relación tómese 1 o 2 aspirinas con agua aunque se sienta bien puede evitar un infarto.
8. Si pesa mas de 100kg y se acerca a los 50 años no tenga mas que 3 relaciones al més. Ya no tiene 20 años
9. No es romántico morir de placer
10. Si ya es mayor y ud sigue las indicaciones anteriores con mucho gusto estaremos dispuestos a proporcionarle la habitación.
11. Si eres joven haz caso omiso de este letrero y disparate sin drogas
12. Si tienes mas de 65 años 1 o 2 veces al més es mas que suficiente!

Sergio y Nayelii 19-Nov-06

There – if you can read Spanish, you've got a magnifying glass handy and you know about these things – you can see if the advice makes sense!

There was an en-suite bathroom, if that's not too grand a term. It had no light. The toilet had no seat, it didn't flush and there was no toilet paper, although being a bus traveller I carried my own. Only one tap remained. I was hot from my exertions and I took a cold shower (there was no hot water). The shower had no screen. You stood in a well but the water squirted onto tiles on the floor and ran from there into the bedroom. You could minimise the flood by setting the shower at half squirt. For further cooling, I set the fan to the highest speed and let that dry me.

I had the room next around the corner from the discommoded lovers. Their discommodity had not dulled their ardour and, with our windows at right angles and both open, late into the night and again in the early morning, I could hear Spanish endearments along with utterances of a more international nature. The couple seemed determined to get the utmost value from their 100-peso investment in a room too indecent for mere sleep. They left early, suggesting that their assignation had been as improper as it had been vigorous.

After a less than refreshing sleep I returned to the bus station. My next bus seemed rather long and once we were in the country the driver needed all his skill to take the vehicle round the many hairpin bends, one of them so tight that he had to cross to the wrong side of the road and hope there was nothing coming the other way.

Sitting next to me on the aisle seat was a slim woman of about 30. When we stopped at Arriaga I asked her to let me out. I got off the bus and stretched my legs. Not knowing how long the stop was I didn't dare look for a public toilet but got back onto the bus. When she saw me coming Slim Woman got up again to let me in. With a gesture of my hand I declined her offer and pressed on to the bus toilet, cracking my head on one of the cursed television screens. When I finally returned to my seat, Slim Woman got up again and asked me if I was all right, putting her hand on the bump on my forehead in a tender gesture that almost made the accident worthwhile.

I fell asleep and woke up at Pijijiapan, a wonderful word, particularly in upper-and-lower case because above the 'I's and 'J's are five dots in a row. At last I could see the Pacific – and very reassuring it was too. We crossed another dried-up river. I saw a cow with straight horns sticking out sideways and measuring almost a metre tip to tip.

Slim Woman started mothering me, buying me *Totopo de Crema y Quesillo*, and writing down those words for me on a scrap of paper. This 'delicacy' consisted of rectangles of ham in gooey cheese, packed in coloured paper. She let her knee touch mine. Then she wrote a note on a scrap of paper and passed it to me, *'Mi nombre es Mercedes Zárase Julián. Vivo en Acapetahua, Chiapas. Me dio gusto conocerle y rezo a Dios que le acompañe en su viaje.'* (My name is Mercedes Zárase Julián. I live in Acapetahua, Chiapas. I was very happy to meet you and I pray God that He accompany you on your travels.) We had a slow conversation interrupted by long searches in my dictionary. Then she got off.

The landscape grew softer. There were bits of lush, thick jungle. A cow standing in a shallow river appeared to be puzzling over her own reflection. Then we came into rain. At five o'clock we arrived at Tapachula. There was a flood around the bus station. Baggage handlers in wellington boots passed the cases from the luggage compartment onto a dry platform. At the front of the station a man with bare feet and his trousers rolled up was vainly trying to sweep away the water. I could see the 'Hotel Dux' on the other side of the road, but because of the flood I had to go a long way round to get to it.

That night I was lying in bed when I experienced a rush of something to my head – presumably my own blood. My chest felt tight and my heart thumped rapidly. I sensed a headache coming on. I wondered if my blood pressure was going up the wall – or worse still through the roof – and I was going to suffer a stroke that would leave me dead or paralysed thousands of miles from home. I tried relaxing and breathing deeply. It's difficult to relax when you think your number is up, but the breathing helped and all the symptoms faded away leaving me greatly relieved.

Much of the time the hotel was in the charge of a man so small and so boyish I took him to be about fourteen. In the morning I asked if I might stay another night. He handed me a receipt for 250 pesos. I gave him two 200-peso notes, the smallest change I had. All he had to do was to hand me 150. But he made the understandable mistake of saying something in Spanish. Because I didn't understand what he'd said I made the understandable mistake of querying it, in so far as my linguistic competence allowed. Numbers flew between us – 50, 150, 200. These we wrote down on the back of the receipt, which ended up looking like a mathematical puzzle. Hot, deaf, ignorant, frustrated and old enough to be his grandfather, I was getting more and more agitated. I got him to turn the television off in the hope that if I heard him better I might understand what he was saying.

'It's only 200 pesos (or 150 pesos) for the second night', I thought he said.

'Something, something, *cambio*,' he definitely did say.

I think this had to do with fetching change. As he didn't go to do this, I offered to go. But he said he would. By then there were only 200 pesos on the counter. He asked me for the second 200. I refused.

'You've got it!' I mimed, as loudly as I could.

'No, you've got it,' I believed he said in Spanish.

This was a ridiculous argument. 200 pesos seemed like a lot of money but if I'd stopped to think I would have realised that it was only worth about £10. I had five pockets in my trousers. I emptied two pockets, bringing out a comb, an old bus ticket and a ball of fluff. I pointed to the till as if to say, 'I saw you put the money in the till!'

He looked at me as if I had the most outrageous nerve in Mexico.

And I, as if to say, 'Look, I will prove to you that you have the money', emptied my other three pockets. And then – the shame, the feeling of utter foolishness! I found that the missing 200-peso note had mysteriously found its way into my front right-hand pocket. I handed it over like a naughty child caught red-handed.

'Something, something, *cambio*,' he said again, and walked out of the hotel.

This gave me time to get out my dictionary and remind myself of the Spanish for 'I'm sorry!' He came back and handed me the change.

'*Gracias, señor,*' I grovelled. '*Lo siento!*'

He gave me the sweetest of sweet smiles.

The streets of the Mexican towns I'd seen were noisy, narrow, dusty and run down. The concrete was cracked and the drains smelled. The shops were cluttered with cheap and vulgar goods. But look at the people, with their broad faces made for laughing and smiling, many resembling the images I'd seen in the museum in Tampico. I found Mexicans good-natured, relaxed, easy-going, living as if every day was a fresh delight, joying in each other's company, happy in their skins. They were very kind to me. Whenever I was frustrated with the language difficulties they were patient, helping me when they could or just smiling and waiting. They never made me feel small. Again and again I felt I was among friends.

I had lunch in a café at the intersection of two streets near *el parque* (the main square). Two sides of the building were completely open to the street and the fans blowing across it made it a comfortable place to sit and watch people go by. Two Mexican musicians arrived, carrying between them a wooden xylophone, which they set up on the pavement. It was an attractive old instrument in a light-coloured wood decorated with marquetry and to some extent held together with string. I decided later it must have been a marimba.

Standing side by side facing me across the instrument, the marimbists played a duet, one player attacking the upper register with four hammers (two in each hand), the other the lower notes with three hammers. The upper register was particularly easy on the ear, like tuned wood blocks; the lower had a more metallic sound, which blended with the higher notes surprisingly well, while emphasising that we were hearing a duet. After playing a few cheerful traditional numbers, one of the musicians drew a resonator from the instrument, a long hollow block pointed at one end and open at the other, and using this as a begging bowl went round the café's customers. I gave a contribution but few of the locals did. The two then picked up their instrument and moved on.

Two minutes later another duo arrived with another marimba, also tied up with string. This time they set up on the pavement two metres from where I was sitting, forcing pedestrians to step into the road. This second duo seemed very relaxed. Between numbers they chatted to passers-by. Then the lower-register player of the first duo came back and talked to them, as friends rather than rivals. After a couple of minutes the 'low' player of the second duo went off and the 'low' player of the first took his place and played until the man he'd replaced came back. The second duo went round collecting and then left.

Soon after that a third duo, who looked like father and son, turned up with a third marimba and two trumpeters. Again they set up close to my table. They asked for requests. They played a sentimental number involving only one trumpet. Then the other trumpeter took over. I gave them 10 pesos. The guy collecting seemed pleased with this. I was the only person to applaud them, so they applauded me. Smiles and waves from them – and from me – and off they went. Marimbas are like buses – you wait for ages, then three come along!

In the park, under a large covered area two small male dancers and a drummer were performing, in tall headdresses and leopard-skin skirts over black shorts. Their chests and feet were bare, brown and glistening with perspiration. The drumming was frenetic, the dancing relentless. For a time one of the dancers played a pipe, something like a penny whistle, except that it had a miniature drum fixed to the end. He played both at the same time. A male and a female clown, both whited up, were waiting their turn. A couple of unicycles lay on the ground. The players had drawn a good crowd. I was the only European. I felt conspicuous and a bit uncomfortable, standing there with my notebook, so I left a great show earlier than I would have liked.

That evening in a restaurant I came across more male performers, looking like members of an official band, in black trousers with loops of gold braid up the sides and white shirts with white cravats. There were two trumpets and four acoustic guitars, including a bass guitar, which looked cumbersome in the hands of the bass guitarist, who was on the small side. Three of the guitarists took turns to sing. Of course, two trumpets without mutes will drown one singer, so the trumpets were confined to the instrumental passages between the vocal lines. The music was unsophisticated, jolly and easy on the ear.

It became clear that they were there to entertain just two couples at one table. After a sequence of numbers the musicians stopped playing and sat down at the next table to eat. They didn't treat it as a proper meal, however, because the trumpeters and one of the guitarists kept their instruments in their left hands while they ate. After 15 minutes they were on their feet, performing again. One of the couples started dancing. The second couple joined in – a little man with a woman some 20 cm taller and 20 kilos heavier, who kept her shoulder bag on her shoulder. Immediately four waiters went over, apparently just to applaud. Suddenly the big woman voiced her disapproval of something the little man was doing – I couldn't see what. Then he slapped her great backside with his hand. She biffed him with her bag.

A few minutes later, the other man, who seemed to be the one with the authority, stood up and started pontificating. After a while I saw him walk unsteadily to the toilet. When he came back I sensed that he was becoming maudlin. Voices were raised in argument. One of the trumpeters seemed very bored. A guitarist looked at me as if to say, 'Enough is enough.' I smiled out of sympathy and he nodded in acknowledgement.

All the musicians appeared fed up but none left, as if they felt a responsibility to see the job through. The only thing that restored equilibrium was picking up their instruments again to play another number. The whole room seemed to be revolving around the ill-mannered foursome. My own waiter was too busy dancing attendance on them to bring me my bill. The man at the centre of the party called for another number. After playing this, the band packed up their instruments and made as if to clear out. Eventually I got my waiter's attention, but he seemed preoccupied.

'Who are these people?' I asked.

'I'll get your bill,' he said and strode away quickly.

The big woman then walked out on her own, managing to look dignified except for a garment label poking out at her collar. The band walked across the restaurant and waited by the door. But after a few minutes some of them came back. They seemed torn between wanting to leave before things got nasty and feeling obliged to stay out of duty. They stood around for a while, then finally left for good. When my waiter came back with the bill I tried again.

'What's going on?' I asked.

'Where do you come from?' he asked, changing the subject.

'England.'

'I thought you were from Italy.'

'Well,' I said, 'that music reminded me a little of Italian folk music. Why won't you tell me who these people are?' I persisted. 'I shall be in Guatemala tomorrow. I'm just fascinated. I know you're being very professional …'

'You like Mexico?'

'Yes, I do – very much. But it's the people – you are so nice, so sweet. Do you know what I mean? The mothers with their babies, the young lovers, the married couples, the friends – you are all so affectionate …'

Then he was called to the private party. I would never find out the identity of the rancid big cheese, who had everyone running around after him. Nobody who had worked in the catering profession would expect a waiter to leave his customers and leap to attention. Was he a jumped-up tycoon, who had bought half the restaurants in Tapachula and controlled the local entertainment industry as well? If he were a Mafia boss – or similar – wouldn't he have had more henchmen with him? And a bit more style? Was he a drug baron, perhaps? The Governor of the State of Chiapas? Answers on a postcard, please.

I woke in the night to realise that I'd been bitten. I'd lots of small, raised pink spots. They didn't bother me as such, except that I imagined that they were bites by mosquitoes carrying malaria, insects that bite at night – or Dengue-Fever-carrying mosquitoes, which bite by day. I had started taking anti-malarial pills a week before I entered the malarial zone, but there was no cure for Dengue Fever, which can be fatal, and there was no way to protect against it either, except avoiding the bites – and I'd been bitten!

In the morning I was up at seven. Outside there was a general discussion in progress conducted entirely by motor horn. I put off going to Guatemala and decided to have a third night in the Hotel Dux, because I was ahead of schedule – I'd no idea that the Mexican bus service would have got me this far so quickly. But I found a money exchange and swapped most of my pesos into Guatemalan quetzals (not to be confused with German pretzels). I found myself in the town square again. On the big platform there was a sale of paintings, jewellery, dolls and other artefacts. On the stage were three men playing a single marimba with a fourth on electric bass guitar. Two girls in school uniform came up to me to practise their English. One wanted to be a businesswoman. It was difficult to talk against the noise of the announcements. Then four middle-aged women in traditional costume came onto the stage and danced to recorded music consisting of a singer and the ever-present marimba. The girls came back and presented me with a figure of an owl and a biro bound in white and glittering gold threads, with the word 'CHIAPAS' superimposed.

'We're volunteering,' they told me, without explaining what for.

I was touched and a little embarrassed as I couldn't think what to give them. In the evening I returned to the corner restaurant, where I'd first heard the marimbas. I asked for the fan above me to be put on, but they had electrical problems. A man was standing on a chair fiddling with the wiring, presumably with the current switched off. The waiter fanned me with the menu card. I fanned him back. In how many countries would that happen?

Finally, it was time to move on. In the morning I walked across the road to the bus station. A doleful white fellow with a long, narrow nose got on, so tall that his hair touched the roof of the vehicle. I made some notes and while I was thinking what to write next I held my pencil in my fist against my ear. Immediately a woman offered to let me use her mobile phone. The bus was only a third full. We were to do the journey to Guatemala City in one go, including crossing the border. There was a long announcement – too quiet for me to catch a word. So I went down the bus to talk to the tall guy with the long nose.

'Excuse me,' I began, 'do you speak English?'

'Yes,' he said.

'Did you get any of that?'

'No, it just washed over me.'

'Are you American?'

'Yeah. You English?'

'Yes. I'm going round the world. You just visiting Guatemala?'

'I'm going to Costa Rica. I've heard it's beautiful.'

'I shall be in Costa Rica eventually.'

'Well, if you need any help …'

'Thanks, that's very nice of you.'

Soon after, we came to the border. The old nervousness came back – physical as much as mental. I knew I was entering a new and poorer country. The actual crossing seemed to represent a stressful and irrevocable step. Everyone else got out of the bus, so I did so too. I didn't know where we were supposed to go or what we were supposed to do. I lost our party and pressed on in the hope of finding them. Eventually I went the wrong way and someone had to put me right. A bit later I almost caught up with my American friend, who signalled to me where to go. Boy, was I relieved to see him! I was required to hand over 260 pesos for the privilege of leaving the country. Then a number of local men appeared and started telling me what to do. They were all round me. One asked me how many pesos I had. They didn't believe me when I showed them a handful of coins. I counted them. A man said he'd take them all – and did so. I didn't know what this was for. Then, out of the blue as it seemed to me, he gave me a quantity of quetzals.

'How many quetzals have you got?' he asked.

'Lots,' I said and patted one of my pockets.

'How many?'

'Why do you need to know how many quetzals I've got?' I asked, getting anxious.

'How many?'

'I don't understand why you need to know!'

'Okay, you can go.'

'I'll come with you,' one of the other men said.

I thought he might offer to carry my bag and then get nasty when I refused to let him.

'What's your name?' he asked.

'John,' I said, getting more anxious.

'Mine's Marco.'

'I'm just going to my bus,' I said, trying to break away without upsetting him.

'I'm your friend,' he said, keeping up with me.

That made me really suspicious. Just then I saw three travellers ahead of me.

'Those people are on my bus,' I said, 'I'll go with them.'

But when I got up to them I found they were going the other way. If I stayed with them I'd end up back in Mexico, while my bus would continue to Guatemala City, carrying my rucksack with it. So I just kept walking fast with one thought – to catch up with my bus before anything unpleasant happened.

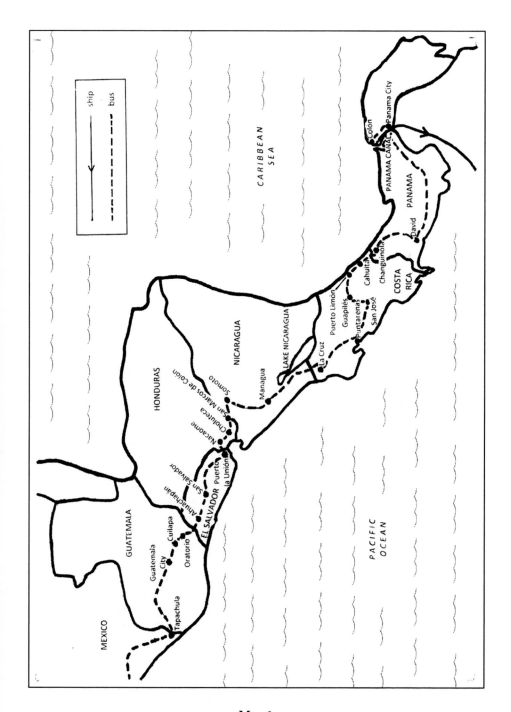

Map 1a
Central America (detail)

4. Guatemala

May 1 – 4

I found my bus and got on it, and, luckily, the man at the border who'd claimed to be my friend didn't get on the bus with me!

Guatemala struck me as greener than Mexico. It seemed to have an innocent air. I saw fewer signs of man's imprint. There were more trees and less bare earth, fewer rocks and less rubbish. There were tree-covered hills and sparkling young rivers. Children were playing in one. But I saw the same hump-backed, flop-eared cattle.

I moved to the passenger seat just behind the driver. This was much higher than his and I was able to look over his head. I'd avoided Mexico City but I arrived in another vast, sprawling, polluted metropolis – Guatemala City.

The first three hotels I tried had no vacancy and seemed to be locked up. I wondered if there was a festival in progress. In the fourth I tried, someone let me in but told me to wait. I sat in the corridor in a queue behind two couples. There was another queue for the toilet. There was one toilet, basin and shower between 12 people. A woman, mentally or otherwise disturbed, was making a lot of noise as she emerged from one of the rooms. She lay on the floor, pulled up her skirt and continued to call out. The man with her dragged her out through the gate. I thought it very sad. Meanwhile two men were trying to get the rooms ready for those waiting. They had to knock on doors and ask the people to come out, although it was the middle of the afternoon.

After half an hour I got into a room. It cost 50 quetzals (less than four pounds). It was a small room with a double bed, a table, a large mirror and a television on a shelf. I complained that there was no way of locking the room from the outside. The guy fetched me a padlock and key. The room had no window or other means of ventilation. Every time I went through the doorway I used the door to waft relatively fresh air into the room. When I was in the room I left the door open. When I was ready to go out I squirted fly spray around and locked the door behind me with the padlock.

As far as I could see, everywhere in the city was closed. I asked the guard at the town hall where the tourist office was. When I got there I found it too was closed. All the shops were shuttered. But Guatemala City had a McDonald's, which, being part of an international chain, was open. I went in and had just a cup of black tea as my stomach was unsettled. The only other outlets I found open were a supermarket, a Burger King and a garage. I bought a paper and found that Tuesday May 1st was a holiday. By now I had a terrible headache. I hoped this was due to dehydration as that is easy to treat. I bought a bottle of water and some *pan tostado*. I went back to the hotel and lay on my bed with the door open. When I felt a little better I went back to McDonald's to eat something small.

My room was next to the gate. Every few minutes, it seemed, somebody would ring the bell to be let in. I asked when the check-out was. 9am tomorrow. I was amazed because I'd had to wait until 4pm to get into my room. The only explanation I could think of was that the staff had had most of the day off as it was a holiday.

Next morning I was out of the building by 7.15. It was the familiar scene of traders pushing trolleys piled high with wares and equipment, while others were setting up their stalls. I breakfasted at *Pollo Compero*, yet another fast-food outlet. It took me fives times as long to work out what I wanted to eat as it took the waitress to bring it.

I went to the tourist information centre to find out where the best hotels were and which route to take to El Salvador. I also got a tourist map of the City. By 10.30 I had moved into room 709 of the Conquist Hotel. I had read that in Guatemala it was a good idea to register with the British Embassy, so I started to walk towards it. Half of the main double street was taken over by a protest march, ten abreast. A large number of women in traditional dress were carrying sunshades; other marchers wore baseball caps. Some carried banners, some blew whistles. As I watched, for some reason they all broke into a run. The security forces were out in force, many of them in vehicles stuck in a traffic jam caused by the march. The sight of so many guns and truncheons made me feel uneasy. In the local paper next day I read that the protestors were members of the teaching profession.

I walked to where the map said I would find the Embassy. I searched all round the block without success, so I broke for lunch. The waitress rattled off a list of what was available. I didn't understand a word. I asked her to bring me a menu and got out my dictionary.

'Do you need any help?' a woman on another table called over to me. She was beautifully dressed and carefully groomed.

'Well, yes, please,' I replied, 'that's very kind of you. I've just asked for a menu because I can understand that better.'

She came over and stood by my chair.

'This restaurant does grilled fish and grilled meat,' she told me.

I saw she had fish.

'I'll have what you're having.'

She ordered it for me.

'Would you like to sit down?' I suggested. 'You could bring your food over.'

She did. Unfortunately the traffic was noisy, the air con' was yelling its head off and the woman had the light behind her so I couldn't lip-read. But I did learn that she lived in the town where she was born and came into the City every week for two hours of English lessons. She was desperate to practise and I was desperate for company. She told me she had two sisters and a brother. She'd four children of her own, aged from 13 to one. Her mother was looking after the little ones. She said there were seven or eight quetzals to the dollar. The way to pick up a woman is to go to a country whose language you don't speak and get out a dictionary.

Thus refreshed, nutritionally and emotionally, I tried again to find the British Embassy. I had in my mind's eye a grand, well-guarded building flying the Union Flag. There was only one building it could be – that hidden behind a high, solid, metal fence, with no way in. I'd turned it down the first time I saw it because I thought an embassy was supposed to be a presence, not a furtive operation. I was looking at the solid fence when someone called out to me and pointed to a door in the fence, which was now open although it had been closed before. I ran to it and got there just as a Guatemalan guard was closing it.

'*Embajada Británica?*' I asked, and showed my passport so that he'd know I had a right to be there. He took the passport, studied it and waved me through the doorway. I put my hand out for the passport. I didn't want to lose it a quarter of the way round the world. He said something in Spanish and pointed me to the front door of the building. I put my hand out again.

'You talk to them about it,' he said – or words to that effect.

Remember, I didn't yet know whether this was the British Embassy. There was no sign on the building. I was compelled to leave my passport with this gorilla and hope to get some sense out of the staff inside. There were two smart women on the reception desk. No sign that this was the Embassy.

'Excuse me,' I said, 'do you speak English?'

'Yes,' one of them answered.

'Oh, thank goodness. I'm looking for the British Embassy – and that sentry has got my passport.'

'Do you need the passport now?'

'Well, yes,' I said, 'I'm going round the world. I must have my passport – and he's got it!'

'Well, we'll talk to him.'

A third woman joined us, as if she didn't want to miss anything.

'Is this the British Embassy?' I asked.

'No, this is not the British Embassy, this is a company.'

'Do you know how I get to the Embassy?' I asked.

'Have you an address?'

'No, just this.'

I showed the map with the symbol for embassy (a castle with a flag flying). They looked at it. Then they got out some telephone books.

'Maybe the map is old and the Embassy has moved,' I suggested.

I wanted to get back to my passport. The third woman saw the state I was in and put her hand on my arm. I began to calm down. And the three of them put their minds to the problem.

'Isn't it next door?' I believe one of them asked. 'I think it's the building next to us. That'll be it.'

Two of the women came out with me to face the gorilla. He handed me my passport, apparently none the worse for being captured. I thanked him in Spanish and the women in English. The ape opened the door in the fence. I wished I could have given him a banana to show there was no ill feeling. The women came out with me, took me to the building next door and pointed me to the entrance. The Guatemalans seemed just as friendly and helpful as the Mexicans, if not quite as childlike or ready to laugh.

The building next door was an oval glass skyscraper. A sign at the entrance said, 'The Bank of Such-and-such'. The woman at the desk of Such-and-such looked at my passport and then at me.

'You can go up,' she said. 'It's on the Nth Floor.'

Notice, I'm not telling you the details – for security reasons. A security officer felt my bag for weapons, while I passed through a scanner like those you get in airports. He showed me to a lift, which took me up to the Nth floor. When I got out, I faced further security. I still had no hard evidence that I'd reached the British Embassy – no name, no flag, no picture of H M The Queen. All this could have been a front for some criminal organisation. Then they let me in to the Holy of Holies. I found myself in a small reception area, like that of a struggling firm that couldn't afford premises of its own and had to rent a cramped suite in a mighty corporation. There was, however, a photograph of Her Majesty, wearing an expression that seemed to say, 'We know, dear, *we* are not amused either!' In a Perspex folder on the coffee table I found a paper called 'British Muslims', featuring a blue-eyed, serious-minded female, wearing a *hijab*. I picked up a note about El Salvador (the next country I planned to penetrate).

A single glass window (no doubt bullet-proof) opened like the windows in a post office. I expected a disembodied voice to say, 'Attaché number one, please!'

'I'm a British citizen,' I announced through the window. 'I'm travelling in Guatemala. I've been advised to register.'

'Ah,' Attaché Number One said, 'I'll give you the form.'

I filled it in and passed it back through the window.

'Thank you for coming to us and registering,' said Attaché Number One.

Something of an anti-climax. Of course, I didn't *have* to go to the Embassy. But supposing my passport had been stolen? Then I would really have had to go to the Embassy. How could I have found it without any document to get me past the gorilla? And how could I have got into Such-and-such inc to ask my way? The moral is – never let your passport out of your sight. Easier said than done!

Guatemala City was big, noisy, hectic and polluted. To cross the road you had to watch carefully and make quick decisions. There was no sign saying, 'WALK; DON'T WALK'. The traffic controllers wore fluorescent yellow tunics bearing the letters 'PMT', presumably to indicate that they were a bit irritable at a certain time in the month. The buses sent out black fumes so thick that it was probably healthier to ride on one than to have one drive past you. I caught one of these heavy smokers to go back to my hotel. The seats were mid 20th Century, tubular-framed chairs screwed to the floor, their backs and seats made from an unyielding plastic. Back in my room, I had a siesta. It wasn't just the heat that made me tired but the need to be on my guard all the time, especially at night, looking over my shoulder, not passing doorways or dark corners, always looking purposeful and confident, even if I didn't feel it.

At breakfast in the hotel next morning every table had a lily so gorgeous I first thought they were fake, but I was impressed by the haphazard way the pollen was sprinkled on the inside of the petals. The fact that the flowers gave off a heady perfume removed the last trace of doubt.

Midday, I left on a bus to Cuilapa. This was a regional bus (as opposed to local or long-distance), decorated so garishly and ornately that from the outside it looked like a fairground ride. Inside, the illusion was sustained by a fairground-style accompaniment to a song on local radio. A vendor got on to sell sugared buns individually wrapped in polythene and packed in home-made plastic baskets on a rope slung over his shoulder. He got off two stops later and presumably took another bus back, continuing this routine until he had disposed of all his stock.

I had put my rucksack on the rack above me. My other bag was on my lap. The bus became so full that passengers sat three to a seat, with many more packed standing in the aisle. I was glad I'd applied deodorant that morning. The driver sounded the horn by pulling on a tangle of coloured streamers, which operated a switch mounted above the windscreen. Next to the streamers a crucifix was swinging, near enough for the driver to grab if things got really scary. While the vehicle was in motion there was always a breeze; at speed this developed into a wind. Hoping I was on the right bus, I was relieved that we took a turn in the direction of San Salvador (the capital of El Salvador), where I was ultimately heading. The bus shook a lot so I was glad of the high-backed upholstered seats. Amazingly, the guy next to me was asleep.

The conductor, who looked about 19, conducted himself and the passengers with cheerful good humour, squeezing between them to move along the bus. A man who looked my age but was probably younger stood up in his seat, took off his baseball cap and had one of those heart-warming conversations with me, in which neither party has the smallest idea what the other is saying. But we smiled and shook hands. I put my hand over his knuckles to seal our relationship.

A boy of about 11 and his well-upholstered mother appeared from nowhere and started to push their way down the bus. The boy had two buckets laden with drinks in screw-top bottles. The mother had a basket lined with towels containing a great jug and a quantity of disposable plates. Despite the banging, shaking and swaying of the bus, she managed to pour something from the jug onto the plates and take money from her customers, all the while balancing the basket on the back of a seat.

Luckily the man in front had heard me ask for Barbarena so he signalled to me when we arrived. I stood up. The man next to me let me into the aisle. My rucksack had become jammed on the rack and I needed two hands to drag it free, so I gave my small bag to a third man to hold. Once the bus stopped, I struggled forward with both bags to become stuck myself in a queue to get off. I was compensated by finding myself directly above a pair of the smoothest, brownest breasts I'd ever seen – a pleasing end to a cramped journey.

I sat on some steps at the side of the road to make notes. As the bus pulled away, coughing up a blast of black smoke, I checked that I had my passport, bank cards, camera and the change from a 100-quetzal note that I'd stuffed into the zip pocket of my bag because in the crush I couldn't reach my trousers. When a car parked next to me, I could feel the heat radiating from the engine. I ate some dry toast and drank some wonderfully wet water.

Then I walked round the entire town of Barbarena looking in vain for a hotel. I did, however, find the best restaurant in town. I enjoyed some lovely hot soup with unsolicited rice. Then I had a large piece of stewed chicken covered in onion rings (full of flavour but mild, under-cooked and succulent), green beans, more rice (pale yellow and flecked with grated orange peel) and a large leaf of lettuce (softened by the heat of the other items on my plate). Outside it was thundering and raining. As soon as I'd put my knife and fork together, I looked up the Spanish for 'excellent'. *'Excelente'* – I could have guessed it!

The idea of stopping in Barbarena was to see a little more of Guatemala, as I seemed to be shooting through the country. But as there was nowhere to stay I took another bus, just 10 km further on to Cuilapa. On the edge of the town I spotted the Hotel Max. As I walked up to the door, the proprietor came out to greet me, as if he'd known I was coming. He showed me to a room on the ground floor. The door had a second, much smaller door set into the middle of it. This small door was glazed and the glass painted yellow. The small doorway was protected by a small wrought-iron railing. A free-standing fan drooped on its stand, but it did a good job of keeping my feet cool.

The shower and toilet were separated from the sleeping area by a wall as high as the door. The shower was electric. I could see the wires, joined by twisting them together close to the actual sprinkler and covering them with insulating tape. I'm not sure whether its insulation properties held good when the tape was splashed with water or dampened by steam. The main switch of the shower was within the shower area, easy to reach while showering. The apparatus had three settings: *'cálido'*, *'disconecto'* and *'tibio'* (hot, off and tepid), controlled by a second switch on the top of the sprinkler, near where the wires had been connected, again easily reached while showering. The water flow was controlled by a red lever set into the wall. They'd thought of everything – except safety! I was relieved to finish my shower alive.

Five minutes' walk away there was a restaurant, where, although it was a country town, the waitresses wore a uniform of beige polo shirts over black trousers. Like the Mexicans, the Guatemalans favour uniforms, look after them and look good in them. A man got up from his seat and switched the television on without consulting anyone.

A father and his grown-up son came in and ordered something that looked very much like breakfast. Perhaps they were on night duty. The two watched the television. The guy who'd switched it on walked out. I wonder what people watched before television had been invented. The father and son finished their breakfast and left. At this point no one was watching the television. I told the waitress that the meal was '*bueno*' and by gestures and body language persuaded her to turn the television down. Television in public spaces should be treated like smoking – confined to a separate enclosed area or banned altogether. The waitress must have been watching me because as soon as I absent-mindedly put a fingernail to my mouth she sprang from her hiding place to offer me toothpicks and a paper napkin.

At 10.15 next morning I boarded a bus to Oratorio. This time the driver had two rosaries dangling from the mirror on the windscreen. A tiny girl on her own got on, clutching a tall candle and a bunch of dainty flowers, the two items wrapped together in paper. Another little girl kept standing up to put her ponytail out of the window only to have it instantly blown back in again.

I saw men building a house. Three stood at different heights on the same ladder passing buckets full of concrete or mortar mix up this chain to a man at the top of the ladder and lowering empty buckets down the chain to a man on the ground, who filled them. The countryside was as lovely as Scotland, but with no tourists.

When I got off at Oratorio there were two clean young white men with ties and white shirts waiting at the bus stop. They told me they were from Florida and sent by the Church of Jesus Christ of Latter-day Saints (the Mormons). They were doing two-year terms in Guatemala. One, who had completed 13 months, wanted to find a job and get married. The other, who had done only six months, wanted to see other countries. I said the Mexicans and Guatemalans were wonderful people.

'If George Bush,' I declared, 'had spent two weeks with these people, he would not have ordered the bombing of Iraq. A simplistic proposition they did not challenge.

'I love the buses here,' I continued, 'they're like something out of a fairground.'

'They're old school buses from America,' said one Mormon.

'Well, they really make them go,' I added. 'You get the best bus services in poor countries, where people can't afford planes and cars.'

Before I could produce any more sweeping statements, their bus arrived and we said 'good-bye!' The best thing about Oratorio was its name. Nothing against the place, but there wasn't much to it. I crossed the road and went into a café that smelled of wood smoke. I ordered a can of peach nectar from a girl with a sleeveless top and natural armpits. I asked for a straw but they had none, so I asked for a glass. This was a mistake because the glass she brought was dirty. I used the glass after surreptitiously wiping it. I hoped I wouldn't die.

While I was waiting for a bus to take me on towards El Salvador, I noticed a man walking along on the other side of the road, with a *machete* on his belt. When the bus arrived I climbed aboard with my rucksack. A man grabbed it and gestured to me to go further into the crowded bus, which I did. I lost sight of both man and rucksack, but at the next stop I saw the man again, this time taking the rucksack off the bus and running with it towards the back of the vehicle. I hoped he was the conductor. (They don't wear uniforms.) I managed to get off the bus and follow him. I thought he was going to put my rucksack on the roof but, no, he opened the back door of the bus and pushed the rucksack in, gesturing to me to get in after it. I climbed the ladder, got in and found a seat close to my luggage.

As in Mexico anything larger than a rucksack (and there was a lot like that) was carried on the roof. We approached a metal river bridge, constructed like a long cage, which the bus had to pass through. While the bus was still moving, the conductor opened the back door from the inside, stepped out onto the ladder and with the agility of an ape climbed it, kicking the door shut as he did so, in order to get onto the roof, where he checked that no piece of luggage caught on the cage, taking care not to get hit himself. Once over the bridge he opened the door from the outside and stepped into the moving bus as if it was all in a day's work – as no doubt it was.

The bus soon began to climb. In one town we went along a street so narrow that there were centimetres to spare between us and the displays of merchandise on either side. There was a queue of three-wheeled taxis behind us as, together with the parked cars, we blocked the road, while the conductor unloaded a long roll of wire netting from the roof and passed it through the back doorway to lie between the seats, ready to be taken off the bus altogether at the next stop.

We made a dramatic descent to another river. When the bus arrived at my stop there were men waiting to pounce. Being the only white man, I naturally was the first to get attention. As I got off the bus through the back door with my rucksack and my bag, a man grabbed them both. As soon as I'd climbed down the ladder I managed to get my luggage back off him, but he hurried me forward past the bus. Then I realised we were at the frontier. He said something about quetzals and dollars. Then others joined and crowded round me like paparazzi hounding a film star. Smiling, as much to reassure myself as to pacify them, I made some 'steady on, chaps, what's all the hurry?' gestures and pointed to where I hoped was the official desk. But, no – they wanted to change my money there and then.

'Passport, passport!' they cried, making me think they wanted to take it off me. I was vastly outnumbered. I'm smaller than average; luckily they were too. So at least I could see around me. There was a single counter in the immigration building and, to the amusement of the woman on duty, I succeeded in reaching it, still pursued by the gang, who stood back a little for once. I handed her my passport. She stamped it and gave it back.

I should have got my currency in Guatemala City but I'd been preoccupied with registering at the Embassy. From then on I'd rushed through the country. I looked up the word for 'currency' and, although I should have known this, asked if the dollar was the currency for El Salvador.

'*Si, señor.*'

'The US dollar?'

'*Si.*'

Then she disappeared. I made the gang wait while I put my passport away. Then another guy came up to me with a grin on his face.

'You speak English?' he asked.

'Yes,' I said.

'Where do you come from?'

'England.'

'Do you want dollars?'

The woman came back, still looking amused, which I didn't find reassuring. This crowd, I realised, had no official status. They were just moneychangers who hung around the frontier waiting for mugs like me.

'I'll give you one dollar for 7.7 quetzals,' he said, showing his pocket calculator.

'What do I do?' I said, thinking aloud, 'these other guys were here first. But you speak English, which is very nice.'

Why was I coming out with this stuff? Because the pressure was beginning to tell on me. A beggar woman was hanging around on the sidelines. The man who spoke English turned to the others.

'That okay?' he seemed to ask. They agreed. Everyone was grinning now – except for me. I started to count out my quetzals onto the counter. The man who spoke English held out his hand for me to count them straight onto it. I declined.

I seemed to have an enormous number of quetzals. I counted them into piles of 500. Yes, I had 1,617 of the buggers. He pressed the keys of his calculator.

'A hundred and twenty-four dollars,' he said.

I accepted the dollars. The guy sent me on my way and disappeared. The beggar woman was still there. I gave her three quetzals, which was rather mean, but I was punch drunk by then. An exchange rate of 7.7 seemed fair – the woman in the restaurant had said 'seven or eight'. But, when later I came to work it out, I found that although 7.7 was the rate he offered it wasn't the rate he'd delivered. He should have given me $210, not $124. He'd swindled me out of $86! He had taken a 41% cut for himself – or for the gang if he shared it out. I see why they do it – it's the perfect crime, no paperwork, my word against theirs – and if I were smart enough to complain, then the worst that could happen to them is that they would have to give me the amount they'd swindled out of me. It made me angry, of course, but as well as that I was alarmed at not being in control.

Meanwhile, I'd no idea I'd been swindled. I thought I was in El Salvador by then, the currency touts had left me so confused. But there was nothing to see or do. No tourist office – or anything official. No bus or bus stop. So when a three-wheel taxi came along and offered to take me on I accepted. For two dollars he took me to a bridge over the inevitable river. We were stopped on the bridge by an official and I had to part with my passport. Luckily no gust of wind wrested it from his hand and I got it back safely. In seconds I would be in the smallest country in Central America, El Salvador.

5. El Salvador

May 4 – 9

The three-wheeled taxi dropped me just inside El Salvador. I walked to a bus stop and took the bus to the town of Ahuachapán. After a pleasant lunch I walked to *El Parador Hotel y Restaurant* and checked in. I was upset about losing money at the border and very tired. I was glad to find a peaceful place to stay. I washed a shirt, two pairs of socks and some underwear. After half an hour's siesta and swimming 20 lengths of the pool, I felt better.

At 5.45 I went into the restaurant to find out when dinner was.

'Cuándo la cena?' I asked a waitress.

My pronunciation must have been faulty because she showed me the menu. This made no mention of opening times, so I closed it and handed it back to her.

'Cuándo la cena?' I tried again. *'Hora,'* I added this time and pointed to my watch for further clarity.

She passed the menu back to me. I looked at it again. Again I passed it back to her. This must have seemed like the depths of rudeness. At this point a girl came in and sat down at one of the tables. This answered my question. The restaurant was already open. I smiled as if to convey that I had what I wanted. She tried to show me to a table. But I didn't want to eat then. It was only 5.50. So to show that I wasn't hungry yet, I put my hand on my stomach and indicated that I would go and come back. I hoped putting a hand on your stomach in El Salvador didn't mean, 'You and your stinking restaurant make me want to vomit!' I smiled again, pointed to the doorway and made as dignified an exit as I could.

At 6.55, I turned up again to eat. The same waitress greeted me. We smiled at each other as if to say, 'the less said about that earlier business the better'. She brought me the menu. This time I did not pass it back to her, but started to study it. She raised her notepad. But I was in a strange country. I didn't speak the language. I needed time. Let her come to England, glance at a four-page menu and immediately decide what she wants to eat. I can't do it, and I've lived in the country for over sixty years! I didn't know how to say, 'Look, I'll need some time on this and it's going to be easier if you don't stand there, pencil poised, making me nervous. Couldn't you find something else to do for three minutes – better make that five?' So I got out my dictionary, stuck my nose in the menu and hoped she would get the message. But she didn't so I ordered something quickly, just to show there was no ill feeling.

Meanwhile the canned music did its inept best to calm me down with 'I like to be in America', which put me in mind of the lecture by Rita Moreno I'd enjoyed so much on the QM2. This was followed by a weird version of Beethoven's 'Moonlight Sonata' arranged, for some reason, for piano and orchestra. Then four men in bright blue overalls labelled 'Schlumberger' came in and sat down. A moment later a huge television screen appeared from nowhere. I moved to a seat facing the other way. Luckily nobody turned the sound up. Meanwhile we had a blast from a Tchaikovsky piano concerto, a burst of a Rachmaninov concerto and a few bars wrenched from the popular slow movement of Mozart's 21st piano concerto, the one that was used when the doomed lovers run through the meadow in the film 'Elvira Madigan.'

For once I had no problem finding my way back from restaurant to hotel. I had a good sleep and in the morning I took breakfast on the terrace beside the pool. I saw the Schlumberger boys again. They obviously hadn't been schlumming it, but had stayed the night in the hotel and were now doing maintenance tasks around the place. I decided to press on to San Salvador. I took a three-wheel taxi to the bus stop. The driver took me three-quarters of the length of an unmade-up back street, the state of which grew more impassable as we advanced.

'I have to stop,' he explained. 'Go to the end. The bus is just there,' he added, pointing to the left.

Where he dropped me there was no sign of a bus, a stop or traffic of any kind. But as I picked my way around the puddles I soon learned why he didn't want to take his vehicle any further. I could hear noise and then I came to a street at right angles, impassable for another reason – it had been taken over by a market. A jollier, more colourful sight you could hardly wish to see. I pushed my way between the stalls and through the crowd until I found a bus, apparently jammed in forever. It was empty except for the driver.

'San Salvador?' I asked.

'*Si,*' he replied, matching my concision.

I produced a banknote. He pointed to a kiosk. I bought my ticket there and became the first passenger on the bus. The next to come aboard were ambulant traders. They were followed by an old beggar woman.

The driver started the engine, sounded his horn and drove slowly enough not to knock into any stall. The bus brushed against the crowd but injured no one. A young man came onto the bus to sell socks, followed by a woman with a towel wrapped round her head. We went through the town, which was green with trees and brightened by roses in the gardens. It would have been fascinating to stay longer, but I had a whole world to go round. I got the impression that, compared with Guatemala, El Salvador was generally more organised and in a better state of repair. There were signs of American investment, aided perhaps by El Salvador's recent adoption of the US dollar as its currency.

Once we'd left Ahuachapán it was non-stop to San Salvador, less than 100 km. It was a good road – dual carriageway with a grassy central reservation. The last section was lined both sides with trees and had more trees in the middle. I saw an American industrial park. Pictures of Jesus Christ abounded. The journey took an hour and three-quarters and cost only $2.30.

In Central America, San Salvador is second in size only to Mexico City. I walked from the bus terminal until I found a road with city buses on it. I caught one that said *'Metro Centro Antiguo'*. Near the Metro Center (a shopping mall – I'm using the American spelling advisedly), I came across the *Hotel Real Continental*. I was offered the choice of a 'city view' or a 'garden view'. I chose the city view and was given a room on the eighth floor with a view not only of the city but of a volcano as well.

I had lunch in the Metro Center. Then I took a bus hoping it would take me to the 'Historical Downtown Center', which I'd learnt contained the national theatre. I saw nothing like that, but I was enjoying the tour until I realised I'd no idea where I was. Two guys on the bus took pity on me and told me to get off when they did.

'Where are you going?' they asked.

'I am looking for the Downtown Centre,' I told them.

'It's dangerous.'

According to the Travellers Handbook, in El Salvador 'robbery and murder are not uncommon.'

'I thought there'd be shops.'

'No, it's just stalls. There are shops in the Metro Center.'

So I took another bus to the Metro Center, where after much hunting I bought a tourist map of El Salvador before finding my way back to my hotel.

The next day I awoke refreshed. I decided to move on east towards Puerto La Unión, where I hoped to get a boat to Costa Rica. I'd seen a lake on the map near a town called Ilopango, not far from San Salvador, and thought it would be nice to take in the lake on my way. After three attempts – on three separate buses – I managed to find the centre of Ilopango, with its pleasant square and covered market, where I had lunch for $1.20. I gave the woman $2.00 and paid 50 cents for a 30-cent apple. There wasn't a hotel. I saw a man with no arms, merely bandaged stumps so the accident, if that was what it was, must have been recent.

I was determined to find the lake. I tried walking but came to a dead end. Someone told me to take a bus and where to find one. I came to a road going in the right direction. No sign of a bus or bus stop. I started walking. The road began going downhill. I thought this encouraging because I guessed the lake would be at a lower level. After a while the road turned into a dusty track. People stared at me as if they'd never seen a white person before – or one so stupid.

Eventually I was stopped by two men standing doing nothing in an open-fronted hut by the side of the track. One of them beckoned me over. I went towards them but not right up to them as I didn't want to be drawn into the hut. One of them asked for the time. I showed my watch. I was glad I'd left my gold watch at home. We got into what passed for conversation, the subject of which, I believed, was my desire to see the lake. One of the men, for no reason other than kindness, began to walk with me along the road, repeatedly putting his hands together as if in prayer. I can only guess that this meant, 'Please, God, let a bus come along!' The road grew steeper and, as I knew this poor fellow would have to walk up the hill again, I tried to persuade him to let me continue on my own. I hardly need to add that it was very hot. But he would have none of it and we pressed on, the weight of my rucksack encouraging me down the hill.

Then a bus caught us up.

'Bus! Bus!' my friend yelled.

I hailed the bus and shook the fellow warmly by the hand.

'Thank you, thank you!' I said and squeezed onto the bus, which was full but still took me.

The lake was beautiful, with a sandy beach, trees overhanging the water, little cliffs and an island. The water was extra welcome because of the heat and the effort I'd made to reach it. It was Sunday afternoon and children were having a good time in the shallow water. A group of all ages had a boat – some sitting in it, others standing in the water holding onto the sides. I would have liked to go in but I had a cold so I stayed in the bar on the edge of the beach, sitting at a table under a roof of palm leaves and sipping a chilled beer.

Two men on the next table were very friendly. One of them called two little boys in from the water. A third man joined them, who had some English.

'I'm looking for a hotel,' I told him.

'You should go back to Ilopango,' he suggested.

'Is there a hotel? I couldn't see one.'

'Yes,' he said, with something less than 100% conviction.

'Thank you. I'll get the bus back.'

I settled down again to enjoy the scene.

'He's going now!' the English speaker suddenly cried out, indicating the father of the boys. 'He'll give you a lift.'

I turned to the father.

'Okay?' I asked.

'That's okay,' I think he said, in Spanish. 'We'll take you to a hotel.'

'In Ilopango?'

'*Si.*'

So I had my first ride in the back of a truck. A little girl sat in the cab between the driver and another man. The two boys, their father, the father's friend and a fifth man, who turned out to be a policeman or security guard, sat with me in the back. I was perched on the curved metal housing of one of the wheels holding onto my small bag with one hand and the side of the truck with the other, while my rucksack lay on the floor. Up the steep, winding and bumpy track we went at good speed, the hot air rushing past us. It was exhilarating and the warmth of these people's kindness was undeniable. As we came into Ilopango, it became clear that none of them knew a specific hotel.

'You can get a taxi to the centre,' one said. 'There's a hotel in the centre.'

We came to an attractive square.

'Is that the centre?' I asked.

'Oh, no!'

We went on and, seeming to leave Ilopango behind, we got onto a much faster road with lots of traffic. I saw a sign to San Salvador. I was puzzled but quite relaxed with my new friends. Then, on a dual carriageway, we slowed and turned left into a gap in the central reservation as if to do a U-turn. But we stopped. The security man got off. I was urged to do the same. I took a photograph of the two men and the two boys. They handed me my luggage and I said 'good-bye!' Then the security man saw me across the other line of traffic to a lay-by where a taxi was waiting. The man spoke to the taxi-driver, said 'good-bye!' to me and disappeared. I put my bags on the back seat of the taxi and sat in the front with the driver. Off we went, but I soon realised that we were going back to San Salvador. I didn't see a single hotel along the way – even as we came into the city itself. In fact the first hotel I saw was the *Hotel Real Continental*, where I'd stayed the previous night. I immediately decided that if the driver dropped me there I would wait until he had moved on and then go and look for another. But he took me to a little place with its own security guard, the *Hotel Miramonte*, 200m from the *Real Continental* – back almost exactly where I'd started from, but after a delightful interlude.

I dumped my bags, washed my hands and went back to the Metro Center, because I'd lost my map. Unfortunately, I'd also lost *El Abácus*, the children's bookshop where I'd bought it. I couldn't understand how, without taking stairs, escalator or elevator, I had moved from first floor to ground floor. This led me to postulate that the Metro Center consisted of three malls, one on three levels, two on two levels, but not the same levels, each mall connected to the other two. Confused? So was I. To avoid searching any section of this three-dimensional maze twice, I noted descriptions as I went about, but there were so many sections and I didn't know which level I was on, so the descriptions were little help.

In one shop a sales assistant told me that *El Abácus* was in Section 8. That's all the information I needed, I thought. Unfortunately none of the sections appeared to have numbered signs and none of the staff I spoke to knew where Section 8 was. I might have been condemned to end my days in the Metro Center, for unlike Theseus, I hadn't laid a thread to help me find my way out of the labyrynth. As in the best epics, I was saved by an unexpected turn of chance. I stumbled on a general bookshop, where I bought a tourist map of the country with an excellent plan of the City on the back – something I could have done with earlier. As soon as I opened up the map, a young male customer came up to me.

'Do you want some help?' he asked. 'Where are you going? What are you trying to do?'

He was a genial, educated man. He told me how to get to La Unión. He suggested a place worth stopping at on the way. He told me the numbers of the buses I'd need and where to catch them. He rounded off this briefing with a consideration of big express buses as opposed to small local ones. This encounter lifted my spirits and cleared my head to the point where I managed to find my way out of the Metro Center, although I came out on the wrong side and ended up walking three-quarters of the way round the outside of the vast complex. From there I crossed a dual carriageway and marched off in what I believed to be the direction of the hotel. Soon I had to ask the way. I think I got the wrong answer because I had to ask three others before I found the place.

There was a restaurant nearby. It was already dusk at 6.45pm and a man with a gun was lurking in the shadows. I hoped he was the security guard, not the local gangster. I sat outside under a large canopy. When the waiter saw me struggle with the long Spanish menu, he brought me an English one. Then he began to struggle because when I ordered in English he didn't know what I meant. I more or less solved the problem by choosing from the English menu, then finding the same dish in the Spanish menu, using the price as a check that I'd got the right item. But when I'd ordered, the waiter clarified the order with supplementary questions in Spanish, explaining what the dishes consisted of. It was now my turn again to struggle.

'You do realise,' I believe he said in Spanish, 'that "Tempranillo" means "little fish"? And the other dish you've chosen is a stew made of seafood – you do realise that? It takes half an hour to prepare.'

According to the English menu it was worth the wait. By now I had a streaming cold. I hoped the tissues I'd brought with me would last me through the meal. In Central America many restaurants have the considerate custom of placing a rack of little paper napkins on your table, so I started on them. The Tempranillo was what I knew as scampi – dry and crunchy. It was like eating dog biscuits and made a great noise inside my head. While the scampi was dry as toasted sawdust, the seafood stew was as wet as the primordial swamp. When the dish arrived it looked as though the creatures of a murky red sea were climbing out to save themselves, the shrimp onto the back of a mini-squid, which in turn was clambering over something that looked as though it shouldn't have been in the sea at all. It was quite hard to break up this evolutionary tangle, with just a spoon and my fingers. The trouble with seafood is that they always seem to leave the packaging on. There was even some packaging with nothing in it – an empty crab shell, doing nothing but getting in the way. Worth the wait? I didn't think so, but I was in no hurry.

In the morning I was impatient and bad-tempered. I felt it was not going to be a good day. I was right. Breakfast was excessively delayed. I think I was the only guest in the dining room. Indeed I was the only person there, because the woman who 'did breakfast' hadn't turned up. I dropped hints by going to Reception and asking the receptionist if I was waiting in the right place. After 20 minutes I went back to Reception.

'*Desayuno* (breakfast)?' I asked.

'*Momento.*'

I went back and waited. Eventually the woman turned up.

'Where did you get to?' I wanted to snap. 'I've been waiting 25 minutes!' Luckily for her I didn't have the required Spanish.

'*Desayuno, por favor!*' I said with as much venom as I could spit out.

I needed to send some things home so I went back to the dreaded Metro Center to look for the post office. The hotel had given me directions from the main entrance of the mall. Unfortunately, it wasn't at all clear which of the entrances was the main one. But, by trial and error, I found the post office. It didn't sell envelopes so I set off to find a stationers. You might think that I'd have mastered the labyrinth by then, but I spent half an hour failing to find a stationers. I did, however, find a bookshop. I looked up the Spanish for envelope but the assistant didn't know what I was on about, so I drew a picture. Luckily I'm better at drawing than speaking Spanish. She showed me a range of envelopes and I bought one the right size. There in the shop I addressed it, put a hat, a notebook and some papers in it, sealed it and set off to find the post office again. But the envelope was made of paper so unaccountably feeble that my thumb went right through it.

There was now a queue of 30 people in the post office. Luckily the hole in the envelope was at one end and the man who served me was able to fold the envelope over the hole and stick it down with sticky tape. Then there wasn't much room for the 19 stamps needed to make up the correct total. Even when wetted with a wet sponge the stamps wouldn't stick first time so I was forever pressing them to the envelope and letting go to see if they were secure. By the time I'd got them all stuck on the envelope I noticed the beginnings of another hole in it. Then the envelope wouldn't go through the letterbox. So, I squeezed it gently, fed it gingerly into the opening and hoped for the best. As I came out of the Metro Center I was still in a bad mood.

Soon after that I saw two children sleeping on the pavement. Their faces looked strange as if they had been drugged. I found this disturbing and immediately stopped feeling sorry for myself. I realised I was an affluent visitor, who – any time he wanted – could go home to nurse his cold in a place where the envelopes were strong, the stamps stuck easily and it wasn't difficult to find your way around.

On the bus to San Vicente a notice said, '*Gracias por no fumar.*' The ambulant vendors surpassed themselves, offering bananas, strawberries, cold water in polythene bags, sweets, even belts. For a dollar, one offered a bunch of bananas much bigger than you would ever see in Britain. I tried to buy a single banana. Everybody laughed. I should have taken a bunch, broken one banana off for myself and given the rest away. The bus had no conductor but there was a turnstile to negotiate at the front. You had to pay the driver before he released the turnstile. If you were a child small enough to squeeze under the turnstile you got in free. The vendors climbed in at the back door. Calling out their wares, they pushed their way to the front and then to the back, before getting off.

In San Vicente, I found a hotel that faced directly onto the main square. A girl of about twelve was sitting at a table, cutting out and sorting newspaper articles. The woman at the bar had no key for my room. I told her I must have a key and went to the bar for a beer. I was hot and tired from the bus ride. I'd had my rucksack on my knee most of the time but I'd avoided deep vein thrombosis by twiddling my toes inside my boots. Sipping my beer and looking out through the open front of the hotel, I began to unwind. Little children played on a verandah that ran across the front of the building and joined to other verandahs in front of the adjacent premises. The little ones were thus protected from sun, rain and traffic. Once I'd got the key to my room, I rinsed my clothes and had a shower, both in tepid water – all there was. Then I flopped onto the bed and fell asleep.

At 6.15pm I was out again and into the main square. The light was fading. A particular cloud seemed to be getting darker and moving nearer. In the square a little girl was leading a little boy with her hands over his eyes for a game. I went into the church. There were lots of plastic flowers and too much religious symbolism for me, so I came out again. In the middle of the square there was a white stone clock tower, taller than the church. Many of the figures were missing from the clock face. On the paving and steps around the tower, two teenage boys with very long, thin legs were practising stunts on their skateboards.

At 6.30 the sky was indigo. By 6.35 it was dark as night. A warm wind got up. Banners hung across the streets began to flap restlessly. I sat in the square waiting for the storm. When the lightning came it lit up the clock tower, which looked dramatic against the black sky. I moved to the hotel seconds before the rain arrived. Then I remembered to go to my room for my insect repellent. There followed a series of very short power cuts, in between which the light was off more time than it was on. I managed to spray myself with insect repellent in the dark. Somebody came along the landing carrying a blue light. It turned out to be a little girl with a mobile phone, but she was gone so quickly I got no benefit from the illumination.

When I went downstairs again I found that the street was flooded, but the verandah, several steps higher, was not. I walked along it to a friendly cafeteria next door. I had a lovely meal consisting of lots of bits and a beer – all for $2.23. More lightning and more power cuts. When the power went off the big fans continued turning through inertia.

After the storm no water came out of the taps in my room, but there was a water dispenser on the landing, which dispensed hot water as well as cold. I woke in the night to the sound of running water. I thought at first it was a cistern refilling but after ten minutes of feeling around for a light switch I turned the television on and saw that I'd left a tap on at the basin while the water had been cut off. Once again I was in an airless cell with a careless smell. The fan and the 'air con' cooled you down and gave an illusion of freshness by circulating the stale air.

In the morning I was keen to get up and out, having slept some nine hours altogether. I got half a bottle of hot water from the dispenser for a shave. Then I decided to have a shower. I'd wetted and soaped myself and was looking forward to rinsing off the lather when the water ran out again. Luckily, I'd a little left from shaving. For breakfast I went again to the cafeteria next door. The boss handed me a newspaper, perhaps because he thought I looked like an intellectual. On the front page, I read that El Salvador had signed a sixth free-trade agreement with Taiwan.

By 10.30am I was on the bus to San Miguel. The female ambulant vendors, I noted, wore a uniform of frilly aprons edged with ribbons and lace and furnished with two pockets for change. The vendors had powerful voices. A woman got on to sell pills. Despite the noise of the engine, the traffic and the chatter, I heard every word. I didn't understand any of them, but judging by the length of her speech she was selling a panacea. Donizetti could have written an opera about it – *'L'Elisir d'Amor del Bus'*.

San Miguel was big, noisy, dirty and smelly. I had a pleasant lunch of the hot-buffet type that suited me because I could order by just pointing. When I went for a bus that afternoon someone tried to snatch my bag. Luckily, it was only an over-enthusiastic taxi-driver, whom I refused.

El Salvador is the size of Wales so I was not surprised to have gone from one end of the country to the other in four days. When I got to Puerto La Unión I had a long, dusty walk to the port. As a lorry came along I moved to the side of the road, shut my eyes and mouth, and waited till it had gone past. Further on, I smiled at a pleasant-looking couple of my age. The man told me the ferry to Costa Rica was *'finito'*. I said I would look at the port, then take a bus back to La Unión Centro to find a hotel. I went on towards the water, but was turned away by a foreman on the port-development project. I followed the road, which ran parallel with the coast and up an incline. Queues of lorries were waiting to be loaded by a mechanical digger, while others were driving away full of soil. I was leaving the port behind, but for some distance the road remained dusty. Finally, like a mirage, the words 'Comfort Inn' appeared – as welcome as an oasis in the desert. A man who lived beside the hotel drive told me that the hotel had a restaurant, so I went in.

The Comfort Inn had been open only a year. It had been built for the port-development work and presumably for the extra business that would accrue. It was a small, beautifully appointed hotel with a little pool. It was in a good position on higher ground overlooking the inlet known as the Golfo de Foseca, beyond which lay Honduras and Nicaragua. From my room I saw a team of men in white shorts and singlets running along the road.

I told the receptionist that I had hoped to take a ferry to Costa Rica but had heard that it had stopped. He told me that the other ferry (to Honduras) had also been stopped. I e-mailed Thomas Cook, whose 'Overseas Timetable' (railway, road and shipping services) had been an invaluable guide to planning my journeys all the way from Fort Lauderdale, to tell them that the ferries out of La Unión weren't operating.

For once I welcomed the welcome drink. They'd no vermouth so I had a glass of a pleasant – and chilled – white wine. The bar was at one end of the restaurant. Three men and two women were relaxing over drinks. One of the men had the loudest laugh I had ever heard. The women didn't laugh, but they smiled loudly. It was good to be near people enjoying themselves but soon it got too much, so I moved to a table at the other end of the room. I had 'cerviche de mixto' – shrimp, fish, tomato and coriander, marinated – so they said – in freshly squeezed lemon juice, but I thought it tasted like lime. Then I had beef medallion with green-pepper sauce, mashed potatoes and vegetables, with a pleasant cabernet sauvignon. The waiter confirmed that all ferries had been stopped, presumably because of the port development. They didn't charge me for my second glass of wine, so I pointed this out, which caused a stir, but I wanted to be honest – I felt I was representing the United Kingdom.

I woke before 6am to see men in white singlets and shorts again running along the road. I decided they were cadets from a naval barracks, running to the sea and back at the cooler ends of the day, as part of their fitness training. At breakfast I had to ask twice for coffee and when it finally arrived I'd finished eating so I took my cup out to a table on the verandah. It was 7.50am. The sun was so low that I wasn't shielded by the roof of the verandah and the rays so fierce that I was glad to be able to move into the shade of a pillar. A squadron of millipedes was touring the paving. The developers were busy developing. When I moved to the pool area, once again I could see lorries queuing to take soil away.

I took a bus back to La Unión. I saw men walking around with *machetes* as naturally as if they'd been umbrellas. It was not a place to get into a fight. I went to the water's edge and took a photograph of a flotilla of small boats, one of which might well have taken me across the Golfo de Foseca to Honduras or Nicaragua for a fee. But where would they land me? Would I have been able to continue my journey from there? Would the authorities let me ashore? I decided to fall back on the ever-reliable bus network.

I had to re-plan my route through Honduras and Nicaragua but once again I'd lost my map of El Salvador. This wouldn't have mattered if I was going to take a boat to Costa Rica but as things were I went into a shop and asked for the map I needed. If a shop gets no visitors from outside the area there is no demand for maps. As had happened before, the assistant looked as bewildered as if I'd asked for the Pope's old betting slips. When she'd recovered, however, she took a pile of papers from a drawer and let me look through them. I found a simplified wall map of the country intended for schools. This showed me that El Amatillo on the border with Honduras was the place to aim for.

It took two buses to get there. As usual the currency sharks attacked me. I waved them all off, except for one who followed me but not uncomfortably close. A pleasant and beautiful woman behind the grille looked at my passport. While she turned to speak to another traveller one of the sharks tried to hand me a piece of paper. I refused it, pointing to that part of his chest where he would have worn a badge of authority if he'd had any. When the beautiful woman had stamped my passport, the shark showed me a wad of notes.

'No!' I said, remembering my experience leaving Guatemala.

'The rates are different over there,' he said, pointing to Honduras.

'Too right they are!' I wanted to quip, but instead I said, 'I will not deal with you people. I had a bad experience at the last frontier – I was cheated out of $86!'

Asserting myself like this felt good, although was I wise to enter a new country without a single note in its currency? But I had settled an old score and, throwing caution to the wind, I began to walk across the bridge towards Honduras.

6. Honduras

May 9 – 12

Once I'd crossed the bridge I found another currency shark waiting for me. I waved him away and was mighty relieved to find a Western Union Office, where I changed $100 into Honduran *Lempira*. I deliberately kept some dollars back, intending to build up a fund of this widely accepted currency to fall back on. I got a bus to the nearest town, which turned out to be Nacaome. At first it seemed to consist entirely of stalls. One offered beer but no food; another offered food but no beer. But I persevered and found a large Chinese restaurant with 'air con' where I had 'chicken curry'. That is to say I had chicken with a stir fry of carrot, peppers and onion in soy sauce; a salad of crisp, shredded lettuce, cucumber and tomato, and a portion of chips – nothing anyone in England would call 'curry' but the chips were hot, crisp and a lovely colour.

After this strange lunch I went to the town square and stood looking around and wondering which direction I should take to find a hotel. A little man in a beige uniform came up to me.

'I'm Such-a-name, Police,' he announced. 'Do you need some help?'

'Yes, I'm looking for a hotel.'

'Come with me.'

We started walking.

'Police,' he reminded me.

Each time he said the word I mentally downgraded his position in the Force. We came to a hotel and went in. He asked if they'd a vacancy.

'No, señor.'

'Come on!' he said leading the way again. As we walked he turned to me. 'Police,' he reminded me with a knowing look. We came to a second hotel. He asked if they'd a vacancy.

'Si, señor,' said the woman behind the counter.

'Muchas gracias, señor,' I said to the policeman, hoping he would take the

hint and leave us to it, but he was studying the contents of the fridge. I turned to the woman to discuss the room.

'I'd like a drink,' the cop announced, adding, 'Police.'

He was now down to police cadet. Once more and he'd be out of the Force altogether. The woman said something to me about the room.

'Could we have something for the *policía*?' I asked.

She asked him what he wanted. He told her. She gave it to him and offered me something. I shook my head and paid for the policeman's drink. It's one thing to co-operate with foreign police; quite another to socialise with them.

The woman put me in an annexe across the road. There was only one tap. The basin wobbled, supported only by its own waste pipe. We had a power cut lasting several hours. There was a water cut too. I woke in the night worrying about the dreaded dengue fever.

The next day, armed with another schoolchild's map, which showed the regions in different colours, some of the towns, but not a single road, I set off to conquer Honduras. I spotted an infants school run by 'Save The Children'. When we reached Choluteca I was dropped at the *'Mercado'* (Market) Terminal. It was 10.30 and already very hot. I wanted to go to the *Centro Municipál*, mainly to get away from the *Centro Mercado*. Even in the shade I was getting hotter and hotter. I saw a bus going to the *'Ciudad Nueva'* (the 'new' city). That sounded good. There could be a restaurant, a hotel, who knows – a smart new square and some cultural life? I jumped on the bus. It was good to be moving again. I spotted two dogs facing in opposite directions but awkwardly trapped in *flagrante delicto*.

Once we got away from the stalls and the big buildings of the old city, we came into a pleasant, newer area boasting bungalows with names and gardens, as well as dwellings under construction. On, on it went. I wondered when we'd get to the New City. The tarmac gave way to shingle. The shingle gave way to an unmade-up road.

The conductor had tiny fingers on one hand, like toes. He could count money using what looked like a great toe as a thumb. He either had a congenital deformity or he'd lost all his fingers and had his toes grafted onto his hand as replacements. Yet he was the cheeriest bus conductor I ever met. When I asked him for the Ciudád Nueva, he kept coming back with questions – presumably asking me which bit I wanted.

'El centro,' I said.

Then the penny dropped. There was no centre, no square, no church, no hotel, no restaurant, no bar, no shop. No city at all – just residential development. We stopped. The last of the other passengers got off leaving the driver, the conductor and me. They told me they didn't go back for two hours. I bought a bag of water. You bite the corner, squeeze the bag and suck the water out – easier said than done. The water was warm and tasted of polythene. There were two other buses waiting to return to the old city and I caught the first to leave.

I got off before we reached the *Centro Mercado*. Then I went out and found a 'smoothie' bar where I bought a *'Combinación con Naranja y Fresa'* (orange and strawberry – delicious!). I came out and found some steps in solid shade with a continuous breeze. I was content to sit and do nothing. After a while I fell asleep, dropping my notebook on the pavement. When I woke up I picked it up, moved off and came to a hotel. In the lobby an old boy was reading the Bible in Spanish helped by what I took to be a commentary. He let me have a room and took my money. The hotel was built around a courtyard dominated by a great water tank on concrete stilts.

When I went out again I saw a donkey pulling an empty cart away from a church. Beside the church were two heaps of building materials, which I presume the donkey cart had just delivered. Another church had a pond so full of terrapins that they were standing on each other's backs, sometimes as many as four-high. I walked around the town taking photographs. There were two little girls in school uniform, one of them squatting by a wall.

'¡Hola, señor!' the other one called out.

'¡Hola!' I replied.

'She's doing a wee-wee!' (or the Spanish equivalent).

I know that was what she said because immediately the other girl, in one movement and as decorously as possible, pulled her knickers up under her skirt and stood up. She had a grin on her face as a trickle of liquid made its way to the edge of the pavement.

In front of a Chinese restaurant, a group of people were sitting at a table. They looked as if they knew each other very well. I thought some of them might work in the restaurant. A stout man in the party was cooking on a barbecue. I sat down at a table. A young woman got up from the barbecue party to take my order. A big drinks lorry pulled up beside me and a man brought in crates of bottled drinks on a trolley. Another carried stacks of expanded-polystyrene dishes – perhaps for take-away meals.

When I'd nearly finished my meal, an attractive woman with big soulful eyes came over from the barbecue party to speak to me. 'Where do you come from?' she asked me.

'England,' I said, 'It was kind of you to come over to speak to me.'

'Where are you going?'

'Nicaragua, Costa Rica, Panama. Then by ship to New Zealand.'

'I'm from Nicaragua,' she said.

'Are you visiting?'

'No, I live here.'

'How long have you been here?'

'I came here with my two brothers and my sister. Nicaragua is not a good place to be – too much wars. I married a Honduran, but he died.'

'Do you ever go back?'

'I go to see my mother. My father died – some time ago.'

'Will you marry again, do you think?'

'Honduran men no good. They won't work. They're like babies. But I've got a bike,' she said, brightening up.

'A bike?'

'A motorcycle. I deliver food.'

'For the restaurant?'

'My name's Carla,' she said, as if to put a seal on our acquaintance.

'I'm John.'

'That's my sister,' she told me.

It was the girl who had served me.

'My brother … ,' she said.

A young man was sitting on a scooter.

¡Hola, Señor!' I cried, and then asked Carla, 'Is that your bike?'

'Yes,' she said.

'It was very nice talking to you.' I said, getting up.

'Be careful in Nicaragua!'

At 6.15 the next morning, the man who'd been reading the Bible when I first arrived at the hotel sang several verses to the tune I knew as 'John Brown's Body'.

'Glory, glory, hallelujah!' he went, at the top of his croaky old voice.

For breakfast I found a big restaurant well supplied with fans. I smiled at two men in their fifties on the next table. They invited me to join them. They turned out to be French Canadians doing some sort of social development work. We spoke English. One of them told me that he had woken that morning to a sharp pain in his cheek. He found he'd a barb in his skin, which he couldn't immediately dislodge. He had some knowledge of the insects of the area but could not think what had attacked him and was going to consult a biologist he knew. He was relaxed and looked perfectly well, but it set me thinking about all the unknown dangers lurking around the corner. Such encounters with strangers didn't amount to much but they helped to keep me sane.

I went back to the Mercado Terminal, where some kind people helped me find the bus for San Marcos de Colón, but there was a long wait. I managed to get my rucksack on the rack and eventually we set off through residential roads. Some of these were partly blocked with big heaps of soil. A single-track road grew so bad that we turned back by reversing around two corners. A big man sat down next to me. I moved my bag.

'Gracias,' he said, 'or where you come from "Thanks very much!"'

I thought from his accent that he was from Yorkshire but he took out a copy of 'La Tribuna', a Honduran national paper in Spanish and said not another word. Every five minutes he mopped his face with a towel. The bus became congested and when a thin man came along, the big man moved closer to me to let the newcomer perch on the end of the seat. Very cosy! The ambulant vendors couldn't get onto the bus so they offered their wares through the windows. Like many other buses ours bore the words 'Díos es Amór' in big letters on the windscreen. Some had it in English – 'God is Love'.

After three-quarters of an hour we got onto a dual carriageway; after an hour we were in open country. In the haze the mountains seemed mysterious. I saw pigs un-tethered by the side of the road. By now there were twenty people standing inside the bus. We stopped in the middle of what I classed as 'nowhere'. The driver lifted a large metal lid inside the bus next to his seat. This turned out to be 'the bonnet' because underneath I was surprised to see the engine. In the crowded vehicle the fumes spread only slowly. Girls pulled faces of disgust or tried to fan the fumes away. The conductor took off his long-sleeved yellow shirt and his clean, white under-vest and put on a black T-shirt he obviously kept for repair work. He picked up some rags and poked about in the engine. Some of the passengers got off. The driver started the engine. This produced noise, heat and more fumes. More people got off. When it looked like it was going to be a long job, we all got off.

There was a shelter made of spars of timber but very few of the party could squeeze into that. I went behind it where there was some shade. The land fell away from the road. Below us lay a house and its garden. A turkey, its head a pale French blue, its crop pink, was wandering about in the undergrowth. A line of washing was stretched between trees and a woman was in the garden doing some more – by hand, of course. She was wearing a short-sleeved top and denim shorts. She threw a little of her washing water over these garments to cool herself. Further down the garden an older woman was washing her grey hair, maybe her whole person, under a tap in a home-made bath-house with no roof – three sides brick, the fourth a cloth screen, above which a wet brown arm appeared from time to time. It was bad luck on these people that our bus had broken down on a spot overlooking these domestic activities.

After an hour a replacement bus arrived, slightly smaller than the first. I and many others squeezed in through the back door of the faulty bus to retrieve our luggage. I got in the back of the new bus with my bags and people passed their luggage up to me. There was a live puppy wrapped as a traditional parcel with a hole cut for its head to stick out. I ended up sitting on a milk churn facing the back door, which was apparently fastened shut, although it rattled with each bounce of the bus. Two children were standing by this door (which opened outwards), one holding onto the emergency release handle. They played at making kissing noises on the glass window of the door. The bus was doing about 50 miles an hour. I was anxious that if the door opened the children would fall to their deaths. The children's grandmother seemed relaxed but when the bus slowed down she suddenly thrust her hand between the door and the children. She couldn't reach the smaller child so instinctively I put my hand out from my side and found myself holding Granny's hand – all this because she'd seen a young man on the bus about to open the door while the vehicle was moving, prior to jumping out when it had slowed down enough. When he did jump, he left Granny the job of closing the door again. The children did not fall out. The woman and I exchanged expressions of relief.

I gave my seat on the churn to a young mother. Without warning, a man opened the back door from the outside, got in, pushing between the children and dragging a long pole into the bus after him. Then he banged on the roof of the bus to tell the driver to move off. With all this excitement I had little time to enjoy the spectacular scenery. We slowed down. Lots of passengers looked out of the window. There was a police car and six police officers. A truck was upside down on the side of the road. Bus rides are so boring in Britain.

When we arrived at San Marcos de Colón, which is near the Nicaraguan border, there was a minibus to take those wanting to cross. But I thought it would be too late to find a town and a hotel on the other side. Somebody told me there were three hotels in San Marcos, so I investigated all three and picked one in the highest part of the town, called 'The Shalom Hotel' (literally 'The Peace-be-with-you Hotel'.)

My host took me up two flights to my room.

'We're Christians,' he said.

This made me think he was a Protestant. Catholics wouldn't mention it.

'There's a wonderful view from up here,' I said.

'Yes, yes. Would you like some drinking water in your room?'

'Oh, yes please.'

'I'll put it here on this table,' he said, indicating one on the external landing. 'Then you can get it when you want it.'

I looked out five minutes later and, sure enough, there was a jug of water with a lid to keep the insects out. The external landing led to a large empty room under a broad, curved, plastic roof. This vantage point, one of the very highest in the town, offered a superb vista – roofs, cypresses, palm trees waving in the wind that was getting up, tree-covered hills and mountains beyond them – all made more dramatic by the darkening sky as dusk and a storm approached. The rain came quickly and soon was heavy, producing a loud clatter on the roof, which rattled and let the rain through in places. Meanwhile a brown river had formed on the steep, cobbled street that I'd come up. In another street, whose streams fed this river, a white duck outside a house was finding plenty to eat. As the rain died down, first a dog came out, then chickens and finally people. I went in search of an Internet café. I'd an e-mail from Andrew Weir Shipping, the company whose ship 'Tikeibank' would take me on from Panama, giving me the contact details of an agent in Colón, where I would go aboard.

'Tomorrow I shall cross into Nicaragua,' I told my family and friends back at base.

I came upon a big building with its doors wide open. There were rows of chairs. Some people sat on these; others were walking around. On a platform a woman with a microphone was holding forth. The only word I caught was *'Señor'*, but this came so often it cannot have been addressed to any mortal in the room. She had an insistence and inner conviction that reminded me of the evangelical preacher I'd heard in Florida. Clearly, *'Señor'*, in this context, meant 'Lord'.

I was the first customer in a large restaurant. The waitress took my order (soup and a main course) and switched on the CD player. She brought me a complimentary starter and, when I'd finished that, an appealing rice dish with bacon, onion and prawns. In Europe we consider soup to a be a starter. But in Central America, I'd learnt, they often serve it with the main course or they bring the main course before you've finished the soup. That evening they brought the soup after everything else. This was not so odd when you consider that it was half way to being a stew, containing as it did whole pieces of chicken.

The following morning I was woken at 4.15 by a loud dog-erwauling from the farm and for all I knew some urban dogs as well. They seemed to be set on barking to the end of time. They eventually woke the cockerel up, who must have been disconcerted, not only because traditionally he is the first to wake but also because he could hardly make himself heard above this canine cacophony. A second cockerel joined in. He seemed to have avian laryngitis because he made a rasping sound. I'm sure a vet would have advised him to rest his voice. The sky was still as black as night. Then the dogs suddenly fell quiet and left the cockerel to it. A mosquito was flying around my bathroom looking for trouble. I turned off the light and shut the bathroom door, an option not usually available to me. Something set the dogs off again, but eventually I managed to go back to sleep.

I had breakfast in my host's living room. We talked while his wife, a sweet homely person, brought the food. He was happy to sit and smile, as if he thought of himself as a vessel through which God poured out His love, while his wife did the mundane work. Their daughter helped while the boys played. Women's lib has not reached all corners of the globe. I had corn flakes, toast, grape jelly, coffee (slightly sweetened out of a thermos flask) and orange juice.

'How long have you had the hotel?' I asked.

'Five years,' he said. 'People love to come here. They hear about it through the church.'

I hadn't seen another guest.

'"Shalom" is a good name for a hotel,' I said.

Neither he nor his wife looked Honduran. He had auburn hair. They had two boys and a girl. All three had black hair. Perhaps they were adopted. He gave me a banana to take with me. It reminded me that Honduras is a banana republic par excellence.

His parting shot was, 'Jesus loves you.'

I smiled. He grinned. It was Saturday morning but I found a bank open. They didn't supply Nicaraguan currency and, when I tried to draw *Lempira*, the system wouldn't accept my bank cards. So I set off for the Nicaraguan border with only $200, 45 *Lempira* and a traveller's cheque card in dollars. I decided to head straight for Managua, the capital, and my best chance of using my cards. I got into a minibus headed for Espina on the border with Nicaragua.

At the frontier there was no official exchange office – despite a sign that said

'Western Union'. I didn't want to be cheated again. I checked the exchange rate with the police. Then, on my own in my own time, I carefully counted out $100. I went back to look for a dealer. A young boy found me a single trader. I made him write down his rates and how many *córdobas* he'd give me. Then we did a deal that I was happy with. Nevertheless, I still felt anxious as I stepped onto the bridge that would take me into Nicaragua.

7. Nicaragua

May 12 – 15

It was the middle of the day. I started waiting for a bus. Although I was in the shade, I could feel a fierce heat from the tarmac. There was a bar but I preferred to go hot and hungry than suffer the Muzak, which was very loud. I talked to some friendly lorry drivers, their vehicles parked in a queue. Some of them tried to persuade me that a taxi would be better than the bus. When one started quoting prices and then began to drop those prices, I realised that he wasn't a lorry driver at all – he was a taxi-driver.

I wasn't going to say to them, 'I don't trust you.' All I could come up with was, 'I like buses,' which must have sounded strange.

Looking across the road I saw real lorry drivers pull up their T-shirts in an attempt to cool their bellies. Some lay in hammocks slung in the shade beneath their lorries. Looking under one lorry I could see the legs of a horse, standing on the other side of the lorry in full sun, with no grass to eat.

When the bus arrived I nearly missed it because I was the only person at the bus stop actually waiting for a bus – I think all the others were taxi-drivers. As we went along I noticed more of the scarlet trees I'd photographed in Oaxaca in Mexico. I saw more people riding horses than in the other countries. A turkey was spreading its tail.

When we reached a town called Somoto I checked into a hotel, refusing the first room because it didn't have a fan. Next door to the hotel was a lovely restaurant – a circular space 15m wide under a high conical roof thatched with palm leaves and supported by wooden pillars like telegraph poles. The wind came in through unglazed windows and cut across the circle. It was mighty pleasant to sit in this well-ventilated building, sipping a beer.

I had an early start the next day so I didn't want to oversleep. I needn't have worried! The rooms ran along both sides of a dark corridor. The only ventilation consisted of louvred windows onto that corridor. There was no outside window. Any sound in the corridor or in any of the rooms off it could be heard throughout the sleeping quarters. Some young couples came in late and talked loudly before settling down for what I assumed would be the night. But I was woken by an alarm call consisting of a loud, metallic buzzer followed by a recorded voice, English not American, saying very clearly, 'It is time to get up. The time is 5.35. After a few minutes the loud, metallic buzzer sounded again. Again the recorded message, 'It is time to get up. The time is 5.35.' This was followed ten minutes after the first alarm not by the loud metallic buzzer but by the recorded sound of loud church bells, followed by, 'It is time to get up. The time is 5.35. Five – three – five!' although I knew that it was actually 5.45 by then. The alarm had done its job. The young couples were awake. I could hear them talking and laughing. Through the louvres I watched them politely call on each other, politely knocking on each others' doors or having polite conversations through each other's louvred windows, to make sure everyone was awake. I wish they had politely turned the alarm clock off at the first alarm instead of letting it run through its repertoire. By 6.15 one of these people was sufficiently awake to whistle a popular song – not so well that he got the tune right, but well enough for me to recognise that it was supposed to be 'The Campdown Races'. Eventually they left and a blissful hush fell. I could have gone back to sleep but unfortunately I had to get up myself then to catch my bus.

By 7am I was on an express bus bound for Managua, the capital of Nicaragua. On the adjacent bus bales of hay were being piled up on the roof. On our bus the music was loud, but it was country-and-western, which sounded appropriate once we got started. The selection included 'I beg your pardon, I never promised you a rose garden.' For an express service we stopped surprisingly often for the odd passenger waiting on the side of the road, and in the towns we squeezed along narrow streets. The traders came aboard as usual. The windows of the bus were tinted against the sun (or maybe for security reasons), which marred the view. But I did see cultivated land, very fragmented, and pointed mountains – presumably volcanic. A horse lay dead at the roadside. The horses I was to see later were small and undernourished, unshod, sometimes lame, standing motionless in the sun or pulling carts of building materials.

Quite often on a bus there'd be a dude, who fancied himself, sitting on the (internal) bonnet, where everyone could see him. It wasn't very comfortable there, so much of the time he'd move to stand by the door as if usurping the conductor's position. Wherever he was he could chatter to the driver and the conductor – or to those passengers in the front rows and those getting on or off.

He could chat up the girls and he did. But on that day, when we entered a town, the dude took over from the conductor, who got off the bus. This made me suspect that the other dudes I'd seen had been off-duty conductors taking a free ride, perhaps on their way to work on another bus. While we were waiting at a bus station the first conductor got back on again. One of them came down the bus saying, '*Something, something ...* Managua.' I failed to find out what this meant.

'Does anyone speak English,' I called out. 'I just want to know – does this bus go to Managua.'

I'd tried to pronounce the name correctly, I really did. Several people corrected me. I hoped there weren't two places of similar names.

'We've just got to wait,' someone said.

Then a lot of people got on the bus and we were off again. We came to a market. There was a strong smell of onions – mainly because onion sellers were holding them up to the windows of the bus, which was now too crowded to allow the traders in. Other items such as salt cellars were passed around and then back out of the window. As we moved off a big bunch of onions fell off the luggage rack but nobody was hurt.

When we got to Managua, it took me ten minutes to find my way out of the bus station. I took another bus towards where I believed the city centre to be and got off when, looking up a side street, I spied the Hawaiian Hotel. It was run by two bald men, who I guessed were gay. The taller of the two (I'll call him Miguel) was Central American and spoke some English. The shorter (I'll call him Mr Chan because he was Chinese) tried to join in, as if he was jealous of his partner's rapport with me. Mr Chan walked slowly but always wanted to be in on anything his partner was doing, so he spent his time trying to catch up with what was going on. He wandered about in only a vest and Y-fronts, although he did not look at all well and had a bad cough. His face was wrinkled and pale as pastry. And whereas Miguel's baldness looked like his chosen style Mr Chan's looked like a sign of illness or a side effect of its treatment. He gave the impression of someone taking a break from his sick bed. I wondered if he had aids. The two were very concerned about me.

'Where are you going?' they asked me when they saw me heading for the front door – as if I were about to step into a war zone.

'I'm going to the bar on the corner to get some more drinking water. I used mine up for washing, as you've got the water turned off.'

'Ohhhhhhhhh!' said Mr Chan, pointing to my draw-string bag and keeping his mouth open as if hoping the correct English words would come out. He seemed to be trying to warn me to close my draw-string bag tightly before I risked my life on the street. The bag was pretty tight already.

In a rival hotel opposite there was a children's party. I heard the song 'Happy Birthday' coming from a CD player, in a version with about five verses. The bar on the corner had a shop run by a good-looking guy, young, with quite good English, who looked after me – once I'd got his attention, because he was usually busy impressing the girls sitting at the counter on stools. Nicaraguan people didn't seem as happy as those from the other Central American countries I'd visited. Life was hard for most of them, but they had a sense of pride, or at any rate style. The men affected big brimmed hats and *machetes*. Most women wore their hair tied back, which suited their faces very well. Some had dyed their hair brunette or blonde, no doubt inspired by pictures of American film or pop stars. This made them look brash and vulgar. Both genders were dreaming of a better life. For some reason I felt alienated as I walked about. Everything I'd heard about Nicaragua was making me nervous. There were explosions. I hoped it was fireworks.

I felt psychologically better after a meal at the bar, but I had to hurry back to the hotel because I had diarrhoea. I'm afraid I didn't quite make it. Imagine – no light in the bathroom, dim light in the bedroom, no running water, and I had only one pair of trousers! There was no water all night except for one hour when Miguel turned it on. I washed my trousers, remembering to take the bank notes out of the 'secret' pockets. I flushed the loo, had a shower and saved two bottles of water for shaving and washing my hands when the water was off, removing the labels in case later I thought they contained drinking water. I improvised a washing line using my two bootlaces and a lace from one of my trainers.

At seven o'clock in the morning I heard a pumping sound and the water came on again. I had another shower. I knew that I'd be sitting very close to people on a bus. How awful, I thought, to live with limited water supply all the time – and yet the little girls go to school with clean white blouses and socks every day. Mr Chan was padding about in his underwear and slippers. If he'd worn a T-shirt and boxer shorts he would have looked dressed, but Y-fronts! He caught me making for the front door again. Miguel was not around.

'You want to go somewhere?' Mr Chan asked me. 'There!' he said, apparently pointing to the security fence.

'That?' I asked.

'No – out there. He – driver.'

Mr Chan made a steering motion with his hands. There was a man in the street. He came over – presumably a taxi-driver.

'No,' I tried to explain. 'I'm going to the corner. There!'

The taxi-driver pointed.

'No, where it says, "Coco-cola". I'm going to get breakfast – *desayuno.*'

The taxi-driver went back to his car. I wondered if Mr Chan ever put his clothes on. Maybe, Miguel had confiscated them to keep his partner a prisoner.

As I was having my breakfast, a man of about 40 was spreading out bits of a cardboard box in a shady spot under an overhanging roof. It was only 8am but already exceedingly hot. He took off his shirt, but kept his trousers and boots on. He scratched his bare chest. He didn't look at all comfortable. He was like somebody who wasn't sleepy but knew it was bedtime. His knees were drawn up and to one side. He was using only half the length of his cardboard bed. Eventually one leg went out straight. People went by. He took no notice of them, nor they of him. He looked bored rather than dejected as if the worthwhile day he had planned for himself had been postponed not cancelled – all he had to do was sleep it out. As I left he slid down the cardboard and lowered his head but he still had one knee in the air. When I got back to the hotel Mr Chan, still in his underwear, let me in. By 8.50 he was wearing a white T-shirt and white slacks. Maybe they'd just come back from the laundry.

I felt uneasy and wanted to get out of the country. But to do so I needed a map of it. I asked Mr Chan, who padded off and a minute later padded back again with a splendid map, which showed El Lago de Nicaragua, the country's vast lake, the towns and the roads, but no frontier town, but I guessed that a narrow strip of land between the lake and Costa Rica would contain at least one exit point. I copied the details I thought I'd need into my notebook.

I joined a minibus. We were packed in like corn on the cob. The comfort and sensuality of touching the thigh of a woman next to me was more than undone by the pressure of the knobbly knees of a bony man sitting facing me. The woman closed her eyes – either to sleep or to imagine she was somewhere else. As for the conductor, he gained a measure of comfort by sticking his torso out of the window and holding onto the roof rack. His feet were not resting on the floor. If he had had a stroke he would have fallen out of the window. I was the nearest passenger so it would have been up to me to catch his legs and pull him back in.

When we got to the town – Jinotepe, I think – I bought a map of Nicaragua showing the regions and for once I was able to buy a map of the next country on my route (in this case Costa Rica). I checked into the Motel Santos Yapia, so new it smelled of plaster. A big man with a black beard was working to finish the fitting out. In my room a welcome mat had been stuck onto the floor. However when the door was fitted one end of the mat had had to be cut away, so the word 'welcome' was cut short. The toilet wasn't screened in any way so I felt as if I would be sleeping in the bathroom. Instead of the usual complimentary sachet of shampoo they gave me two complimentary condoms, on the basis, presumably, that it's more important to have protected sex than to wash your hair.

When I went out, the landlord wrote the name, address and telephone number of the motel in my notebook in case I needed to ask my way back. I found a proper hotel and wished I were staying there – until, that is, I tried the hotel restaurant. I was the only guest – at least in that part of the dining room. I ordered soup and asked to have it first. As soon as I'd ordered it the waiter rushed out to place my order. When he came back I ordered my main course. He brought the soup and according to the best traditions of those parts, when I was three-quarters of the way through it, arrived with the main course. He didn't plonk it down, but stood holding it, while with his other hand he laid a knife and fork around my soup plate and fiddled with other items on my table. I sensed that what he wanted to do was to take my soup plate away and put the main course in front of me. But it was seafood soup and rather good. I refused to let it go. But there's a limit to how fast you can gulp hot soup, even when blowing on each spoonful to cool it. It was a battle of wills. When he realised that he wasn't going to win he put the main course down and went away. I like a little pause between courses but the main course was already quite cool enough. This was a grilled slice of pork 7 mm thick, as tough and dry as a carpet tile, mainly because it had no sauce of any kind. To make matters worse the waiter had forgotten to bring my wine. I got up from my table and looked up and down for him. I went and asked the receptionist. He said he would get the waiter. While I was waiting, I went back and tucked into my salad.

Just when I'd managed to put the thought of wine out of my head, the waiter appeared and showed me a bottle of Chilean red.

'That'll be lovely,' I said.

He took it away and presumably carried it around with him while he hunted for a corkscrew. Then he remembered they kept one in the bar – for emergencies. He opened the bottle out of sight and brought it in with a wine glass, elegant as to style, mean as to capacity. The wine was very good. So were the chips. They were cold, of course, but that was hardly their fault. The carrots and the marrow were delicious and not a second overcooked.

I'd just put my knife and fork together when the waiter brought the bill. Why? They charged so little that the whole exercise cannot have been economically viable. But didn't they want to sell me something else – desert, cheese, coffee, some more wine? Earlier the receptionist had apologised for the delays and said the *other* waiter was ill.

That night seemed very hot. I lay on my bed with a fan directed at my nakedness. Sometimes the only way I could be comfortable was to get under the shower and then stand wet in front of the fan. There was a small window set into the door but the window had no mesh so when it was open insects could get in. A determined thief could have put a hand through the window to release the catch on the door knob and opened the door from the outside. The window had a sill or shelf on the inside so a murderer could have reached in to place a canister of poisonous gas, where it would have killed all the people in the room, namely me. The only safe thing to do was to lock the window with its sliding bolt. Then there was no ventilation – only circulation of the trapped air by the fan. I had odd pricking feelings in my skin. Each time I felt one of these I thought a mosquito was biting me, but I never saw one. Were these the first signs of Dengue Fever? My tummy was unsettled. Perhaps the seafood soup or the pork carpet tile was at fault. At three o'clock I took Immodium.

Later, I looked at my watch. It was half past five. I'd fallen asleep with the light on. There was a nasty creaking noise. The door, window and all, was opening, apparently on its own. I ran to it, in so far as you can run in a small space, and pushed the door to. I clicked the catch shut and opened the window expecting to see a shifty figure with a mask and a bag over his shoulder labelled with the Spanish for 'swag'. But there was no one there. The air outside was cooler. I left the window open and some of that cool, fresh air came in. Anyone passing could have seen me and my lavatory pan, but I didn't care. I went back to bed. At ten to six the door rattled. I didn't know why – until I heard someone tapping on my door. That would be the landlord, I thought.

'It's all very well for him,' I thought, 'he's probably slept like a baby in a room with a window that had a mesh and could be left open at night. He might even have air conditioning! It was now a bright but hazy morning. I decided I might as well get up. After all it would soon be too hot to move. I had just stepped into the shower when there was a definite knocking at the door. I didn't answer. Why should I? I was in the shower. The knock came again. The window in the door opened and a cylindrical object was passed through the opening and placed on the little shelf. The phantom gasser had struck.

'Coffee is here!' a voice said.

'Oh that's very nice.' I called from the shower. 'Thank you!'

It was the big workman with the black beard. I decided he must be staying at the hotel while he was working on it. Perhaps he didn't like the thought of the guests lying abed when he had to be working.

At 10.15 I set off for La Rivas. We were buzzing along nicely, the minibus full, not overfull, when we were stopped by the police, who inspected the vehicle, then took the driver and conductor away for questioning. A woman passenger began screaming what sounded like abuse at the police. Luckily the interview with the bus crew was held at some distance so I don't think the police heard her. After ten minutes the driver and the conductor returned not looking at all shaken and we continued our journey. Whether the matter had been settled by the payment of a fine or the passing of a bribe I never discovered.

At La Rivas somebody on the bus told me where to get off and got me on the right bus for La Virgen. In this strange and troubled country it was uplifting to see Lake Nicaragua. I got off the second bus and walked from the road to the water's edge. The lake was so big I couldn't see the other side. There were two islands in the shape of mountains, one sharper and more obviously volcanic than the other. A flop-eared bull was tethered on the beach. That is to say it had a rope around its neck. Whether the other end was fastened I never found out. Some cows were free to wander. There were tiny waves on the lake and numerous rocks broke the surface. A horse was standing in the water while a man washed it with soap and lake-water. A woman was washing clothes while her two boys played in the water. I bathed, leaving my rucksack on a rock close to hand. If the water had been any hotter it would not have been safe to bathe a baby in it. It was too shallow to swim but perfect for lolling under the surface. I kept a T-shirt on so that I wouldn't be sunburnt and when I came out the wet shirt was pleasantly cooling.

I walked along the beach and came to a hotel, appealing to look at, except that the swimming pool had no water. There was a restaurant with tables inside and out, but I didn't see a single guest and they weren't open for non-residents. There were some staff and one of them, with civility and good humour took me to the gates, that is, saw me off the premises. I did find a bar, however, away from the beach, on the road, where the man produced a beer and his wife got out of a hammock to prepare grilled steak, with rice, purple beans and salad.

I took a bus to Sapo, the next place on the lake. This had no hotel either, so I pressed on. Someone told me there was a hotel in Peñas Blancas (white rocks), further along the lake's edge, but again I came across none so I went on to the border. I had found Nicaragua fascinating but unhappy. I was looking forward to Costa Rica, well known as an eco-tourist destination. But it was late in the day and by lingering at the lake I had ended up rather late at the frontier and was not looking forward to finding a hotel in a new country in the dark.

8. Costa Rica

May 15 – 25

As in the other countries I'd passed through, there was a muddle at the frontier. The 'in' and 'out' lanes were not separated or clearly signposted. Again people without badges were hanging around to tell you where to go and what to do. Instead of a clear pathway as you have in airports there were various unnamed buildings, with large non-specific areas between them, some with facilities such as a garden, a casino, a shop or a café. I didn't know whether I was in Nicaragua, Costa Rica or the no-man's land between. There was a sign, however, that said, 'Pedestrians and Buses'. I followed this but realised I was going the wrong way when I came to a big notice saying, 'Welcome to Nicaragua'. I worked out that paradoxically this meant I was in Costa Rica. As I did a U-turn, I could sense dusk approaching and I'd no idea which was the nearest Costa Rican town likely to offer a hotel or which of several buses to take. I saw two tall attractive young white women, who looked like students.

'Excuse me,' I said, 'do you speak English?'

'Yes,' replied the taller, 'we're British.'

'Where are you from?'

'Sussex.'

'I'm from Dorset. Where are you heading?'

'We've been all over South America, but now we're going back to Santa Cruz' (the capital of Costa Rica). 'To the Embassy. My friend's had her passport stolen.'

The friend looked dejected.

'Oh, no!' I said, 'That's terrible.'

'I put my bag on the rack just for a moment,' the friend said, 'just for a moment!'

'The bag was stolen,' the taller girl said, 'and her passport was in the bag.'

I secretly congratulated myself on always keeping my passport under my shirt. I had seen very few Europeans since I'd got off the QM2. These two wore three-quarter-length trousers, very practical. There was no way they could blend in with the local population. The taller girl had natural blonde hair in a bob and shining eyes as blue as forget-me-nots. She seemed relaxed and comfortable.

'Do you know if that bus is going to stop at a town where I might find a hotel?' I asked. 'I don't want to be looking for somewhere to stay in the dark.'

'You could come with us. We know where we're staying in Santa Cruz.'

'That's sweet of you. But I'd have to find my own place to stay. I'd be better getting off at the first town.'

'We both speak Spanish. We could ask for you.'

'That would be fantastic.'

They told me that their bus was due to stop at La Cruz so I travelled on it. I didn't try to sit with the Sussex girls. The girl who'd lost her passport was still sore and I thought she might resent me chatting to her friend.

With some help I found what I think was the only hotel in La Cruz, Amalia's Inn. In this simple establishment, places had been found for a number of large semi-abstract oil paintings, which put me in mind of the sixties and gave the place an unconventional, Bohemian air. I guessed the owner was a painter or perhaps the widow of one. The notion that the hotel was a 'one-off' was enhanced by its position overlooking the Bahía Salinas, a bay on the Pacific coast. My room was on the first floor and looked over a balcony to a view of the ocean. Enchanting at night, in the morning it reminded me of a 19th century travel painting, showing the hotel garden and its palm tree carrying fruit, the land sloping away with cattle, green trees, brown grass, pink sandy beaches on the wide bay, the grey sea, the grey-blue sky and a most artistic rainbow.

I took a bus to Liberia (an inland town, not the republic in West Africa). Costa Rica (the 'Rich Coast') appeared more sophisticated than the other Central American countries I'd seen. There were fewer ambulant traders and less shouting. The fields were clearly defined and some had properly constructed fences. I saw no rubbish. I guessed the people were tourism-minded – nearly everywhere was tidy, purposeful and presentable. The other countries had looked as though they weren't expecting visitors. At Liberia the bus station was busy but not chaotic. Its café was well organised, with each member of the staff knowing what they were doing, multi-tasking without getting in each other's way, all activities interlocking like machinery.

It was a lengthy ride from there on to Puntarenas, because we went 90 km out of our way to take in another town. However, for part of the way I sat next to a young woman from Massachusetts, who was living in Costa Rica with her husband. They both worked on-line so they could live where they liked and for three months they had made a temporary base in Costa Rica in order to explore the country. While I was there, she advised me, I should see the Northern (Atlantic) coast, because it had some wonderful beaches and it was good way to enter Panama.

Puntarenas sits on a peninsula, which protrudes like a tongue into a large bay on the Pacific coast. When I arrived I was greeted by the usual cries of 'Taxi! taxi!' and as usual I decided to do my own thing. It was getting dark and I wanted to find a hotel quickly. I saw yachts and cabin cruisers on the inland side of the tongue so I deduced that there was money around and therefore hotels, but I guessed these would be on the Pacific side so I headed straight for the sea front. There were palm trees, a sandy beach and a view of a headland. I was surprised not to see a hotel straight away so I started walking towards the tip of the tongue. In a side street there was a hotel run by a French Canadian, who said all his rooms were taken.

'What sort of hotel are you looking for?' he asked.

I wanted to say, 'No worse than this one.'

'Well, like this one, or I don't mind paying more money,' I said tactfully.

'If you continue along the front you will see hotels. Keep going.'

I came to various eateries – always a hopeful sign – then I found a hotel on the sea front with a swimming pool. A pool is a big investment and a nuisance to maintain, so it's a sign of a certain standard. After the places I'd stayed in, I was looking forward to a bit of class, or if not class then comfort. The hotel didn't serve dinner, however, so I went to a restaurant. On the menu was onion soup and sea bass in garlic and butter. The onion soup was off so I had the alternative. I thought it a harsh thing to do to the subtle sea bass, to smother it in garlic, but I decided to try it. I ordered a glass of white wine. The waiter brought a litre bottle of something already started, I didn't know when. He produced a tiny glass and poured some wine for me to taste. The 'bouquet' was medical, the taste unsubtle but the wine was dry and drinkable so I said 'yes' to a proper glass of the stuff. The sea bass came with carefully cooked carrots and crisp chips. As soon as I tasted the fish, it cried out for wine. And once I'd tasted the fish, the wine improved immeasurably. The two were made for each other. Whether this happy marriage was the result of luck or good management was not my concern.

My hotel did, however, serve breakfast. Before I went to the dining room I stepped out for some air. For the first time I could see a picturesque island. I walked down the beach towards the water. Palm trees grew along the high-tide line. The sand was a comforting deep brown colour. A man with a barrow was patiently sweeping, but another was doing press-ups. Set into the sand were permanent goal posts. These signs of recreation suggested affluence. Poor people don't exercise; they work.

The dining room had a long, unglazed window, which looked over the road and the beach to the sea. I sat at a table by this window to enjoy the view and the fresh sea air. Unfortunately the noise of the television blocked out the sound of the waves. Had I come all that way for breakfast television? No one was watching the programme except for the staff. Maybe it kept them sane. Central-American Spanish is a hard sound. The language has so many syllables that the overall effect on someone who doesn't speak it is a staccato battering of the ear drums.

A young woman on the next table, with a slim, trim figure wore her jeans so low that that everyone could see the parting of her buttocks. As she was Costa Rican this posterior cleavage was an elegant shade of brown – so that was all right! I was more taken with one of the waitresses. Her hair was black, shiny and tied back, her features strong and balanced, her eyes a classic leaf shape. She wore a white shirt and white shorts, which emphasised a squidgy bum. I fantasised about having an encounter with her. I didn't have to wait long.

A member of the dove family flew in through the window and tried to share my table, alighting on the back of a chair, even strutting around on the tablecloth. I have nothing against fauna in general but I resented the presumption of this pigeon and didn't think it should be encouraged in a place were food was served and eaten. I shooed it away but it kept coming back as if it lived there and I was the intruder. The waitress (the lovely Leaf Eyes) came over and instead of driving the creature out placed a large helping of cooked rice on top of the letter 'L' of the 'HOTEL' sign just below the window. I didn't know whether this was to divert the pest from me, to poison it or to provide its usual breakfast. I gave Leaf Eyes a look – half disapproval, half lust. The bird left my table, ate as much of the rice as it could and then dropped out of sight. I finished my meal in peace. The next morning I returned to the same table. So did the pigeon.

After the first breakfast, I went out to explore. On the beach fishermen were mending nets stretched between trees to keep them more or less off the ground. I saw a house surrounded by cacti growing so close together that they provided an effective security fence. A man selling hats had much of his stock stacked on his own head. I heard the song 'Puff, the Magic Dragon' made famous in the sixties by Peter, Paul and Mary. I found an Internet café and enjoyed the coolness of an air-conditioned building. I e-mailed the shipping agent in Colón and my support group in England.

'I am taking a day off,' I told them. 'I am ahead of schedule so I can afford to do this. I've been on the road for seven weeks. A second night in a comfortable hotel and a short break from buses will do me a lot of good. The wash basin is nice and large, which helps with the laundry.'

In the afternoon a wind had got up. The flag in front of the hotel was fluttering, the pole itself swaying. I went to the beach. More rubbish had come in on the last tide – the wheel of a toy tractor, a blue pen top, a lump of wood the size and shape of a small alligator, a synthetic sponge, a toothbrush bearing the word 'PEACE', a plastic spoon, the remains of a mattress, a single flip-flop, a long red pepper, a high heel, a dead fish with its eyes closed, a piece of wood once painted blue with six nails in it, a red plastic bottle, a fruit I didn't recognise, a green pepper, a small rubber ball, which I put in my pocket to serve as a universal basin plug, a broken drinks crate, a turned wooden spindle from the back of an upright chair, a doll's leg with pelvis still attached, a large lime, bottles with tops, a small mango, a vegetable I didn't recognise, heads of sweetcorn, and, best of all, chunks of tree trunk that the sea had worn smooth as sea mammals. These lay on the sand as if they had every right to be there. A log resembled a vertebra of one of the larger dinosaurs. An arm chair I'd seen earlier had shifted position.

The sea reflected the grey of the sky, although the water was brown where it churned up the sand. The freshly wetted part of the beach was the colour of slate. A woman jogged by, then another dressed to jog but walking and holding her hip as if she had a stitch.

A bird was hanging in the air. With its thin tail and a forward-pointing peak on the middle of the front edge of each wing, it looked like a pterodactyl. As I came back up the beach I saw two men walking about on a corrugated iron roof, as if planning repairs. Because of the slope of the roof, the swaying of the palm trees behind it, the quivering of their leaves and the drifting of the clouds behind them, the scene had a bizarre, unstable air. A flash of lightning didn't disturb the men but added to the sense of unreality.

I sat on a low wall under some overhead wires, but I wasn't close to them. If the lightning were overhead, I considered, the wires would take the electricity not me. On one side of the sky the clouds looked heavy, a dark purplish grey. On the other they were silver. The islands and headlands looked like cardboard cut-outs carefully arranged with the darkest nearest to give a sense of perspective. There were double flashes. The wind grew stronger and it began to rain. I realised that if the wire burnt through it might have fallen on me, still live with the sky's electricity. The storm was only one or two miles away. Then there was sheet lightning, very bright. The thunder grew louder, sometimes like gunfire, sometimes a kettle-drum roll, once like furniture dragged over floorboards. Now the flag was wrapped around the post, wet and limp. The headland and island were blanked out in the mist as if the cardboard cut-outs had been blown over. The wet sand looked like raw liver.

I went back to the hotel, put my valuables in the safe in my room and got ready to go into the pool. I was just about to enter the water when I felt rain on me. I'd forgotten that like so many buildings in Central America, the central part of the building was open to the sky. This meant that the pool was exposed to the elements, such as lightning. This would go for anything wet and higher than the water – that could be me. I gave up the idea of a swim and went back to my room. I looked out of the window. It was dark early. The hotel and street lamps were on but sea was unlit except when the lightning rendered it as bright as the sky, making the horizon visible again. For a second, lit as if by moonlight, it appeared white like snow.

When the rain had steadied from heavy to moderate I set out for my evening meal. I found a grander hotel than my own with a larger pool and a dining area outside. The guests were protected from the rain by a giant sunshade on each table. A couple dining with their grown-up daughter were speaking French. There was also a young couple standing at the bar, very much in love. I know this because she was fondling the nearer of his two buttocks.

Strangely, as at the other restaurant the previous night sea bass with garlic featured on the menu and the onion soup again was off. I ordered the alternative soup and asked to have it before my main course. You see, I never give up. The waiter served someone else then disappeared into the depths of the hotel garden holding an umbrella over his head. I wondered if he was going by a back way to the other restaurant, so I timed him. The young lovers moved to a table to play cards.

The waiter returned with the umbrella in one hand and my soup in the other. It tasted identical to the soup I'd had at the other establishment the previous night. But the waiter had taken only two and half minutes to collect it. There wasn't time for him to go to the other place and be back in that time. I never discovered where the waiter went – maybe to a kitchen between the two establishments, and serving both. Nor did I discover how, with all his complications, the waiter still managed to observe the local custom and bring my main course while I was only two-thirds of the way through my soup. The card players got up. Once again the girl's hand went straight to his buttock. It was a balmy night and I wished them joy.

Next morning I had a proper swim in the hotel pool. Its shape was more or less a right-angled triangle and, as I had the pool to myself, I swam up and down the hypotenuse.

I asked at Reception where the tourist information office was.

'Where to do you want to go?'

'I want to see a rainforest.'

'I know the man.'

'What man?'

'The man who knows all about the rainforest. He can take you. He's a friend of mine.'

'Is there a rainforest near here?'

'Oh yes. He can take you. Do you want to speak to him? No obligation.'

So it was that I arranged to meet Ronald from Varso Travel in the hotel half an hour later.

'What do you want to know?' he asked.

'Well, I will be going into Panama from the Caribbean side of Costa Rica. I want to know where the national parks are, because I'd like to see a rainforest on my way across the country.'

'There are rainforests,' he said, taking up a map and pointing to an area between San José in the centre of Costa Rica and Limón on the Atlantic coast. 'You could go that way on the bus and the bus could drop you off and you could see the forest and another bus pick you up. I don't know how well the bus co-ordinates, but ... it would be possible. Yes, ... you could do it that way.'

His tone implanted enough uncertainty, to make me receptive to his next suggestion.

'We have a national park here, you know – the Carrera National Park, 40 km away. There are monkeys and macaws and toucans and iguanas ...' he said.

'Wonderful!'

'We could go this afternoon.'

'How much will it cost?'

'That will be $60 per person,' he said.

'Right, that's $60 then,' I said.

'No, it's $120 – for two people.'

'But there's only one person.'

'You don't have a wife?'

'My wife is dead,' I said bluntly, then I added, 'If you find me a wife, I'll pay $120.'

Following so closely on the announcement of my wife's death, my little joke threw him.

'There must be other single people who want to do the trip,' I suggested. 'Shall we say $90?'

So the cost of not bringing my wife was halved on the basis that she had a good excuse not to be there. But it wasn't my idea of $60 per person.

'All right,' I said.

'I'll pick you up here at the hotel at 1 o'clock,' he told me. 'It might be me or it might be my son – okay?'

'Do I have to bring anything?'

'We'll supply water and a waterproof.'

'I've got my own waterproof.'

'It may be raining, of course.'

'Well, it is a rainforest,' I quipped.

'It often rains in the afternoon.'

'I don't mind.'

'Unfortunately the animals do. They don't like the rain. You can never guarantee seeing the animals anyway. But you'll see the forest.'

'Yes, I'd like to see the forest.'

'Well, we'll come for you at one o'clock.'

'Thanks. I'll see you then.'

I had lunch in the hotel so that I'd be on the spot when Ronald came for me. We drove to the other side of town, where I transferred to a four-wheel-drive vehicle, driven by his son Mike, who then took over. They were Costa Ricans despite the English-sounding names. Varso Travel, Mike told me, had developed from a taxi business, a natural progression, I thought. Mike drove to a retail warehouse. I waited in the car while he bought long plastic cagoules for two people. We picked up Heido, a big pleasant man, who was to be our guide as he knew about the animals. Then we drove to a woman's house in a wood to collect some bananas. I guessed these were to tempt the monkeys to show themselves. Then we headed for the forest. I'd realised by then that I was the only tourist in the party. No wonder Ronald had wanted to charge me $120!

'Costa Rica doesn't have an army,' said Mike. 'That's why we don't have any wars. We have security forces trained in the United States, but no army.'

It was quite a thought.

'Would you like to see crocodiles?' Mike asked.

'Yes, certainly I would.'

'We'll stop on the way.'

The sky got darker. A light drizzle materialised. We stopped just short of a bridge. Heido put on one of the new waterproofs. I put on my own. Mike stayed in the car.

'This is the best way to see crocodiles,' said Heido.

We stood on the bridge and, from this safe viewpoint, looked over the edge. There in a muddy river were big, mud-coloured crocodiles. We crossed the road and looked from the other side of the bridge. There were some more. I couldn't see much detail, but it was exciting to see the creatures at all. I was careful not to drop anything – there'd be no going after it. We got back into the car and drove to the national park. Mike got out and bought tickets. It was raining steadily now. Mike left Heido and me to go into the rain forest. Just as we came up to the gate Heido pointed. On the tarmac was a lizard some 40 cm long, with fancy bits on its back and throat.

'Iguana,' said Heido.

The animal disappeared into the foliage. A moment later, we were in the forest and soon we had left the human world behind. The only man-made objects were the concrete path, the bridges over the streams and notices in Spanish and English explaining aspects of the forest. There was a calm but steamy atmosphere. As we walked into the forest, it became denser and darker. Despite the thick leafy roof above us the rain still came through. There were dozens of plant species but I recognised only one – the mangrove balancing on its exposed roots as if walking on stilts. I knew that trees grew very tall in the forest as they competed to reach the light, but I wasn't familiar with the buttress tree, star-shaped in section with protruding buttresses, which steadied the lofty trunk against toppling, as man-made buttresses support a castle wall.

'Look!' said Heido, pointing to the path ahead of us.

Bright green fragments of leaf were moving across it in a constantly changing mosaic. When I peered closer I could see that the reason the fragments were moving was that ants were carrying them. Other ants without leaves were going the other way – presumably to fetch more leaf fragments.

There were few sounds apart from the bubbling of a stream over stones – and mysterious bird calls. We saw no macaw or other bird. In fact we saw no fish, amphibian or reptile. The iguana and crocodiles had been outside the park. We saw no racoon or monkey – I don't know what became of the bananas. We didn't even see a squirrel. The only mammals Heido and I saw were each other. Come to think of it, we didn't see that many ants, because most of them were hidden under the leaf fragments they were carrying.

'I'm sorry about the rain,' said Heido. 'The animals don't like rain. They hide.'

Poor things! That's like being an eagle and not having a head for heights. We went on in silence. All we could see now were plants; and yet to be immersed in this serene and humid atmosphere was a memorable experience. This world had existed long, long before the birth of man. I know it was special because the strangest thing happened towards the end of our walk. I gradually became aware of the sound of road traffic. This seemed weird, out of place and out of time. It was like waking from a dream. We emerged from the forest at another point on the road and walked to the car park. We were back in the 21st Century, in a milieu dominated by man.

I'd booked a third night in the hotel. By the time I got back there the weather had brightened up. I changed into swimming trunks, went downstairs, crossed the road and walked to the sea. The water was warm and calm and I felt as if I'd got the ocean to myself. I'd bathed in the Pacific before, in San Francisco, where the sea was rough. This was the first time I'd actually swum in it. Although I was to spend weeks crossing the ocean, I guessed that this would be my only chance to get into it.

When I was dressed again I looked out and saw a strange object on the sea. It was a bit like a boat, except that it didn't seem to be moving and it had a pair of arms or wings sticking far out on either side above the water and at angle to it. There was a bright light on the vessel. I decided it must be a fishing boat and the wings must have been there to support nets. The light, I guessed, was to attract fish.

I felt relaxed in Costa Rica. More people spoke English and there were a lot of middle-class visitors. Two young Canadian men were staying in the same hotel as me on an eleven-day holiday for water-skiing and other sporty pursuits.

The next morning, on the grass of the sea front, a man had stretched five lines of rope between two trees and was pegging sunhats, baseball caps, sunglasses and jewellery onto the lines of rope. I'd been watching him for ten minutes when I recognised him as the 'mad hatter' I'd seen earlier with a stack of hats on his head. He was clearly a master of retail display.

I checked out of the hotel and set off for the capital, San José. At the bus station there was a snakewise arrangement of seats so passengers could queue sitting down – very civilised! Through the bus window I saw the grass was green from all the rain; the hills densely covered in vegetation. A little boy and a little girl were standing on a seat next to a wide-open window. The mother was on the aisle seat, fast asleep herself. The children could have fallen out one by one and she would have woken to find them missing. Europeans fuss over their children much more than Central Americans.

As we came into San José we passed close to the airport. This seemed strange after I had set myself to avoid air travel of any kind, like a reformed alcoholic finding a gin and tonic poured out for him. The bus terminal was near a large cemetery, where the citizens had honoured their dead with imposing, elaborate masonry and ironwork.

I set about uncovering the geography of the city. The cemetery was on a road so busy I guessed that it would lead to the centre. One way led to skyscrapers, which suggested the business centre, usually not far from the historical and cultural centres. I took a bus in that direction and got off when the buildings began to look smart. Then I studied the numbering of the streets called 'Avenida' and walked in the direction of the lower numbers until I came to Avenida Central. At right angles to the avenidas were streets called 'calles' and I did the same with them until I found 'Calle Central'. Thus I came to the centre of everything. From there I found the Cathedral, the National Theatre, one or two grand hotels and the Hotel El Maragato, with its narrow frontage squeezed into a gap in Avenida Central – and that's where I stayed, very economically, at the heart of San José.

The hotel provided no tourist information. Outside a small arcade I found a sign in English that said 'Tourist Information – 2nd Floor'. I went upstairs but saw nothing of the kind. I asked. Nobody knew anything about it. I went back to the notice and read it again. 'Tourist Information – 2nd Floor.' I got very cross and started to pull the notice down, but managed to restrain myself before being apprehended.

I went back to the hotel and looked at the local paper. Nothing. I went to the National Theatre. A poster advertised a Cuban ballet. That would be wonderful – no language difficulty! But they weren't coming for four days. I went up to an official in the foyer.

'Excuse me,' I asked, 'Do you speak English?'

'Yes.'

'Can you help me, please? It's difficult to find out what's going on in the City.'

I hoped he'd hand me a leaflet giving details of shows, concerts and art exhibitions.

'Everything happens here,' he said.

It was a good line, but I didn't believe him.

'There's an international poetry festival starting tonight.'

'Well, I like poetry,' I said, 'but this will be in Spanish so I won't know what it's about.'

'It's about poetry,' he said.

I couldn't argue with that.

'Have you got a leaflet?' I asked.

'Here – it's free. You don't need a ticket for the Festival.'

'Thank you very much.'

'It starts at 6 o'clock.'

There must be something else, I thought, and went out into the rain to explore. At 3.30pm I finally found the tourist information office, closed, although it was a Saturday. A sign in the window said in English, 'Open Sunday 10 – 4'. I went to the cathedral thinking there might be a concert, but there wasn't. Then I spotted the Teatro Popul Mlico Salazar. This was presenting a drama with a large cast telling the story of San José. I thought it would probably include movement, spectacle, music and dance – a better bet you might think for a non-Spanish speaker than the poetry festival. I managed to obtain a long synopsis in Spanish and decided that I would go to the play if I could make my own literal written translation. I knew I wouldn't have time to do this before that day's performance but there was one I could attend the next day (Sunday). Meanwhile the opening session of the poetry festival was that evening, so I thought I might as well go to both events.

The festival was due to start at 6pm. We were asked to be in our seats 15 minutes early. So to be on the safe side I got there at 5.35. It was a traditional theatre opened in 1897. The circular auditorium on four levels was sumptuous in red, gilt and grey, intimate but grand. On the circular painted ceiling plump women, angels and other figures floated in the sky amid diaphanous sheets of fabric. I got myself a seat in the stalls near the front in order to see and hear well but on the aisle so I could get out if it all got too much for me. There was an amazing turnout. Some, like me, wore casual dress but many more had got themselves up for an occasion. Organisers wearing smart clothes and airs of importance walked up and down the aisle. After I'd been waiting there 45 minutes I realised the seats were hard. Two presenters, a man and a woman, came on and took their places behind free-standing microphones, so relaxed and professional that I took them to be actors. At 6.25 a man with a camcorder filmed the front rows. The hostess or chairperson brought five dignitaries onto the stage to sit behind a long table with a cloth on it. The house lights dimmed,

Mexico. When I was in Oaxaca I kept returning to this elegant square.

Mexico. I'd grown the moustache so that I wouldn't stand out from the crowd. In practice it wasn't quite enough.

Guatemala. One of many old school buses bought from the United States, still rattling along and providing the main public transport.

San Marcos de Colón, Honduras.
The view from the roof of my
hotel.

Puntarenas, Costa Rica. Lifeguard station.

Puntarenas. Mending fishing nets,
with a little help from the trees.

The combined road/rail/footbridge from Costa Rica to Panama looked sturdy, but before you got to the middle, you realised planks were missing and there was no passing place – even for pedestrians!

Panama City. The bone man, showing me his bones.

Panama City. Prosperous-looking skyscrapers, a contrast to dwellings only 50 miles away – see next photograph.

Colón, Panama. This two-storey block was home to eight households. It was not far from here that I was attacked.

The lounge and bar of the Tikeibank, shared by officers and passengers. Clockwise from bottom left-hand corner: the Captain (his hand only, but what a steady one!); Graham, raising his glass and looking a little blurred (probably from alcohol); Lyndall, vet and keep-fit fanatic from Florida; Steve, the purser, on his favourite watch – behind the bar; two nice-natured cadets; Dolores, the English Chief Engineer's feisty Texan wife; Claudie, la dame mystérieuse; Hugh and Bridget, making the most of every calm and civilised moment on the ship before returning to Mugabe's Zimbabwe.

M V Tikeibank making her transit of the Pana Canal, carrying a mixed cargo and seven passeng

Tahiti. The Botanical Gardens. 'All
mimsy were the borogoves.'

Melbourne, Australia. I found a purse
in the street and wondered if I should
hand it in at the police station.

North Island, New Zealand. The
Coromandel Peninsula, beautiful and
a little unreal.

Melbourne. Earning good money as an industrial spy.

Great Ocean Road, Victoria. It wasn't the cap and pants the young people envied but the trendy pink notebook.

Great Ocean Road. One of 'The Twelve Apostles', possibly, James the son of Zebedee.

Adelaide. The Botanical Gardens. In Australia humour was never far away.

Cook, South Australia. The signpost told you all you needed to know. Behind it, the train that had brought me to this little outpost in the Nullarbor Plain.

Cook. The longest straight stretch of railway in the world.

Fremantle, Western Australia. A pictorial history from 'The Dreamtime' 60,000 years ago, through the colonisation of Western Australia in 1829, to present times and 'Reconciliation'.

On the Indian Ocean. In the bowels of the ship it was hot, quiet and strangely unsettling.

a hush spread through the auditorium. I'd waited 50 minutes for this – it had better be good.

The two presenters did everything they could to speed up and lighten the tone of the evening's proceedings. They nearly succeeded. They set the scene. They introduced the overall organiser, who spoke for five minutes. Then they introduced another of the dignitaries, who spoke for a further five minutes. And so on down the line until all the dignitaries had said whatever it was they had to say. I hadn't a clue what this was but I was able to judge how interesting their speeches were by studying the body language of the others on the stage. By this means I deduced that at least two of the five were there because of their positions as secretary of state for earnestness and bureaucracy – or whatever – rather than their deep appreciation of the poetic arts. Thus I concluded that while I was bored moribund by all the speeches, the Spanish-speaking audience would have been bored moribund by only 40% of them. One statistic is incontrovertible – altogether the speeches took half an hour. I had therefore been in the theatre for an hour and 20 minutes without hearing a single word of poetry.

After further announcements by the actors a number of poets, who had dressed down, and one, very presentable in a light-brown suit, a man who turned out to be the poet from Estonia, came onto the stage and took their places on a line of chairs. The presenters introduced them as a group and then individually, whereupon a single poet would come forward to the microphone, while the presenters stood aside.

One element of a poem is the collection of sounds it makes when spoken, sounds that in obvious or subtle ways enhance the meaning, emotion and imagery of the poem. With no knowledge of what the poems were actually about I was able to concentrate on these sounds, while assessing the fervour with which the poet read his poem and the extent to which he, and the audience, were moved by his creation. The poems of the American poet were in English. Unfortunately he failed to stand near enough to the microphone. I had the feeling that his work was both powerful and original, but I heard scarcely a word. Thus I and the many people in the audience who had English as a second or first language could not hear his poems clearly. The Estonian stood up in his light-brown suit and introduced his poems in Spanish and then read them in what I took to be Estonian or Russian.

I sensed that all the poems were very good and some were excellent. Along with the rest of the audience I applauded the poets individually and collectively when they left the stage. The effort of concentrating as well as I could on so much foreign speech had given me a headache, but I felt in some sense it had been worth it. The presenters rounded off the proceedings and sent us away to our well-earned dinners. No they didn't! They introduced another batch of poets, and soon the first of the second batch was up on his hind legs reading his poems to a flagging audience and trying, no doubt, not to flag himself. As soon as he finished I strode out before the next poet could get started. Two and a half hours without an interval is enough in any language!

At 8 o'clock, as I came out of the theatre, the city was busy – and dark of course. There were beggars lurking in dark corners. I felt I had to look lively. I was so flustered that, when confronted by a beggar with only one hand, I nearly handed my gift to the space where his missing hand would have been.

The next morning, being Sunday, I went to the Tourist Information because I knew it opened at 10. Unfortunately, the people who ran the office hadn't read their own notice and the office was still closed. I went back several times during the day. It never opened. Meanwhile I sat down to work on my translation. It took a long time because I had to look up most of the words. Eventually I'd penned the following:

New Town of the Opening of the Forest

270 years ago a hamlet, poor and without much hope of growth, was established at a crossroads in a fertile area of the then-called Valley of Acsari between the Rivers Torres and Maria Aguilar. When given to the community, for those years famous as the New Villa of the Opening of the Forest, for a hermit, in order that the neighbours would not have to make the long journey to hear Mass in the old capital Cartago, to be dedicated to San José. In this humble way, began the life of a population that, from a country hamlet passed to become capital of an independent nation, which has sustained her free will in the democracy, social justice, the continuous unrolling and the peace.

The dramatic art production, direction and execution with social conscience on the story dramatised from quality to urban myth of those transferred from farming community to cosmopolitan capital thanks to scenes that like a mirror showing the identity of whose power and of whose sound the people that (damage soul and life to be human reality) that today we recognise as San José.

My first translation from the Spanish – dire, isn't it? But it gave me some idea what the play would be about. So I went back to the theatre to buy a ticket for the 5 o'clock performance. This was the last one – and a play about the founding of the City would certainly draw the crowds, so I guessed there would be wonderful atmosphere. I was right about that – there was not a single ticket left. Just as well I'd done the translation – otherwise I wouldn't have been able to tell you the history of San José! At least I'd been to the opening of the International Poetry Festival, so that was something! It sounds greedy, I know, but I didn't feel completely satisfied. I was in the capital city – I had to have my culture fix.

I set off for the National Museum. I knew from the map that I had to go six blocks and I strode along, counting as I went. But when I'd done so, the museum wasn't there. Nor had I seen the other landmarks I expected on the way. There was something seriously wrong with the City. I decided to do a check. I got my compass out. Either San José had swung through 180 degrees when I wasn't looking – or I'd got the map upside down. I'd got the map upside down! I'd gone the right distance – but in the wrong direction! Still, I was now only twelve blocks away from the museum and I'd seen a bit more of the City. When I eventually got to the museum it was closed, but near it I stumbled on a little theatre. I asked two men in the foyer if I could have a look at the auditorium. It was a bit run down, but when it was full of people the atmosphere would have been great. In Britain it would have been a fringe theatre. Photographs advertised a 'musical cabaret'.

'Is it on tonight?' I asked.

'Yes,' they said, 'but not here.'

They gave me instructions and off I set. I found myself in a run-down, insalubrious quarter of San José. I felt insecure but I managed to keep on the move, only stopping to go into shops to ask the way. I found the theatre and bought a ticket with an hour to spare. Across the road was an Asian restaurant. The boss welcomed me at the door. I told him I had less than an hour before my show started. He led me straight to a room called 'South Asia', decorated appropriately and, mercifully, with no television. The menu included dishes from Thailand, Japan, China and Indonesia. I had a soup with prawns and then a Thai beef curry, with two species of Thai bean – an encouraging foretaste of a continent I hoped eventually to reach. The family on the next table consisted of a very dark West Indian man, a very dark Costa Rican woman and their two beautiful very dark little boys. The boss caught me on the way out.

'I know you are in a hurry,' he said, 'but would you mind giving me your comments some time?'

'I may not be here again,' I said, 'so I'll give you my comments quickly now. You gave me a really warm welcome. The service was very attentive. The ambience was most appealing. The food was excellent. I could not fault anything.'

'Thank you very much, sir. Enjoy the theatre.'

Billed in San José as 'cabaret', in Britain the show would have been called 'revue'. That sounds outmoded but it was bursting with whatever the Costa Ricans call 'joie de vivre' and presented in a thoroughly professional way. It might not have succeeded in London but it certainly worked here. The company consisted of a comedian, two character comediennes, a female singer and six vivacious female dancers, who played any bit parts required and supplied links between the long solo turns so the whole thing never flagged. With their high heels, pretty brown legs and cutesy blonde wigs they lent a tongue-in-cheek glamour, sustaining what appeared to be an unfeigned infectious glee. The comedian had such an expressive face, hands and whole body that I think he must once have been a dancer himself. The women sent themselves up unmercifully. The audience was pretty thin – I guess nearly everyone was at the Teatro Popul Mlico Salazar – but the show had the audience laughing freely. There was a baby in the row behind me. It and I were the only two people who didn't get the jokes, but we both followed the show in our individual ways. I know this because the infant was quiet as soon the show started and remained so. Maybe its mother was one of the dancers – or maybe it fell asleep.

You would have thought that when I got back to my hotel I would have had enough entertainment – if that's the right word – but I was on something of a high so I put the television on and caught an arts programme. I heard the celebrated European pianist Alfred Brendel play a Schubert impromptu and someone else beautifully sing a chunk of the same composer's 'Winterreise' cycle. Finally, deeply satisfied after all my efforts in pursuit of the arts, I fell asleep.

The next morning in a shopping arcade I handed in my boots to be mended by one of two smiley, jokey and loveable brothers, sitting low and hunched, surrounded by the tools of their ancient trade, in a den reeking of leather and glue. The two exchanged significant looks and grinned up at me. Each on his own could have claimed a place in a book of fairy tales. Together they were a double act of Dickensian richness – 'The cobblers, Grinwarm and Chortlip.'.

'We're mad!' Grinwarm confided, looking pleased with himself.

'I'm going round the world,' I told them. 'I need my boots to be in good condition.'

If I'd asked for seven-league boots, they wouldn't have raised a single one of their four bushy eyebrows.

'That's it!' said Chortlip with satisfaction.

'Eleven o'clock,' said Grinwarm, nodding.

They had my boots ready for me within two hours. In this time I went to the tourist office – open at last – and asked what there was of interest between San José and Puerto Limón, on the Caribbean Coast, where I was headed. They gave me a leaflet for another national park – a second chance for me to see the animals. There was an overhead rail through the forest and, I read, I could stay the night in a lodge. Then I would be out in the forest early and catch the little blighters before they all scurried away from the rain. The wisdom of such reasoning was reinforced as, after an early lunch, it began to rain gently. I set out on foot for the Caribbean bus terminal. The rain was refreshing, but with every step it grew heavier and I began to hurry. It was not very long before the thoroughfare I was walking along had filled with water. I could see the bus station ahead, on the other side of the road. I found a place where the water wasn't too deep and through a gap in the traffic I managed to run through the flood to the other side of the road. I started to walk along the pavement towards the entrance to the terminal when two buses rushed within a metre of me, ploughing through a deep trough of water and sending up a great wave, which drenched me to my chest. I bought a ticket to the nature reserve and was soon on the bus, where I sat, wet through, wiping my glasses and trying to dry my hearing aid with damp tissues. Through the rain we went, along winding roads, up and down, through a tunnel, across part of the forest until the driver – bless him – set me down close to the entrance to the park, which I don't think was an official stop.

At the gate building, the man on duty looked surprised to see me.

'I've just come from the bus,' I explained.

'Well, it's a bit late,' he said. 'I don't know whether you'll be able to see anything. There are no vehicles at the moment.'

'Well, I was hoping to stay the night in the lodge,' I explained, 'then I could see the forest in the morning.'

'Have you made a reservation?' he asked me with much civility.

'No,' I admitted.

'You can't stay in the lodge without a reservation.'

'May I make a reservation now?' I asked with some nerve. 'It's only three o'clock.'

'Just a minute, I'll ask. What is your name?'

'John Barclay,' I said, showing my passport.

He picked up the phone and held a conversation in Spanish. The lodge appeared very appealing – dry, cosy, calm and comfortable.

'No, I'm sorry, Mr John, you cannot stay in the lodge without a reservation. You can go on the overhead rail but you can't stay in the lodge.'

So I went back to the lay-by where the bus had dropped me and stood there in the rain. On the other side of the road was a lovely waterfall, speeding over feathery plants. I'm sure the waterfalls were looking their best – after all, the rainy season was in full flood. I was sodden by the time a bus came along and I must have made a pathetic sight. I hailed the bus, but it failed to stop. In all I hailed five buses, none of which stopped for me. I decided to wait for one more and then go back to the park entrance before it closed, in order to cadge a lift to a town from one of the staff – or beg to be allowed to spend the night on a seat in the reception area. The sixth bus stopped.

'Where do you want to go?' the driver asked me.

'Anywhere,' I said, 'a town with a hotel?'

I got on and sat on one of the steps, level with the driver. After a few minutes he turned off the road into a bus station. No one got off. He signalled to me to follow him to the ticket counter. I was trying to explain to the man behind the counter … whatever could be explained, when a man appeared.

'What do you want?' he asked.

'I want to go to a town that has a hotel,' I said.

'You could go in a taxi – it's only so-many *colones* to Guápiles.'

He was a taxi-driver. There's one under every stone.

'Thank you. I like the buses,' I said pathetically.

I wanted to stay with the driver, who had taken pity on me and had now gone out of his way to help me. The man at the ticket counter mentioned a price. I paid it and got back on the bus. The passengers, who had been delayed five minutes, were sitting patiently. I then worked out why the other five buses hadn't stopped. The buses have no conductor and the drivers do not handle cash. You can only use pre-bought tickets. The bus dropped me opposite a hotel and pointed me in the right direction. I tried to show the driver the profound gratitude I felt.

I walked into the hotel like a well-drowned rat. A slim, young woman at reception started in Spanish, then switched to English because her English was marginally better than my Spanish.

'50,000 *colones*,' she said.

'Okay,' I said, opening my back pocket.

'I mean 15,000 *colones*,' she corrected herself.

'Even better!'

At that point I would have paid anything. When I got into my room I took everything off and hung it up. I emptied my bag and turned it inside out to dry. I emptied my money belt. I spread my banknotes, maps and other papers on the bed. I interleaved the pages of my passport with paper tissues. The contents of my rucksack were still dry inside a black plastic bin bag. I pulled this out and hung up the rucksack itself to dry. There is a limit to the number of places to hang things but the television stand, table lamp and the handles of drawers were all brought into play. I turned a stool upside down and put my boots upside down on the ends of the legs. I put the fan on and opened the window louvres. Rather late in the day I held my hearing aid in front of the fan for a minute then hung it up somewhere. With all the banknotes and documents drying, the place looked like a forger's den. I had a warm shower and put on a shirt I'd bought in San José, also my waterproof trousers, which unfortunately I hadn't been wearing, and my trainers. Then I went out to see what was what.

The swimming pool and the fountains looked very pleasant, although I'd had enough water for a week. I walked round the pool to a covered eating area on the other side. I was fascinated to see eggs in trays, glass-fronted fridges filled with food and bottles of wine set out in wine holders. The slim, young woman had spotted me. She walked purposefully towards me.

'Is the restaurant open this evening?' I asked.

'You cannot eat here tonight,' she said.

'All right, I'll have a look outside.'

'Are you hungry?'

'Well, I need to eat,' I said, thinking this was a concept with which everyone in the hotel business was familiar.

'There's a baker,' she told me.

'Well, I'll have a look at that,' I said, trying not to poo-poo her ideas.

By now I was walking away from the covered area towards the gate, but she was keeping up with me. Indeed she was at my side as if I were a VIP who had to be watched closely and steered towards some planned outcome that she and her organisation desired.

'What do you want?' she asked, as if she were determined to get at the truth.

'I want to have a look.'

'What do you like?' she persisted.

'I just want to go for a walk,' I said.

The security men (yes, in the plural) were watching. I noticed a padlock on the gate.

'I'll take a little walk,' I said as calmly as I could and moved again towards the locked gate.

She walked with me.

'But what are you going to do?' she persisted.

'It doesn't matter what I'm going to do. I just want to go out – to go for a walk – *"faire une promenade" en français.'*

'No, no!' she exclaimed.

Till then our conversation had been in the hotel garden, but now she beckoned me into the reception area.

'Just a minute!' she said.

She dialled a number and spoke to somebody in Spanish. I couldn't work out what was going on. She passed the receiver to me.

'Hullo!' I said.

'*Alo!*' a woman's voice said, 'ow are you?'

'I'm fine,' I said. 'I just want to get out of the hotel.'

She said something else in English but in an accent so thick that over the telephone I couldn't hear what it was. The security guards stood riveted. Indeed everyone was watching me.

'I can't hear you,' I said.

'What do you want?' said the woman with the thick accent.

'I want to go out of the hotel – for a few minutes. Look, I have a room. I have the key. Normally you can go out when you want to … '

'Let me speak to Such-a name.'

I passed the receiver to Slim-young. They conversed in Spanish. We were building up to something but I didn't know what. Slim-young passed the receiver back to me.

'What is wrong?' Thick-accent asked.

'Nothing is wrong,' I declared, getting desperate. 'I have a room. I have a key. I like the hotel. I'm very happy – but I want to go out! It's normal, isn't it, when you stay in a hotel? You have your key – you can go out when you like. Look, your hotel isn't serving dinner, so I <u>need</u> to go out. IT'S LIKE A PRISON!'

Thick-accent said something.

'I can't hear what you're saying,' I said.

She said something else.

'I'm sorry,' I said, 'I cannot hear you. I'm a bit deaf. I think I'd better find someone who speaks English.'

'All right.'

I put the receiver down. Everyone was staring at me. One man looked as though he had been following what was going on.

'Do you speak English?' he asked me.

'Yes,' I said. 'Well, thank you for … '

'What is the problem?'

'I just want to go out of the hotel.'

'Well, you can go out.'

'Thank you!'

I turned to Slim-young.

'I'm sorry,' I said, 'I have very little Spanish.'

I walked out, feeling a fool, but at least I was out. It was an anti-climax. I had got what I wanted but in a way that was far from satisfactory. It was another reminder, if I had needed one, that language is vital to understanding. It also taught me that struggling too hard to communicate in speech when the parties have no common language can be counterproductive, building up misunderstandings and preventing the limited accord possible through facial expressions, body language and gestures. In other words if one of us had been an Inuit and the other a Hottentot, the whole ridiculous business wouldn't have happened.

My account of the next two weeks will be sketchy, because the relevant notebook disappeared (in circumstances I shall describe at the proper time) and I had to rewrite my notes from memory a week or two later.

What with my silly adventure in the rain and my silly misunderstanding with the hotel receptionist, I was feeling very low. My hearing aid seemed to have packed up, although it still made fizzing noises. I gave up my notion of seeing the animals of the rain forest and set myself the much more achievable task of getting to Puerto Limón on the Caribbean coast, where I could lick my wounds. I found a hotel in Limón, facing the main square. It had a vast window, which let in an enormous quantity of heat, but it did allow me to observe two men fixing telephone lines. A security man watched the hotel building from a seat in the square. The door to the residential part of the hotel was kept locked. If I wanted to go in I had to ask the security man to unlock it.

I still felt I was ahead of schedule so I spent another night in Limón, moving 200 metres to a better hotel near the sea. I was allowed to move in at midday. In the afternoon, I set off to discover the port. This, it turned out, was kept separate from the town of Limón (where I was staying). There was a fence between the two, forcing me to walk inland through a derelict area to a busy road parallel to the shore. This took me over a wide brown river with a big curve between the bridge, where I was standing and where the river entered the Caribbean. There was an old yellow house on the bend, reflected in the water. With the trees and various boats, the scene had the makings of a pleasing composition in the style of an old European master. I got out my camera and climbed down a slope into a jumble of working boats. On higher ground there was a group of what I took to be local boat people. As I moved about between the vessels, looking for the best viewpoint for my picture, I kept an eye on these people in case one of them objected to my taking a photograph. I became aware that someone was watching me from the road. He made a fist with his thumb sticking up and then drew the thumb across his own throat. He nodded in the direction of the boat people, then made the gesture again. The message was clear – 'Watch out, mate, or they'll kill you!'

I raised a hand in acknowledgement and, keeping well away from the cut-throats, I squeezed between their boats and climbed up the slope back onto the road, putting my camera away as I did so. Then I marched smartly back into the town avoiding as much of the derelict area as I could. The warning might have been a joke – or perhaps an exaggeration – but it was not worth risking my life for a photograph, however picturesque.

My new hotel had a communal balcony looking out to sea. I saw a black man wearing a hat like a tea cosy and scrutinising a board he was holding up. When he turned the board, I could see what looked like the preliminary sketch for a painting of a bird with outstretched wings. It reminded me of the creature I'd seen at Puntarenas but it had teeth so it was either prehistoric or pure fantasy. The man seemed satisfied with the sketch and carried the board to a place beside the sea wall three metres from the 'camp' where he had some, or maybe all, of his other things, including a Bible open at a certain page and a small plastic ukulele. I saw him chatting to so many people that I assumed he was a well-known local character. Later I saw him spreading out pieces of a cardboard box, presumably to make a bed.

I ate in the hotel. Two men, black and older than me, came into the restaurant. One sat and played a drum, using a single hand, with more variety of colour and expression than I had thought possible. The other stood and played a guitar, which for some reason had been painted white. They both sang. They gave us several numbers before the guitarist went round with a hat. They then played one 'last' number, which encouraged someone to make a request. More requests followed and the recital was still going on when I left. I walked round the outside of the dining room to be met with the pathetic sight of my friend, the artist, with his toy ukulele, watching through the window and playing and singing along with the two performers inside.

In the morning, after I'd had my breakfast, I watched the artist get up, take his shirt off for a wash, urinate against a wall and shake the last drops from his penis. He was so unselfconscious that I felt guilty for watching him. At no time did I sense that he was envious of those like me who could afford to stay in the hotel.

I took the bus to Cahuita, also on the coast and that much nearer to Panama, but a very different place from Puerto Limón. Cahuita was a village where the only industry I could discover was tourism. There were restaurants, bars, car hire shops, tour agents, American and other visitors, laid-back West Indians, hippies, drop-outs, and others who enjoyed an easy-going lifestyle. Looking for somewhere to stay I came to a house offering tours and free tourist information. It was run by someone known as 'Mr Big'. I went round the back of the house, where I found a big, black man and a beautiful, smiling black woman, who had obviously captivated him and was half way to captivating me.

'You must be Mr Big,' I said. 'I'm Mr Small.'

We shook hands. The woman smiled even more.

'I'm looking for a hotel,' I continued, 'are there any round here?'

'There's no hotel,' Mr Big said, 'but there are cabañas.'

I'd never seen a cabaña.

'Come with me,' he said. 'There's very good cabañas here, next door, right by the sea.'

He took me to the woman next door and introduced me. Then he went back to his own woman, a move I could readily understand. And so it was that I spent my first night in a cabaña. There was a line of them stretching down the garden towards the sea. Mine was the nearest to the water. It was as well ventilated as a wind tunnel, a vital feature in the steamy atmosphere. The walls and the window shutters were made largely of narrow strips of wood alternating with narrow strips of air. The window was unglazed. There was a single bed at ground level, as well as a bathroom with a shower, loo and washbasin. On a half-floor reached by a fixed wooden ladder was a double bed. Both beds were supplied with mosquito nets. The whole thing including the window could be locked. There was a verandah boasting a hammock.

If you walked five metres down the garden you came to something that was almost a beach. The water was calm and warm, but you couldn't swim more than a stroke or two because of submerged rocks. I also tried out the hammock. I enjoyed the rocking motion but after a while the curvature of the thing hurt my back.

On the wall just above my bed, centimetres from my face, was a tree frog less than three centimetres long with its legs flexed. I knew it was a tree frog because instead of the webbed feet I was used to seeing on pond frogs its toes were separate and had spherical pads on the ends. It stood on the wall as easily as an ant.

In the morning I saw the landlady in the garden.

'All right?' she asked.

'Yes,' I said, 'it's very nice here.'

'My husband's going snorkelling – in the boat – do you want to go?'

'No, I've got to move on, but thank you.'

I took the bus to Sixaola on the Panama border. This was the last land/land border I would cross until I got to Asia. For once there was order at the border. A sign was helpful enough to say, 'To Panama'.

The bridge over the River Sixaola had a single lane intended to take three kinds of traffic. A railway track was narrow enough to allow road vehicles to straddle it. Between the sleepers there was nothing to stop you falling to the muddy water below. Outside the rail track, on either side, were two narrow wooden footpaths, missing many planks. In places there was nothing to tread on. You could keep to one side of any motor vehicle until the path gave out altogether, when you had to walk either on the rail itself or the narrow strip intended for one wheel of a motor vehicle and hope that no such vehicle came along.

I'd a rucksack and my hand-luggage bag, so I'd only one hand free to steady myself, but this didn't matter because most of the way there was nothing to steady myself against, except a bit of slanted fencing, which itself looked in need of steadying.

Despite my fear of heights, everything was going well until I saw some women and children walking towards me. But as I was halfway by then, strictly speaking I should leave what happened after that until the next chapter.

9. Panama

May 25 – June 6

I edged to one side of the narrow planking intended for one wheel of a motor vehicle. Then I kept still, out of respect for the women and children coming towards me, but also out of respect for the drop to the river below. There was nothing to hold onto except my bag. I grinned and looked scared at the same time. The advancing party did not hesitate. They passed me with all the assurance of squirrels passing a wood pigeon they'd met on the branch of a tree. Once they were behind me I pulled myself together and continued until I was on firm ground.

On the Panamanian side I found no official money exchange such as Western Union. I asked in a small supermarket where I might change money. The manager said he would give me dollars for Costa Rican colones. This surprised me because my book said the currency of Panama was the balboa.

'Are they the same as US dollars?' I asked.

'Yes,' he said.

'And you can use them in Panama?'

'Yes.'

He must have thought me an idiot. I wouldn't be surprised if eventually all the Central American countries adopt the US dollar. They would then enjoy the practical advantages we have in Western Europe with the euro. I guess it's anti-American sentiment that's holding them back.

I stayed the first night in Changuinola in the North West corner of Panama. I had to get to Colón at the northern end of the Panama Canal. By this stage I had acquired a map of the country, which showed there was no major road along the north coast to Colón. I had to drop down to David on the south coast and take the arterial road to Santiago, then on to Panama City at the southern end of the Canal

The details of my stay in Changuinola were in the notebook that disappeared. I do remember, however, that the journey from there to David was stimulating, even uplifting. It took hours in a minibus and included several stops, on winding, undulating roads, steep in places and taking us up to 1,200 metres, much of it through national parks. The view changed continually. The scenery was spectacular and wholesome, being un-marred by man. Dwellings and shelters by the side of the road were made from natural local materials such as timber thatched with palm leaves; I saw no metal, plastic or concrete. Thus they blended into the landscape. There was very little litter. The grass was a vivid green. Anywhere wild was jungle. The hills and mountains were clothed with trees. Again and again for more than half of the way we glimpsed a bright blue Caribbean with some of the islands that make up the archipelago, Bocas del Toro (the mouth of the bull), that looked like a holiday paradise. Indeed from this one journey I concluded that the country had enormous tourist potential.

In David I stayed in a hotel next to the bus station. Once I'd dumped my luggage I walked into town. It was a disappointment. The town square was boarded off for renovation. All around were shops packed with cheap, imported goods. I heard a band producing strange sounds. When I got nearer I saw there were two young men on trumpet and saxophone and two older men (their fathers perhaps) on drums. They sounded as if they were making tentative steps towards jazz. One of the wind players would play a few phrases. Then the other would take over repeating the rhythm but altering the notes. This happened over and over, but it didn't add up to anything. Meanwhile the older men sounded like the rhythm section of a military band. I'm usually a sucker for street entertainment so I was sad that these four hadn't yet got their act together.

I wandered away from the centre of town into a suburban area. I soon came upon a long covered way like a bus shelter 400m long but snaking to fit the pavement. It gave protection from sun and rain and led to a recreation ground, where a game of football was in progress involving all ages. I continued along residential roads observing scenes not so very different from some in England. A man was cutting back a tree watched by his wife. I continued until I came to a shop, where I bought a bottle of cold water. When I came out I went on walking and saw another man cutting a branch of a tree. This struck me as an amazing coincidence until I realised that I'd seen the man before. I hadn't carried on – I'd accidentally retraced my steps. Too much of that and I'd be back in Texas.

It was a very warm evening. I had dinner under the verandah of a restaurant.

'Where are you from?' a man asked.

'England,' I said.

'England!'

'Yes, I'm English.'

'English!' he exclaimed, as if I'd said I was a Martian.

He shook my hand.

'Your first time in Panama?' he asked.

'Yes.'

'You like it?'

'Yes, it's very nice.'

He shook my hand again.

'You drink red wine?' he asked.

'Yes,' I said.

'You like red wine?'

'Yes, I do – with meat. I have white wine with fish and red wine with meat.'

'I don't speak English.'

'You're doing very well.'

'You speak Spanish?'

'No – only with a dictionary.'

He shook my hand again.

'Welcome to Panama!'

A simple conversation, but I think we both felt better for it. When he'd gone I realised I had toothache. I'd had my teeth checked before I left so this came as a surprise. It was a mild toothache, but worrying faced with the prospect of being on board ship for three or four weeks and therefore out of reach of a dentist. I decided to press on to Panama City, where I'd have the best chance of getting my teeth looked at.

The next day I went in one hop to the capital. The windows of the bus were obscured so I couldn't enjoy any view, so instead I set myself a puzzle. Knowing that I was heading for the Panama Canal, a friend had e-mailed me the famous palindrome 'A man, a plan, a canal – Panama'. In case you don't know, a palindrome is a word, phrase or longer piece of writing that reads the same forwards as it does backwards. I set myself the challenge of coming up with a palindrome of my own. It made the journey go quicker but I didn't finish the task until later. I e-mailed my friends with the following – all concerned (I made out) with the press coverage my adventure had attracted up to that point, explaining that most periodicals had ignored my odyssey, although …

'Time & Tide' did edit & emit.

'Hello!' ran, 'OAP drawn onward – pa on a roll, eh?'

R A C strapline: 'Nil-parts car!'

Star did, 'Rats!'

I'd found it impossible to improve on the original. The bus terminal at Panama City was near the airport, so I guessed correctly that it was some distance from the centre, but I stubbornly refused taxis and set off on foot in the direction of the skyscrapers I could see. I had to negotiate dual carriageways, flyovers and toll roads. It's easy to cross a road at a toll gate, where the traffic is slowed down for paying, but then I found myself on one of those grassy spaces between fast roads at a junction, areas where no one goes except maintenance workers. It was hot and there was no shade so I drank some warm water and carried on. Eventually I reached the populous parts of the City. I suddenly realised that everyone was much younger than me so I wasn't surprised to discover that I'd blundered into the university. I pressed on and came to an area of hotels and restaurants. Avoiding the grandest hotels I checked in to El Hotel Milano.

I was in touch with the shipping agents at Colón. The latest schedule gave me at least a week to get my teeth seen to. Colón was only 50 miles away so I was within striking distance of my rendez-vous. The toothache I'd been experiencing was almost gone. At dinner that night, by way of a change and attracted by the pepper sauce served with it, I ordered steak. A man joined me on my table because all the others were taken. He was overweight and ordered something very light. When my steak arrived the first mouthful gave me a nasty shock. It was agony to bite on that side. I was determined however not to waste a perfectly good piece of steak so with the steak knife I'd been given I cut thin slices across the grain and chewed them on the good side of my mouth, with my head tipped sideways. By this slow and fastidious process and with the help of a glass of Chilean red, I eventually consumed the whole steak, by which time my table companion, who must have thought my eating habits very strange, had finished his meal and left.

Now it was a matter of urgency to get to a dentist. The first trouble had been a wake-up call; this was an emergency. I was so lucky that it happened when it did. Ten days later I would have been on a ship with no remedy except to go down to the engine room and ask someone to bang me on the head with a spanner every time I returned to consciousness.

There was a family dental firm in the same street as my hotel. The next day I called there at 9.15am. I was seen by a dentist so good looking and charming that I expected many of his patients said 'ah!' without waiting to be asked. I can't remember his name, so I'll call him Dr Charmer. By 10am I'd been examined, x-rayed, photographed, shown the pictures and given an appointment the next day with a dentist who specialised in root fillings. What sort of person would want a job like that? I can't remember the root specialist's name either, so I'll call him Dr Rootman.

Fortunately both dentists spoke excellent, clear English. I was lucky that good English is common among professional people in so many countries. Dr Charmer had built up in me a confidence so complete that I was inclined also to trust Dr Rootman. Rootman persuaded me that, as I couldn't pinpoint the sensitivity to one tooth or its immediate neighbour and as I was going to be cut off from dentists for up to four weeks, the sensible course was to give me (or rather sell me) root canals in both. This, to use an appropriate metaphor, was hard to swallow. But what choice did I have? I could either trust these guys or I could fly home to my regular dentist, who in any case was not British and was less sophisticated, experienced and charming than Charmer and Rootman. I decided to let Rootman loose on my mouth. He gave me powerful injections and I didn't feel a thing – at first. All I had to suffer was the ache of keeping my mouth open and the fear of choking on my own fluids.

'Don't close, my friend,' he kept repeating, 'don't close!'

I was allowed to swallow between the two operations. The second filling was painful; the anaesthetic was wearing off. By the time I left the surgery with temporary fillings and was back in the waiting room forgetting to pay the $750, I could hardly think straight – let alone keep still. But Dr Charmer had given me 24-hour painkillers and a note to the hospital for something stronger if I needed it.

As soon as I was back in the hotel I took a painkiller. Then I hung the 'Do not disturb' notice on my door, put the television on and (to keep my mind busy) alternated between looking at the picture and looking at each of the four corners of the screen before clicking the 'next channel' button and going through the process all over again. By 4pm I knew I could manage without the hospital. And by the evening I was in a wine bar eating a meal of soup and *spaghetti bolognese.* The next day I felt I didn't need the third and final painkiller. In Panama they prescribe pills by the exact number. The poor pharmacists must wear out countless pairs of scissors cutting up blister packs.

Apart from the cities in the United States, Panama was the most Westernised, up-market and sophisticated of any I'd visited on my travels. At night the downtown area shimmered like Leicester Square. By day it was very hot. I kept out of the sun as much as possible. Many of the shops were air-conditioned. I bought boat shoes and a brightly coloured outfit of shirt and shorts for my imminent sea voyage.

Every time I headed for the Via España (the Oxford Street of Panama City), I passed an Italian ice cream parlour – every time, that is, that I managed to resist the temptation to go in. For $2.50 you could relish two scoops (the same flavour or different). You ate these with a dainty spoon, which made the experience last longer. I sat on a high stool in the window. My favourite flavour was the lemon, a watery as opposed to creamy ice, with that cleanest and zingiest of flavours, superior, I felt, to the cruder, more metallic lime. The coffee ice was good but the others I tried, such as blackberry, were too subtle to overcome the coldness of the confection. For me only the lemon truly came through. I met a young American couple there, who turned out to be staying at the same hotel as me. I told them in unequivocal terms the conclusion of my research and on my last day in the City I was gratified to see them in the parlour enjoying a blob each of – guess what – the champion of champions, lemon. The range of ice cream was displayed in fat swirls, which showed off their texture and vivid colours to luscious effect. I was not allowed to photograph the counter but, as you can tell, I have my memories.

Over the next few days my mouth settled down. I had to stay in the City a week to have the temporary fillings replaced by permanent. The City has many faces so there was much to occupy me. I decided to go to the 'old city'. In other countries the term promises charming buildings that have withstood time and much else, quaint streets where today's artists and artisans produce and sell their work to tourists, perhaps a concert in a church, a climb to a vantage point with a view of a river and the new city that grew up later. Panama's old city may have offered all that at one time, but I came to a cluster of well-ruined ruins. I don't have the temperament for archaeology so I wandered away to look at the water. An elderly West Indian man spotted me and came out of the trees carrying a plastic bag. He carefully took the contents out one by one and laid them on the ground – skulls and other bones or part skeletons of birds and mammals. He explained in Spanish what each was but mostly we communicated by gesture.

He pressed me to take a photograph, which I did. He wanted me to photograph the relics with the water in the distance. I suggested I take him with the bones. I got him to squat behind them and hold out his bony hand as if showing them to the camera. I felt that I had really humoured him. He saw the whole thing differently and started dropping hints, which at first I failed to take. So he picked up a discarded plastic bottle, removing the lid and turning it upside down to demonstrate the utter emptiness of the vessel.

'You want me to give you money for a drink?' I asked in English supported by a bit of mime.

He nodded. I gave him two dollars, thanked him for his pains and strode off. Near the ruins a long public hall had been given over to local artisans to display and sell their traditional art and craft. The building had been divided up into some fifty stalls packed mostly with embroidery in brilliant colours on black, a highly distinctive look. I wanted to buy something for the two little daughters of a British couple I was hoping to stay with in Sydney. I looked at every display. The crafts people couldn't understand why I didn't buy anything, and I didn't have the vocabulary to explain. Eventually I came away with a purse decorated with a tree frog in two shades of green and a tiny blue stuffed elephant.

On my way back to the hotel I got on a bus, but some people soon told me to get off so I did. I had no idea where I was or which bus I should take and I found it hard to read the destinations amid the decorations and cluttered wording on the fronts of the buses, but a woman who had got off at the same time waited at the stop with me and checked every bus that came along – 'not this one, not this one' many times until eventually she called out, 'this one!' and I got in, leaving her behind. I gave her a cheery wave through the bus window. Like many other people I met, she'd been very kind.

I knew that I would be passing Panama City by ship via the canal so I wanted to get where I could see other vessels doing just that. I took a bus to Santa Ana and found the old dock area, where at stalls of imported goods you could buy anything from a bed-head to a door hinge. I went on to San Felipe, a promontory sticking into the sea. Here I found official buildings such as the Presidential Palace. Uniformed guards patrolled the area. The *Teatro Nacional* was a splendid and substantial building painted in bold colours. Outside it there were large busts of European artistic giants such as Shakespeare, Rossini and Molière. Sadly there was no performance for several weeks because of building work.

In the gardens on the promontory I saw other tourists. I stopped and listened to three old men singing and playing a concertina, a guitar and a sort of rattle. I discovered later that they were better at making music than they were at walking.

I continued on round the coast through Chorillo, a poor area, where I was the only tourist. I didn't feel safe so I kept moving. I got onto a road to El Puente de las Americas, a bridge across the Canal to the Western side. I knew I would get a good view of the shipping from this bridge as all vessels would have to pass under it. The traffic on the road was so slow that I was overtaking it on foot. There was no pedestrian way on the bridge but with the traffic at a crawl I thought I could safely squeeze beside it but before I reached the bridge a policeman turned me back.

Not to be put off I headed for what looked on the map to be a residential area called *La Boca* (the Mouth). It was indeed a residential area but between it and the Canal I discovered an entire container port not marked on my map. The way was blocked by fences and the gates guarded. My view was blocked too so I gave up and took a taxi back to the hotel.

The next day I found a restaurant with good shade in front of it and settled down with a coffee to write some postcards. A man who'd been standing next to a car on the other side of the road came across to speak to me.

'Excuse me, sir,' he said, 'I'm sorry to interrupt you. Do you need a car?'

'No,' I said, 'I've just sat down. I'm not going anywhere.'

'I understand that, sir, and I don't mean to trouble you. But I am a professional driver with my own car and if you are going somewhere …'

'Well, I'm staying in a hotel near here – I'll just walk back.'

'Of course, sir, I do understand. Only I am a professional driver and you might want to go somewhere another time …'

'Then I'd just ask the hotel to get me a taxi.'

'You could ask me.'

'Look,' I said, 'thank you very much, but I'm leaving Panama City tomorrow.'

'I understand, sir. Sorry to trouble you.'

He went back to standing next to his car. After a while another man, possibly also a taxi-driver, joined him and the two of them stood talking and, when I finally left the restaurant, neither of them had been hired and they were still talking. No wonder the first had been so courteous and persistent to me.

I went to the waterfront, passing between some slender, graceful and stylish skyscrapers – more elegant than anything I'd seen in Houston. They seemed so close that that if your stapler jammed you could lean out of the window and borrow one from your opposite number in the other building. It was my last whole day in the City and my last chance therefore to see the ships on the Canal. Walking along the front in the direction of the Canal I saw a line of vessels off a headland known as Amador. They seemed to be queueing to enter the Canal from the Pacific. I saw that I could get near to the ships if I got onto the headland so I found my way there on two buses.

Amador is a small peninsula with a long narrow isthmus offering views one way into the mouth of the Canal and the other way into the Bahía de Panamá. I could watch ships of all sizes and clambered over rocks to photograph them. I also saw pelicans. I had a beer in a first-floor restaurant with a view over the water. It was thrilling to be so close to the waterway I would travel in a few days' time.

At dusk I took two buses to get home. At least that was the idea. The second was labelled 'Via España', the big shopping street near my hotel, but looking out of the window of the bus I never saw anything like it. We went to parts of the City I didn't know existed. After three-quarters of an hour we came to an area of out-of-town superstores, beside a dual carriageway. I thought I'd better get off the bus. There wasn't a single skyscraper on the horizon to give me a sense of direction. It was like being dropped in another country. No one called out, 'Taxi, taxi!' I stopped one and asked the driver to take me to the downtown shopping area. He said, 'No!' as if I'd asked him to take me to Colombia. Someone told me I needed to be on the other side of the dual carriageway. I crossed this busy road and got a taxi the other way. We went very fast via a toll gate and the driver dropped me at my hotel. He charged me six dollars. I gave him seven, greatly relieved to be 'home'.

The next morning, after a visit to the hairdressers, I went back to the dentists, where Dr Charmer himself replaced my temporary fillings with permanent. He gave me a copy of my dental photographs and x-rays to take with me. He also gave me a prescription for a week's painkillers in case I needed them on the ship and told me to bite carefully.

From the bus to Colón, we'd glimpses of the Canal and some of the rivers feeding it. I found myself next to a West Indian man of my age. He told me his grandfather had worked on building the Canal. There were two teams on the project, he explained, a West Indian team and a team of locals. The teams were kept separate because the West Indians were much more susceptible to the local infectious diseases and many died. Many must have survived, I deduced, because I saw a much higher proportion of black people in Panama than in the other Central American countries.

My companion was a member of the Society of Friends of the West Indian Museum. A leaflet he gave me explained that the museum was inaugurated by the Panamanian Government in 1980 'as a tribute to the West Indian immigrants who came to Panama to build the railroad and the Canal'. The museum is in Panama City. If I'd known about it earlier I would have gone there. The Society of Friends was formed in 1981 to raise money to keep the museum going while promoting West Indian culture. Anyone sympathetic to these aims can become a member for an annual membership fee ranging from $15 to $499. Any member who gives $500 or more becomes a 'benefactor'. Considering the debt international traders owe to forebears of the West Indian community in Panama I hope the Society has found a way to ask for contributions from today's users of the Canal.

'Be careful when you get to Colón,' he warned me. 'Everyone is very nice. Some will offer to help and … well, it's a port – just be careful.'

'Thank you,' I said, 'I will.'

When I arrived I quickly found Avenida Central, a long, wide street with an area like a long, narrow 'square' (geometrically impossible, I know), extending down the middle, with trees, seats and the odd sculpture, which acted as a useful landmark. I saw two policemen and gave no thought at the time to why they went around in pairs. I checked in to the Milan Hotel, which looked to be the best of a rather basic bunch. It had entrances from two parallel streets, one via its own restaurant, a cosy place with bar stools at the serving counter and a line of tables stretching to the door of the hotel proper. The restaurant was run by a cuddly, mumsy type, whose dyed chestnut hair made her seem European. She looked after me and I felt safe there.

I had a room on the third floor. Peering through the louvred windows I could study a scene of Dickensian squalor. Facing the side of the hotel was a two-storey block of flats, cramped and in poor repair. Some of the doors were off their hinges and resting against their doorways. You could not say where the residents' living space ended and where a general yard littered with rubbish began. A single bench and some old boxes served as outdoor furniture.

I had a spyhole in my door, which I suppose was a useful security measure. When I looked through it I saw that the door of the room opposite was open. A woman was sitting on the bed. Her legs were bare, one stretched out, the other bent at the knee, which pointed upwards, a pose somewhere between casual and provocative. A man of about my age was standing at the doorway, conveniently to one side, allowing me still to see the woman. I heard bits of their conversation.

'How much do you charge?' the man asked.

I thought this was a cheeky joke on his part to a woman who had carelessly presented herself as a lady of the night, when she was nothing of the sort, but as the conversation continued in a matter-of-fact way I concluded that there was no irony on the part of either of them. I couldn't hear the woman's reply but it must have been on the lines of 'x dollars', because he asked, 'For how long?'

'Half an hour,' she replied.

'I've got a girlfriend in such-a-place.'

I saw the man go away. Then a younger man came along, went in and the door shut. When I went out a short while later, the door was open. The younger man had gone and the woman too. Perhaps he'd asked her to come to his room. In the woman's place was a large cuddly toy in the shape of a panda. Now pandas are notoriously reluctant to mate so it seemed an unlikely mascot for a sex-trade worker. Later I saw her again on the bed, her face changing colour and brightness as the light from her television screen played across it. As I was going to bed at 11.30pm it was still hot. The children from the Dickensian flats were playing naked in the street with a hosepipe.

The next day I went looking for Cristobal, the port where I was to join my ship. According to my one and only map, it was somewhere north of the town on a peninsula stretching into the Caribbean. I got my compass out and headed up Avenida Central in a northerly direction. There were a number of schools, and the variety of religious denominations represented, including Islam, reflected the mixed population of Colón. I found a ship, propped up and abandoned on a beach to rust, but no port.

When I came back a thin, restless man came up to me in the Avenida Central.

'You Okay, man – how you doin'?' he asked.

'Fine, thank you,' I replied.

'Where you come from – England?'

'Yes.'

'First time in Panama? How you like it?'

'I like it very much.'

'When you back to the States then?'

'I'm not going back.'

'You going to Panama (City)?'

'No, I've just come from there.'

'Where you going?'

'I'm getting a ship to New Zealand from Cristobal. Now I can't find Cristobal. It's not on most maps. I need a good map.'

'I know a place where's there's a big map. I'll take you there.'

'Thank you.'

'I gotta go to Panama. I just need two dollars for the bus. You wouldn't give me two dollars? My auntie died. She had a business but she died. So there's no money coming in. If I could get to the States I could get a job in Macdonalds – work my way up. People think I just spend it on marihuana. You're going round the world. I'm fifty – I haven't done anything with my life. I wanna make something of myself. What's it like in the States?'

'Well,' I said, 'if you work hard, you can earn more money there – but everything costs more. And the bus service isn't so good; it costs more.'

'What would it cost in the States to go to Panama?'

The question sounded confusing, but I knew what he meant.

'Oh, I don't know,' I said, 'five, ten dollars?'

'I'll show you where the map is – earn that two dollars.'

He led me through the streets to the premises of a state-run tourist organisation. The door was locked. My new guide gestured through the window. Someone let us in.

'Hi! How you doin'?' My guide began. 'My friend here needs a map.'

He turned to me.

'There you are,' he said, 'there's the map.'

There it was, mounted on the wall. It was one of the biggest maps I had ever seen.

'But that's a map of the world,' I protested. 'I don't need a map of the world. I want a map of Colón – not the world.'

'Have you got a map?' he asked the tourist people.

They gave me a map of the country of Panama as a whole with a tiny inset map of Colón, all of which I already had. It did, however, have Cristobal marked, near the bus station where I'd arrived.

'Thank you very much,' I said.

'Come outside,' I said to my 'friend'.

I led him out to the street.

'I didn't want to give you money with those people watching,' I explained, pulling out a wad of notes.

'Five dollars,' he said, 'that'll do.'

'No, we said two dollars,' I argued. I gave him two. He looked at me with hurt and disgust, as if I'd said, 'Father Christmas doesn't exist – and neither does God!'

But he took the two dollars and walked off. He'd done all right – I'd given him the money for a 50-mile bus ride. But I didn't think he'd ever get to the States. He might not even get to Panama City. Cristobal was less than ten minutes' walk from my hotel in the south-east corner of the town. I found the Shipping Agent's Office. I introduced myself to the agent and confirmed our arrangement that I should be there by 12 noon the following day.

On my way back I noticed a street that seemed to have been abandoned. It was full of potholes, puddles, mud and rubbish. I could see no shop in it, nor a single person. It was like a strip of waste land but it lay only three streets from Avenida Central. If nobody else went down this street, I certainly didn't want to.

When I went back to the hotel, the lady of the night said, *'Alo! Alo!'*, demonstrating that she was a 'lady of the afternoon' as well.

'Hullo!' I said and slipped quickly into my room before I made her think I was looking her over, although I had had time to gain an impression of someone with a warm personality and a big cuddly body – nothing much to hurt yourself on there, I thought.

I was bored. I went back to the Avenida Central and hung about for as long as I could make myself. The other people were hanging about out of habit – or because there was nowhere else to go and nothing else to do. There were lots of them and almost anywhere that passed for a seat was taken. Eventually I found a space on a seat, which already had a man sitting on the back of it. I kept an eye on him, but he showed no interest in me. I had my draw-string bag with me with a few odd items in it. When the strings were pulled tight, the hole closed up and you needed two hands to open it, but I kept it away from people. People looked at me as if I were strange. I was strange. I felt strange. As far as I could make out I was the only European in the town. I must have stood out like a raw sausage on a plate of well-cooked ones.

I was looking forward to going to sea. I'd had nine weeks on the road, guarding my valuables, always keeping a look out, struggling with the language. I'd overcome my initial fears. I'd travelled from Fort Lauderdale to the Panama Canal and apart from losing $86 at a frontier crossing, nothing bad had happened to me. I couldn't help feeling I'd done rather well. One more night on land and then I'd be joining a British ship. If I kept my cool I'd soon be able to relax.

Still bored, I went to a café and enjoyed a papaya smoothie, although they don't call them that. There was too much sugar for my taste and I could only get it down with the help of the iced water that came with it. I decided not to hang about outside any longer but play safe and go back to the hotel. When I got back to my room I found that the light bulb of the bedside light needed replacing. I took it downstairs to reception and asked for a new one. The receptionist indicated that someone would come and fix it. I was back in my room, sitting on the loo, when there was a knock on the door.

'Just a minute!' I called out in English.

When I had finished and had washed my hands, I opened my door. There was no one there. I stepped into the corridor and looked up and down. The lady of the night appeared, now a 'lady of the early evening'. She gave me a generous smile. Indeed everything about her was generous – her make-up, her bust, her hips, even her waist. She had long black hair and rich brown skin. She wasn't exactly pretty, but she was without question voluptuous. She said something in Spanish and pointed to the floor above.

'The man called to fix your light bulb,' she must have said, 'but as you weren't there he's gone upstairs to see to something else; he'll be back in a minute.'

At this point the man appeared with the light bulb. The lady of the early evening gave me another huge smile.

'You see, sweetie,' she seemed to be saying, 'how well I can take care of you.'

I followed the man with the bulb into my room, while the lady of the early evening went into hers, presumably to watch some more television and wait for business to hot up. I tried to read. There was nowhere to sit except on the bed. I put the air conditioning on. When it got too cold I turned it off. There was nothing I wanted to watch on television. I had a sense of anticlimax.

I wanted to have a decent meal on my last night, to round off this section of my odyssey, to celebrate my success so far. After being spoiled for choice in Panama City, in Colón I hadn't found a restaurant that really appealed to me and I'd seen most of the City. There was one quarter I hadn't explored and I decided to check it out. I emptied the draw-string bag and repacked it. I wouldn't need my camera so I hid it in the room. I'd need my dictionary, my reading glasses, my notebook, a pencil sharpener and my waterproof. I had a pencil in my pocket. I locked my door and set out for my last dinner in Panama. It was dark but there were plenty of lights in the Avenida Central. I went up the one section of it I had not explored before. There was not a single restaurant.

'I'll look quickly in this side street,' I thought, 'and if there's nothing there I'll give up looking for somewhere new and go back where I've been before.'

The street was darker than Avenida Central but I could clearly see there was no restaurant. But with my built-in aversion to going back on my tracks I pressed on past the end of the abandoned street I'd avoided earlier. It looked just as grim from this end. I was moving quickly out of habit in dark places. The next street, I thought, would take me right back to the part of town I knew. I was well into this street, when I could feel some anxiety building up. There was no shop – none lit anyway, no street lamp, no traffic. It was dark but I could see figures standing at the side of the road, people hanging around as if they'd nothing to do. There were puddles to dodge and these brought me nearer to the people than I wanted to be. Mostly they seemed indifferent to me but there was a man, my size but much younger, who looked at me so intently, intensely, that immediately my anxiety turned to outright fear. My pulse was racing. I felt I was in real danger. It was too late to turn back. In any case I would have had to pass the young man again. I held on tight to my draw-string bag and, careful not to stumble on the uneven surface, I moved as quickly as I could without breaking into a run. Ahead of me was the street I knew, with lights and lots of people. Suddenly, like things happen too quickly in dreams, I felt something or somebody pulling hard on the bag. Fear cut right through me, like the terror that takes over just before you wake out of a nightmare. Without thinking I tightened my grip on the draw strings. Well, if I thought anything, it was, 'these are personal things – they're no use to you!' Then what I took to be a fist hit me on the side of the face. I let go the string immediately. My glasses had been knocked off my face. Without them I couldn't see in the dark. I didn't know where I was. The nightmare was real.

NO WORRIES

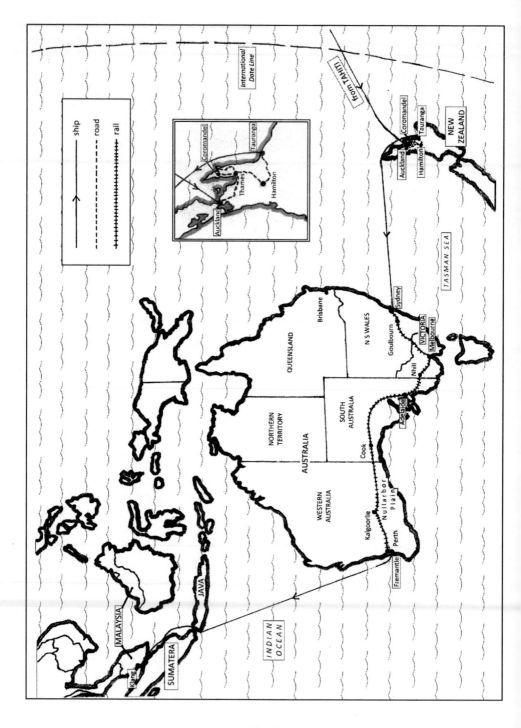

Map 2
Australasia

10. The Panama Canal

June 6 – 8

I was shocked by the speed of it. I was hurt that someone should take by force from me something so personal. I felt hopeless to have lost control of my belongings. I was upset at losing my travel notes – I couldn't quickly think what other items had been in the bag but I'd a feeling my camera wasn't among them. And I felt a fool to have so carelessly blundered into dangerous, unknown territory at night.

All these thoughts and feelings seemed to come at once. At some point I had glimpsed a brown face but now my attacker had gone. In the dark street, with lots of people around, I was bewildered. And without my glasses, I couldn't see to find them. I looked on the ground but could see nothing. I didn't recognise the shops or anything else except that it was a busy street. But I managed to find my way back to the Avenida Central. I started to move along it looking for a distinctive sculpture that marked a street that would take me almost to my hotel. Then two West Indian women came up to me and handed me the missing glasses. These kind souls must have witnessed the attack and seen the glasses fly off my face. I was touched to receive such practical kindness. I was in a whirl but I managed to get out a *'Gracias, múchas gracias!'*

The glasses weren't broken. One leg was bent but I could put them on and then I saw which street I was in – the familiar one near the hotel. I'd been attacked only ten metres from safety.

The women, bless them, took me to two policemen – maybe the same two who had sent me to a hotel I couldn't find. The women explained to the police what had happened. The men showed less interest than if the women had asked them whether they liked their sandwiches cut into squares or triangles. The five of us then proceeded to the hotel at a pace set by the policemen, slower than they would have gone at their own funerals. At the hotel the hotel's security man, who spoke both English and Spanish, took over. The receptionist watched through the glass of her booth. The only people who showed any compassion were the two women who'd rescued my glasses and brought them to me. They had done their bit and after a while they slipped away.

'What did they take?' the security man asked.

'My reading glasses, a dictionary, a notebook and a waterproof.'

'Oh, nothing of value then! Well, you cannot go there,' he said.

'I see that now,' I said, 'but I didn't know. I really think the hotels should tell visitors. It was obvious I was a visitor. If someone had told me, I wouldn't have gone there.'

'You shouldn't have been there.'

'I know now. I made a mistake. But we don't know – you should tell us.'

'I did once,' he said, looking fiercely at me as if I personally had created the no-go area. 'I told someone not to go there and he assaulted me.'

He seemed to think that ended the discussion. I was in a terrible state but I wasn't going to let it go at that.

'Surely,' I said, 'a way could be found to tell people what the no-go area is – maybe the hotel manager, a notice, a warning?'

The policemen, whose contribution amounted to the square root of bugger-all, faded away completely. I had run out of energy. The security man had run out of interest. I went up to my room. My advice to anyone visiting an unfamiliar city or port is – ask whether there is a no-go area and where it is. Don't be like me and find out the hard way! Also, let the mugger have what he wants straight away.

On the stairs I met the lady of the night. She gave me the most loving smile and said something in Spanish, which might have meant, 'Are you coming to see me later? You look as though you could do with a little tenderness.'

'No comprendi,' I said.

'Oh, you don't understand – you are English!' she said.

She took my hand and gave it an affectionate squeeze, all the while maintaining a sweet, reassuring look. I gave her a rather more English smile and went into my room. I never saw her again.

I had little spirit for anything, but I went down to the hotel restaurant and ordered something easy to eat and a beer. But the story of the Englishman who'd been attacked must have reached the ears of Mumsy Type because without being asked she brought a bowl of soup, saying something soothing to me in Spanish.

I had a terrible night. I'd a swelling on my cheekbone and a bruise was building up under my eye. The skin to the side of the eye was cut, the eye itself bloodshot. I had an unpleasant headache and felt a little sick. These last two symptoms, I knew, could indicate brain haemorrhage. My blood pressure, normally controlled by a drug, could well have been raised, making a haemorrhage more likely. Supposing I died, would my sons ever find out what had happened?

The fear I felt when I was being attacked was still with me. Although I had treble-locked the door, I started at every noise, frightened that my assailant, coming away with worthless booty – mere reminders of my European affluence – could have easily found out which hotel the police had taken me to, would talk his way into the hotel on the pretext of an urgent appointment with the lady of the night, break down my door and my resistance, take everything I had of real value and leave me dead – or at least in no state to board my ship the next day.

But worse than that, I tortured myself with the realisation that it could have been far worse. The guy could have drawn a knife to cut the string of the drawstring bag, even stuck the blade into me. He could have pulled me into a deserted building, where he and his mates could have done what they liked with me. And all the time it was my fault for being so irresponsible. I should have eaten in the hotel with Mumsy Type. I knew the town was dangerous. I'd been warned by the man on the bus. I could have found out where the no-go area was. I already had a clue from seeing the parallel road deserted in daylight. But to enter the area in the black night of 8pm, swinging a fascinating bag under the noses of these poor and desperate people, was looking for trouble. If I'd been killed, my family would never have seen me again. What a terrible thing to do to them!

Somehow the night came to an end. I shaved and showered and felt as if I was in charge of a tiny part of life. I went down to breakfast and asked Mumsy Type for familiar, comforting foods like orange juice and scrambled egg on toast. I still felt badly shaken and couldn't face going out of the building to check my e-mails or to the optician to get my glasses straightened. My headache was no worse. It was 14 hours since the attack so if I was going to lose consciousness, I thought, I would have done so by then. I managed, slowly, carefully and methodically to pack. I left all my change in the ashtray for the chambermaid. I was ready at ten o'clock. I lay on the bed and tried to relax. I looked at my watch every few minutes. At 10.45 I went down to the restaurant and asked Mumsy Type to make me a sandwich because I guessed I'd have a long wait at the agent's office. I bought a banana from her and a carton of apple juice because she didn't sell water and I didn't dare go the short distance to the nearest shop that did. I went back to my room, packed this picnic into my bag and, although I was desperate to get away, made myself wait until 11.15.

Taxis are as common as raindrops in Panama. But I couldn't bring myself to step out onto the pavement, so I asked the receptionist to get me a taxi. I don't know what she thought of this, but she didn't ring up, she just stepped out onto the pavement and in less than a minute came back in to say the taxi was waiting. I could see it standing outside the hotel in the middle of the one-way street, no doubt blocking the traffic. Whether I liked it or not I had to go. So, calling out, *'muchas gracias'* and *'adiós!'*, I somehow got into the car with my bags to go one-tenth of the distance I would carry them under normal circumstances.

The agent wasn't around but his sidekick welcomed me, looking a bit surprised.

'I'm a bit early,' I said.

'Well, the ship's in,' he said, 'so you can go over about one o'clock. We'll take you in a car.'

'Do you mind if I wait here? I was mugged last night and I'm scared to go back into the town. Is there somewhere I can sit? I won't get in your way.'

He put me in an empty office. I felt safe there. I had notes to write but the memories were still too painful. So I read a chunk of my book, ate my picnic lunch and listened to a thunderstorm. At 1.40 a man drove me to the docks and all around them, looking in vain for MV Tikeibank. I hoped it hadn't sailed without me. Once we'd exhausted all the possibilities, the driver had a conversation on his mobile and then gave up trying to take me to a freight ship and took me instead to a small water bus, which, for me in my fragile state was about as reassuring as asking me to get into a giant baking tin. This already held a woman in some official capacity and a nautical boiler suit. The driver handed me over to two men, who took me and the nautical woman out into the bay in the baking tin. While it was lovely to say, 'good-bye!' to Colón, or rather, to leave Colón without saying 'good-bye!', I was out of the fire, but into the baking tin. One of the guys took my rucksack and laid it on the upper deck.

'You go inside,' he said.

'Will that be all right there?' I asked.

'Yeah, don't worry about it.'

'That's everything I've got!' I added.

I went inside but I was still in a fearful state and couldn't help worrying about my rucksack. If there's a swell when we get further out, I thought, that rucksack will be sliding about. One wave and it'll be in the drink – and I won't be there to stop it! I opened the door and looked onto the upper deck. The rucksack had gone! Oh no! I turned to look for one of the crew. There on the lower level was my rucksack – they must have brought it down without telling me.

When we were what seemed more than a mile from the shore we sighted MV Tikeibank. As we got closer I could see that the pilot ladder, a wooden staircase supported by ropes from the deck, had been lowered to the water. We got near enough for the nautical woman to step from the baking tin onto the ladder. I would have done the same but at that moment one of the men handed me a pair of gloves. If I was to climb the rickety ladder I would need as good a grip as possible so I put them on. There were crewmen on the Tikeibank to receive us but no one in either vessel attempted to hold onto the other or tie the baking tin in close. Once I'd got the gloves on, one of the Tikeibank crew standing on the bottom of the ladder grabbed my hand-luggage bag. Immediately the gap widened until it was too far for the jolliest of jolly Jack tars to leap, so I didn't try, even though there were two members of the crew of Tikeibank waiting to catch me. We pulled away from the ship and went round in a circle to try again, but we couldn't get near enough. It was something to do with the engine not being a match for wind and current. They had the lid off the engine and one man was tickling it while the other was trying to steer us close to the ship.

'Go back in!' they called.

I went back under cover.

'Come out! Come out!' they yelled.

I came out.

'Go back in! Go back in!'

I went back in. The next time they didn't bother to call me. After four attempts we swung out into the waterway and set off, as far as I could tell, back again to the land. Well, at least my hand luggage was aboard and would make it to New Zealand, even if I didn't. Then with acres of water all around us we met up with a larger baking tin and I was obliged to step carefully into it. It was a superior tin and this time we got close enough to Tikeibank at the first attempt and I stepped onto the rickety ladder. Someone offered to take my rucksack but I felt it safer to keep it on my back than to take it off with all this deep water around. Also, I needed both hands free to hold onto the rail as I climbed the rickety ladder, trying not to look down any more than was necessary to see where I was putting my feet. I told you I had a bad head for both heights and depths; now I had to contend with the two phobias at once.

I took the climb one step at a time. There were members of the crew at the bottom and top of the ladder but the bit in the middle I did all on my own. I was greatly relieved, after being so close to all this wobbly wet stuff, to be standing on a ship made of cold metal, but the cheeriest thing, for me in my anxious state, was a door opening just as I approached it. A jolly man with a nautical beard, a nautical belly and a warm demeanour stuck out his hand. I told him later how much this greeting meant to me.

'Welcome aboard!' he said. 'It's John, isn't it?'

'Yes,' I said, 'hullo!'

'I'm Steve, the Purser. I'll show you to your cabin. We'll go through the lounge on the way.'

The lounge was a cosy L-shaped room with a small bar in one leg of the L, a computer desk and a table with a stack of British board games in the other; and some comfy chairs in the middle – all ship-shape but in a homely, reassuring style.

'We've got a list for drinks,' Steve explained in his Scouse accent. 'You just help yourself and put your name down. You're on the deck below, next to the Chief Engineer. We're very relaxed here. The Captain likes a joke and so do we all. So you get ragged one day and it'll be someone else the next time. This is your cabin ...'

'Oh, it's lovely!' I said.

'We've got a buffet dinner tonight on the bridge deck.'

'When's that?'

'Six o'clock.'

It was another world. My cabin was clean, wholesome and nothing like any of the places I'd slept in the previous nine weeks. In a small space I'd a single bed with a raised side edge at the head end to stop me rolling out and a bedside shelf that folded out of the way. There was a long low couch for visitors or for just throwing stuff on, a wide desk with a bowl of fairly fresh fruit, a table lamp, a bedside lamp, a clock, a video/DVD player, a small fridge, tea- and instant-coffee-making equipment, a thermos of iced water, a wardrobe, drawers and a shower room with toilet, washbasin and bathroom cabinet. There was also air conditioning. If only hotels employed ship designers, they could fit many more people in and make more money while charging each guest far less. A window – sorry, porthole, which could be opened, looked onto the bow of the ship.

I took off my boots and collapsed onto the bed. What a relief to be there! You could not design a better environment to help someone to get over a trauma. I had one worry – was I healthy enough to cross the Pacific? My headache was bad. I'd look a right fool if, out in the Ocean, I developed a brain haemorrhage and died. The injured eye stung when faced with a bright light. Photophobia is a sign of meningitis, which I knew could be caused by dengue fever. I guessed it might also be caused by a bang on the head. I took no painkiller so I could monitor my progress or decline. I rested. Rather late in the day, I breathed deeply to lower my blood pressure.

The buffet was served on the bridge and eaten just off it. Life was easy-going on MV Tikeibank. As long as the passengers didn't get in the way of those on duty, we were allowed on the bridge at any time. The roof of the bridge, or the 'monkey island' as I learned to call it, afforded wonderful 360° views. I saw the pilot arrive to take us through the tricky bits of the Panama Canal. It was a warm night and, beers in hand, we enjoyed the approach to the Gatún Locks. Kurt, a New Zealander, who'd watched with amusement my protracted efforts to come aboard, welcomed me with an easy friendliness. In my fragile state this meant a lot to me. Those who had made the transit before said it was more impressive by night. There was a starry sky and I saw the Southern Cross for the first time. Three locks lift vessels 26m to Lago Gatún, the lake in the middle of this amazing waterway. With the lights high up on the hills, those along the banks, the floodlights on the locks and the ships themselves lit up, it looked as though we were approaching a giant golden staircase leading to a mythical city of joy and beauty. As we came nearer I could see that the staircase was a terrace of steps each big enough to take a ship considerably longer and wider than the Tikeibank. As we entered our end of this mighty stairway, tugs nudged us into position. Along the sides of the locks were tracks for locomotives known as mules, which aligned the ships by hawser, steadied them and towed them all the way to the highest level. A parallel staircase took those going the other way and dropping down to the level of the Atlantic.

The Canal had been a daring concept and a giant feat of engineering. The final gates going west for instance, those facing the Pacific with its extreme tidal fluctuations, were 25m high. Each gate weighed 730 tons. The management of a heavy two-way traffic was an impressive operation.

'I'm keeping a journal,' said Hugh, a 79-year-old white Zimbabwean passenger. 'It's difficult to express in words how wonderful the experience of going through the Canal is.'

'Well, of course,' I said pompously, 'as a writer I relish the challenge.'

But when I sat at the computer, composing an e-mail to my supporters, I was prepared to admit that Hugh had a point. In my case it was overshadowed by my need to get myself together again after my assault. I was subdued as well as a bit shy of the officers and the other passengers.

In the Lake we were held up by fog. Later we waited hours for a fuel tanker to come along. We needed at least enough fuel to get us to Tahiti. Although the pipe was thicker than a man's thigh, the process took further hours. Then we'd to wait our turn before being allowed to enter the Gaillard Cut, which would take us to the three locks at the Pacific end. Because of the delays we passed through the Cut and the locks at night, so again – thanks to numerous lights of all kinds – we witnessed the waterway at its most glamorous. We took two days to go 50 miles and although I'd done nothing to make all this happen I felt a sense of achievement when finally we entered the Pacific.

11. The Pacific

June 8 – 20

Freight ships are not allowed to take more than 12 passengers unless they have a doctor on board. As doctors are expensive and accommodation is limited anyway, these ships take 12 passengers or fewer. Cabins have only become available because developments in technology have allowed ships to operate with fewer officers. On the Tikeibank I was one of seven passengers.

What sorts of people go on a freight cruise? In general, quiet, sensitive people who are not in a hurry. Hugh, the white Zimbabwean, was quiet but had strongly-held opinions, which he expressed articulately. He was stoical about his country's situation. His daughter sent him reports of galloping inflation. Hugh was open to the idea that Zimbabwe's economy could have collapsed by the time he got home. He had a progressive bone-marrow disease and wanted to do the round-the-world cruise while he could. He had been a widower for two years. His friend and next-door neighbour Bridget appropriately had the cabin next to his. A trim little body, who celebrated her 70th birthday during the voyage, she was sharp and quite capable of standing up to Hugh in his more authoritarian moments.

Graham was another widower. He'd also lost his wife two years previously. Before she died he had booked a similar cruise for the two of them and when she died his friends had encouraged him to go on his own. He said it had been therapeutic but he hadn't enjoyed it much and now, feeling stronger, he was going on his own again. You might think him a glutton for punishment because he'd spent his life at sea or close to it. He'd been a steward on an ocean liner, a fisherman with his own boat at Eastbourne and a lifeboatman. As an old salt he naturally fraternised with the officers and the officer cadets and for us passengers he provided a running commentary with useful insights into what was happening both at sea and in the ports. He always had a view on what the captain was up to but was open-minded enough to revise it as new facts emerged. He had a warm, fruity voice and a twinkle in his bright blue eyes. His weather-beaten face had a ruddy glow from the sun, the wind and regular tipping of the tankard. Slightly hunched and bow-legged in his white sleeveless vest and shorts, he was an unpretentious easy-going fellow.

Lyndall, about fifty, was the youngest in the party. A vet from Florida, she was slim and a fitness enthusiast, who rowed many nautical miles on the rowing machine in the ship's gym. She spoke of 'working through the pain barrier'. She told us she was also a horsewoman; indeed with her long face and her toned body she resembled the creatures she rode. We didn't have a lot to say to each other but, being capable and practical, she seemed to enjoy helping me use the computer that was available to passengers in the officers' mess.

Kurt the Kiwi was a writer of non-fiction, on his way from France, where he spent much of his time, back to his native South Island. A gay Jewish man, two years previously he'd lost his older partner of many years and still keenly felt the loss. In fact he was travelling to escape the pain. He trained as an opera singer but told me that there wasn't room in the profession for both Kiri te Kanawa and him! This confidence must have been ironic because she was a soprano while he sang bass-baritone. He'd entertained on cruise ships. His main interests now were horses and harness-racing.

Then there was a French woman, Claudie, a regular traveller on freight ships, cuddly as a pillow, sweet as a *crème brûlée*, with a gentle, musical voice, the hardest person to get to know. She had auburn hair and very fair skin, so she used to sit in the shade when on deck.

Finally, there was Dolores, the wife of the Chief Engineer, who accompanied him on one voyage in three. She also went on challenging, adventurous holidays with her daughter. She was a Texan of about sixty, with dyed blonde hair. Her face and her wiry limbs were a deep tan and wrinkled as a walnut. I saw her on the Monkey Island with her skirt pulled up to top up her pigmentation. She used her Texan drawl to effect when emphasising words or phrases. The trick worked equally well, whether expressing surprise, horror or disapproval. Her husband, David was also thin, his head like a barely covered skull. He would give you a meaningful look or a grin. Then there would be nothing, as if he was fading away. All this gave him a ghoulish mien. He could have gone to a Halloween party without a disguise. I don't know what his wife saw in him unless she liked the idea of someone good with his hands, who could revive a moribund engine in the middle of the ocean.

The captain was a big man with a boyish fringe. He was laid back and had a jolly sense of humour. When he came into breakfast he would greet us with, 'Morning, campers!' (or some such jovial expression). He had a wide taste in music. I know this because he left the door of his cabin open and the sound of his CD player could be heard all around the deck. When you got nearer you could hear him tapping away on his computer. For someone who spent most of his time at sea, he had an amazing knowledge of what was happening in the United Kingdom. When one of the non-British passengers asked me a question about how something was done in England I would do my best, only to have the captain helpfully fill out my answer with more facts and greater clarity. There were four cadets, gentle young men, who used to drink with Graham and Kurt.

All of these people, together with Steve, the Purser, ate in the officers' mess and were entitled to use the officers' lounge. I didn't see very much of the crew, except for three young Russian stewardesses, who served the meals and cleaned the cabins and the lounge. I can't remember their real names so I'll call them 'Upanova', 'Supernova' and 'Legova'. I was fascinated to observe these females in a male-dominated workforce. In the dining room they wore a traditional uniform of short-sleeved white shirts and short black skirts with white aprons. Thus I got to know the shapes of their legs very well. Legova, the girl who cleaned my room, was petite and sweet. None of them spoke much English but they knew some polite idioms.

'May I come in?' Legova would ask, and when I thanked her, she'd say, 'You're welcome.'

Although we passengers weren't able to access the Internet ourselves, we were able to send and receive e-mails on the ship, courtesy of the Captain's radio messages to the shipping company's headquarters. My address list of regular contacts was on my web-mail, which I couldn't access from the ship. The only e-mail addresses I had were those of Rupert and Edward, my two sons, and a friend called Monica. I e-mailed all three asking them to send me the other addresses but I got no reply for two days and as we headed out into the Pacific I felt cut off from my base. I was also suffering from a delayed reaction to the mugging, which had awakened a feeling of hopelessness and emotional pain which sat on my chest like a boulder. As a result I was still subdued and diffident with the officers and the other passengers. I struggled to bring my notes up to date or mooched about the decks.

Claudie told me that we were soon to pass near to the Galapagos Islands on the port side, although not near enough to see them. There is nothing on earth bigger than the Pacific Ocean. It was marvellous to contemplate the great blue disc of visible water, of which we were always in the middle. The possibility of falling in deliberately, not accidentally, and the terrible finality of it exerted their old fascination although I'd no interest in a real suicide. I even imagined the irrevocable step of throwing my camera overboard, along with its irreplaceable images.

It helped me that the simple, but civilised, life of the ship pressed on regardless. The Captain liked to do things right. Meals had a sense of occasion. At dinner the officers wore short-sleeve white shirts with epaulettes, black ties, shorts and sandals. There were two tables arranged in a T-shape and covered in white table cloths. There was a choice of dishes, shown on a single printed menu taken around by a stewardess, who showed it to us as she took our orders. Sometimes I sat next to the Captain. He explained that to spread the effect of the additional hours to take account of our progress westward the three eight-hour watches were each increased by 20 mins. I thought this very fair.

The next day I rose to a bright morning. I went up to the monkey island and breathed the very fresh and clean air. This put some edge onto my appetite for breakfast but when I went down to the dining room, no one was there. I'd forgotten about the hour change.

There was nothing to do on the ship except eat the meals, which I enjoyed, and sunbathe, which I avoided as I couldn't be bothered to put on sun block. You could read, of course, and there was a little library. The books were mostly at the popular end of the spectrum. There was also a random collection of videos. I was reading Stephen King's novel 'Carrie', a terrible, bloody and utterly absorbing story, told without compromise. I found it strangely liberating. I felt too self-conscious to use the gym and hadn't brought suitable kit. I got permission from Steve, the Purser to post a notice in the lounge, announcing that I hoped to organise a Scrabble tournament and sought entrants.

The bar prices were cheap and there was nothing else to spend your money on, except in port. Kurt would come into the lounge to fix himself a drink, his bald head gleaming and his bare chest glowing. His white three-quarter length muslin pants worn with sandals looked comfortable and appropriate to the climate.

'Oooh, it's hot out there!' he would declare as if he didn't expect the tropics to be so mean as to treat him like that.

David and Dolores shared a double cabin next to mine, the outer half a living room, the inner half a bedroom. She seemed to have taken a shine to me.

'Do you like teas?' she asked me at lunch one day, apropos of nothing.

'Yes, I do,' I said.

'I'll give you some.'

A few hours later she knocked on my door and handed me three different blends of tea in teabags with individual Harrods' wrappers. That evening I came out of dinner with Dolores. Almost as soon as we'd left the dining room, I saw Legova moving in the corridor behind us.

'Did you see that?' Dolores asked as we began to climb the stairs.

'She was just going into the dining room,' I said.

'She was going into someone's cabin,' she said.

'Oh!' I said, not finding such behaviour worthy of comment.

The dining room was at the level of the crew's cabins.

'She was going to entertain someone,' Dolores persisted.

'She was going into the dining room!' I insisted.

'I've been on these ships too long!'

Dolores, I was learning, was a person of black-and-white opinions. I let the matter rest, but I couldn't help thinking that, if Legova was entertaining someone or being entertained by him, it was hardly a matter for moral censure. The appealing Legova was committed to a life at sea for months at a stretch, away from friends and loved ones. Why shouldn't the poor girl seek male company, even a little nautical nookie, whether of the paid or mutually desired variety – especially in view of the number of male crew members in the same position as her?

Dolores was a tough cookie. She told me that, when she found out that for years her first husband had had a woman on the side, she stopped sleeping with him but stated that she didn't want a divorce. By keeping this pretence up consistently she drove him to concede a financial settlement far in excess of what she would have got if she had started proceedings. She had an interesting take on my mugging in Panama.

'I held onto my bag,' I said. 'Everyone says you should always give in to a mugger.'

'You could have brought your knee up into his groin,' she argued.

'He was behind me,' I pointed out.

'You could have hooked your foot round his leg and made him overbalance. Women have an advantage. They can drive a high heel into the guy's foot.'

At 8am (ship's time) the next morning we all went up to the bridge for the crossing of the line – the Equator, that is. We watched the reading on the satellite navigation system switch to a line of zeros and then from north to south. Someone opened a bottle of champagne, provided by Bridget, who'd been given it by the ship to mark her seventieth birthday. So we sipped champagne and I realised that for the first time in my life I was in the southern hemisphere. Some of the other passengers took photographs, not of the sea because it looked like any other bit of sea, but of each other. No one signed up to enter my Scrabble tournament.

I usually kept out of the way when Legova cleaned my cabin. That morning I returned to find her finishing off, while a new pink towel lay, carefully folded into a rosette and looking up at me from the middle of my bed, in what seemed a tender, intimate gesture. I tried to engage Legova in conversation but, with our profound lack of mutual language, the best I could do was to complain that my jug of iced water leaked. And the best she could do was to take it away and replace it with a jug that didn't. I photographed the towel.

I had been warned that at a certain time in the afternoon I should present myself in the stern on the poop deck. I was advised to wear something I wouldn't mind getting damaged. I was not in the mood for an initiation ceremony. I felt it presumptuous of the Captain to subject his passengers to ritual humiliation. It seemed to me to be out of character for someone who otherwise treated us cordially as guests. I didn't find the business funny but I guessed that if I tried to avoid it I might be persecuted in other ways. I went down to the poop deck (lovely phrase!) with the four cadets. I started sounding off to them in tones that were only partly self-mocking.

'In your case,' I joked, 'this business could be regarded as a career move, but we, the passengers, are *paying* to be here!'

They smiled politely. When we arrived a small crowd had gathered. Steve and others were preparing the means of torture. Four upright chairs had been placed in a line. A big Russian tar called Sacha was dressed as King Neptune with a long grass skirt, fish netting, Christmas decorations, crown and artificial beard. The Captain had a sheet of paper in his hand. The four cadets were ordered to sit on the chairs. Then their hands were tied behind the chair backs and their ankles to the chair legs. The Captain read out a list of trumped-up charges, which probably contained elements of truth – such as matters of over-indulgence in alcoholic beverages and sleeping when they should have been on their watch. All I could do was to observe their punishments and tremble.

First the Purser made each cadet drink a spoonful of two noxious liquids – according to Kurt's blog, vinegar and raw vodka. Then someone shaved areas of their heads. The bosun ladled quantities of goo, coloured bright blue-green and purple, onto their heads to drip over the rest of them. Finally the cadets were released and hosed down with sea water. Next it was my turn and that of Lyndall, the only other passenger who that day had crossed the line for the first time, together with two of the stewardesses. I was wearing nothing but a pair of seersucker bathing drawers, the only garment I was prepared to have ruined. The consolation was that I found myself next to the fragrant and flagrant Legova.

I assumed we would get the same treatment as the cadets. I was charged with organising a Scrabble tournament despite knowing I was bound to win. Lyndall was charged with something like wearing out the rowing machine. Upanova and Legova, I believe, were charged with offences in connection with waiting duties and solecisms in the English language. For us the noxious medicine was merely olive oil. I had so little hair removed that afterwards, even with the help of a mirror, I could detect no damage. The small quantity of coloured goo I was subjected to was all below chin level. And the hosing down was welcome as it washed most of it off. We had been let off lightly. And the Captain had led the proceedings with a light touch. Crossing the Equator was of significance and had to be marked in some way. As I write, however, my seersucker bathing drawers still hold small impregnations of a sticky coloured substance.

That evening the sun sank behind the horizon like a compact disc slipping down the back of a bookcase. It left a lovely pink glow. Dinner took the form of a barbecue on the bridge deck. As is often the case with barbecues, the best thing was the smell of the food cooking. The party separated into two groups – the officers and passengers standing or sitting with their food and drink in their hands, and the crew standing Russian-style around a large high table, on which they placed their food and drink. They sang, appropriately, a Russian version of the Beetles' song 'We all live in a Yellow Submarine'.

The next day I was presented with a certificate which read:

m.v. *"Tikeibank"*

On this day the 12ᵗʰ June in the year of our Lord 2007,...... John Barclay ...... First Class Passenger on board the mighty vessel, did cross the line of the Equator, in Longitude ..099..Degrees ..50..Minutes West of the meridian of Greenwich.

It is customary for landlubbers who attempt to gain uninvited entrance to his Oceanic Majestye's Domain, to be arraigned before an assembled court of true seafarers to answer to various and often numerous crimes against their fellow seafarers. Punishment is traditionally administered by the ship's surgeon and his assistants.

As a result of accepting the punishment with outstanding courage and fortitude, ... John ... is now allowed to sail the seven seas and in all waters connected there-with, without let or hindrance and shall be offered every assistance by His Oceanic Majestye's loyal subjects.

Signed this 12th day of June in the year of our Lord 2007, on board the good ship "Tikeibank"

Captain Peter G.H.Stapleton
Master Mariner & BSc

The marble-like patterns of white water on blue, produced as a wash by the ship, were quite as lovely as anything I'd seen from the QM2 and on this much smaller vessel I could view them from lower down. I saw flying fish for the first time. They looked like silver birds, although I understand they leap, rather than fly, to reduce the chance of being caught by predators – what an exhausting way of life! I also saw dolphins, but very much in the distance.

The next day I found the 'swimming' pool. It was so small that after two strokes you would have had to turn round. And I blundered into the gym, where Dolores was keeping her stick-like frame in trim, so I crept away. I was not exactly bored – I was enjoying Frank Muir's autobiography 'A Kentish Lad', which I'd got from the ship's library – but I felt I should be doing something with my voyage – as if travelling 8,000 miles to New Zealand weren't enough! I settled down on the shady side of the ship. I'd look up from my book and spot the top edge of a whale. I'd glue my eyes to it, only to find it was just the crest of one of the zillion waves surrounding the ship.

In all of the voyage we never crashed into an abandoned floating container. We were never set upon by pirates. We never ran out of fuel. No one fell overboard or was pushed. It was a dull voyage, but a mighty pleasant one. An abundance of fresh air, a mighty, uninterrupted dome of sky, the countless waves, the rocking motion of the vessel, all made it a perfect environment to be alone with your thoughts. Since we'd left Panama I hadn't seen a single ship. I don't even remember an aeroplane. Talk about getting away from it all!

One afternoon, the sky was a delicate sky blue, but as it approached the horizon it grew paler until it wasn't blue at all, but pearl grey. In the middle of this was the ship with its funnels sending up restless grey clouds of its own. I wanted to fix a camera to the radar antenna to make a 360° photograph of the sky about a quarter of an hour before sunset. Nearly all the clouds appeared low and were lit from one side, making fascinating formations, sometimes dramatic, sometimes whimsical. The wind seemed to be getting up. I held onto the ladder to the radar antenna. It was throbbing with the general vibration of the vessel. Bridget came up.

'Nice sunset!' she said and went down again.

I stayed, as I usually did, to watch the sun disappear completely, the gold turning to pink and finally grey.

Within 24 hours the four cadets got their heads shaved to get rid of the damage done during the crossing-the-line ceremony. I was lounging in the shade, reading my book, when Upanova came along, gave me a courteous nod, collected a mattress and carried it up the steps to the Monkey Island, presumably to pinken up those white squidgy legs of hers. When I came to the end of a chapter, I decided to go up the other steps, all nonchalant-like, to see how the process was going – in the interests of this book, you understand. I thought by then that she'd be flat out with her eyes closed, but instead I saw she was sitting with one knee up while she rubbed sun cream into her thighs. I didn't want her to think I was spying on her – although I was – so I shot down the steps before she could see me.

The boat shoes I'd bought in Panama City were not very comfortable. I took them off whenever I could. I was sitting at my desk in my socks, when I noticed that my cabin smelled stale and unwholesome. I opened the door but the music, presumably from David and Dolores' cabin, was worse than the smell, so I shut the door. Finally, I decided to go and find out if an e-mail had arrived for me. I stepped into the corridor to see one of the engineering cadets looking macabre in an off-white boiler suit and a pink bandage over his recently shaved head.

At meals I liked to talk to different people but as I was usually one of the last to arrive I would often end up sitting opposite Steve the Purser, who always sat in the same place so that he could see into the galley. He was responsible for the conduct of the Russian stewardesses. He was a bit impatient with them, in a patient sort of way. He told me to say, 'No', rather than 'No, thank you,' as if the girls were thick as well as linguistically disadvantaged. He was thrown by me because I often didn't get his jokes – not because they were no good, but because, with his Liverpudlian accent and my impaired ears, I didn't hear them properly.

On Sunday nights we had free wine with our meal. As a result people lingered after they'd finished eating. I got talking to Kurt, Lyndall and Steve.

'How old are your children?' I asked Steve.

'31, 13 and ten,' he said.

'Do you miss them?' I asked.

'Oh yes! I don't see the oldest much. The young ones are joining the ship at Auckland and coming with us to Singapore.'

'I bet they're looking forward to that.'

'Yes, they are.'

'And you?'

'I'll get to know them again. I'm away two-thirds of the year. When I go home I do the cooking and the housework and all the jobs that need doing – there's nothing else to do. I don't have any friends, 'cause I'm away so much. And the family – they've got their own lives. I interrupt everyone's routines when I go home.'

I think we must have repaired to the lounge at some point. Kurt at least would have had more drinks, because I remember him looking at the other people as if we were part of his own dream. We talked writing. He told me he was finishing a history of musical theatre.

'Have you got any other projects in the pipeline?' I asked.

'No, not after this one,' he said.

'You're not going to write another book?'

'I've done all that. I don't see the point of doing it again.'

He told me later he was struggling to find a purpose in life.

'Are you a widower?' he asked me.

'Yes,' I said and added something about my family.

'If you're gay,' Kurt said, 'you don't have that.'

He started to cry quietly.

'I'm sorry,' he said miserably. 'I thought I was doing so well.'

'You are doing well, Kurt,' I reassured him, 'but it's an up-and-down thing – not a steady process.'

I wrote up my memories of my visit to the rainforest. After this I didn't exactly feel on top of things but I did feel a little less underneath them. I still wasn't integrated into the group of passengers and I was living for e-mails. So far I'd heard only from Rupert and Edward.

We would be more than three weeks in the Pacific. The time was going slowly. With an effort I'd get out of bed at 7.20am in order to get to breakfast at 7.35. Then I'd go back to my cabin to clean my teeth, take my pills and tidy my room before Legova came to clean it. I'd go to the lounge, read the captain's News Digest, which he passed on to us. I'd reply to any e-mails, go back to my cabin, close the door because of the sickly stale smell in the corridor, kneel on my sofa to look out of the porthole, go on deck to read until it was time to go back to my cabin to make myself a cup of coffee. Eventually I'd get in the mood to write up my notes. I'd realise I hadn't shaved. I'd shave. I'd sniff my armpits to see if I needed a shower. I'd shower. I'd go to lunch, struggle to hear what people were saying, go back to my cabin, clean my teeth, go to the lounge to check my e-mails, back to my cabin, try to open the porthole, lie on the bed, fall asleep, wake up, go on deck for air, read, listen to the rumble of the engines, stare at the water hoping to find anything that wasn't water, go back to my cabin, make myself a cup of tea, sharpen a pencil, try to do some work, go to the library, look again through the videos, with a big effort do something practical like go to the laundry room to do my washing, drying and ironing, talk to someone in the corridor, go back to my cabin, kneel on the sofa, look out the porthole – and continue in this vein until it was time to go up and watch the sunset. Then drink before dinner, dinner, read, watch a video and go to bed.

Kurt on the other hand would turn his daily activities into little milestones on the journey of life. He'd come into the lounge, red-faced as usual.

'I've done my exercises,' he'd announce, 'I think I'll have a beer.'

One afternoon I was on the bridge deck, when the Captain came out.

'Wiss, wiss, wiss,' he said or words to that effect and continued on past me. I got up from my lounger and followed him like a disciple. He led me to the starboard side of the ship and pointed.

'That's Such-a-place,' he said. 'It's an atoll.'

There was a flattened piece of land, visible but virtually unnoticeable, like a thin extra layer of sea laid on the horizon for a degree-level spot-the-difference competition.

'That's exciting,' I said, 'to see land after such a time. Thank you!'

He gave me a knowing grin and went back onto the bridge by another door.

One evening the sun set at 5.05pm. I stayed and watched the sky darken. Eventually I could see a crescent moon and a bright little light, presumably Venus. From the rocking vessel, both bodies appeared to be swaying in a mauve sky. One by one the stars became visible. Another night I saw the moon apparently swinging like a bare light bulb on a flex.

I woke up wondering where the cabins got their oxygen from. The portholes, I thought, were sealed. We'd been told to keep our doors shut so that the air conditioning would work. I had mine turned off because it made the cabin cold. I resented putting on extra clothing whenever I came in from the heat of the deck. With limitless fresh air outside, I felt we weren't getting much. The captain had a cold – ditto the Purser. What happened to the germs, I wondered. Did they just get circulated around the cabins. I learned later that there was an inlet for fresh air into the system but I never saw it.

We passed within four or five miles of some flat islands, half a dozen of them, some joined by what I guessed was a coral reef. I thought I could make out sand and trees. The crew were laying out thick mooring ropes snakewise on the deck. In the morning we would be in Tahiti.

12. Tahiti

June 20 – 22

I woke early with the sensation that the ship had stopped. I wasn't sure whether we had docked or were still at sea. I put my coffee jar on the floor to see if it would roll. It didn't. As it was still dark I went back to sleep. At seven o'clock, with a big effort I got myself up onto the deck to watch the end of the docking process. A tug was nudging us into position. I could see lines of stacked containers and way down below us what looked like Lego men working on the quay.

We were moored in the port of Papeete, the capital of Tahiti, in the north-west of the main island. I saw someone locking one of the doors to the bridge. It wouldn't do to have a vital piece of navigational equipment stolen or sabotaged. The cabins were being fumigated. Astern of us a container ship was being unloaded. Tikeibank's own cranes came into action. I saw two men fasten hooks to the uppermost corners of a container then abseil down the side of it, using the hoisting wires while they were still slack. Giant folding lids opened to reveal the ship's hold. Inside were a lorry, a tractor, a big earth mover and some other vehicles. When I came off the ship I watched these large items being driven through a great opening in the side of the hull onto the quay.

Eschewing taxis as usual, I set off on foot, dodging fork-lift trucks, which were charging about carrying containers. It would make a good scene in a film – the hero running down a narrow lane between two walls of containers, chased by a forklift truck dangling a container above his head.

I had to show my passport at the Immigration Office in the harbour. Then I did something I hadn't done for two weeks – I went for a brisk walk – and very liberating it felt too. I skirted the edge of the harbour and came into the town. I'd a full day in Tahiti and wanted to make the most of it. I drew some Polynesian francs and bought a notebook in the market. In the tourist information centre I found out that, of the two round-the-island tours, one was cancelled and the other was over-subscribed. So I decided to do something much more fun – to make my own tour. The island was shaped like a lumpy grapefruit kissing a lumpy lemon, with Papeete on the side of the grapefruit away from the lemon. I found a public bus that would take me anti-clockwise around the coast to the Gauguin Museum and Botanical Gardens, which lay close to where the 'grapefruit' joined the 'lemon'.

There was no conductor on the bus, suggesting that Tahiti was economically closer to Costa Rica than Nicaragua. A man sat next to me wearing shorts, his thighs apart, his hairy knee against mine. Why do men sit with their knees apart, even in a confined space? Is it a biological urge to keep their testicles cool? We stopped near the airport where a girl got on with a big black box containing, according to the label, 'Logitech adrenaline-pumping sound' with a 'ported sub-woofer'. The global economy was alive and well. Eventually the world will be wearing a baseball-cap, blue jeans and plastic flip-flops, sitting on concrete, eating chips, drinking coco-cola, and talking to itself on a mobile phone purchased electronically with American dollars.

There was only one main road, the coastal road that we were taking. There were creeks, islets, palm trees and houses beside the sea. The waves broke a long way out, so either the beaches on the south side of the island were very flat or there was a reef. In a pretty place called Papara, I saw helium balloons on separate strings, suggesting a party – customs around the world, like merchandise, are also becoming the same. Looking inland, I noticed steep hills covered in trees and other vegetation. Behind the hills I made out mountains, their peaks hidden by clouds, which contributed to the romantic character of the island.

I was the only customer in the restaurant beside the Botanic Gardens. The waitress looked and sounded like a student from France on a holiday job. I took great pleasure in ordering my meal in the local language, French. I was further encouraged by the speedy arrival of some French bread. On the table was a small arrangement of bird-of-paradise flowers in a block of oasis wrapped in palm leaves. The ceiling of the restaurant was lined with an assortment of fabrics printed in floral designs. They hung down wherever there were beams to hide. The pillars supporting the roof were disguised by climbing plants. These people were keen on wrapping. The restaurant was next to the sea. I sat by a window where I could hear the tranquil sound of water lapping below my elbow. The man-made music sounded like a westernised version of a Polynesian song rendered in French.

I was doing really well with that language until, when my 'mahi-mahi' (a local fish) with green pepper arrived, I accidentally said, 'Gracias' instead of 'Merci'. The menu had said, 'poivre vert' (green pepper) but I started looking for green peppers (*'poivrons verts'*). The fish was 'delish'. The *'frites'* (chips) were the best I'd ever tasted. It's a long way to go for a portion of chips so I was really glad I had some while I was visiting the country. The rice was cooked to a T, so I didn't mind having chips and rice at one meal. There were also taros, purple-grey with a texture – and to some extent a taste – like soap rescued from the bath water, an impression which the coconut sauce did little to counter. The white wine helped a lot.

Through the window I watched a woman in a turquoise dress carrying a child and wading in the calm sea from a half-submerged log. Suddenly a black chicken, with that startled expression her species go in for, alighted on the back of another chair at my table, looked around and flew down to the floor.

After my lunch, taking photographs as I went, I walked quickly round the botanical gardens. They were varied, lush and reached the water's edge, where I saw canoes, each with a single stabiliser on one side, like an extremely disproportionate catamaran. There were realistic streams running through the gardens, wonderful trees and giant bamboo.

Right next to the gardens was the Gauguin Museum. The Japanese-style buildings and more gardens to the water's edge evoked a serene atmosphere. The museum contained personal items, documents, photographs, reproductions, original sketches and block prints – everything but paintings, which is probably a good thing because Tahiti is remote from almost all of the world's art lovers.

Born in Paris, the son of a French journalist and a Peruvian Creole mother, Paul Gauguin grew up in Lima (Peru), joined the merchant marine, returned to Paris, became a full-time artist, moved to Pont-Aven in Brittany and later went to Panama in search of the primitive, enrolling in the Canal project, from which he was dismissed after two weeks – maybe the work was just too primitive for him! All this was before he lived in Tahiti and the Marquesa Islands, where he died in 1903, long before the development of international air travel.

When I went back to the road, I saw two women on the verge, selling small red fruit. The women reminded me of those painted by Gauguin during his time on the island. They told me the fruit was called rambutan and gave me one to try. It was like the lychee except that the flesh clung to the stone. I bought some to eat on the bus and take back to my friends on Tikeibank. One of the women told me where to catch the bus. I didn't have time to visit the 'lemon' and with one change of bus continued on round the 'grapefruit' back to Papeete.

I'd the best seat on the bus, the only one on the coastal side that was raised. Soon two women got on. After a while for no apparent reason one of them swung round and gave me a big smile. We passed gardens, jungly bits with a tight unstructured mix of lush green foliage, then neatly trimmed hedges. I saw two boys sharing a bicycle, which reminded me of Mexico. Six men riding in a truck reminded me of my adventure in Nicaragua. Someone jogging reminded me of Costa Rica.

On the north side of the island the coast road ran close to the water all the way, winding along the edge of cliffs, dropping down to run around inlets, across narrow bridges and over clear rivers before they entered the sea. Here the beaches were steep and the waves broke close in. The water was white with froth, the sand the colour of charcoal. I saw people bathing and surfing. There was a lone canoeist.

We were heading into the sun, which made the water sparkle. When we drove around small headlands, the driver was forced by the narrow winding road to go slowly allowing me to enjoy the view, which eventually turned into a sunset.

I returned to the ship a changed person – cheerful, optimistic and confident. I don't think this was due to the scenic attractions of my excursion but to the fact that I had exchanged my passive existence afloat for a day of exploration and doing my own thing. I was back in time for dinner. I put the rambutans on the bar with a note saying, 'Help yourself.' The four cadets went ashore after dinner for a booze-up, hoping, I gathered, to meet some friendly women.

We'd a lot more containers now but the men were still loading and unloading. I could see right down into the bowels of the ship. The men sat waiting for the next hoist to arrive. From the monkey island, where I was watching, it was a long way down to the bottom of the hold. Around the harbour edge, lights were reflected in the water. The lights of the houses up the hills were more thinly spread out. And a white cross of light, presumably on a church on the hill, seemed very high up.

The next day I woke at 6.30am. The hook of the hoist was swinging freely. One of our crew with a brush on a long handle was painting parts of the crane. A man was sweeping the tracks that took the cover of the hold. Then another man pressed a switch to close a folding platform, which up till then I'd thought of as solid deck.

At 8.15 I left for town. In an Internet café I collected messages and sent replies. I was in a dark corner, trying to cope with a French keyboard on which the letters were arranged differently. I kept pressing the 'Q' instead of the 'A', and the punctuation keys were in different places as well. It was taking so long that I decided to make a note of the messages and reply to them from the ship. I was back on board just ahead of the deadline of 10.30. I didn't want to be left behind.

13. More of the Pacific

June 22 – 30

High winds were forecast, so we storm-stowed everything we could.

'It was good to get back on the buses,' I told Kurt in the bar.

'I really admire what you're doing,' he said.

'As we're leaving the ship together, I expect there'll be some sort of party. If I perform a poem would you like to do a party piece?'

'Oh, no!' he said, 'I couldn't.'

'But you used to stand up in front of a lot of people and sock it to them…'

'Yes, but not now.'

'Well you could read one of my poems.'

'No. You see, I'm not an actor; I'm a singer.'

'That's a shame! Okay.'

I decided to get a crew cut. At the appointed time I went down to a little room near the swimming pool to see the ship's part-time hairdresser, Valery. He was waiting for me and gave me a big grin when I arrived.

'How do you like it?' he asked.

'Like Kurt,' I told him. 'Do you know Kurt?'

He immediately reached for the electric clippers and set about my neck and ears. Then he took scissors and comb to the top of my head. I guessed he had to cut my hair down a bit so that it wouldn't clog the clippers. Two cadets passed through on their way to the pool.

'Oh, you're having it shaved!' one said.

'Yes,' I replied, 'but I don't think he understands.'

Valery picked up the razor and comb and made a few brief passes over my hair.

'Mirror, mirror!' he exclaimed and led me to the changing room.

I looked at myself. Valery read the look of disappointment on my face. I looked at the mirror, then at him. I pointed to his hair, which was short as a short-pile carpet.

'Come back!' he said and beckoned me to his salon. 'It's okay. No problem.'

'Like the boys,' I said, pointing to the pool.

In two minutes he had 'mowed the lawn'. We went back to the mirror. I looked like an elderly duckling. You could have played croquet on my head. I gave him a big smile and a thumbs-up sign. I shook his hand for good measure.

'Do you like beer?' I asked him.

He put his hand out.

'I'll get you some beer.'

'Steve ...'

'I'll talk to Steve.'

I went up on deck and saw Kurt. He'd had that style for forty years. Later, James, the best-looking of the cadets, saw me reading on the monkey island.

'Like the hair!' he said.

'Thank you,' I replied. 'I can feel the air on my scalp.'

'You're one of us!'

There are few things a young man can say to a 64-year-old that are as heartening as that. At 12 knots we were not rushing because the two Andrew Weir ships ahead of us had been delayed and the company didn't want the vessels to bunch up like the Mexican marimbas. The sun had nearly slipped behind the edge of the world when a man with a shaved head came out, looked at the sun and did something with a sextant and the gimbal-mounted compass, as if checking that the heavens were behaving themselves.

The next day I went down to breakfast.

'Sorry I'm late,' I announced, 'I was combing my head!'

As the days went on, more and more men had the standard haircut – even the Captain! I soon felt normal. The ship was pitching moderately. You could see the waves that were doing it – broad, creeping mounds of water, their surfaces dimpled but never broken – smooth enough to reflect clouds in white tracks all the way from the horizon. I didn't see a white horse all day – normally there were droves of them. As I held onto the ship's rail I could feel grit on my palms. When I looked at them I saw they were sprinkled with cubic white crystals of salt. How did they get there? I hadn't felt any spray!

I knew that the Tikeibank was an old ice breaker, but I hadn't realised how much went into keeping her in service. I spotted the captain walking down from the bridge in old clothes rather than his uniform shirt and tie.

'He's been working with us and the crew,' James told me at lunch, 'to clear the ship of the rubbish left over from unloading at Papeete. He expects there'll be an inspection in Auckland. There were five tons of chain to be shifted and hung up.'

'Gives a new meaning to the phrase "chain gang"!' I quipped.

'These old ships,' said James, 'they come down on hard.'

'The Bank Line has flags of convenience from the Isle of Man,' the Captain explained. 'This authority is proud of its place as third highest for standards of safety and so on. So they take a tough line on their ships in inspections. Trouble is – the people conducting the inspections are not experienced seafarers. They've got little understanding of the background to their standards or the point of view of those of us who have to manage the ships. Untidiness is immediately obvious to anyone so if they see a ship looking messy, they're going to search harder for more serious faults. It's an ageing fleet and we have to work hard to keep it going.'

The next morning at 8.45 we stopped. I was in the lounge. I noticed that the usual judder had ceased.

'The engine's still running,' Graham explained, 'but it's not driving the ship.'

I went outside with him. One of the crew was chipping old paint off metal.

'We're broadside on to where we should be going,' Graham said. 'We're drifting round.'

In relation to a pool of oil and dirt, which must have come from the ship, we were hardly moving – pitching and tossing but not going anywhere. It felt strange. It was raining gently and the decks were wet. 'Adrift in the Pacific', I thought, would make a good title for a story in Reader's Digest.

There was a rainbow. I went up to the monkey island. Lyndall was there in a bikini with a wrap around her narrow hips. The sun came out again and it was warm even in the wind. Close to the ship was a narrow carpet of yellow flecks of paint. 80 minutes after we'd stopped I noticed the yellow carpet move towards the stern. Looking back I could see a feeble wash in a curve. We were turning. Soon we were pointing WSW – back on course. I'd been hoping the trouble would have developed into a full-scale emergency. It turned out to be a mere pit stop.

I did my washing and ironing. Then I felt nauseous. Was this the famous *mal de mer*? Perhaps, I thought, if I were on deck and could see the horizon, the nausea would go away. I sat on a lounger that was under cover, only to find it had somehow got wet in the rain. So to dry my bottom I went round to the sunny side of the ship and stood facing a metal wall.

'John!' a voice called.

I turned round. It was the Captain.

'A whale – over there,' he said, pointing to something ahead on the starboard side.

It was grey, like the sea. I found it difficult to make out an animal shape but I couldn't help being aware of the tremendous energy of the beast when it came almost completely out of the water.

'They do that to knock the barnacles off,' the Captain explained.

It did this trick several times and as the ship continued so we got nearer to the whale. When it lined up with the sun it became invisible. Finally it did its best trick of all – squirting an elegant fountain from its blowhole. A few more jumps and then it was gone. I'd wanted so much to see a whale and now, thanks to the captain, I had.

About this time we crossed the International Date Line. The Captain took the decision to cancel Monday 25th June. As we worked our way westward every few days we'd enjoyed several days that were 25 hours long. Suddenly, instead of being twelve or 13 hours behind British Summer Time, we were eleven hours ahead.

The next day was grey and the sea rougher. At breakfast I noticed that the tablecloths were soaking wet – purposely so, to prevent slipping. Later in my cabin my coffee slid across the desk in a race with itself for the edge. I caught the saucer, which in turn caught the coffee that spilt.

You are not allowed to bring soil or plant life into New Zealand so I cleaned my boots, scraping, washing and scrubbing them with a nailbrush. Supernova and one of the Russian crewmen were preparing the cabin next to mine for a new passenger joining at Auckland. I could hear Russian speech interspersed with giggles. With the life they led, they had to seize whatever fun they could find.

I still hadn't found the opportunity – or the nerve – to enquire how the ventilation worked. Where did we get our oxygen from? Why did the air on the staircase smell so foul? Had the system been passed by any health authority? What was it like for the crew, languishing in the lower depths? Because of the change in the weather I was spending a lot of time in my cabin. There was a mega-glut of fresh air just outside my window – sorry, porthole. All I had to do was to open it. That day I finally did something about it. Being nosey, when I saw the door of Hugh's cabin open, I looked in.

'Excuse me, Hugh,' I said, 'I notice you've got your window open. How did you manage that?'

'Lyndall's got a thing …'

'Oh, thanks. I'll ask her.'

I tracked Lyndall down.

'Sorry to bother you, Lyndall,' I said, 'have you got the thing for opening windows?'

'You mean portholes?'

'Yes.'

'It's in the gym – do you know where that is?'

'Yes,' I was lying, because I'd forgotten.

She knew I didn't use the gym. I didn't want her to think that I didn't even know where it was. She'd already registered that I called portholes 'windows'.

'It's a thing with a curlicue,' she added. 'It's in the box with the weights.'

'Thank you very much.'

I went down to the second deck and started to look around. If labelled at all, the doors were labelled in Russian. I didn't know the Russian for 'gym' – because I didn't know the Russian for anything. I went round and round trying to work out by a process of elimination which one was the gym. I didn't want to knock on a door and disturb some poor slave who'd been up all night – or a member of the crew getting his leg over Legova. One door had a very clear notice that said in English, 'Please turn off the lights when you leave this room'. I deduced from this that it was a public room. I opened the door quietly and peeped in. It was the first time in my life that I was pleased to see a set of gym apparatus. And there in the box with the weights was the thing with the curlicue. I took it back to my room – sorry, cabin – and eventually opened the window – sorry, porthole. A great roar of the sea and a great rush of wind came in. My cabin faced forward so that even if there was no wind I could have as much air as I wanted. I soon settled for having the porthole opened just a crack.

Despite my new supply of fresh air, I felt nausea building up. It helped to lie down. From there I could watch fluffy white clouds calmly bouncing up and down as if riding in a heavenly lift. The shower curtain floated about like a ghost. Of course, what was really happening was that the curtain was hanging still while the whole ship moved. I ate a satsuma. It was surprisingly juicy and flavoursome considering it had probably been picked many weeks before – no scurvy on this ship, I thought! I managed to get through lunch without mentioning seasickness once. I certainly wasn't going to tell anyone I'd got a plastic bag hidden in my pocket!

After lunch I knelt on my sofa and looked out. The sun appeared, lighting up some furious action on the starboard side. It was magnificent – thick clouds of white spray above, while below, the froth unrolled like a carpet, as brilliant a white as the icing on a wedding cake. Up and down we went, like a bucking bronco in slow motion. I expected to see the containers topple into the waves. When I went to the library and opened the cupboard four books leaped to the floor. During the night a glass of water I thought I'd wedged securely went on its travels. The cupboard door rattled. I thought I heard someone slam a cabin door and someone else whack a tin tray with a wooden spoon. I hoped someone had remembered to put wedges under the wheels of the tractors and the other vehicles in the hold.

Only half the usual suspects turned up for breakfast. I learned later that Graham had twisted Kurt's arm, literally, to persuade him to have another drink – a terrible thing to do to someone like Kurt, who had a strong urge for alcohol, which he carefully managed. The arm in question had been injured previously. This second incident was so painful for Kurt that he stayed in his cabin all morning. Graham did the same. I was sitting at the computer later, when the old salt put his head round the door.

'Albatross!' he announced.

Two birds were following us, crossing and re-crossing our wake, so far away that they looked like seagulls, not the champion gliders they are with their two-and-a-half-metre wingspans. They came nearer then and you could see they were dark on top and pale underneath. Never touching the water but gliding so close to it that, as they turned, their wing tips were centimetres from it, a majestic, graceful, seamless show of aerobatics. The secret of spotting wildlife is to tell everyone that you really want to see a grizzly bear or a Queen of Spain Fritillary butterfly and then someone will call you when the creature appears.

I wrote a haiku (a three-line poem of seventeen syllables, arranged five, seven, five, traditionally about the natural world):

> *Tireless albatross*
> *air-dancing across the wake*
> *lets the ship go first*

I spent most of my last day writing another poem for the party that would be given for Kurt and me – a buffet dinner in the lounge with free drinks. I was swaying with the ship when I read it out, so I clutched the poem in one hand and held onto the wall with the other.

BON VOYAGE, TIKEIBANK!

We've had a great time and we'd just like to thank
the Captain and crew of the brave Tikeibank.
She's getting on now but, like other old dears,
with constant repainting she'll look good for years.

The Captain knows land matters 'well as the sea.
He fills the whole ship with his music for free.
There's Steve, our dear purser, his jokes getting worser,
his bluff Scouse one-liners could hardly be terser.

While Dave likes to slave in the bowels of the ship,
Dolores no bore is – she shoots from the hip.
And no one forgets the four gallant cadets –
whatever they do they are everyone's pets.

The guys in the boiler suits swabbing the decks,
who get all the shit jobs and think about ... Russia.
The girls in the galley, who don't shilly-shally,
all dancing attendance, a real corps de ballet.

The passengers, well, we're a well-ordered bunch,
with no one but me ever late down for lunch.
There's Kurt with his shirt open, showing his chest,
while Graham can slay'em in mariner's vest.

And Lyndall, as keen as she's fit and she's lean,
doing eight or nine knots on the rowing machine.
Then straight 'out of Africa' not one but two
intrepid explorers – yes, Bridget and Hugh.

Oh Lordy! There's Claudie, so French and so sweet.
More pleasant companions you'd not hope to meet!
Before anybody slips out for a wee-wee,
before we arrive in the land of the kiwi ... ,

It's yo-ho-ho-ho and a bottle of rum –

South Island, North Island, Kurt and I come.
Before we depart, though, we'd just like to thank
you all once again. Bon voyage, Tikeibank!

It went down well – probably because I'd mentioned everyone. People asked for copies so I typed it up there and then on the computer and Steve ran off copies. On that last day, everyone seemed to want to open up to me. Lyndall let me see the photographs she had taken of an albatross. Graham told me his life story. Hugh said that he and Bridget lived in a retirement village of like-minded people. Whenever President Mugabe introduced a new measure the villagers got together and worked out what to do about it. And I looked at my map of China with Dolores.

'I always had something of my own with me to eat,' she told me, 'and you can live a long time on rice. Always take your own stuff for the toilets. I'll give you some wipes for your hands. Why don't you stay on the ship? After Auckland we call at New Caledonia, Vanuatu, Papua New Guinea, Indonesia and Singapore.'

She came up with a list of exciting and exotic possibilities for the two of us. I can't remember what she said, but the following will give you an idea of the sort of thing.

'We could dig up the buried treasures of Boga-Boga,' she might have suggested, 'race elephants across the high jungles of Kalimantan, and dine with cannibals on the flesh of their previous visitors.'

'You're a very adventurous lady,' I said. 'I'm sure we could have a great time, but it wouldn't be *my* adventure, *my* challenge, anymore.'

Besides, I wanted to see New Zealand and Australia. The next morning I put on my spotless boots, said my goodbyes and went down the rickety ladder for the last time.

14. New Zealand

June 30 – July 6

Arriving in Auckland was a weird experience. So much seemed familiar and of course I'd no language difficulty. Even the sparrows and pigeons looked British, although some of the people clearly had Chinese or south-east-Asian roots. I drew some New Zealand dollars and there, looking up at me, was my Queen, although Her Majesty did look strange, as if the journey had unsettled her. The oddest thing, so far from the United Kingdom, was to find what at first glance looked like a provincial British city I happened not to have visited before. After being on the move for three months, it was like coming home. It all seemed tidy, well organised, visitor-friendly, wholesome and a bit old-fashioned, so when I entered a public telephone box I was shocked to see a large human turd on the floor.

The weather was cool and wet, but not bad for midwinter. People were sitting outside under sunshades for dinner. I had to, because the inside of the restaurant was full. There was a New Zealand couple on the next table.

'Excuse me,' said the man, 'but you remind me of someone in "Coronation Street".'

'Well, I am English,' I said.

I'd no idea which character he had in mind, because I've never watched 'Coronation Street', although I have watched the Australian soap 'Neighbours'. These days culture (if that's the right word) is passed round the world like a box of chocolates. Young people in dinner jackets or party dresses were collecting in the street. A small crowd arrived in a mini-bus. There was much greeting and counter-greeting. Those holding drinks gave each other one-armed hugs. The chatter and squealing grew louder. Soon the party had spread across the street and was blocking the traffic. Who says New Zealand is a quiet place? Kurt had told me that Auckland was not the real New Zealand. Well, it was good enough for me.

I had ordered a ticket for the theatre. I had to wait 25 minutes for a pizza, but I needed to collect the ticket by a certain time. So I paid my bill early and covered my food with a second plate. The waitress put a reserved sign on it. The Skycity Theatre was just round the corner. I got my ticket and came back to finish eating my meal.

The play, featuring the Auckland Theatre Company, was called 'Who Wants to be a Hundred?' Written by Roger Hall, it focussed on four old boys in a nursing home, suffering the frustrations and indignities of age – arthritis, stroke and short-term memory loss. One of the four was a rich old bugger, who couldn't be bothered to look after himself. It was very funny at times but also poignant, as when near the end one of the men starts to sing 'Abide with me' and one by one the others join in.

The Skycity Theatre was part of a modern entertainment complex called appropriately 'Skycity'. I came out a different way and found myself on a balcony with a fascinating view from above of a giant gambling casino. Hands reaching out over green-baize tables, the white shirts of the croupiers, the red carpet, the rotating glitter balls, the carefully planned and constantly changing lighting (enchanting enough to draw people in with a promise of literally glittering success, not so crude as to distract the punters). A dragon had flashing red eyes and a flashing yellow flame coming out of its mouth. TV screens were showing rugby – what else? A refreshment trolley was going round. It would have made a wonderful opening scene in a film.

I wanted to be in Sydney by 13th July so that I could visit Mary, my niece by marriage, her husband Simon and their two little girls, before the family returned to England. This meant I had quickly to find a ship to take me there. While I was still on Tikeibank, Claudie had lent me a book about freighter travel. This contained contact details for a New Zealand agency for freight passengers and I'd e-mailed the boss, Hamish Jamieson, while I was still aboard. He pulled out all the stops for me and when I arrived in Auckland I found he'd booked a berth for me on Sunday 8th July. This meant I'd eight days in New Zealand. In that time I couldn't possibly do justice to the Country, even to North Island, but it was better than nothing.

The Backpackers' Centre in Auckland was full so I booked into the Hotel Mercure. My room was on the vertiginous 13th floor, but with so many skyscrapers around it didn't seem that high. I had views in three directions over rooftops to the bay, which was sprinkled with sailing boats.

Breakfast, a well-run buffet, included an assortment of prepared fresh fruit, moist scrambled eggs, toast you could prepare yourself on a toaster built like a big wheel at a fairground and coffee freshly made from beans at the touch of a button – add water to taste. Wonder of wonders – there was no television!

On Monday, the water was sparkling. Ferries purposefully criss-crossed the harbour. Two black-backed gulls were padding about on a flat roof. Hamish had e-mailed me some forms for my passage to Sydney. I filled them in, signed them and sent them off, including a Letter of Indemnity, which contained the following declaration:

'I hereby undertake to make no claim of any nature whatsoever against you your servants or agents whether of (sic) not such claim be occasioned by the negligence, act of default of you or any of you, not (sic) to claim against any person whom you or any of you may be liable to indemnify by contract or otherwise and I also agree to relinquish any right which a (sic) I may acquire to participate in salvage money.'

This doesn't make a lot of sense, does it? And the first bit implies that the mariners could get out their cutlasses, chop me into pieces and feed me to the sharks, and I wouldn't be able to sue the company. Hamish assured me that the Letter of Indemnity was illegal but we agreed that I had to sign it if I wanted to be on that ship.

Somebody on Tikeibank had told me that the Coromandel Peninsula to the east of Auckland was beautiful, so I set off after lunch. The bus station was full of backpackers and other young people. When we got out of the city it began to rain so I didn't see much of the countryside. What I did see was green and pleasant, reminding me of the Lowlands of Scotland. Brown rivers with sloping muddy banks did not. The weather reminded me of Northern Ireland.

I had to change buses in a town called Thames. In the interval I did the British thing of ordering a pot of tea and a piece of cake in the bus station. The second bus was a small vehicle run by one Turley Murphy, who drove his own vehicle as part of the public service. He wore a blue shirt with white lapels and a white cap with a chequered band as if he were a member of the British police, except that the band had his name on it.

'Where are you staying?' he asked me as I got on.

'Coromandel,' I said.

'Could be tricky,' he warned me and then proceeded to debunk his own warning. 'We get there after five and the Tourist Information will be closed. There's the Such-and-such Ranch – that'll cost you so-many dollars. There's the Such-another Lodge and the Yet-another Lodge. There's the So-and-so hostel. I imagine there's a hotel if you don't get in to one of those. Oh, there is a hotel, but it's called the "Such-a-name Pub" – it's that sort of hotel.'

It sounded plenty for one person. There were only four of us on the bus and before we set out he began a commentary on the places we would pass through. Thames, he explained, had grown up as a centre for the New Zealand gold rush of 1860, which led to heavy immigration from Britain. It was now a regional centre for commerce, with lawyers, doctors, dentists and banks. The railway had been closed and the railway station turned into an interesting residence.

'The mining took place at this level,' Turley Murphy said, 'at the foot of those wooded hills you see.'

As he drove he continued in this vein, eloquently, not wasting a word and throwing in colourful stories of the places we passed through. At the same time he played a CD of romantic music, which later was replaced by a man's voice singing with a light touch and clipped diction like Noel Coward. There were binoculars available for the passengers' use. Perspex folders of newspaper cuttings hung on the back of the front seat. All provided free! Turley Murphy's microphone wasn't close enough to his mouth. I sat as near to him as possible, leaning forward to catch as much as I could over the music and noise of the engine. I noted what I thought worth noting, but my notes were useless!

'*marshalling yard – Thames School of Mines – Captain Cook – charts – engine driver – New Cyprus …*'

Doesn't mean a thing! Ah, well, I can't go back now! I do remember a marvellous drive along the west coast of the Coromandel Peninsula. Big bays, little coves, sandy beaches with loose rocks, well-kept roads, neat wooden bungalows, trimmed lawns and, anywhere there was space, a conical tree like a Christmas tree but more perfectly formed.

Eventually we turned inland up a winding road and soon found ourselves behind an articulated lorry, which blocked the view ahead but allowed us more time to enjoy the views on either side. To me it was a curious landscape, hummocky, with steep but rounded hills like heaps of something, a pine forest exuding innocence – all as green as you could wish, except that the grass, while apparently perfectly healthy, was a pale shade, like the artificial surface of a tennis court. The low light of early evening brought out the relief and gave the scene a romantic, dramatic appearance, while the faint haze on the hills added a magical effect. It was like a full-size model of somebody's dream country.

When we got to Coromandel town, I checked into 'The Lion's Den', a hostel with fairy lights on the wall. I took a room for myself for 40 New Zealand Dollars (about £15), then immediately rushed out to the supermarket to buy food for breakfast. When I got back I went into the living room, a large studenty space incorporating a communal kitchen. On the wall were the heads of two wild boars and a stag, neither of which are indigenous species. It was lovely to sit round a big table talking and drinking tea. Two young New Zealand men, hearty outdoor types, were on a diving instructors' course. A young male blond I'd seen on the bus turned out to be German. There was also a German girl, not his companion.

'It has been vet most off se time,' she told me.

I wasn't a bit surprised, having seen how green the countryside was. She continued in a gloomy vein. I imagined she was sitting on some personal unhappiness because I couldn't understand how anyone could be gloomy in such an enchanting part of the world.

An American guy of 18 or 19 had been in North Island for ten months. His mother had come out to see him and the two had been exploring the region together. She was a primary school teacher (ages 5 – 12), who worked entirely in the school library, helping children find information for their projects, teaching them how to use the Internet and showing them how to get more out of reading. Lucky children!

She had started something called 'Travelling Book'. The notion was to release books like doves and electronically follow where they went. There was a website address inside the book's cover and a note encouraging people to report where they found the book and what they thought of it. She hoped the children would learn some geography, not in the traditional dry way of gathering facts, but through the news of the travels of actual people and actual books. It all sounded fanciful to me especially as the books would mostly be for adults. But when she produced a cardboard box of paperbacks for me to choose from I began to warm to the idea. I would need something to read as I crossed the Tasman Sea. I chose 'The Glass Castle' by Jeannette Walls, an autobiographical account of the early life of a girl growing up to be a strong, balanced young woman despite the idiosyncratic, erratic and very different parenting styles of her mother and father, which amounted at times to abuse and neglect, a story made all the more amazing by its non-judgemental, candid and matter-of-fact telling. It took away the inherent tedium of my next sea voyage. I found it more moving even than 'Tess of the Durbervilles'. I had a good howl when I'd finished it.

In Sydney I passed the book on to my niece, Mary, before she returned to Manchester, having, as I thought, registered myself and the book with the Book-crossing web-site. When I got home I found that 41 copies of 'The Glass Castle' had been registered by various individuals and organisations. I could find no record of my registration or of the particular copy whose impressive world travels I had so boldly instigated. This probably tells you more about my level of computeracy than the efficiency of the system. Meanwhile if you happen to pick up one of the many Glass Castles knocking about the globe it might – just might – have reached you via Coromandel, Sydney and Manchester.

But to return to Coromandel, the next morning I had a hot shower in the communal shower. A notice on the outside of the door said, 'Please knock', but nobody did. Nobody came in without knocking either. For breakfast I had the instant porridge I'd bought in the supermarket – 'just add boiling water and stir for 30 seconds'. Amazingly it tasted all right – probably because it had fruit in it. I followed this with a toasted teacake without butter, a mug of tea made from a teabag I took to be complimentary, a banana and an orange.

It was cold so I wore a vest, two shirts, my jumper, my jacket and my pyjama trousers under my regular trousers. Remember it was the middle of New Zealand's winter. Thus protected, I walked to the tourist information centre. The woman who attended to me could not have been more attentive, or indeed more womanly. The encounter scored nine out of ten on the pleasantness scale, so I was glad it was prolonged by a misunderstanding.

'Have you got a map of the area showing the footpaths?' I asked.

In view of the climate and apparent safety of the region, I wanted to continue my circumterrestrial wanderings on foot – at any rate as far as the next town or village.

'You mean "walking tracks"?' the womanly woman asked.

'Yes,' I said, pleased to learn this variant on British English.

'Here you are.'

She produced a small black-and-white plan of Coromandel showing the streets and other features of the town.

'There are several tracks. This one's very nice.'

I stared at the plan. Eventually I made out three walking tracks, apparently not leading anywhere except a short way out of the town and of course the same short way back into it.

'Have you got a bigger map?'

'Yes,' she said, showing me a map of the whole peninsula identical to the one I already had.

The roads were marked but not a single walking track.

'Have you got a map that shows the walking tracks as well as the roads?'

She looked at me as if my question had no meaning, but as pleasantly as ever.

'Are there no long-distance walking tracks?' I persisted.

In France, you can buy a map showing a network of *Grandes Randonnéées* that will enable you, in theory anyway, to walk from Brittany to Provence.

The womanly woman's look of incomprehension turned to amusement.

'All the land is owned. You can't walk on it.'

'Well, I'll just have to go on the roads then.'

'I don't think you could do that.'

The amusement had turned to concern.

'No one walks on the roads,' she told me. 'It's dangerous.'

'I'd face the oncoming traffic.'

'There's nowhere to step out of the way. The roads aren't for walking. Any driver seeing you would …'

I didn't wait to hear what any driver would do to me. I'd got the message.

'Is there a bus to Whitianga?' I asked.

Whitianga is a Maori name. The 'wh' is rendered as the British 'f'.

'Yes. It leaves from here in an hour and twenty minutes.'

'Do I pay on the bus?'

'You can buy a ticket now.'

'May I leave my rucksack here for a bit?'

'Yes, of course.'

In New Zealand outdoor activities range from bungee jumping to harness racing via white-water rafting. But if you want to do a bit of ordinary old-fashioned walking you should go to an old country, like Wales or Austria, where 'walking tracks' have been around for centuries, not a well-ordered, young nation like New Zealand.

I had a pleasant amble along the pavements of Coromandel. I was due again to visit more friends of a friend. They were called Pat and Angus, and they lived in Hamilton. As a present for them, I bought a locally produced box of toiletries aimed at easing the aches and smoothing the skin of the gardener, guessing (rightly as it turned out) that the two of them were horticulturally inclined.

The bus was a mini-bus. I asked the driver if I could sit in the front next to him to make the most of the wonderful scenery. He took us up a hill past strange primitive-looking trees and through a forest. A notice said, 'FIRE DANGER TODAY – LOW'. I saw black turkeys in the open air, unlike their British counterparts, which are kept in vast sheds. Then we came down to the water's edge – this time on the eastern (Pacific) side of the peninsula.

When we reached Whitianga I found an Internet café and checked my e-mails. Hamish Jamieson had sent word that my ship would no longer leave from Auckland but from Tauranga a hundred miles further down the east coast from where I was at that moment. And it would do so that Friday, not Sunday as I'd previously been told. Friday was the day I was to go to Hamilton, so I rang Pat and arranged to see them a day earlier. Hamish had been very helpful so I told him that I hoped to go to Hong Kong from Australia – preferably from Darwin or Brisbane.

'There aren't any ships to Hong Kong,' he said, 'but we'll get you something.'

'I've got to go to Melbourne,' I explained, 'to get my visas for Asia. I don't know how long that will take.'

'Well, let me know when you know when you want to go.'

I saw a lot of children. Somebody told me they were on holiday. New Zealand schools have four terms. The children therefore have four holidays with only two weeks in July (their winter) but six weeks over Christmas (their summer). I checked into another backpackers' hostel. Once again I took a double room for myself rather than join a dormitory. I have no objection to sharing a room with strangers, but strangers have been known to object to sharing with me – because I snore.

It was warm and sunny and I walked to the water's edge. The beach was particularly crunchy under my boots. There was no sand or shingle – only billions of sea shells or fragments of them. I took a ferry across the bay and taking my life in my hands walked up a hill – *on a road!* It was a residential area and, as you will have deduced, I wasn't mown down or otherwise done in. I saw oranges and grapefruit hanging on trees. I talked to a gardener. He said it was an ideal climate for growing citrus fruits – but also bananas, peaches and apples. That is to say, in one place you could grow fruit from the tropics, the Mediterranean and the temperate lands. I think it must be the mild winters and the rain. I found some beautiful beaches.

An Italian restaurant in Whitianga proved to be an excellent bet. I was impressed by the woman who served me, a bright competent Italian in her late twenties. She had the assurance of someone born into a family of restaurateurs. I wasn't surprised later to learn that she was in fact the proprietress. I ordered 'pumpkin, parsnip and sun-dried tomato soup' followed by baked rabbit with Kalamata olives, rosemary and garlic, toasted polenta and carrots.

'Would you like some wine?' she suggested.

'Have you got half a bottle?' I asked.

'The only half bottle I have is the chianti. It will go well with the rabbit.'

The décor was classy, nothing frivolous. On the walls were framed prints of Italian streets. The garlic bread that came with the soup was subtle and crisp. The soup itself was thick and hot, served in a deep, heavy bowl to hold the heat. The three flavours were nicely balanced. A long sprig of rosemary lay on the surface, adding a delicious aroma. The rabbit was served with hot dark-red olives. The polenta was sliced, like bread. The carrots, in thicker than usual strips, were glazed in a syrup. It was difficult to get the meat off the bones without picking them up but the proprietress saw this and quickly brought me a finger bowl. Somewhere I read the words 'Aris Restaurant – Fine Italian Cuisine – Alberto and Olivia Usseglio.'

Alberto, evidently the chef, appeared and went behind the bar to pour himself a well-earned drink. Olivia told me they had been going eighteen months. I admired the assurance and professionalism of the operation. I was impressed by their courage in launching a business so far from home in a sparsely populated area (albeit one of outstanding natural beauty).

As usual I had no difficulty in getting to sleep. I woke to the sound of knocking on my door. I didn't remember asking for an early call. I got up and opened the door. It was a young man.

'Sorry about that,' he said, 'but your snoring is really, really loud.'

'I'll try and stay awake,' I said, 'while you get off.'

I sat on the bed thinking, 'I'd love to get to sleep.' The building was made of wood, with partitions rather than thick walls. My snoring must have reverberated like a vacuum cleaner trapped in the belly of a double bass. I tried to read. Soon my head was flopping about on my shoulders. I had an early start in the morning!

I caught the bus at 7.30am. Pockets of mist made the countryside appear more magical than ever. It was the driver I'd had the day before. He granted me a backpackers' discount. He told me that the New Zealand honey industry was threatened by bee diseases from the United Kingdom and the United States, possibly introduced deliberately to destroy the commercial advantage New Zealand had enjoyed when free of disease.

The native wild life was distinctive – I saw strange trees, including tree ferns and trees with leaves that looked and tasted (apparently) like cabbages. Species such as sheep had been introduced, of course. I saw alpacas and some very English-looking cows. The driver told me the Indian mynah bird had been introduced.

We crossed the Coromandel Peninsula on higher ground. The driver stopped the bus at a viewpoint while he had a cigarette. He pointed out islands and kiwi-protection notices. Being the national emblem, these birds were protected. They were brown, shy, mainly nocturnal and nested in the ground. Thus you hardly ever saw them. This, the driver explained, was taken advantage of by those opposing building proposals. Nobody had seen a kiwi in a particular spot, but as soon as a developer announced his intention to build, the kiwis 'appeared' and had to be protected. Thus a dowdy, flightless bird the size of a chicken was responsible for saving numerous beauty spots and viewpoints without actually being there. According to my man, it had saved the Punuraku Scenic Reserve – whatever that was – without realising it. What a worthy and modest creature! The kiwi has done far more for New Zealand than the lion ever did for England!

By the time we got back to Thames I'd had a circular tour of the peninsula. I changed buses. The driver was none other than the articulate and well-informed Turley Murphy. This time a woman passenger discussed recent local history with him. I'd brought breakfast to eat in the break between buses. In the event there was no break and, as eating or drinking were not allowed on the bus, I became hungry, but the discussion helped me to keep my mind off my stomach. I gathered from the conversation that Turley Murphy was a retired businessman who drove buses because he enjoyed it. A girl got on and showed him a card.

'I can't accept that,' he said. 'You can come on – I'll pay for you. They won't let me have a card-reader.'

I saw a rotary milking shed like one I'd seen on a dairy farm in Dorset, imported from Australia. This one had been built in Tauranga, where I was heading after Hamilton. So the Northern hemisphere doesn't always lead the world! We picked up a lad with a rucksack.

'I'll pay for it,' Turley Murphy said again.

Every time I came into a town there was a sign saying, 'Engine breaking prohibited.' What a virtuous nation!

In Hamilton I booked into the Commercial Hotel Victoria. I had a fantastic meal in a French restaurant called 'Paris'.

Next morning, Angus met me at the bus station and drove me to his house where Pat welcomed me with coffee. They treated me like a cousin they hadn't met before. They took me up a hill to Till's Lookout to get a view of the whole of Hamilton, and very clean and respectable it looked too, then for a walk around Hamilton Lake. I later learned that a track to the west of Hamilton, taking in Till's Lookout, was being upgraded as part of a national plan to establish a 'hiking trail the length of New Zealand by 2010'. So I have to eat my words – or some of them.

Finally, to Hamilton Gardens, which were magnificent, partly because they offered lovely views of the Waikato River but mainly because they contained the Paradise Gardens, a collection of distinct garden 'rooms', close together but discrete, each celebrating a national gardening style of a particular period. Thus in a small area we had seven gardens ranging from the 'Chinese Scholar's Garden' (10th-12th Century), through the 'Italian Renaissance Garden (15th-16th Century) to the 'American Modernist Garden' (20th century). I was deeply impressed. This was lucky because Pat turned out to be on the committee.

We had lunch in these gardens and then Pat and Angus generously took me to Tauranga ('Pat likes driving'), right to the door of the Sebel Hotel on Trinity Wharf. I ordered tea for the three of us and checked in without asking the price of the room, because my only concern then was to make sure Pat and Angus had a break before they drove the 108 km back to Hamilton. It was a beautiful, high-class establishment on the edge of the water and it was very agreeable (for me and, I believe, for my new friends too) to sit over a pot of tea in such calm and elegant surroundings.

To be on the safe side I told someone at reception I would have dinner in the hotel. Then I walked into the town, which took seven minutes. It was upmarket, trendy, clean, tidy and not a bit like any other port I'd passed through. I found an Internet café and e-mailed my supporters that I was having a great time and that I'd be boarding the 'Cap Beatrice' in the morning. There were some appealing restaurants along the sea front but I felt committed to the Hotel dining room.

The waitresses looked highly arresting in light-blue shirts, black trousers and long white aprons. The waiters wore the same with rather less impact. A waiter took my order. Then he left me in peace until the water waiter, who had clearly been trained on the QM2, brought me, unsolicited, some severely chilled water. I kept my head down every time I saw him approaching with his frosty jug. Another waiter glided up.

'Have you ordered, sir?'

'Yes, thank you.'

'Would you like a newspaper to read?'

'No, thank you very much.'

I had hapuka fillets (fish), delicious in spicy saffron butter with cherry tomatoes and prawns.

'Everything all right, sir?'

'Yes, thank you.'

The desserts were unashamedly wicked, desperately tempting, definitely fattening and certainly expensive. If I'd had more of the Te Mata Woodthorpe

Sauvignon Blanc I might have yielded. Instead I ordered a long black decaffeinated coffee.

'Would you like milk on the side?'

'No, thank you.'

This was always happening to me. I'd ask for black coffee and they'd offer me milk! When I had drunk it all I put my cup down. A waiter came up to me. I smiled at him.

'I've finished,' I said, with as much finality in my tone as I could muster.

'Can I get you anything else?' he persisted.

'No, thank you – I've done very well.'

I got up and left the dining room before he could press the matter further. So, you see, I had three memorable meals on three successive nights. I went to Reception.

'I've got a geography question for you,' I said. 'Do you know where Sulpher Point is?'

This was where I was to report the next morning.

'Yes, it is here,' the receptionist said.

With a nicely manicured index finger she pointed on the map to the point on which stood the hotel where we both found ourselves. I couldn't have chosen to stay in a more convenient location. This assuaged the guilt I felt at choosing such a luxurious flophouse and then making the mistake of eating in it. The dinner was $70 for two courses including tip. You'd think for that money they could have had someone playing a Maori harp in the dining room – preferably a Maori!

In the morning I was up at seven. I showered, dressed, cleaned my boots in the basin, cleaned the basin and cleaned the basin surround. I put the boots on my balcony to dry and went down to breakfast.

'Good morning, sir. Is this your first breakfast with us? Don't worry, we'll be gentle with you!'

I guessed arrangements would be more basic on the Cap Beatrice.

15. The Tasman Sea

July 6 – 9

Why I needed to be aboard five and half hours before the ship sailed I never discovered. The third officer gave me a New Zealand Passenger Departure Card to fill in and showed me to my cabin. Then he left me on my own. I hoped no one would ask to see my medical certificate, because I hadn't got one. I'd been allocated the third engineer's cabin.

Through my porthole I watched the loading process. The basic shape of a gantry crane is a bridge consisting of a horizontal platform supported by two vertical columns that move on parallel tracks along the quay beside the ship. The platform, known as the gantry, is extended by means of an arm above the ship. When the arm is not in use it is swung up until vertical, making the crane look like a vastly oversized giraffe. The gantry contains a track on which a car runs back and forth, while from that car a lifting system is suspended, which can raise or lower a 'grabber' capable of picking up loaded containers. A fleet of feeder trucks bring the containers one at a time and place them on the quay for the crane to collect. The grabber lifts a container, raises it high, and carries it away from the shore until it's in the right position to be lowered accurately onto the deck or added to a stack of containers. A foot in each corner of the underside of the upper container engages with a peg sticking up from each corner of the upper side of the lower container – like Lego® bricks, but with the bumps in the corners. The whole process is controlled by a single individual high up in a cabin suspended just under the gantry. The cabin has a glass floor so the operator can see what he's doing. I find it difficult sometimes to park a car (an operation normally confined to movements in two dimensions not three) so I can only marvel at the skill of the crane operator.

You may have known all this but do you know how fast they work? I timed the procedure. A single crane loaded a container every 80 seconds, that is 45 containers in an hour. As far as I could make out, the only factor that ever slowed this relentless programme was a delay in the arrival of the feeder trucks bringing the containers to be loaded.

This research made the time go quicker for me. At 12.30 someone called me for lunch and led me down two decks to the dining room. I found that I was the only passenger. Three places had been laid on a table that would have taken eight. Nobody said anything to me. I turned to the guy next to me.

'Hullo!' I said, 'my name is John. I'm the passenger.'

He still didn't say anything. Maybe he didn't speak a word of English, but surely he could have smiled or given me a friendly grunt. The officers, I knew, were Russian. A few words in that language would have been better than nothing. I don't know who he was. The third person, further down the table was in a trance. He didn't eat anything. He didn't say anything – not even to the person who hadn't said anything to me. Some pleasing soup was on the table in a metal tureen with a lid to keep the heat in. This was followed by a piece of roast chicken with a few delicious little potatoes and a dessertspoonful of runner beans. There were jars of pickled beetroot, red cabbage, gherkins and black olives. The guy next to me took almost all the olives, repeatedly and rapidly dipping his fork into the liquor. I managed to get four olives for myself using my fork but then, after 'Olivier' (as I decided to call him) had finished, there were far fewer to aim at and he was more practised than me. The dessert was billed as 'fresh fruit' – in practice an orange. The guy next to me took two oranges and left. It was a cheerless meal. I imagine Trappist monks have more fun.

Back in my cabin I left my door open in the hope that someone would come in. I began to list the colours of the containers I could see. While shades of red were the most common there were many other hues. I continued to add to my inventorial palette by viewing containers on the quay or on other ships. This was the final list:

white
pale grey
deep yellow
buff orange
brick/terracotta
dark red
chocolate
dark green
French blue
Prussian blue.

The neat stack of containers in randomly assorted colours with no space between was an artistically pleasing sight.

After an hour or so I saw the Chief Officer standing in the doorway.

'Have you eaten?' he asked.

'Yes, thank you,' I said, 'when is dinner?'

'17.30.'

I expect I looked surprised.

'Breakfast 7.30, Lunch 12,' he concluded.

'Thank you.'

With that timetable the ship would have made a good old people's home – and burials are easy at sea. I stayed in my cabin as I knew I'd be called to see Customs and Immigration. I lay on my bed and played the alphabet game. Somebody (it had to be me) names a category – in this case it was 'places in the world' – then you have to think of one beginning with A, two beginning with B and so on. I had 'Auckland; Birmingham, Brazil; Canada, Coromandel, China … and so on. I fell asleep before I'd completed 14 places beginning with 'N'.

At 2.45pm the telephone rang. Customs and Immigration wanted to see me. I handed in my completed departure card. The officer looked at it, then up at me.

'Six days in New Zealand,' he said, 'and it rained every one!'

'I hadn't realised that,' I said.

Once I'd been 'done' I went out onto one of the decks. It had been raining and the surfaces were wet. The sky was grey. The mountains were becoming invisible. The cranes stood close together in the 'giraffe' position. The mist thickened until the mountains disappeared altogether. Cap Beatrice moved sideways away from the dockside. Then, as we steamed forward, the four 'giraffes' looked magnificent and the mountain reappeared. As we accelerated, a wash developed, bigger than that of the Tikeibank, but then the Cap Beatrice was a bigger vessel.

The third officer took me through the safety procedures. He was conscientious and made sure I signed against all the items he covered, but when I asked questions he became impatient.

'I've got to see the other passenger,' he said.

'There's another passenger?'

'A groom – a horse groom.'

I'd paid 765 euros for a three-day voyage on the ship. I had no rubbish bin, no tea-making facilities, I couldn't use the lounge and I had to have my dinner at 5.30! I went down to the dining room to see if I could get a cup of tea. These things are only important when you're bored. There was a box of teabags and a coffee machine but no kettle and nobody to ask. At dinner there was a man with a T-shirt saying, 'born to be wild'. I wondered if he was the groom.

'Hullo!' I tried.

I found him a glass of water. He gave a minimal response. He helped himself to both rice and potatoes. I didn't blame him – the other vegetables were in short supply.

'Tea?' the steward offered me.

'Yes, please. No milk.'

'Sugar?'

'No, thank you.'

'Honey?'

'Yes, please. I'll have it on some bread. Dinner is very early on this ship.'

… and a one-course dinner at that – if you didn't count the bread and honey. I hoped I would lose weight. So different from the British sense of style and conviviality aboard MV Tikeibank! You had to arrive at the dining room early because the food was all put out at the beginning of the meal, on plates on the table. A man of about 50 came in and sat at the other table.

'Hullo!' I said.

He said the same in Russian – certainly no more. I'd had a slice of bread with the cooked food and two slices with honey to fill me up. The honey improved the bread, which appeared German, solid and on the stale side. The tea was great.

The third officer, who'd been responsible for my induction, came in and spoke in Russian to the man of 50. He didn't speak to me, even though I knew for a fact that he had good English. He didn't even look at me. There was no small talk on the ship; indeed there was little of any size. It occurred to me that no one had shown me round the ship or told me what facilities I could use. Imagine crossing the Pacific, I thought, on a ship like that! When I was back in my cabin a man I hadn't met before brought me a table lamp with suckers so powerful that the appliance would have survived the Poseidon Adventure.

At breakfast next morning the steward offered me bacon and fried egg. For the first time somebody spoke to me on a matter other than the business of the ship.

'Your first time in New Zealand?' he said.

I guessed it was the groom. His hair was nearly as short as mine. His face was craggy, with the strong colour of someone who led an outdoor life.

'Yes,' I said. 'Unfortunately I'd only six days. But I did see the Coromandel Peninsula – wonderful! But I have to get to Australia to see some people before they leave. Are you going there?'

'Yes. With the horses. I've just been feeding them.'

'Were they all right?'

'Yes. It's calm.'

'Where are the stables? All I've seen is containers. They're not in a container?' I smiled.

'Yes. They're closed in, partly – but when they're on board you open it up and they can see out.'

'How many have you got to look after?'

'Only five this time.'

'Is this your job?'

'No. I'm a farrier. I'm doing it 'cause the usual guy's in Japan.'

'And the horses – they just stand there?'

'They're fairly confined, but they're happy standing for three days. It's not stressful.'

'You'd know?'

'Yes, they'd be sweating. For longer distances they fly.'

How wonderful to have someone to talk to! When I'd nearly finished my bacon and eggs I saw that the Russians were having something else. I looked at the menu on the wall and saw it was buckwheat. Also on the menu was muesli. I would have had that if I'd known. The horses were getting more personal attention than me!

When I went into my cabin I saw that someone had been busy – made my bed, tidied the place up, moved the lamp to a new position, produced a folder of papers for me to read, put non-slip mats on the bedside table and given me a blanket. The ship wasn't so bad. I didn't feel neglected any more. They'd even hung up a pair of overalls for me! Then I realised I was in the wrong cabin. I shot out. Luckily no one saw me. I'd blundered into the electrician's cabin. Supposing I'd started to look at those papers and someone had caught me? I'd have been arrested as a spy. From what I'd seen, the officers didn't have much in the way of a sense of humour.

From my cabin I could see the horse container – a new meaning to the term 'horse box'! It was green and bore the legend 'SEAHORSE' in large letters. The upper half of one side had been lowered and I could see the animals over the top. It was like a stable with six stalls in a row. Someone was tightening the stays holding the containers – ready for the 10-metre waves we could expect on the Tasman Sea!

I went out onto a little deck on the port side. A fine sight was a lone yacht, its sail bright white in the sun. I could clearly see islands and headlands – most picturesque. We followed the coast for 300 miles.

After lunch I went back on deck. Now I could see high cliffs and attractive beaches. I tried to work out where we were. I pulled out my little hiking compass but I wasn't sure if the metal of the ship was deflecting the needle so I looked at the sun. It didn't make sense – the sun was in the North! Then I remembered that we were in the Southern Hemisphere. The sun had every right to be in the north. I expect people in Australasia relish a 'north-facing garden'. The other weird thing is that the sun moves anti-clockwise. A European sundial wouldn't work. But then a sundial built for the Southern hemisphere would look very odd. Nine o'clock would be where you'd expect to find three o'clock – and vice versa! You'd have to view it in a mirror to tell the time – and then the numbers would be back to front!

I went back to my cabin to read. I fell asleep and when I woke up a bottle of water was rolling across the floor from side to side. I went to rescue it and found myself running downhill into the wall of the cabin. I put the bottle somewhere safe, knelt on my sofa and looked out of the porthole. The stacks of containers were rising and falling, tipping one way then the other. There was a solitary stack four containers high. The top one was so elevated that from my viewpoint it seldom dipped below the horizon and therefore blocked my view. This container hadn't been lashed down. Even the cushions on my sofa were held in place with Velcro. I waited for this one container to leap into the sea but it never did. I pulled the cushions away from their official positions and rearranged them at one end of the sofa converting it into a *chaise longue*. Then I could put my feet up safely, despite the rocking of the ship.

But after a while lolling on my new sofa didn't seem enough so I knelt on it wedging my elbows into the surround of the porthole. The waves didn't look very big but between them were deep round craters the size of a public swimming pool. Again and again, the bow of the ship rose into the air only to plunge down, causing a thick curtain of spray to shoot upwards. At this point the ship seemed to be checked by the sea. And the whole vessel shook. It felt as if we'd jammed the brakes on – one thing you can't do at sea. The jolt meant that for a moment the force of the wave in one direction was greater than the momentum of a 39,000-ton container ship in the other. Turbulence on an aeroplane is simply uncomfortable – this was exciting.

Unfazed by this commotion was an albatross, its reflexes as finely tuned as those of a high-wire artist. I know these amazing birds usually follow the ship but I believe it's the wash that attracts them. In these conditions there was plenty of white water at the front of the ship and more than once I saw the creature cross in front of the bow – as if it were doing so for the fun of it, swinging about like a kite on an invisible string.

I went down to the mess for a cup of tea – to the amusement of the cook and the steward. These two were Filipino – warm and friendly. They helped me make three-fifths of a mugful of the essential beverage. The steward encouraged me to sit in an armchair. I saw that the coffee table was held tight to the sofa with a length of elastic. I think the bigger pieces of furniture were fixed to the floor. A long calendar was swinging on a coat hook. I picked up a newspaper. I read the pictures and looked at the words. I know that's the wrong way round but this was a Russian paper.

'Do you want to watch a movie?' the cook asked.

'What is it?' I asked.

'Here.'

He drew me into the crew mess. Nine Filipinos were sitting in front of a television screen. The cook offered me a seat and left the room. The film had already started. It was a story of the sea. You would have thought the jolly tars would have had enough of such a setting. The crew mess had a dartboard. On a sofa I saw a guitar. What a life, being stuck on a ship for months on end! But if there's no work at home … The Filipinos didn't take their eyes off the screen. It was an American film about a sea-rescue training school. We saw men being lowered from a helicopter into rougher seas than those we were ploughing through. The Filipinos were obviously following the action better than me. They laughed at things I didn't find funny – when something went wrong or during romantic scenes. They even laughed during a training scene where the grim realities of sea rescue were simulated in a swimming pool and, in the tradition of the genre, an authority figure, being cruel to be kind, overdid it and nearly killed a cadet. It was good to see the *matelots* enjoying themselves – even if their way of doing so was alien to me. They were a hundred times jollier than the Russian officers.

At breakfast the next day I accidentally sat in a new position.

'That's my place!' said the third officer in a voice devoid of charm.

'I beg your pardon,' I said and moved.

Olivier didn't even bother to look up. The third officer tucked into a plate of buckwheat and said nothing more. When he'd eaten half of it he hurried out.

He was either overworked or a workaholic.

I looked out of my porthole to see the farrier busy with the horses. I met him when I went down to the mess for coffee.

'Where are the horses going in Australia,' I asked, 'not for a race?'

'They're being moved to Australia,' he said. 'There's a brood mare, a foal, two are going for harness racing.'

'And they're all right?' I enquired.

'After two days they've got to know me.'

'I expect they're pleased to see you.'

'Yeah.'

'I watched you cleaning them out.'

'Two of the deck hands helped me. They don't have to. They swept and washed the deck. I had a shower after that and felt good.'

'Have you always worked with horses?'

'Yes. My wife runs a riding school.'

'Do you ride?'

'I do, but not much.'

'What do you do when you're not working?'

'I like to stalk deer. I hunt and shoot them. There are too many in the country. Guns are controlled.'

'So New Zealand hasn't got a gun culture like the States?'

'No.'

He finished his coffee.

'We live on venison,' he said, 'and fish.'

'Very healthy!'

'We have lamb sometimes – just for a change.'

I went on deck to sun myself and take the air. The ship had been built in 2007, so this may have been its maiden voyage. Certainly it was in excellent condition. Everything was painted white or terracotta. The third officer appeared.

'How fast are we going?' I asked.

'Twenty-two knots.'

'I thought we were doing a good pace. And we get into Sydney tomorrow evening?'

'Noon.'

'Ah, good. Thank you.'

I'd had a conversation with the third officer! Things were looking up. When I went for my afternoon tea the captain started talking to me from his table. I couldn't hear him so I went over and stood opposite him. I still couldn't hear very well. He had the light behind him so I couldn't read his lips at all. His thick Russian accent didn't help. Eventually I took the liberty of sitting down. The officers didn't wear uniform and I'd only worked out that he was the captain by a process of elimination, although he did have the most assurance. A tall man, he wore a long-sleeved shirt, not tucked into his shorts, which didn't match, and the sort of slip-on shoes you could step into. He looked as if he'd thrown some clothes on quickly to answer the doorbell. His hair was much longer than the others. And unlike them, he had a charming smile.

'We have overtaken another ship,' he told me, 'but we are coming into bad weather. If it's bad in Sydney we may have to wait outside. We were due to arrive in the evening but they say they've speeded up their operation and we can come earlier. If we're ahead of schedule,' he said, 'we'll divert to view some islands – even stop for a few hours.'

'I appreciate your taking me,' I said, 'for a short segment of the voyage.'

'We are a commercial operation. Time is money. We have to sail in bad conditions. I don't want an old lady of 75.'

'She might break her leg,' I suggested, to keep the conversation going.

'It's a new ship, but we got scraped coming through the Panama Canal.'

'I came from Panama to Auckland on MV Tikeibank.'

'I know the Bank Line – old Russian ice-breakers. We are not geared up for passengers.'

'I appreciate your taking me,' I repeated

'It's fine for three nights.'

He asked me where I was heading. He seemed to be as glad to talk to me as I was to talk to him. His temperament was quite different from the other officers. Maybe he found them as heavy-going as I did. Perhaps he wasn't Russian. He asked me about my plans. I made the mistake of saying that Australia was a big country. Coming from the United Kingdom that's how it seemed to me.

'It's four-fifths of the size of the United States,' I said.

'Australia is not a big country. Russia is a big country!'

I knew then that he was definitely Russian.

'Ships do go from Australia to Hong Kong,' he assured me. 'Do you want to borrow some newspapers, magazines, books – or videos?'

'I'd be very interested to see the papers, magazines and books,' I said, 'but I haven't got long. I wouldn't have time to watch a video.'

'Come!'

He took me up to his dayroom. It was very bright and airy. He let me have a box of reading matter to take back to my cabin. Everything was at least six weeks old. There were several issues of 'Fairplay – the International Shipping Weekly'. An article said the Chinese container ports were growing fast. By 2015, it claimed, four of the top five in the world would be Chinese (Shenzen, Shanghai, Hong Kong and Qingdao), with Singapore expected to come in at number three. Another article explained that expansion of the Panama Canal had triggered a hike in charges for shipping. There were five issues of the magazine. None spoke of passengers on freight ships, although cruise ships were mentioned twice.

At dinner I made Olivier smile by passing the jar of olives to him without being asked. It takes time. They'll be all over me by tomorrow lunchtime, I thought – just as I leave the ship! The steward told me that he and 'Cookie' had worked as a team on another ship. He was now six months of the way through a nine-month contract. He was the only steward on the Beatrice. He showed surprise when I told him there were three stewardesses on Tikeibank.

The next morning there was a rainbow. It was a complete arc beginning and ending in the sea. The sky was such a dark shade of grey that it merged with the violet band on the inside of the arc. I could feel tiny drops of water on my face. I didn't know whether it was rain or spray. I put my arm out. It definitely felt like rain – and the sea was a long way down. Then I licked my arm. It tasted salty. So it was spray after all.

Being at sea is an opportunity to think. I imagine it's nearly as good as a desert for contemplating one's place in the universe. I like to think; I do a lot of it. But to feel okay about myself I also need to be active. I was looking forward to Australia. When later we could see land I felt a sense of wonder. The visibility was poor but I could make out a gap in the coast, which must have been the entrance to Sydney Harbour. We stopped and waited three miles from the land. I took the opportunity to finish packing. It had been too turbulent before. Now we had only the up-and-down motion from the rising and falling of the waves, not the effect of riding over them. It was raining now and mist came down. Every now and then a big wave would jolt the ship making its contents shake, including me.

I saw a little boat heading towards us, bravely riding the waves. Sometimes it would dip out of sight leaving visible only the head and torso of the stout soul at the helm. He gave a wave as he came alongside the Cap Beatrice. I didn't see the pilot come aboard but I did see the helmsman of the little boat wave again before turning it to return to the harbour. We had been yawing but after a while I sensed a more purposeful motion, then I felt the ship turning and heading slowly towards the harbour. It was now tossing dramatically. I felt sorry for the horses. As we got closer I could see the 'giraffes' waiting for us in the rain. Once we were in the channel, the sea became calmer. I heard a clanking noise. It was my friend, the farrier, emptying the horses' drinking buckets onto the deck. Two tugs appeared and between them they turned us round and began to pull us in backwards.

I saw the green 'SEAHORSE' container lifted into the air as it was. A chestnut head with a white blaze was moving about as if the animal was bewildered. I'm sure I would have been. Bored with waiting to have my luggage checked, I sat in my cabin doing the Sudoku puzzle in one of the newspapers the captain had lent me. He said he'd have them collected. I had the sense to leave my door open and after some time the Captain himself came along the corridor and spotted me.

'When are you leaving the ship?' he asked.

'When they let me,' I replied. 'I was told to wait in my cabin, to have my baggage checked.'

'What for?'

'I don't know – animals?'

'Do you want to have dinner on the ship?'

'Thank you, but I've got friends to meet.'

He came back in a few minutes.

'I think they've forgotten about you,' he said. 'I'll call the bus for you.'

I thanked him and when I saw the farrier I shook hands with him. I handed the keys of my cabin to the first officer and started down the ladder. I was about to enter a country I was particularly keen to visit.

16. Australia

July 9 – August 12

The port bus dropped me at the immigration office. I showed my passport to a man behind a desk.

'Welcome to Australia!' he said in a matter-of-fact manner, 'Can I get you a cab?'

'That's kind of you,' I said. 'I want to ring my friends. Where's the nearest telephone?'

'Oh, there's no phone around here. You can ring from here if you like.'

He dialled the number for me.

'There's no reply,' I said. 'May I ring their mobile number?'

'Go ahead.'

I spoke to Mary. I knew she'd be getting the dinner ready, so I told her I would make my own way to her house.

'Shall I call you a cab?' the immigration officer offered again.

'Yes, please. I'll need to get some cash. I've only got US and New Zealand dollars.'

He rang the taxi company.

'Gentleman has got US and New Zealand dollars, needs to stop at an ATM. That okay?'

He put the receiver down.

'Be about ten minutes. Wait at the gate. I'll you show you what it looks like.'

He brought up a picture of the gate on his security screen.

'Thank you very much.'

'No worries!'

What a friendly and helpful welcome! The taxi-driver took me to a filling station for money and then to Balmain, one of the more central suburbs of Sydney, where Simon and Mary had rented a pleasant house in a quiet, tree-lined street. It was lovely to see them and the little girls. I gave the purse I'd bought in Panama City to Rosie and the elephant to Charlotte. Mary made a lovely meal and we drank my New Zealand wine. After the taciturn company on the Beatrice, it was good to be with people who were on my wavelength. Even more, it was wonderful, if a little unreal so far from home, to see my niece, whom I'd known all her life, and to be with family.

I found Sydney as attractive as I'd been led to expect. The irregular shape of the harbour and the hilliness of the surrounding land meant that there was a fascinating view round every corner. One of the pleasantest ways to get about was on the ferries that serve stops around the waterfront. The next day Mary took me and the girls by car to one of these ferries, which carried us across the water to Sydney Opera House. This well-known landmark, stunning from every angle outside, seemed a bit dull once you got inside, especially at a time when there was no performance. We walked to the Botanic Gardens, delightful in their own right but greatly enhanced by views over the water with its ever-present landmark, the Opera House. After a picnic lunch, the girls rolled several times down a grassy slope and I rolled down it once. I hadn't done this for a long time but I remembered to put my arms above my head. I forgot, however, to take the hard objects out of my pocket and they dug in on every revolution. Then we took a miniature train around the gardens, with a commentary by the driver. In a tree was a colony of fruit bats, wrapped in their own wings like parcels, each one dangling from a single claw.

Walking back to the ferry stop we saw a guy balancing on a bicycle on a high stand steadied by five lines held by members of his audience. To make it more interesting, while he was balancing, he juggled an apple, a knife and a flaming torch. Two aboriginal men with a backing tape were performing nearby, one on a didgeridoo, the other on a pair of musical sticks. The didgeridoo-player produced a noise like a whale gargling. The sound was amplified with a microphone placed at the end of the instrument, so it could be heard above the general clamour of a vibrant city and the announcements at the ferry station. Back in Balmain we had coffee and chocolate brownies in an attractive thoroughfare called Darling Street.

Mary and Simon had spent six months in Sydney. He was an Ear, Nose and Throat surgeon who had gone there to work and study with a professor who had pioneered cochlear-implant surgery in the City. I was visiting during the couple's last week and I helped them clean the house they had rented, which they were obliged to leave in a high standard in order to reclaim their deposit. The next day, while Mary took the girls to a magic show, I spring-cleaned my room and swept the front and back gardens, also using the broom to get cobwebs off the outsides of the walls. Another day I vacuumed the sitting room, moving the heavy furniture, and I scrubbed the kitchen table.

'I'm a horse,' cried Charlotte. 'You can be a rabbit!'

Mary was most appreciative of my efforts but at that point in my travels these domestic activities made me really happy. I also took the chance to do some personal housekeeping. I went to an opticians and got them to bend back into shape the glasses that had been damaged by the mugger in Colón and I changed my New Zealand dollars into Australian.

I was impressed by Sydney's Taronga Zoo. There were lots of trees and because the zoo was situated on sloping ground close to the water line there were numerous glimpses between those trees of the glorious Harbour. The Zoo had its own cable car to take you from the lowest parts to the highest. Of course the familiar Australian fauna were well represented, but there were lots of creatures I had never heard of, some with droll names like the bilby and the quoll.

We went to a bird show presented by the zoo in the open air, in a small well-raked amphitheatre. Spectacular, slick, colourful, varied, it was quite as entertaining as most shows performed by humans. It featured a stork, an eagle, a parrot, an owl and 'Slammer', a black-breasted buzzard, who could break an egg using a stone in its beak as a hammer. The birds flew very close over our heads. There was a continuous live commentary, presented in the easy, laid-back style you'd expect in Australia.

'Don't duck – the birds will just fly lower!'

There was an informal dinner in a local restaurant so that the whole family could say 'goodbye!' to Simon's professor and the cochlear-implant team, including the Prof's wife (who had helped him to build up the practice by organising and preparing his patients), a young doctor doing research, a technical expert, an audiologist and her partner, who himself had had two implants. Having studied medicine myself I felt completely at home in this gathering.

'I've heard a lot about your work,' I said to the Professor, 'but I wondered what activities you have to help you to unwind.'

He said, 'Alcohol!'

I hadn't had any family life since March and the five days with my relations brought me joy and contentment. On Saturday 14th July the whole family took me to the station and said goodbye. I set off with renewed spirit for Melbourne, where I could obtain visas for the Asian countries I would pass through.

The train was labelled 'Indian Pacific', after the two oceans it connected. It squeaked continually but the seats were comfortable and the windows big. The suburbs looked good in the sun. The steward took orders for hot cooked lunches and there was also a cold buffet.

When we got into open country, the trees were green and the grass brown, which didn't seem strange to me as it was July – I'd forgotten that it was the Australian winter. Some fields were green; presumably they'd been watered. There were farmsteads and ranches with cattle and horses. After a while the countryside became what I would term 'agreeable'. We passed through woods of eucalyptus. Further on I upgraded 'agreeable' to 'attractive'.

We gained enough height to allow distant views for the first time. We came through wild country with bare rock faces to enter wide-open downland. I broke the journey at Goulbourn, because the train from there to Melbourne left at a reasonable hour the next morning. For 30 Australian dollars (worth a little less than American dollars), I got a room with no washbasin, but there was an electric blanket. I had the use of a bathroom and a kitchen.

I went for a walk and found myself skirting a long, narrow field. Without any encouragement from me a horse in this field kept me company, walking with me until it came to the end of its territory. At this point it stuck its head over the fence towards me. As I'm not a horsy person, instead of petting it, I merely photographed it. I went on to a river, where a notice said:

> 'Willows in this area have been poisoned as part of a
> noxious willow eradication programme.
> CAUTION!
> Dead willows could fall without warning at any time!'

It was not clear whether it was the willows that were noxious or the eradication programme. The town was spread out with easy parking, a bit like the small American towns I'd seen. A shop sold 'Real Ugg Boots'. As I didn't know what an *ugg* boot was I went in to ask. A man told me that it was a form of footwear made of sheepskin. There were six pictures showing at the cinema, all of them Australian – a measure of the size of the country's film industry.

It was getting cold. When I got back to my room I switched on the electric blanket and flicked through the TV channels until it was time to go out to eat. I put on four extra layers and went to the nearest place, the Carlton Hotel Motel, which had a bar and bistro. There was a giant TV screen showing a rugby match between the Bulldogs and the Penrith Panthers. On the other side of the bar a window opened onto a betting shop and there were machines in which you could place bets without involving another human. Nine screens showed, among other things, race details, rugby, harness racing and the ancient British sit-com 'Are You being Served?' The wide screens distorted the picture giving rugby players broader chests and the horses longer bodies. To avoid the rugby I went round a corner to an area with seven gambling machines. At one of these a young woman was sitting on her own. A notice read:

> *'Your chance of winning the maximum prize on a gambling machine is generally no better than one in a million. This venue operates a self-exclusion scheme for patrons who may have problems with their gambling.'*

One machine stated that the maximum prize was $10,000. On each of the machines a card said:

> *'Excessive gambling can destroy family and friends. Is gambling a problem for you? CALL G-line (New South Wales) Counselling Service 1800 633 635.'*

So, Australia caters for gamblers in more ways than one!

The barman was talking to the woman, who had broken off gambling to buy a drink. I don't know whether he was counselling her, chatting with her or chatting her up. Then she returned to the machine and settled down to get some more gambling done, with a drink in her left hand while her right hand worked the machine. Her left leg was raised, the ankle resting on her right knee. The toes of the raised foot were resting on the tray where the money would come out if she won. After a while she did win something and moved to the next machine. It was Saturday night. What a sad and lonely business! My own hotel had nine gambling machines. Goulbourn is clearly the Las Vegas of New South Wales.

I was in bed by 9.20. The electric blanket had taken the chill off the under-sheet, but I was glad I'd kept most of my clothes on. I slept well and woke the next morning at 7.30. It was again very cold. I went to the communal bathroom and ran the hot tap. Cold water came out, which got colder the more I ran it. I decided the room temperature was too cold for a cold shower. Luckily I thought of trying the cold tap, which ran hot immediately.

For breakfast I enjoyed free bread, free use of the toaster, free margarine and free instant coffee. If I'd paid five dollars extra I could have had free bacon and eggs as well. An Australian woman came in – very friendly.

'I used to live in Perth,' she said. 'It's warm there. It's cold in Melbourne. We have four seasons. I like that. In Queensland it's hot all the time.'

At the railway station a sign said:

'NGUNANA GANDANGORA

This plaque acknowledges that the land occupied by the Goulbourn Railway Station is a significant site for the Ngunana and Gandangora people and is known as the gathering place for the corroborees and special ceremonies that were held in neighbouring nations. Wednesday 9th July 1991.'

I asked the man at the ticket office for a ticket to Melbourne. He checked the computer.

'Sorry,' he said. 'There are no places. I can let you have a night ticket. A sleeper is $40 extra, first class. If you've got a pillow, you can make yourself comfortable. It'll be all right.'

I hadn't realised that I would have to book. I was disappointed by the thought of travelling at night because I wouldn't see much of the countryside.

'May I sit in the waiting room for a bit?' I asked.

I knew there were two fires there and I needed time to work out how I was going to spend the day. A woman told me that a car had been taken off the train. She said she never booked. She was interrupted by an announcement that the train I had hoped to catch was late. A while after this a railway official came into the waiting room and told me that if I waited until the train came in there might be a place for me. There was. I couldn't imagine this personal service in the south of England.

You see much better from a train than from a bus. It was a landscape to paint, with outcrops of rock, big rounded rocks, rocks grouped like sculptures in a sculpture park, loose stones or a stream cutting deep into the sandstone. There was little in the way of greenery, but there were so many trees that it looked like parkland, except that many of the trees were dead, standing, again like sculptures. Trunks lay dry and grey like dinosaur carcasses, reminding me of the beach at Puntarenas in Costa Rica. The austere landscape changed to winding tracks, fields of sheep and cows, even alpacas, also wild rabbits.

'I've got to change your nappy,' a woman said to her child.

I was pleased to hear her use the British word 'nappy', not the American 'diaper'. This fitted the view I'd left Britain with, that Australia was as different from America as Britain was.

After we'd passed through a place rejoicing in the delicious appellation 'Cootamundra', we found ourselves on a flat plain – so flat in fact that at first I thought it a playing field. Then we came to Wagga-wagga, pronounced to rhyme with 'jog a logger'. From time to time the plain was interrupted by ridges of hills. As we neared Melbourne the hills grew bigger and bluer. Then I saw mountains, under a majestic sky more dramatic than any I'd seen in the Pacific.

When I got to Melbourne I checked in at an establishment near the station known as the 'All Nations Backpackers' Hotel'. I paid extra to have a room to myself. There were two bunks. Each had a duvet cover based on the Australian flag. I slept on the lower bunk and spread my kit out on the top one.

There was a large communal living room with a kitchen at one end, two large dining tables, a bank of four computers, some long sofas with no cushion and a case of books, many of them graphic novels, very popular with the people from Eastern Asia. I checked my e-mails. I had now agreed with Hamish of Freighter Travel that I would go from Fremantle (the port of Perth) to Klang (the port of Kuala Lumpur). This was considerably out of my way compared with my original idea of going from Darwin to Hong Kong, but I liked the idea of having more land travel and doing less by sea. I was disappointed to miss out Hong Kong, but I would see four extra countries – Malaysia, Thailand, Laos and Vietnam.

On the door of the bathroom a sign said, 'Unisex Toilets'. By way of washbasins there was a metal trough with four pairs of taps and a long mirror above. Beyond the trough were two lines of doors facing each other. I could hear the sound of water striking a hard surface – evidently someone was having a shower. A length of hose snaked across the floor and a middle-aged woman was doing her best to clean the place. She was very serious and, understandably, looked as though she would rather not be doing the job at all. I began to shave at the trough. Next to me a man was shaving his head and face as if it was a single operation.

'This way,' he said, 'I don't have to worry about how long to leave my sideboards! Where are you from?'

'England,' I said. 'You?'

'New Zealand.'

There was one double shower. One night at 2am I could hear a male and a female voice inside.

'Slow down!' the male voice was saying.

'Slow down?' the female voice sounded surprised.

There are adjustments to be made in any relationship.

The next morning I went to the kitchen to make my breakfast. There were teabags, a hot-water dispenser, bread, margarine and marmalade with a few dirty plates and knives on the draining board.

'Where do you get crockery and cutlery?' I asked.

'From Reception,' someone said. 'You've got to pay a $10 deposit.'

I went to Reception.

'What room number?' asked the girl.

She looked as young as the people staying there. I found out later that some of the guests paid for their board and lodgings by working in the 'hotel'.

'210.' I said.

'John?'

'Yes.'

'$10, please.'

I handed over the money. She put a box on the counter and took the lid off. The selection was pathetic, a few oddments, just about enough for one person – no choice at all. Then it dawned on me that the box and its entire contents were my allocation.

'Keep it in your room,' the girl said.

When I got back to the dining table I found myself sitting with a man and a woman.

'My name's Fabricio,' I think the man said. 'This is Matilde.'

'Hi! Are you travelling?' I asked – or some equally fatuous question.

'We're brain surgeons,' the man confided, 'here for a congress. We're from Colombia.'

'Ah, brain surgeons!'

I thought he was pulling my leg but I trod carefully.

'I'm sorry to be surprised,' I said. 'I just thought it was a little strange for brain surgeons to be staying in a backpackers' hotel'.

'It costs us a lot to get here,' Fabricio pointed out. 'I'm working for the equivalent of a PhD. I'm studying the effects of the endocrine system on memory. I gave a talk in the congress – on how memory is strengthened and modified by use.'

They really were brain surgeons! Or at any rate neurologists. I can't remember how the conversation continued except that we agreed that science was morally neutral although Fabricio took my point that scientists had a responsibility to make the public aware of any dangers inherent in the application of a scientific discovery. I later found that, sure enough, five minutes away in a huge stylish conference centre, the World Congress of

Neuroscience was in brain-storming progress.

While I was working on my personal-details sheets, which I would have to get translated for the four extra countries, the guy with the shaven head came in.

'What are you doing?' he asked.

'Well,' I said, 'I'm going round the world and I …'

'What's that costing you?'

'I don't know. All I know is that I'm not overdrawn yet.'

'But you must have some idea!'

'Well, it'll be about £10,000 – but it's spread over seven months. I've got my pension coming in. And I'm not spending the money I would be spending if I was at home.'

At the first opportunity I went on foot to South Melbourne (near the port), to find the office of a company that specialised in obtaining visas for people. It was a long walk but I like to find my own way around and to see the parts of a city that visitors normally miss. It was a crisp, bright morning. I stopped to have a coffee with a chocolate muffin, which was cut in two, garnished with fresh fruit including strawberries and dusted with icing sugar. In the Bay Street Library I found that the company I was looking for had moved, although luckily not far. I did the last bit by taxi. The driver was a cheery fellow. He soon found out that I was going round the world.

'Are you going to Morocco?' he asked me.

'No,' I said, 'Is that where you come from?'

'Yes, I'm studying engineering. We have a saying in our country, in our religion, "Travel is good for a man, but bad for a woman." – it means, if a woman travels, she knows too much.'

'Yes,' I said, 'I understand. People will say that's an old-fashioned point of view.'

'Some of these sayings are very old.'

As I got out of the car, he gave me a warning, 'Be careful in Asia!'

'You have to be careful everywhere,' I said.

When I got to the visa company I made myself known at the office window. The woman went away and then my contact at the visa company, Simon Corcoran, welcomed me and, aided by a wall map of the world, we discussed my route, which countries required visas, the points of entry, the cities I expected to visit, the possible timings and the dates when I would require the visas to run. He explained that visas for different countries had to be obtained from embassies in different cities around Australia.

'We have agents wherever the embassies are,' he said. 'We have to send your passport around to all of them. But we can save time by processing your applications, two at a time in each city. You'll need to get passport-style photographs.'

He made a complicated process seem straightforward. Meanwhile a colleague fetched me a cup of tea.

'My wife made this cake,' he said. 'Would you like some?'

I walked to the bus stop, where I got talking to a man on his way home from work. He said he had a friend who was worried about getting a visa in time. I gave him Corcoran's contact details to pass on to his friend. We travelled into the City centre together. He gave me a running commentary and told me at which stop I should get off.

That night there was a comedy evening in the pub next door to the All Nations Backpackers' Hotel. Because of my hearing difficulties I sat right in the front, on my own. The compère was a beautiful actress of about 29, called Nikki. She told us she had been in a television soap opera. She had a tough attitude but an endearing manner. It wasn't long before she picked on me. I was sitting very near her and I dare say looked defenceless.

'Where are you from?' she asked.

'England.'

'What's your name?'

'John.'

'Excuse me,' she said, 'but you seem, if you don't mind me saying this, mature. What are you here for? To meet Swedish women?'

If I'd wanted to meet Swedish women, I thought, I would have gone to Stockholm, not Melbourne.

'No,' I said, loud enough for all to hear, 'I'm going round the world ...'

'... making friends?' she suggested.

'Yes.'

'Anyone a friend of John?'

No answer.

'You'll have to put more effort into it!'

It was an ambush I had to admire. And she consolidated her victory by using it as an excuse to go into her stock of jokes about England and Englishmen. But it was nice to have the attention – especially as I fancied her rotten. She could have picked on anyone, but she picked on me! It made my day.

Nothing unmasks a silly old buffer more quickly than his misuse of communal toasters. At breakfast the next day I made myself some of the said delicacy. It came up too pale so I put it in again. This time I sensed it was going to be overdone. I could find no cut-out switch and I couldn't get the toast out, so I turned the toaster upside down. At this point the appliance caught fire. So I turned it right way up, put it down carefully, looked for the plug and pulled it out. This, luckily, extinguished the flames. I got the toast out and cleared up the mess. No one took any notice. The toast was just right.

There were three toasters and you had to remember which one you'd put your bread in. Another day I put two slices in one of the three appliances. I got fed up with waiting so, like the other people, I went away to do something else. When I came back my toast still hadn't popped up. I waited a bit longer. This is ridiculous, I thought, the toast will burn. This time the toaster did have a release button so I pressed it. The 'toast' popped up, white as bread.

'Vot are you do-ink?' asked a dainty German girl with auburn curls, looking at me with disgust.

'Oh, I'm sorry,' I said, 'is this your toast?'

'Yes,' she said, without a molecule of humour.

'I thought it was mine. I couldn't understand why ...'

Another German girl had been watching. She indicated two pieces of brown toast lying on the counter next to another toaster.

'Maybe those are mine. I didn't see them. I'm sorry. I thought your toast was mine.'

The more I said, the stupider I must have sounded.

'No, you haf eet,' the redhead said graciously, indicating the white slices.

I thought that if I took these I'd have to put them in again and wait while the girls watched me.

'No, you have it!' I ungraciously said, 'If nobody wants those,' I persisted, indicating the brown slices, which I was coming to believe were mine, 'I'll have them.'

'No, you have those!' the redhead commanded, with all the authority of a latter-day Führer. This was building up into an international dispute.

'No, that's yours,' I protested. 'If nobody wants these, I'll take them. I'm very sorry.'

So I got my toast. I moved away from the counter. The likelihood of a major incident receded, but I felt I'd let the UK down.

There were many nationalities under one roof. Around the table one morning were an American boy; two German girls with fair hair, blue eyes and fresh complexions – you know, the English-rose type; two Korean girls travelling together and a young Vietnamese man, who was there to look for work and at that moment was wetting some instant noodles.

Most were students and English was the common language. Communication was easy but nearly all of my fellow backpackers were 40 years younger than me; many must have been 45 years younger. So I didn't feel I was one of them. The men, generally, had hairy limbs and faces. Even indoors, some affected bobble hats without bobbles, probably knitted by their grandmothers. The girls had thin arms and perfect complexions. In the mornings they were solemn. I guessed they took their academic work seriously and were now taking seriously the challenge of letting their well-washed hair down and doing the mad, studenty things that they had travelled thousands of miles to do. The people from Eastern Asia were smaller and incredibly cheerful.

After breakfast the next day I cleaned the marmalade off the dining table, spread out my maps and worked out a route from Kuala Lumpur to China, colouring it in with an orange felt tip. I hoped someone would ask me where I was going and give me some tips but no one did.

One night I heard a big drunken noise, like a wild party in full swing. I set off for the bathroom to keep my nightly appointment with the plumbing. A girl standing on a bend in the corridor saw me.

'Go back,' she cried to others out of sight round the corner, 'someone's coming!'

I can't imagine anything so shocking that people as intoxicated as they sounded would mind others seeing. What were they up to? Leading a stolen horse? Creosoting the receptionist? Goose-stepping through the All Nations Backpackers' Hotel totally naked? I never discovered. Sorry, reader.

Another night, at ten to four, a woman cried out at what I took to be the top of her voice, in anguish or pain or possibly drunken hysteria. A man shouted. Women screamed. Men laughed. Someone played the guitar loudly and with conspicuous mediocrity. A door banged.

'Ee bah gum!' someone cried out.

'Whoa! Whoa!' from someone else.

'We're out!' from a third.

Loud laughter. The sound of one object repeatedly striking another.

'I'm jealous!' someone cried.

The sound of moving furniture. Of course, it was a Saturday night. Alcohol was not allowed on the premises, but as the pub was next door and alcohol makes people bolder, plenty of the temulent hydrocarbon was smuggled in, even if they'd had to swallow it first. The noise stopped soon after five. I got up at eight. In the kitchen there was a young fellow looking fresh and lively.

'You look ready for anything!' I said.

'You can sleep when you're dead!' he quipped.

On the kitchen floor was a salad of food, milk and broken glass. Two men staying in the hotel were earning money as cleaners.

'You got the short straw!' I said.

'It's not too bad,' replied one.

They'd obviously cleared up after worse nights. In the dining area it was quiet. I sat next to a man of about my age. He was reading the paper and didn't look at me. While I was at the toaster he used my knife. He still didn't speak. 'It's quiet now,' I said, 'not like last night. They're sleeping it off.'

'It was terrible!' he said. 'Where are you from?'

'England. You?

'Brisbane.'

'Just visiting Melbourne?'

'I'm working here.'

'My name's John by the way. What's yours?'

'John.'

A Brazilian couple were at the same table. I'd found out earlier that they lived in Sydney and were visiting Melbourne.

'This gentleman comes from Brisbane,' I told them.

The four of us then embarked on a chummy conversation about the respective climates in Melbourne, Sydney, Brisbane and the South of England. The Brazilians, it turned out, were leaving that day to go back to Sydney. Before they left I got the man on his own.

'What do you do,' I asked, 'if you don't mind my asking?'

'I'm a bass player,' he said. 'It takes time in a new place to make contacts, so I'm working in a restaurant.'

'And your partner?'

'She's an artist.'

One day after breakfast I went to the bathroom because I hadn't shaved. A creepy young man came out of one of the cubicles. There was no else about.

'Do you remember me?' he asked in English with some sort of accent.

'Yes,' I said, 'I saw you yesterday.'

'In the shower – *remember?*'

'In the shower!'

He gave me a look that seemed full of significance, but meant nothing to me. I felt uneasy and as soon as I could, I got out of the hotel. From then on I tried to avoid him. Even in Australia I couldn't relax completely.

I went to a photographic shop to get the images on my digital camera transferred to a CD to send home for safety. The girl who served me appeared to be of East Asian descent but spoke perfect English with a perfect Australian accent. While we were waiting for the process to finish we got onto the subject of my travels. I pulled out a map of South East Asia and showed her the route I had marked in orange.

'Do you know any of these places?' I asked.

'No,' she said, 'not really.'

'Where do you come from?'

'I was born in this country,' she said, 'but my parents came from Vietnam.'

'Have you any wish to go and see the places they knew?'

'No,' she said, as if there could be no point.

That evening, in one of the many restaurants beside the Yarra River, I ate kangaroo for the first time – not a lot of flavour, but very tender if under-done. Outside, on a wide promenade along the water's edge, there were countless lights and flares that from time to time shot up into the night, startling anyone new to the scene. On the opposite side of the river a grand panorama of illuminated skyscrapers was reflected in the water. It was a wonderful place to stroll, even in winter. One night I saw five musicians sitting in a line on the south bank, playing to a dozen members of the public. Two of the players were wearing woolly hats and mittens. The quintet had collected a lot of money in two open guitar cases. I was making a note of this when a guy came up to me.

'What are you writing?' he asked.

'That they've collected lots of money because they're very good.'

'How do you know they haven't been a year collecting that?'

'I can't believe they'd hold onto to it all that time – they'd drink it!'

'Where are you from?'

'England.'

'What are you doing?'

'Going round the world.'

'Where next?'

'Adelaide, Perth, Fremantle, ship to Malaysia.'

'Good on you, mate!' he said, slapping me on the back.

Later I saw a crowd of 50 or 60 had gathered to listen to the quintet, some of the audience singing along. A person had dropped a $10 note in the guitar case. Another time there was a man dressed as 'Superman' juggling five balls. He threw one very high, caught the other four, did a backward somersault, started the four balls off again and when the high ball came down he caught it, continuing to juggle all five as if nothing had happened.

One day in front of the State Library I encountered a flock of bright pink birds perching in a single tree. Some small brass standards, most of them with brass cockerels on top, had been arranged on the ground in the form of the number 1983. Someone had attempted to light a lot of tea-lights but it had been too windy. There were luminous rings, which would glow later when it was dark. Some brown-skinned people (not aborigines) were handing out leaflets. A brown woman sang, but nobody clapped when she finished. Another, with an Australian accent, handed me a small card saying, 'In memory of Black July'. There was a black ribbon attached. A banner said 'No protection for Tamils in Sri Lanka.' A man handed me two leaflets. He explained that a lot of Tamils had come to Australia in 1983. Since the riots in that year 70,000 Tamil lives had been lost.

'What are the pigeons for?' I asked.

'Oh,' he said, 'they've got nothing to do with it!'

In Flinders Street, just round the corner from the All Nations Backpackers' Hotel, was a café where they looked after me while I was in Melbourne. At a big square table in the window where the light was good, I'd sip coffee and read a newspaper called 'The Age'. The arts coverage was good. The paper also questioned those issues on Australia's conscience, such as aspects of the country's history and its treatment of its indigenous peoples. One day I saw an advertisement in the 'Community Classifieds' of 'City Weekly' promoting the services of a '24-hour brothel'. In a periodical called 'MCV' I found this:

4 THINGS YOU NEED TO KNOW ABOUT
SEXUALLY TRANSMITTED INFECTIONS

1. Use contraceptives and water-base lube when fucking or being fucked to reduce the risk of getting or passing on sexually transmitted infections.

2. Because STIs may also be transmitted by oral sex, fingering or arse play, condoms cannot provide complete protection against infections.

I'll spare you the other two items. 'MCV', I discovered, stood for 'Melbourne Community Voice' (the 'community' in question apparently being Melbourne's male gay community). The paper evidently celebrated an Australian's right to call a spade a sodding sod-lifter.

I was impressed by a government-sponsored campaign promoting the government-funded vaccine against cervical cancer, which for a limited time was being made available to women aged 18 to 26 and girls aged 12 to18 who weren't at school. The campaign was advertised on billboards and free postcards. It featured black-and-white photographs of attractive and vital-looking young women with the words, 'Join the fight against cervical cancer,' and on each bare upper arm a pink plaster (the only colour on the whole thing) declared, 'I did'. The women, who were not professional models, were named and their occupations were given – client administrator, pro surfer, music journalist, TV presenter, public servant, 'uni' student, waitress. I bet that when, a decade ahead, the year-by-year incidence of cervical cancer in Victoria is published there will be a kink in the graph following this campaign.

I knew I would be a month in Melbourne, waiting for my visas. While I was there, I treated the city as if it was an arts festival I'd stumbled on. It certainly felt like that. The festival atmosphere was emphasised by the fact that the City Circle Tram, which operated in the centre, was free – no ticket needed. A recorded commentary told you what was going on in each area visited. A real film festival started before I left and I caught two films. I went to the theatre five times. I enjoyed every show, but, considering that, as we have seen, Australia is the home of plain speaking, I was disappointed that 'Menopause – the Musical', performed by four feisty climacterical women, was mostly about middle age in general and contained nothing on hot flushes, osteoporosis, HRT or the bittersweet pleasure of throwing away your last tampon.

I particularly liked the Malthouse Theatre, a little way out from the City's cultural heart. Like many successful theatres the use of the building was not obvious from the outside and I had difficulty locating the entrance. Once inside, I found myself in a large and lively foyer, which merged with the bar, restaurant and box office. The ambience was enhanced by a long parade of back-lit coloured photographs showing current and recent productions. At times it was thronged by the audiences of all three performance spaces. There were attractive young people, interesting middle-aged people and arty types of all ages.

The play I saw had a single character, played by one Neil Pigot. I managed to catch hold of him when he came out into the auditorium afterwards.

'Excuse me, I'm from England. I just wanted to say ... great play ... and your performance was wonderful.'

'Oh,' he said, 'thank you very much.'

'Well, I know it's nice to get some feedback – especially early on in the run.

There's a lot going on in Melbourne but I'm glad I caught this one.'

'Thank you for finding the time to come and speak to me. Are you enjoying Australia?'

'I'm having a marvellous time.'

The Royal Shakespeare Company with Sir Ian McKellan was at the Arts Centre on tour from Stratford-on-Avon. I couldn't get in to see Sir Ian's 'King Lear' but I had the pleasure of seeing him play the much-smaller part of Sorin in Chekhov's The Seagull, with great presence and delightful humour. Frances Barber was eminently watchable as Arkadina, doing what actors always seem to enjoy, playing another actor on the stage. But the production and the ensemble playing of the whole company made me proud to be British. The director was Trevor Nunn and I enjoyed the bonus of spotting him in the interval, looking a little agitated, presumably because it was the first night in Melbourne. I then sat down to read the programme. Next to me were a young Australian couple.

'Do you think it was really Romola Garai,' the man asked, 'or were they using understudies?'

'Well,' I said, 'I was sitting in the second row and I could see the actress's face. I'm pretty certain it was the girl in the programme.

'Was there too much laughter?' he asked.

'You mean – from the audience? The RSC have certainly brought out all the comedy. It's an awkward play but I think they've done well to bring out the comedy. Nobody laughed in the serious bits, the poignant bits.'

I was flattered that they were consulting me, but more than that I liked the straightforward way they came out with their questions. You wouldn't expect that in England.

A marvellous travelling exhibition on The Great Wall of China included atmospheric wide-angle photographs, some 10 metres across, and films made with actors (Chinese, I assumed) charging about in period costume, which brought the history to life. The Wall was built over a period of 2,000 years from 300 BC – it took two days to build a section no more than three metres long.

Did you know that the Chinese invented iron casting, the crossbow stirrup, the horse-trace harness, the seed drill, the wheelbarrow, the abacus, the ship's compass, porcelain, paper, steel, printed books, paper money, matches, gunpowder, firearms, brandy and whisky? I learnt all that without going to China! Admittedly I had to go to Melbourne, which is further from England, but I was going there anyway. A Chinese guide told me not to worry about the language when I got to China. She said some notices are in English as well as

Chinese. I had a map of China with me and spread it out on a table in the café afterwards, inducing several people to come and talk to me. This time the trick worked.

John from Brisbane recommended the Rialto Observation Tower. On a clear, bright morning I set aside my fear of heights and took the lift up 55 stories to the top. Months afterwards, I feel panicky just writing about it. The lift was in the centre of the skyscraper and you stepped out onto an observation deck offering a 360° panorama of the city. For some minutes I kept well back from the glass walls. I sat at a table in the café to collect myself. I didn't look at the view, just at the other people. Much of the time I had my eyes shut – not what you're supposed to do on an observation deck! Meanwhile children were rushing about fearlessly, which didn't help.

'Imagine if you fell … !' a little girl cried.

'Please!' I moaned pathetically.

I made myself go all the way round. The views were exhilarating. The narrow streets with their tiny cars, the model gardens, the toy railway lines, the miniature seagulls suspended over the little river, a lake and the sea – all looked like an aerial photograph that had magically come to life. The shadow of the building I was in stretched across the next block, over railway lines and beyond the river.

In time I crept towards the glass. You could see even more – if that was what you wanted. A man with a kind, intelligent-looking face asked me to photograph him with the view. I got him to take a picture of me.

'Where are you from?' I asked him.

'Poland,' he said.

'I'll be going through Poland.'

'Krakow is beautiful.'

'Are you visiting Melbourne?' I asked.

'No, I'm working here, but I miss my home.'

Our conversation made Poland seem more real and more appealing to me.

'How long have you got?'

'One week to go.'

'It's not so bad for me – I'm English. You speak very good English, but it's not your first language.'

'Not just culturally,' he said, 'but physically it's a long way.'

One place in the tower I would not go was into either of two metal cages outside opposite corners of the building. The idea, I think, was to let you feel the fresh air, presumably very fresh, and to let you take photographs not through glass. Each cage had a double set of doors like a walk-in aviary, in order to keep the wind out of the main, glazed area of the observation deck. People were gaily stepping through these doors and hurrying to the outer edge of the cage. There was a sheer drop of 250m, with nothing beneath the floor of the cage because the sides of the main building were perpendicular almost all the way to street level. A mesh up to chest height, vertical bars from floor to roof and a mesh under the roof were there to stop people committing suicide – or murder!

'WARNING!' a notice said. 'You must not throw, drop or release any object whatsoever from this building. People below could be seriously injured. If you break this condition of entry you will be removed, prosecuted and sued for the full amount of any damage caused.'

... and presumably not allowed back onto the observation deck.

The café was run by a lone girl.

'What's it like working up here?' I asked.

'Oh, I love it,' she said.

'Does it give you a good feeling, that amazing view?'

'Not particularly. Some days I don't look out of the window at all.'

'I keep back from the glass,' I said. 'I don't think I'll manage to go into the cage.'

'It was a month and a half before I dared to go in the cage – I've got a bad head for heights,' she explained.

I wondered if the subject had come up in her job interview. I loved being on the viewing deck and managed not to think too much about how they built the tower in the first place, or how they cleaned the outside of the glass. I had lunch on the deck and after a particularly relaxing time choosing postcards I calmly walked to the door of one of the cages, opened it, stepped out, went through the second doorway and suddenly found myself in the cage after all! The air was wonderful, but desperately real! I heard the noise of a train, way, way down below. I kept well back from the outside bars, shot a few glances at the view and after a minute came back through the double doors. I rewarded myself with a mug of hot chocolate. I was so pleased that I smugly told the girl who ran the café what I'd managed to do.

'I haven't got a month and a half like you had,' I boasted, 'It was today or never!'

She probably felt like pushing me through the unbreakable glass. I saw a man cleaning the inside of one of the windows.

'I suppose people put their hands on the glass?' I said.

'Yes,' he replied, 'we clean it twice a day.'

'Do you have to clean the outside as well?' I asked out of badness.

'No – somebody else does that.'

If I could do one minute out in the cage, I thought, I could do two. So, allowing time for the chocolate to settle, I went out there again and stayed for 120 seconds. After half an hour to recover from that, blow me down (an unfortunate idiom in the circumstances) if I didn't go out and stay out for four minutes. The wind had got up. I believed the tower was swaying. I spent most of the time looking at my watch instead of the view. When I was safely back on the main deck and had got myself together again I wrote in the 'Visitors' Comments' that the experience had helped me to confront my phobia. It had cost only $14.50. As therapies go it was excellent value.

Another day I joined a party of young backpackers on a minibus trip to Great Ocean Road, a popular tourist route along the coast west of Melbourne. It must be one of the great coast roads of the world – with beautiful beach after beautiful beach. The driver gave the sort of laid-back commentary you would expect in Australia. I struggled to hear it over the noise of the engine, the radio and the backpackers talking. The first stop was Bell's Beach, a long-famous surfing beach, still used for competitions although the driver said the surf was unreliable. In a tourist park we saw wild koalas in the trees. While we were having lunch there was a burst of excitement. A mother koala, with her baby clinging to the fur of her belly, started crossing a road within the park. She stopped, sat down in the road and looked about her. Suddenly a pack of tourists with cameras were moving in on her like paparazzi. She got up and moved on, the little one climbing onto her back. Then she made for the main road. Luckily someone had the sense to head her off and thus a tragedy was averted. Outside the café where we had our lunch, parrots and crimson rosellas perched on some of the tourists while other people took photographs. Later I saw an eagle hovering above a field. We were taken to a temperate rain forest. It was a bit like a tropical rain forest, but cooler, of course.

The highlight was the 'Twelve Apostles' a group of rock stacks standing in the sea. The number has varied over the centuries with the progress of erosion but I don't think there have been twelve since they were named. That was a bit of marketing licence. At all events the 'Apostles' must constitute one of the most photographed geological features in the world, and much easier to snap than the Grand Canyon.

We were lucky to be there when the sun was very low, making the water glitter and the whole scene glow golden. Few of the tourists were actually looking at the Apostles, but everyone was photographing them. The accepted practice seemed to be to have your companion stand in front of the view while you took a photograph of both. This would prove that he or she had been there. Or you got a stranger to take you with the view, trusting him or her not to run off with your camera. Personally I wouldn't show my photographs to anyone who wouldn't be prepared to take my word for it that I'd been there. Luckily I didn't have a companion so I dodged between the tourists trying to photograph the scene unsullied by human figures. Once or twice I crawled along the ground between photographer and human subject, so that I wouldn't mar someone else's picture. This invariably made the companion laugh.

We came back to Melbourne on a main road inland.

'Anyone want to watch a movie?' the driver asked.

I couldn't think of anything worse, but half a dozen people said 'yes'.

'Who wants to watch "Spiderman"?'

Three or four voted, 'yes'.

'Who wants to watch "Shrek"?'

Five or six opted for this – probably because they didn't want to watch 'Spiderman'.

'Who'd like subtitles?'

Someone said, 'yes'.

In the event we had Chinese subtitles, so I hope that helped somebody. It helped me because I didn't want to know what the characters were saying. I moved to the back of the bus and watched the sunset until it was over. There was no light to read by. I closed my eyes but kept opening them to find out what Shrek and his donkey were up to. An inglorious end to a glorious day.

John from Brisbane also recommended I visit the Melbourne Gaol, which had been turned into a museum bearing witness to a harsher age, when unfortunates were imprisoned for offences as slight as vagrancy (being without home or money). The museum illustrated Australia's willingness to confront its own modern history.

Modelled on Pentonville Prison in London, Melbourne Gaol was built in the middle of the nineteenth century. Most prisoners began their time on the ground floor with a period of solitary confinement, locked in their cells for 23 hours a day, with an hour for solitary exercise. Each prisoner was given a copy of the Bible. Illiterate inmates were taught to read. Prisoners could bathe and change their clothes once a week and attend chapel each Sunday. They were forbidden to communicate with each other and were required to wear a silence mask whenever they left their cells.

An entire cell block remained in perfect condition. Apart from communal cells for trusted prisoners and those nearing release, the cells were nine feet by five feet (2.75m by 1.5m). We were allowed to enter most of them. Some had stories in words and pictures on the walls – unflinching tales of harsh treatment, racial prejudice, injustice and executions. There was an opportunity to view the paraphernalia of hanging. The process was critical and required skill. The idea was to break the neck quickly. This depended on matching the 'drop' (the length of rope) to the weight of the condemned person – too long a drop and the head came right off; too short and the prisoner died slowly of strangulation. There were news cuttings, photographs and death masks of those executed at the gaol. The story of Melbourne Gaol's most celebrated inmate, Ned Kelly, was told at length but I found that of Ernest Knox desperately touching. He was burgling a property when surprised by the owner. There was a struggle in which the owner was shot dead. Asked at his execution if he had anything to say, Knox quoted the last verse of the hymn 'Abide With Me'.

> 'Hold Thou Thy cross before my closing eyes;
> Shine through the gloom and point me to the skies;
> Heaven's morning breaks and earth's vain shadows flee;
> In life, in death, O Lord, abide with me.'

The gaol was closed in the 1920s. The last prisoner left in 1924.

Towards the end of my stay in Melbourne I found out that John from Brisbane worked for the Government's Tax Department – not something he'd mention at a first meeting. In Brisbane he'd had problems with his lady friend. That was why he'd asked for a transfer to Melbourne. I saw him in the living room of the Backpackers' Hotel talking to a man about his age – or mine for that matter – with long grey hair and a weather-beaten face. The newcomer's name was Paul.

'I've just flown in from London,' he said.

'London, England?' I had to be sure.

'Yes.'

'But you don't sound English.'

'I'm Australian. I lived in England for 17 years.'

'And you've just come back!'

'I haven't seen my wife for that time.'

'Does she know you're back?'

'I haven't told her yet.'

'Don't just turn up on the doorstep,' I advised.

'I'm going to turn up at the Yacht Club.'

'Well, be careful. Someone will tell someone, who'll tell your wife. What were you doing in England?'

'I had a pub.'

'Where?'

'Near Weymouth.'

'I live in Dorset. Whereabouts was the pub?'

'On the Bridport Road, at Portesham.'

'That's just down the road from me.' (In global terms)

'What are you doing in Melbourne?'

I told him.

'Going round the world without flying at all,' he exclaimed, 'that's incredible! Well, it's an amazing journey to Perth. The train goes so slowly you feel you can get out and walk. Perth is the second most remote city in the world.'

'What's the first?'

He named somewhere in the Arctic.

'Vietnam is mad,' he confided. 'It's dangerous! Watch out for yourself. It's crazy. Keep a look out!'

'You've been there?'

'I was there in the seventies – with the Australian Army.'

'Do you mean it's criminal?'

'Amazing!'

'What do you mean by "amazing"?'

'Oh, you should see the tunnels,' said Paul, 'you could hardly get into them!'

'What tunnels?'

'When the Vietcong were there.'

'Since the war,' I pointed out, 'they've built up a big tourist business.'

'Incredibly big.'

In a travel bookshop, I found a guide called 'Let's go – VIETNAM'.

'If you are travelling alone,' it advised, 'don't tell anyone. Try to blend in with your surroundings. Avoid very crowded or deserted places. Don't be in a railway compartment on your own. Have all your valuables and important papers in a wallet under your clothes. Don't accept a drink from a stranger. Be particularly careful on public transport. Criminals can be very cunning, waiting until people are asleep before …'

It went on in this vein. Lonely Planet hadn't mentioned any of these things. Just as I had before Central America, now at the thought of travelling through Asia I vacillated between panic and determination. The day before I left Melbourne I caught Paul in the living room.

'When are you leaving?' I asked.

'It's all gone pear-shaped' he said. 'I was supposed to meet him at Flinders Station.'

'Who?'

'My mate. He needed to have the fare out (from England) in order to get a visa. He hadn't got the money so I bought him his ticket. He was supposed to pay me back when he got here, but I haven't seen him. I waited two hours at the station. I've been round six backpacker places.'

'Is there anyone in contact with both of you?'

'No.'

'Anybody in England?'

'No. I didn't tell anyone I was going to Oz.'

That should have been a warning to me.

'There's someone I can ring,' he said, 'but I need to charge up my mobile and my charger doesn't fit the Australian sockets ... and I can't afford an adaptor.'

'How much does an adaptor cost?'

'About 15 dollars.'

'I'll give you 20 dollars,' I said, pulling out a note.

'I'll only take it if you give me your address and I'll send you the money.'

In the end I *lent* him $100. Later that day he told me that after our conversation he'd got a job as a chef. I never got my money back.

In the afternoon I walked around Fitzroy Gardens. In the middle of the gardens I came upon Cook's Cottage. This was the boyhood home of James Cook, the explorer. The building had been transported from the village of Great Ayton in Yorkshire in 1934 by the philanthropist Sir Russell Grimwade for the city of Melbourne. The cottage was dismantled in Yorkshire and shipped in pieces to Melbourne, where it was re-built and furnished as nearly as possible as it had been in Cook's time. The flag of the Union of England and Scotland was flying in recognition of the fact that James Cook lived before Ireland was brought in to form the United Kingdom. The garden had been constructed again in the style of the period, incorporating slips of ivy that had travelled with the stonework. Concrete paths with wooden edging, however, had had to be laid to cope with the tread of countless visitors. As you entered the cottage you could hear a recording of a dramatization of an imaginary homecoming of James to the Cook household in Yorkshire before his great adventures. The script was corny but the effect was telling.

No doubt a little homesick myself, I sat in the garden and cried, touched by the thought of this decent but ordinary family producing this amazing son, who went on to make three voyages to the South Seas, explore vast areas of the Pacific and chart the coasts of New Zealand and Eastern Australia, as well as pioneering the care of sailors on long voyages. While I was there, two Yorkshire families visited the Cottage and hearing the accent on the other side of the world intensified my emotions.

The shape of the house seemed odd and a guide explained that the original building had been brought over complete but more than half of it was later demolished to make way for a road, itself subsequently removed to make way for the charming Fitzroy Gardens. Also in the Gardens was a model Tudor village presented by the people of Lambeth in London to the people of Melbourne (Australia being otherwise devoid of Tudor villages), in appreciation of those who had sent food to London during the Second World War.

I'd been to a doctor in Melbourne and got a prescription for more blood pressure tablets. I'd collected my visas. I'd bought a through ticket for trains to Perth. I'd booked a berth on a container ship bound for Klang in Malaysia, which would leave Fremantle in ten days' time. I'd enjoyed my stay in Melbourne. If I'd had to leave Europe, I'd have been happy to make my home in the city. But now it was time to head west.

It was an early start. The steward welcomed us aboard the train in jocular form.

'Do feel free to get up, stretch those legs, do a few press-ups,' he coaxed. 'If you use the toilets, make sure you press the "locked" button, which shows "locked" outside and stops it turning into a social event. We'd encourage you to greet your neighbour – not the person you're travelling with, the other person – shake or squeeze their hand.'

So much more relaxed and friendly than the perfunctory safety warnings on an aeroplane. The café on the train was light, cheerful and well designed. It had a partially closed portion like a snug in a pub, which one passenger had taken over as his office, where he was working on a lap-top. I went to the café for breakfast. Ordering at the counter, I turned to the woman after me.

'I love Australian trains,' I said.

She was petite and about 40. In a short conversation I discovered she was also approachable and cheerful. But that's like saying she was Australian. I took my cereal to a table and started eating. The petite woman sailed up to me.

'May I come and talk to you?' she asked.

Now I am turned on by open, direct, confident women, happy in their own skin. I think they must be wonderful in bed. I never had the chance to test my hypothesis in this case, but I did find out that the lady was a 'beauty therapist', now working from home. She was travelling with a younger friend in late pregnancy for a few days' break in Adelaide. When I moved to the regular seats I almost immediately got into conversation with another Australian woman. We started talking cameras.

'They don't come much smaller than that,' I said, taking mine from my pocket.

'Yes, they do,' she said, pulling out something thinner than a pack of cards.

'Where are you heading?' I asked.

'Darwin. I've always wanted to go on the Ghan *(the train that runs North and South through the centre of Australia)*. But I'm flying back. It's a question of time.'

'You like travelling?'

'Yes, I try to spend as much time as possible travelling and as little as possible working.'

'Where have you been?'

'Most places. Show me your route through Asia.'

I got out my Overseas Timetable and a pen to point with. To find a particular map in this worthy guide, you have first to put on your reading glasses, then look at the world map inside the front cover, find the region you are interested in, note the map reference, then refer to the map index in order to obtain the page reference, then turn up the page and check you've got the right map. If at any stage the print is too small, you have to pull your reading glasses down to the end of your nose and look over the top of them. I did all this with my pen in my hand. For some reason I kept opening the book at the map of India.

'Look out,' she said, 'you're drawing on your pants!'

I felt such an amateur, talking to her. She certainly knew her geography. She was ahead of me all the way. She probably wondered if I'd get to Adelaide – never mind about crossing Asia! Back in the café I saw a third woman looking out of the window.

'There's a hill coming up on this side,' I told her.

In Australia any opening gambit will do.

'It's been very flat,' I went on. 'Now suddenly there's this steep hill plonked there. In England we'd call that a slag heap!'

That was pretty blunt, but she came over and talked to me – about travel, of course. It must be the English accent. At lunch I offered a man the sports section of my paper. He'd already seen it. We got talking. There was a dark-skinned woman on the other side of him. She said nothing. When the man got up and went out, she smiled at me.

'You should go to Mauritius,' she said.

'Is that where you come from?'

'Yes. I emigrated to Australia to be with my husband. I'd met him in Mauritius. My life is here now.'

'Have you got any children?'

'I've got two married daughters here and a son. One of my daughters is about to have a baby. That's why I'm going to Adelaide. My son's the youngest. He's getting me down. He's 22, very taken up with himself. He's just broken up with his first love. So he's "depressed". He suddenly came back to live with us. He went out at midnight in the car without telling me where he was going. He came back at five. Of course I didn't sleep. He lies in bed to midday but I have to go work. It's nice to meet someone on a train to talk to, like I'm talking to you.'

She gave me her address so I could tell her when my book was out.

With all these women to talk to I lost track of the time. I was in the toilet when I heard an announcement but not what it said. When I got back to my seat the train had stopped.

'Where's this?' I asked a fellow traveller.

'I think it's Dimboola' he said.

'Oh, that's where I get out.'

I'd decided to break my journey at Dimboola as, apart from Goulbourn, I'd seen nothing of small-town Australian life. I grabbed my bags and rushed to the door. The train manager was there but he couldn't open it.

'We didn't think you were on this train,' he explained.

'So I'm the only person getting off here!' I said. 'Can't you open the door?'

'I can, but I'm not allowed to.'

But he telephoned the driver, who released the door. The train manager and I got off.

'Just a minute,' I cried, 'I can't find my ticket!'

'That's okay,' he said, 'tell them when you get to Adelaide.'

I looked up and down the platform. There was no sign of any staff. We were in the middle of nowhere.

'I don't like to be without my ticket,' I said, 'it goes right through to Perth. Can I get on again, look for my ticket? I'm sorry – I'm holding the train up.'

We were already running late.

'Let me on again – please!'

So he did. Then he telephoned the driver.

'The passenger's not leaving the train – we can go.'

As soon as the train had got up speed, I found my ticket in my lower thigh pocket. I'd put it there because Australian tickets are too bulky for the usual place, but in the rush I'd forgotten that. I agreed with the manager that I'd get off at the next station, Nhill. He rang the driver again.

'Passenger's going to leave the train at Nhill,' he said, 'so we need to stop there.'

'I'm sorry to mess you about,' I said.

'Oh, we've had worse than that!'

'The job would be boring if you didn't have awkward customers.'

'Exactly!'

'What I like about you Australians,' I said, 'is your "can-do" attitude. In England they tell you all the reasons why they can't do something – and *then* they do it! *You* just get on with it.'

'I'll ring the office and let them know that Saturday you'll be joining at Nhill, not Dimboola, but it might not get through to the people on the train.'

'Oh, thank you very much.'

'No worries!'

At Nhill I took a room at the Farmer's Arms, a real single room. It had a washbasin and again an electric blanket. I threw my luggage down and found my way onto the balcony, where I ate an orange in the late afternoon sun. Then I went in search of an Internet Café. This took me to the Nhill Historical Centre where for a small fee I was able to collect and answer my e-mails. The Centre had a room of archives and four rooms of artefacts displayed as a museum. I admired the place and generally chatted up Mrs Scott, the Secretary. She was about to close for the night but she generously offered to open at ten the next morning especially for me.

I dined in the hotel. The dining room was something between a church hall and a private club. There were three or four large family parties, all ages, spread along lengthy tables like a village wedding. The diners all seemed to know each other. On my table was a glass tumbler with wax crayons for children to use. In a place that, as far as I could see, was in the middle of nowhere, it was heartening to be among some eighty people (I was told there were usually more) all enjoying themselves. You could have veal or chicken schnitzel but there was a choice of twelve sauces. I chose 'spinach and béchamel'. The schnitzel, sauce and a helping of chips you collected from a counter. Then from a large hotplate you helped yourself to the tastiest baked vegetables, including peppers and various kinds of onion – all for $12. You got your drinks from the bar. After this cheering meal I sat by the fire in the saloon bar and fell asleep a few times until it was time to go to bed.

Next morning the secretary of the Nhill Historical Centre was waiting for me. The centre had opened in 1980. The archives contained newspapers, paper records and photographs from 1888. Copies of the Melbourne Argus from February 1952 had several whole pages covering the death of King George VI. In the museum I spotted a fife or piccolo that had been labelled 'recorder' so I pointed out the error to Mrs Scott. Other exhibits included:

a baby's cradle from a local family dating from 1900,
cookery utensils including a herb slicer and a cork inserter,
a home medication kit bearing the slogan 'Wawns Wonder Wool relieves pain from snake and spider bites',
jewellery, lace collars and wedding gowns dating from 1860,
a pair of silver shears, 12 cm long, awarded to one William Merrell for 'longest service and cleanest shearer' at a certain sheep-shearing station,
a photograph of nine men standing behind an eight-ton, chest-high heap of half a million dead mice trapped over four nights by a double fencing system.

I was impressed by what had been amassed in less than thirty years. The name 'Nhill' means the abode of spirits (the mists over the water in the early morning were the spirits of the people's ancestors). As I wandered around the town I came across the following statement:

'The Discovery of Nhill from the Aborigine Perspective shows that the explorers Dugald Macpherson and Charles Belcher broke three protocols:
1 They failed to send prior notice before riding into their camp.
2 They entered uninvited – they should have waited at a distance for an invitation.
3 They arrived when the menfolk including the chief were away hunting, which was bad form.

I went to a have a look at the Sun-moth Reserve. This was a small field within a housing estate. It was reserved for sheep and an endangered species known as the Sun-moth. There was a shelter beside the reserve and a raised and fenced-off wooden walkway that cut into the field and led to a viewing platform for the public. I was glad of the shelter because the sun went in and it rained, followed by hail. The roof of the shelter was made of corrugated metal. The rain raining on it and the hail hailing on it made a great racket in this otherwise peaceful place.

The Golden Sun-moth, I learnt from the considerable amount of reading matter displayed, emerges late October to mid-November. Now this was only August, so there wasn't a single moth in residence, but I found myself taking an interest in the critters. Listen to this! The flight period is only three weeks. When they emerge as adults the female Golden Sun-moths are full of eggs and almost flightless and, for want of anything better to do, they sit about on the base of a clump of wallaby grass. Are you with me so far?

The male, unencumbered with eggs, is quite good at flying. When a female Golden Sun-moth sees a male Golden Sun-moth fly above she opens her two fore wings exposing her two hind wings, which are of a bright golden hue, giving the species its name. When a male sees a female flashing him, in this attention-seeking manner, he does the decent thing (or the indecent thing, perhaps I should say) – he alights and mates with her. Once fertilised, the female walks from one clump of wallaby grass to the next depositing eggs at the bases of the clumps. When the eggs hatch, the caterpillars burrow into the soil and feed on the roots of the wallaby grass.

All pretty straightforward and socially conventional! But let me tell you about the Pale Sun-moth. This emerges in February. It has a similar flight period to its golden cousin. But it has a very different lifestyle. Within the State of Victoria the Pale Sun-moth is parthenogenetic. This means that it doesn't only believe in virgin birth, like the Christian Church, it practises the phenomenon, and seems to be pretty good at it. Females produce only females, so parthenogenesis is essential. These females are strong fliers. With no males to impress they just flit about for the fun of it, presumably in a girly sort of way.

'This housing estate,' the notice said, 'is the only place in the world holding an extant population of the Pale Sun-moth'.

Normally, parthenogenetic species are all derived from a clone of a single mother. Genetically all members of the sisterhood are identical. But in Victoria there are five different moth morphs. Meanwhile Fabian Rose, a local expert, was waiting for February when this carefree sorority would come out to play, turning themselves into single mothers without so much as a sneaky visit to the sperm bank. I wouldn't have learnt any of this if I'd got off at Dimboola!

As if I hadn't had enough sex – or lack of sex – for the afternoon I encountered three boys of about ten, flexing their young vocabularies in a garbled version of the birds and the bees that was equally unlikely.

'She kissed us,' cried one.

'She tried to fuck us!' added another.

'She wanted to take us from behind!' said the first boy.

So there you have it – the upside down world of the Southern Hemisphere! I really shouldn't have been surprised to see daffodils blooming there in August.

That evening I went to the cinema. There was no one in the box office but the woman who ran it was standing in the foyer chatting with members of the audience. She told me that they got films six weeks after they came out

'Some people go to Horsham,' she said, 'cause they won't wait – we can't help that!'

It was a multi-purpose hall. Only the circle was open for the film's audience. I took my place in the front row and looked over the barrier to see that 'the stalls' had no seating and were flat like a dance floor. The film was called 'Romulus, My Father'. The Australian rural landscape was beautifully captured. The film was flawed, however, because it had been shot too quickly. The central character, a boy, appeared not to age at all, while in the same time another character was conceived and grew to be at least one. The story, about how the boy was neglected and exploited by feckless adults, struck me as too horrible, so I walked out half an hour before the end.

'I can't take any more,' I said to the woman on duty.

'I haven't read the book,' she replied.

'It may be easier to stomach in the book.'

The TV was showing Australian football. Two guys sitting at the fire were having an argument about the game. I tried to understand how it was played. There were four poles in a row at the end of the pitch, like two rugby goals without crossbars. You kicked the ball to someone else on your side, who caught it, when there was what I would call a free kick or a penalty, while some young people waved giant pom-poms, presumably to distract the player taking the kick. All those playing wore black long-leg pantee girdles (or possibly cycling shorts) under their Australian-football shorts. That's as far as I got. Unfortunately there was chariot racing on the other screen – less interesting but easier to follow. So I kept switching my attention from one screen to the other with little clue as to what was happening on either.

The next morning the town was so quiet that I spent an hour in the Laundromat® without seeing a single other person. I don't know what a person from Nhill is called – possibly a Nihilist. What were all the Nihilists doing that morning? Presumably, nothing. A notice in the Laundromat® said,

'Please do not put horse rugs in the machine.'

So I didn't. I took a pleasant walk over the Nhill Swamp, which is described on the town plan as 'ephemeral'. The swamp certainly didn't look very swampy when I was there but I stuck to the boardwalk just in case. This took me at a raised level to the agreeable Nhill Lake.

When it was time to leave the town, I made sure that I was on the station platform in good time. I could see that the train's approach would be in a straight line. Bearing in mind that the train staff might not know there was someone due to board at Nhill, I positioned myself and my bags in the sun where I would be seen at some distance by the driver. It was the first time I'd hailed a train. As soon as it came into view I stuck my hand out and hoped that it would stop. Immediately the driver flashed a light. I put my hand down. The train slowed to a halt. The train manager was waiting for me. The whole business left me feeling happy and cared for.

As the train came into Adelaide I saw two teenage girls on the platform looking out for someone they were to meet off the train. They were jerking their heads about trying to see who was on the moving train. I started jerking my head in the same way. The girls saw me and immediately took the joke, giving me a wave. I waved back. In how many countries would that happen?

The City was named after Queen Adelaide, consort of King William IV of Great Britain and Ireland (1830-1837). For some reason the rail terminal is outside the City, like an airport. Someone told me which bus to take and someone else gave me a street map. I checked into the Festival City Hotel and immediately went out to find somewhere to eat. The Woolshed looked busy and fun so I went in. I ordered Strezlecki chuck-beef-and-veg stew in a freshly baked cob – a hollow loaf, with the top cut off, then filled with the stew – and, as if that weren't enough, two and half slices of buttered white bread stuck together like a sandwich. A tiny but feisty girl brought it.

'Oh my goodness,' I said, 'there was I wondering if I needed a starter!'

'You've got to eat it all,' she said, 'otherwise we take you in there and spin you around.'

'Oh,' I said, 'that's something to look forward to!'

I went to the counter to look at the menu. On my way back I met Little Feisty.

'What are you doing?' she scolded. 'You're supposed to be eating!'

The Merlot was from Western Australia and very good. When I'd finished, a man cleared my table.

'That was lovely,' I said, 'but the bread and butter were unnecessary.'

When the man had gone, Little Feisty breezed up.

'So you ate it!' she said.

'Yes,' I said, 'I ate the plate as well! Pity – I was looking forward to you taking me in there and spinning me around!'

When I left, I went into the room where the 'spinning' was done. There was an enormous mechanised beast with a smooth and shiny back. Outside I spotted a sign saying, 'The Woolshed – Home of the Mechanical Bull'. I imagine that, with the three glasses of Western Australia Merlot I had inside me, not to mention all that bread, I wouldn't have lasted long.

I had breakfast in the hotel dining room, which was on the first floor and stuck out over the pavement, with windows on three sides and the winter sun streaming in. I spent the day exploring Adelaide like a tourist, looking for things to photograph and getting upset when the sun went in. I bought a Tibetan shawl in the market to send to one of my daughters-in-law. In a park some people were playing a game involving metal balls.

'Are you playing Boules?' I asked.

'Yes,' a woman said, 'or Pétanque'.

'They call it Boules in the North of France,' I said, 'and Pétanque in the South'.

'Do you want to play?' she asked.

'What, now?' I said, getting excited.

'If you'd been earlier you could have played. A woman had to leave 'cause she'd got no partner.'

'What a shame!'

'We play all weathers, even if it's raining and Wednesday evenings we play by floodlight – that's the beauty of it.'

'I'm afraid I'm leaving tonight for Perth.'

I had a look at the Botanic Gardens. Then I walked along the River Torrens to a widening in the river known as Torrens Lake. In the Festival Centre I saw an exhibition of Aboriginal art. I warmed to a picture by Allan Gunter called 'The Heart'. It was a schematic map of Australia, showing cities as blobs with roads all around and in the centre was Uluru (Ayers Rock).

I took one of the local trains from Adelaide back to the terminal where the interstate trains stop. I had to use my wits to find my train in the dark.

Eventually, without going through an entrance, without passing any of the usual facilities to be found on railway stations, without seeing a departures board or any indicator of which trains went from which platforms, I came to a slope, which took me up to the end of a platform.

'Is this the train for Perth?' I asked a uniformed woman.

'Yes,' she said.

I showed her my ticket. She directed me to the front of the train, where a uniformed man met me.

'Mr Barclay? Let me show you your "room".'

After the puzzle of finding the train it was reassuring to be greeted by name. I had a single 'Red Kangaroo sleeper'. The rooms were cleverly fitted in on both sides of a snaking corridor, each room having a wider portion housing a wash basin, mirror, luggage rack and stowage. The washbasin had taps with springs that turned them off. You can't afford to waste water crossing a desert. From time to time there was an audio commentary, which served not only to educate the passengers but to increase the sense that this was a special journey.

The café was like a club. On the train I got to know a woman I'll call 'J'. She gave me some pointers on Perth and Fremantle. She was living in Melbourne but on her way to WA (Western Australia), where most of her family lived around Perth. Her father was dying and she wanted to be with him and to support her mother. She had lived in WA herself but had moved to Melbourne, because she wanted to be around for her third and youngest child while he went to the University. Remember, the distance from Perth to Melbourne is like going from London to Ankara in Turkey. But the son missed his friends, particularly a girlfriend, so he decided to move back to WA. J meanwhile was enjoying life in Melbourne and didn't want to uproot again.

'If you go,' she told her son, 'you go on your own.'

So he did. This was a disappointment for J but nothing compared to the blows she had taken throughout her earlier life. She was very young when she married a man who had seemed decent enough, but he came to resent the fact that she was smarter than him and he began to bully her. She had a daughter and a son by him before they split up. She married a second husband, a mild-mannered man, quiet and supportive and they had a son. But while this child was still a baby, she found out that this second husband had been sexually abusing J's daughter by her first marriage. She bravely took him to court. He was imprisoned. And then she divorced him. The girl, of course was traumatised, but recovered to the extent of being married twice herself, having two children and doing a demanding job. The middle child, however, turned to alcohol and other drugs, eventually heroin. He'd managed to come off this but J knew he could go back to it at any time.

I think she was glad to unburden to me, a stranger from the other side of the world. She might be thought a poor judge of men, but I'd say she was plain unlucky. She was strong and had brought up three children almost entirely single-handed. At every set-back she picked herself up and made the best of her situation. I'm still in touch with her by e-mail.

I slept reasonably and in the morning saw that we were in a flat and barren terrain, which must have been the Nullarbor Plain. If you know Latin, you'll know that 'Nullarbor' means 'not any tree'. Some parts only had clumps of vegetation no higher than heather; others had no vegetation at all. Very occasionally a tree would appear on the horizon like a ship on the ocean. It would grow larger, speed past us and disappear from view. Close to the track the most prolific crop was broken glass, which glinted in the sun. More than once I spotted a sheet of solar panels in the middle of nowhere, sometimes in conjunction with a mast.

After breakfast I was chatting in the restaurant with J and a couple.

'Look – camels!' somebody called out.

And there they were – six or seven, standing or moving about as if they lived there, which clearly they did. Camels had been brought to the country as domestic animals and later released into the wild. I also spotted a wedge-tailed eagle. I was thrilled to notice kangaroos – the first time I'd seen them in the wild – bounding along, graceful as sine waves.

'Kangaroos!' I called out for everyone's benefit and tapped on the window. 'Two on the left side!'

The other passengers took as much notice as if we'd been on a bus going through the London suburbs and I'd called out, 'Grey squirrel there – climbing a tree!'

I got talking to a man in the dining room who was a lawyer. Two middle-aged couples were sitting near us, looking happy just to be there. One of the women was wearing fluffy bedroom slippers made to look like giant bees.

'You'll never guess what those men do,' said the lawyer, '– they're train drivers!'

They were taking their wives on what I have to call a 'busman's holiday'.

'Cows!' cried one of the wives.

This was much more surprising than seeing kangaroos or even camels. I didn't believe her, but later I saw some cows myself as well as a single horse.

We stopped for a while at Cook, a tiny town, isolated and almost deserted.

I had a quick look and then I strode to the end of the train to photograph the dead-straight track disappearing into the distance, part of the 'longest straight stretch of rail track in the world'. When I got back I noticed a lot of people standing close to the train.

'Have you heard the signal for leaving?' I asked.

'Yes,' someone said.

That was a near thing! I might have been stuck in a lonely place without my luggage, waiting half a week for the next train. There was no hotel so I would have had to throw myself on the mercy of the woman who ran the souvenir shop.

Soon after we crossed the border between South Australia and Western Australia, we stopped in a siding to let the other passenger train pass us. It did this very slowly with a guard leaning out with something in one hand, while she held out her other hand as well, presumably to do an exchange with someone on our train, but I can't think of what. There are two trains west in a week and two trains east. Of course, they're the same two trains.

At Kalgoorlie we had a longer stop with an optional coach tour.

'Are you going to go to Hay Street?' people teased me.

Hay Street, I'd learned, was the street of brothels. I didn't know whether this would be included on the tour.

'I'm a writer,' I argued. 'My readers expect me to know about such things!'

It was dark and the driver drove smoothly and spoke clearly but quietly. She reminded us of how under-populated the region was.

'There are 102 police to cover an area the size of New South Wales,' she said.

At some point I fell asleep. I woke up when the bus stopped. I couldn't say to the driver, 'What do we do now?' because I was sure she would have already told the passengers. So I got off the bus, followed the others to a fence and peered through the mesh. On the other side was the biggest dry hole I'd ever seen. It took a minute of staring into this dark abyss before I realised that what I was peering into was actually my first gold mine. In a draughty shed there were information boards explaining the mining process, which was still going on there.

The weather was so cold I was glad to get back on the bus. But the cold air had woken me up and I tried to pay attention. Kalgoorlie is in a concentrated gold-mining area known as the Golden Mile, the richest square mile on earth. Kalgoorlie had had the most profitable gold mine of all time. I think the driver said that at the height of the gold rush there had been 113 hotels in the town and there were now 26. Similarly the number of brothels had plummeted from some large number to three. The driver took us down Hay Street, the location of these establishments, where wanton women had ways of getting their hands on gold without getting those hands dirty. The driver told us the story of a madam who was a woman trapped in a man's body. The money she made out of prostitution was enough to finance a trip to Eastern Australia and a visit to a plastic surgeon, who cut her loose so to speak. There were still plenty of bars and pubs. The place had a dignified vulgarity. I wish I'd been more awake.

Back on the train, after a second comfortable night sleeping on it, we came into a different world, with green grass and mist lying in hollows. After only two days in the wilds it seemed strange then to enter suburbia with houses and gardens. Perth itself struck me at first as old-fashioned, but it's a city on the move with much building development going on. Usually a railway station in the middle of a city acts as a vast blockage to anything but trains, but in Perth there are interconnecting walkways over the tracks making it easy to get from the area known as Northbridge to the rest of the City.

I stayed at the Wentworth Plaza, where I had a room with a single bed and a desk – very important for last-minute preparations before I left Australia. The bathroom had a chequered floor with enough 20cm squares to play draughts, but not enough suitable objects to act as draughtsmen.

The next day I saw a very high skyscraper, which because the clouds were moving away from it seemed to be falling towards me. Perth had a grand river called the Swan. After lunch at a restaurant on the ferry quay, I saw a fin moving through the water like a shark. It turned out to be a dolphin. There was a pelican fishing the same stretch of water and the dolphin continually surprised the bird by coming up under it. The pelican would fly out of the way, only for the dolphin to go underwater and surprise it all over again. After a while I counted three dolphins and spent ages trying to photograph them.

In the evening I went to an Italian restaurant and then to the Blue Room Theatre, where I saw a one-man play performed by an exceedingly tall actor. Because I'd had three glasses of red wine with my meal I fell asleep a few times so I couldn't follow the intricacies of the plot but I enjoyed the bits I saw. I was filling in the guest questionnaire when the lofty actor appeared. I told him the play was unusual because the story – and the play – had a single thread. As I hadn't seen the whole thing I was sticking my neck out. He told me he had recently given up teaching for a full-time career in the theatre. The way he had created work for himself was to set up a production company called 'Flaming Locomotive', find a director, a technical team and a theatre. I suggested he took the play to the Malthouse Theatre in Melbourne, which I'd enjoyed so much.

The next day I decided at the last minute to go to a concert by the Juniper Chamber Orchestra in the ballroom at Government House. The setting was very grand with polished brass chandeliers, a red carpet and large oil paintings on the walls. The ushers were uniformed government staff. I arrived early because I had to buy a ticket. The concert was due to start at 7.30. At 7 o'clock, through two big polished wood doors, we could hear the orchestra having a last-minute rehearsal, which served as a warm-up for us as well as for the players. Most of the audience were smartly dressed. I felt scruffy in my travelling trousers and hiking boots. Luckily the concert featured sculptures by one Greg James. I hoped people would think I was an arty type. In the lobby was a sculpture by James, a life-size figure of a standing woman. To read the label I had to get down on my knees.

'Iris – Greg James. $47,000,' it said.

As you can imagine, I got up very carefully!

At 7.15 the conductor had obviously decided that the orchestra weren't going to get any better and we were let in. Above the platform were two Australian Flags and two I took to be of Western Australia. It was very dim on the platform. I don't know how the back desks of the violins could read their music. The musicians stood to play, even the tympanist. Only the cellists had seats. Most of the players seemed to be in their twenties, the women wearing long black skirts or black flared trousers. The fact that there were few chairs on stage meant there was little furniture to re-arrange when they switched to pieces for smaller ensembles. They took advantage of this mobility in a piece by Telemann in which the various musical voices drop out towards the end. In this performance, one after the other the performers walked out playing.

My ticket to Malaysia arrived, with a date to sail – Sunday 12th August. I exchanged some of my Australian dollars for Malaysian *ringgits*. I went back to the Blue Room to see another play. I was going to be away from western culture for a long time and I needed to 'stock up'.

The next day I went to Fremantle aboard a ferry called 'The Lady Divine'. It must be the happiest way to get to the port. Perth Water, which is wider than the river that feeds it, expands to become Melville Water. The channel is far from straight so the view kept changing. Waterside properties are always pricey and we passed some of the most expensive in Australia. The boat's captain spoke of little else.

When I was exploring Fremantle, I came across the house by the sea of a painter called Andrew Carter. The building acted as studio and gallery. It was open to the public and I went in. He was in the middle of renovating and decorating another room to show either a single work or something of the creative process. He made preparatory sketches and then painted from memory. In this way the buildings and landscapes he depicted took on a surreal quality, hot and intense but dream-like – that is to say 'weird'. Carter said he had travelled by ship when he was young. He was 24 before he flew. He agreed we all needed time to slow down.

I found a didgeridoo shop, which sold some Aboriginal art but otherwise nothing but didgeridoos. A sign said, 'Free lessons'. I thought this a clever sales gimmick. Elizabeth's Bookshop displayed its paperbacks in trays like CDs, with dividers labelled by author in alphabetical order – Amis, Archer, Armstrong and so on.

In Fremantle people like to eat out – even in winter. The weather was much milder than Melbourne. All the restaurants seemed to be in the Market Street area. That evening the atmosphere was terrific. I had dinner in 'Sandrinos'. It was so crowded I had to sit at a long counter in the window and of course I quickly got into conversation with a couple who came and sat next to me. They were in their fifties. It was the second main relationship for both of them. He was stroking the woman's back much of the time. I gave them a bit of my garlic bread. They gave me a bit of their pizza bread and a glass of wine. It was my last dinner in Australia.

At half past seven the next morning I had a bacon-and-egg baguette and half a paper cup of black coffee. Then I hurried to meet the shipping agent. We were joined by Ben, a young Australian with long hair, and Tobias, a tall, thin Swiss, a bit older. The agent took us in his four-wheel-drive vehicle to our ship, the 'Theodor Storm' and came aboard with us. We had to wait in the 'office', while the immigration officers processed two passengers about to disembark. Once the three new passengers had been seen the agent left. The ship wasn't due to sail until the evening but the immigration officers had to go to two other ports and we got the short straw. Thus I had a day to come to terms with the fact that I was leaving Australia, where I'd been so happy that I'd often forgotten to make notes. I looked forward to my last sea voyage, across the Indian Ocean to Malaysia.

17. The Indian Ocean

August 12 – 18

Ben had the fourth engineer's cabin, Tobias the doctor's cabin. Both looked out onto a wall of containers. I was two decks up, very grand in the owner's suite, which had three portholes looking *over* containers to the sea, the way we were going. The suite consisted of a bedroom with a king-size bed, a bathroom and a day room large enough to hold a meeting of all the officers, if the junior officers didn't mind standing. There was a big desk, an L-shaped sofa and a CD player. Fixed to the wall, above the desk, was a list of useful telephone numbers:

the cook
the second cook
the mess boy
the wheelhouse
the first and second fitters
the emergency generating room
the gymnasium
the tally office
the Suez crew
the workshop
the elevator car
the oiler
the wiper
the doctor
the hospital.

On the first day, which we spent in the port of Fremantle unloading and loading, I got to know my companions. Tobias came from Basle. He spoke German, French, Italian, some Russian and very good English. He was a pianist and a teacher in a music school. He was gentle, charming, tall and slim, with long arms and narrow wrists. As we stood on deck, leaning on the rail, he told me that he had got to know an Australian pianist, who went to Europe every year. The Swiss had spent three months in Canberra studying with him, staying in the Australian's house. Tobias was the son of a protestant minister. He had been married ten years, to a singer. They had no child.

'Do you perform together?' I asked him.

'Yes,' he said, 'sometimes. That was how we met.'

'Three months is a long time to be away.'

'Well, we talked about it. My wife flew out to spend a month with me in Australia.'

'And you like to travel by ship?'

'Yes, for long time I have the idea to travel by ship to Australia. I like the space, the chance to think.'

'Where did you sail from?'

'South Italy – it's not far by train.'

'Is that how you're going back?'

'Yes, but I stay one week with a piano teacher who lives outside Kuala Lumpur.'

Ships are strange places. There was a smell of used horse litter on the stairs. On the door of the Cargo Office a notice said:

'Please be sure that it is necessary come in and if it is true please be careful possible chief officer is here.'

In the toilet it said,

'Don't sit like a frog – sit like the king of frogs. Maintain cleanliness.'

I was on deck for a lovely sunset. There were a few attenuated trails of cloud; otherwise the sky was clear, with glowing bands of colour in the rainbow sequence – red, orange, yellow, green, pale blue, pale indigo. I don't know what happened to violet – perhaps she had the evening off. Against this background lay an island – and the silhouettes of ships, for we were still at anchor.

At five past six I went down to dinner. As on the previous ship, the officers were men of few words (most of them Russian). I was glad to have Tobias and Ben to talk to. The three of us liked to linger over our meals. Tobias asked if he might listen to 15 minutes of a CD in my cabin. Somehow Ben came too. While he looked at my maps of SE Asia and China, Tobias put a Chopin polonaise on the CD player. He stood near it to listen while I sat at my desk like a business executive. When Tobias left I joined Ben on the L-shaped sofa while he explained his plans to disembark at Singapore, fly to Ha Noi, go by bus to Beijing and then fly to London for the wedding of a friend.

'I just want to travel,' he said. 'It's the only thing I want to do really.'

'Do you usually go on your own?'

'It depends. I go with my friend sometimes. Between us we've probably done the equivalent of going round the world. We've got this ambition to go across Asia in a *tuk tuk* (a motorised rickshaw).'

'You could buy one at the beginning of the trip and sell it when you've finished. The only problem would be security. I suppose you can lock them up.'

'There'd be a way.'

'I like linear travel,' I said, 'staying in a place, then going on to the next place, and so on, but never going back on your tracks.'

'I'm doing this voyage because it's different,' said Ben. 'I've never been by ship before. There are three stages when you're travelling. First, when you've just arrived in a place; then, you settle in and get used to the place; finally, you've decided to leave, but you appreciate the place; you think about missing it.'

'What's your ambition?'

'I'd like to set up a travel business, eventually, when I've done a lot more travelling myself. There are tours to unusual, out-of-the-way places or to do unusual, exciting activities. But everything's organised – you have to buy the whole package. Some people like to do their own thing, plan their own adventure, but they need help with certain aspects. I'd do that – with my friend.'

'There's a growing market for exotic holidays,' I agreed.

'There must be a growing niche catering for individual travellers.'

'You'd be like an agent. You'd have to work out how you'd charge your clients.'

Ben had blue eyes, a fair complexion and a mane of long blond hair. He looked like a young Bill Clinton. If he had spoken more clearly and less softly he could have become an actor. I was lucky that my companions shared two of my interests – music and travelling. I was lucky to have companions at all!

I looked through one of my portholes. The stevedores were working flat out to finish the job. I had felt anxious for some time about South-east Asia. While I'd been in Australia there'd been lots of distractions. Now I couldn't avoid facing up to what lay ahead. I listed 15 reasons for wanting to get home safely.

On the train from Klang to Kuala Lumpur. My facial hair grew fast in the tropical heat. My constant companion, however, looked as cool as ever.

Kuala Lumpur. Two guards checking that the park benches were fit for purpose.

Thai travellers wearing yellow shirts in honour of their King.

Bangkok. Left to right: an unexpected guest; Natkritta, an air stewardess on her birthday; the remains of the birthday lunch; Natkritta's younger sister; and their friend, who ran the vegetarian restaurant and wanted to open one in England.

Tuk tuks in Vientiane, Laos. What they lacked in speed they made up for in décor.

Ha Noi. A level crossing at a busy junction. Note the high heels and pointed toes of the guard.

The Vietnamese-Chinese border. The Chinese bus and its conductress in their magenta liveries.

Nanning, China. Balconies are very important to those short of living space.

On the train to Urumqi, north-west China, travelling first class this time. A six-year old boy giving me his full attention, while his parents look relaxed at another table.

Urumqi. Entertaining the locals at the hairdressers.

Urumqi. the People's Park. If you didn't come in when your time was up, the oxygen ran out!

Urumqi. Chinese chess.

The Chinese-Kazakh border. This Kazakh lady and I knew there were some activities that didn't require a common language.

Kazakhstan. The platform was so low that it was easier to step down onto the track than to climb up onto the train.

Kandyagash, Kazakhstan. The railway station where I gave the authorities the slip.

Atyrau, Kazakhstan. A new use for containers – extra storage space for flat dwellers. It was in this town that I escaped from a young man molesting me in the street.

L'viv, Ukraine.
Naturally I stayed
at the Savoy.

Krakow, Poland, where L S
Lowry may have got the idea of
painting matchstick men.

Oświęcim, Poland, known internationally by the name the Nazis gave it, 'Auschwitz' – the end of the line for more than a million Jews and others.

Dresden, painstakingly rebuilt after Allied bombing in the Second World War, now excavated to uncover much older history.

The German trains were fast, smooth and efficient, but they had their softer side.

Then I thought of ten ways to stay safe. I remembered how nervous I'd been about entering Mexico – and yet I'd done it. I looked again at the distances. I'd have to do about 12,000 miles from Klang to London. As I moved from the day room to my bedroom I found myself singing the opening theme of Dvořák's 'New World' symphony – proof, if proof were needed, of a more buoyant frame of mind.

The next day I noticed that we were on the open sea. We must have weighed anchor during the night. We were heading more or less due North and each day felt hotter as we got nearer to the equator. I was an hour late for lunch. Fancy having it at 11.30! With no one to talk to I took notice of the food. There was a clear plum-red soup. I don't know what flavour it was supposed to have. The steward brought a plate of peeled whole cloves of garlic.

'It is for the soup,' he said.

The casserole of chicken with mushrooms and tomatoes was very bland. The salad added some interest. The melon was unripe.

As I travelled around the world I kept meeting others who were travelling or who had travelled and they offered me insights into the countries I had yet to enter. I was due to pass through both Russia and Ukraine. I had dinner with Tobias, Ben and, for part of the time, a Ukrainian officer. He explained that, while many Ukrainians spoke Russian, they were not Russian and they resented the actions of the State of Russia against Ukraine. This was hardly news but it was good to start thinking about these things. As the Captain was Russian and the other officers a mixture of Russian and Ukrainian I could only assume that individuals of both nationalities had found a way to get along, if their governments had not.

When the Ukrainian and Ben had left the room, Tobias told me a weird story from his journey out to Australia. While he was staying in Singapore, a young man had approached him in a shopping mall. The man was friendly, charming and said he was a Christian. He persuaded Tobias to go back with him to meet his uncle, who ran a casino. The family were very hospitable and made the young Swiss feel at home. Then the uncle began to confide in Tobias some of his inside knowledge of casino gambling. He explained how, with a certain technique, the dealer could help a particular punter by showing cards as they went down, without letting the other players see the cards or indeed be aware of the deception. The two of them tried it out with the uncle dealing and Tobias seeing what was being dealt. Tobias was fascinated by this glimpse of a world he knew nothing about.

Then the uncle told him of a man who had cheated the casino by some other means. The casino-owner explained to Tobias a scheme to get revenge and win the money back, using the trick deal he had just demonstrated. The idea was to lure the quarry to the uncle's house for a private game of cards with the chance to win a lot of money off a rich and gullible foreigner, who was passing through the country – a part the sensitive, thin-wristed Tobias, if he were willing, was well equipped to carry off convincingly. Presumably the uncle would lend Tobias the money he would need for this. Presumably also Tobias would be expected to win a vast sum off the quarry and to hand back an agreed amount or proportion to the uncle once his enemy had been suitably punished and had left the game with nothing in his wallet.

You can probably guess some of the dangers in getting involved in a fight for money between two such dishonest adversaries. Luckily Tobias, who until then had been trusting and naive in allowing himself to be drawn into this nest of vipers, finally realised he was out of his depth and managed to escape from the house before being sucked in further.

'Have you told your wife this story?' I asked him.

'No, I haven't,' he said, 'but I will.'

'When you're safely home?'

'Yes.'

'You were so wise, Tobias,' I said, 'to get out when you did.'

In keeping with his tendency to walk into strange environments, Tobias encouraged me to go below decks into the bow of the ship.

'It's very peaceful there,' he said, 'you can't hear the engine. The only noise is the sound of the waves against the ship.

Having a similar tendency to Tobias's, I found a long, winding walkway between the stacks of containers and the side of the ship – at the lowest level on which you could see the water, which seemed very close. It felt very much a working area. A fat hose lying on the deck extended down the walkway. Through a perforation it sent up a fine spray, which rendered all surfaces slippery. Careful not to fall, I walked under some containers to an open space and sat on a capstan. It was indeed quiet and, being out of the wind, the air was hot. There was no one about. I felt uneasy, as if I shouldn't be there, and after ten minutes I carefully made my way back to the accommodation block.

The next day at breakfast Ben began to argue that weaponry lent strength to negotiation, because it acted as an unvoiced threat. I didn't like this argument because once other nations understand this threat they want the weaponry themselves. Thus we get the ridiculous and dangerous situation in which the most powerful country, the United States, tries to stop middle-ranking countries, such as Iran and Korea, from having the weapons it has, even considering using force to frustrate the ambition of the weaker countries.

This discussion started by Tobias telling the story of some primitive people whose youngsters are expected to undergo an initiation rite consisting of a challenging journey to obtain a necklace of seashells.

'We should have initiation rites,' declared Ben.

'Some countries still do,' I argued. 'There's national service.'

'Switzerland has a policy of remaining neutral,' said Tobias, 'and not getting involved in wars.'

'If you're never going to fight a war,' Ben argued, 'it doesn't matter if you have to do national service – you're not in danger.

'That's not the point,' I said, 'it's a matter of principle.'

'There's no harm in learning to handle a gun,' said Ben.

'Pacifists act because they are against war,' I said. 'I can't call myself a pacifist because I don't see how we could have avoided fighting the Second World War, but I marched against the Iraq War.'

'In Switzerland,' Tobias said, 'national service consists of army training. My older brothers did it, but they hated it. I refused on pacifist grounds. They questioned me closely about my convictions, then they allowed me to serve as a civilian working with orphans.'

We went then to watch a DVD of Michael Moore's film 'Fahrenheit 9/11, which took a critical look at America's response to the destruction of the twin towers by terrorists in 2001. Tobias had seen it before but he found it a little difficult to follow. The three of us had the TV room on B deck to ourselves because the crew were working. Tobias asked if we'd mind if he stopped the DVD if he didn't understand something. This happened several times – mainly because the English subtitles were full of mistakes.

I used my big desk to sort out my books and papers, throwing a lot away. I slimmed my copy of Thomas Cook's Overseas Timetable down to 40% of its former size by ripping out North, Central and South America and the whole of Africa and dropping them in the waste bin.

It was cool in my cabin because of the air conditioning. So, although we were nearing Indonesia and the Equator, it didn't feel like it. The air was hot on the monkey island but so windy that again it didn't feel hot. On the lower decks two men in yellow overalls and wellington boots with large white handkerchiefs tied over their heads were using a pressure hose to clean some gear. The spray was blown to one side where it hung in the air briefly above the sea and caught the fierce sun, producing a fleeting rainbow.

After dinner Tobias, Ben and I went up to the monkey island to watch the sunset. Then the moon appeared.

'Venus will be out soon,' I said.

It got fairly dark. The warm wind was lovely.

'Ah, yes, Venus!' I announced. 'There she is – right up there!'

'No, that's Jupiter!' said Tobias.

'How do you know?'

'Venus is never far from the sun.'

I'd never thought of that. Then he pointed out one of the stars of the Scorpio constellation. Later, when more stars appeared, he took me through Scorpio, three stars at a time. He also showed me the Southern Cross and Cygnus with its long neck. He explained that, viewed from the tropics, there was an overlap between the night sky as seen from Europe and that seen in the southern hemisphere. He found Ursa Major (the Great Bear), Ursa Minor (the Little Bear) and the Pole Star. Then he went to fetch his star book. This came as a relief to me because by then I'd got a stiff neck from staring at the heavens.

The next morning before daylight we passed through the Sunda Strait between Java and Sumatra. Our route then lay up the east side of Sumatra and between it and Singapore to the Strait of Malacca between Sumatra and the south-west coast of Semenanjung Malaysia (the bit of Malaysia that's joined to mainland Asia) – the obvious way to go, in fact. In the afternoon we passed a big island called Pulau Bangka. I found spotting islands more satisfying than spotting ships. In time I saw numerous islands, small rocky ones, some wooded, some with sandy beaches. There were big islands too, with tree-covered mountains, perhaps a white lighthouse. Some islands were clear, others dressed in mist. I saw fishing boats with prominent prows. After the Panama Canal, this was the most exciting voyage I'd had.

The steward who served us in the mess met me in the laundry.

'You leave tomorrow?' he asked.

'Yes,' I said, 'after breakfast.'

'Where you go?'

I told him.

'You no go Philippines?'

'Sadly, no,' I said. 'I won't have time. I wanted to go from Darwin in Australia to the Philippines and then on to Hong Kong but I couldn't find a ship. You have to go where the ships go. So, when does your contract finish?'

'November.'

He pulled a face as if to say he wished it weren't such a long time.

'My wife ...' he did a mime, which seemed to refer to the central regions of her anatomy. '... tomorrow.'

'She's having a baby – tomorrow?'

'Yes.'

'Is this your first?'

He held up two fingers. And there he was, so near home – the Philippines were just the other side of Borneo from us. In world terms it was no distance. Goodness knows where he would have travelled between then and November. These people had tough lives, but they kept very cheerful.

'It's hard you can't be with her,' I said. 'Can you telephone – when we're in port?'

'Yes, it cost me $60.'

I thought he was talking US dollars, because that was the currency of the ship. I hadn't got any to give him – I'd only got Australian dollars and Malaysian ringgits. I am ashamed that I didn't find a way to give him some money.

Back in the owner's suite, I looked out of a porthole. We were moving more slowly. The traffic was building up ahead. The sun was on just one of the ships. I went on deck with my camera. The sun disappeared and soon it was raining hard. The visibility was so bad that I couldn't see the front of the ship I was on – let alone the ships I wanted to photograph. When the sky cleared I saw a ship at anchor, behind it the skyscrapers of Klang.

In the evening I had a shower and started getting ready for bed, not knowing whether Tobias and I would be disembarking that night or not. It was a spectacular arrival. A long line of yellow and white lights looked pretty and welcoming. The engine was pulsating quietly, as we glided on very smooth water. The harbour seemed to go on for ever. A long way ahead, as if for our benefit, there were fireworks. At 10.10pm the ship stopped. There were lots of small vessels ablaze with lights, as if we and all the other vessels were part of a festive occasion. A tug was moving very slowly. A little car was parked on the quayside, possibly customs and immigration. Three cranes were ready to unload us. At 11pm, with no word about disembarkation, I got into bed. We touched the side with a little bump.

At 5.20 I got up and looked out. They were working hard outside; the sound of metal striking metal. I watched a crane find a container, pick it up in a hurry and then a large shape rushed close past my window. A little man, presumably Malaysian, was gathering metal stays right under the path of the next container. If the guy at the controls of the crane had pressed the wrong lever the little fellow would have been crushed to death. I'm sure it's happened. Out of the corner of my eye I saw a mouse silently and determinedly hurry across the bedroom carpet. It was the light from the moving crane. Even when I knew it was a mouse-shaped spot of light it startled me again as it hurried back.

I had breakfast on the ship, waited for the formalities and then Tobias and I went down the ladder. For the first time in my life I was about to step onto Asian soil.

UNDER PRESSURE

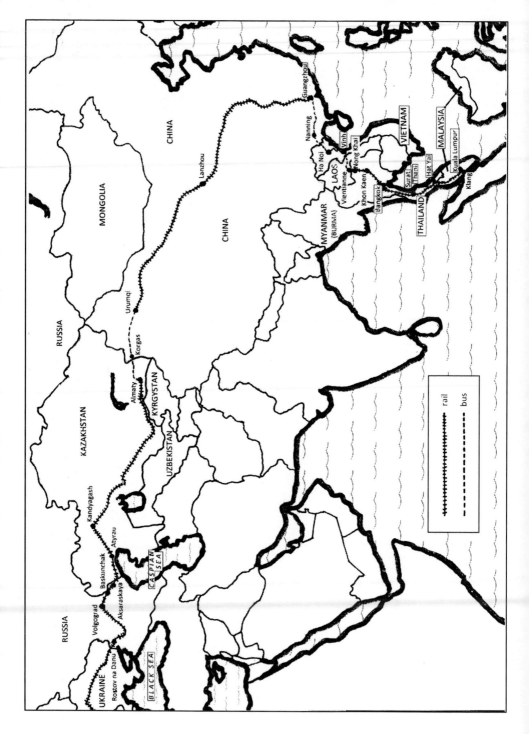

Map 3
Asia

18. Malaysia

August 18 – 22

Tobias and I stood with the third officer at the top of the pilot ladder, waiting for a taxi to arrive to take us to the Immigration Office. I began to think what questions we might be asked. This was a good thing because it reminded me of something very important.

'Have you got our passports?' I asked the third officer.

'Oh, oh, sorry!' he said.

He went back to get them. They always take your passports off you. I think it's to stop you leaving the ship between ports! Tobias sat in the front of the taxi next to the driver and did most of the talking. Imagine my surprise and delight at sighting, through the taxi window, MV Tikeibank, the British ship that had taken me across the Pacific. While I'd been having a good time in Australia, Tikeibank had called at umpteen islands between New Zealand and Klang. She had probably been delayed for repairs and now I'd caught up with her.

When we got to Immigration the driver pulled into the side of the road and parked under a tree. I brought my hand luggage with me but we left our main luggage in the car. We walked across the road.

'Is that all right,' I asked Tobias, 'leaving our luggage with him?'

'Oh, yes,' he said, 'I think so.'

Then someone came out of the building to meet us and took us in. The officials were all smiles. They told Tobias that the taxi was free and he passed this information on to me. I was greatly relieved because it meant it was an official taxi and I stopped worrying about the luggage. Back in the taxi Tobias asked the driver to take us to the railway station.

'That's nice!' Tobias said, indicating the brass head of an elephant on the dashboard.

I knew what it was and wouldn't have said anything.

'I'm a Hindu,' the driver explained. 'In Hinduism we have many gods. This is Ganesha. He will look after you.'

Kuala Lumpur is such a cosmopolitan city that all my time there nobody looked at me as if I were strange. I was relieved to see that the ticket machines were almost identical to those I was familiar with in England. But they wouldn't take a 10-ringgit note so I went to the shop and bought a hard-cover notebook called 'small oblong book' to get some change. The train resembled those on the London Underground except that there was a place on the overhead strap handles for small advertisements on cards. Tobias got off half way to Kuala Lumpur and I continued on my own to the capital. A woman in the street recommended the YMCA. It was a big air-conditioned building with lots going on, such as meetings, symposia and courses:

Thai – with Ms Naruda and Ms Murfa
Japanese – with Mr Lien
Mandarin – with Mr Wang
Cantonese – with Mr Albert
English – with Ms Sarah
Scottish Dance (with someone who preferred to remain anonymous).

The band of the 3rd Kuala Lumpur Boys Brigade company were rehearsing in the hall. Outside, people were playing tennis rather badly on two hard courts. Others were playing football on a pitch covered with artificial grass. It was a realistic green and had been worn brown in the right places. Behind the building was a wheelie bin large enough to bath a water buffalo in. It took three men to trundle it across the road to the refuse truck.

The reception area was decked with the Malaysian flag. Nowhere in the building did I see a cross. However, 'Young Men's Christian Association' was spelled out in full. Within the building was a place to eat called the Lemon Tree Café. The atmosphere was like that of a school re-opened in the holidays for some other purpose.

I felt a little strange in an institution for young male Christians, being myself an old male humanist, but as there was a young female Muslim behind the counter I felt the place was inclusive rather than exclusive. A cleaner came through the café several times, wearing a strange symbol on a thick tape around her neck. This turned out to be the symbol of her office – a bunch of keys. As she carried a black plastic bag of rubbish through the garden I could watch her through the window. The hem of her hijab (headscarf covering hair, ears and neck) was decorated with a shiny thread, which glittered in the sun. I saw women with hijabs, long-sleeved shirts and short skirts over jeans.

I had a room to myself with a wardrobe, a bedside table and a choice of three narrow beds. There was air conditioning with a remote control. I shared a shower, toilet and wash basins. A room labelled 'housekeeping' was packed with mattresses and pillows. Two housekeepers were sitting on the floor, their backs against some mattresses.

The pavements incorporated textured pathways to help blind people to find their way to crossings. I saw a number of such people using these pathways. They had a hard time with the motorbikes, which also used the pavements. I saw placards advertising 'Traditional Massage' and 'Blind Masseur'. Then I spotted the Malaysian Association for the Blind. The signs in Kuala Lumpur were in both Malay and English and most people had some English. Sometimes this English was more correct than British English – a sign said, 'Stick no bill'.

In the evening I wandered down a street looking for somewhere to eat. A guy with a round face, a beguiling smile and only one leg was sitting to one side of the open front of a restaurant. He caught my eye and beckoned me over. In a moment I was inside and he was hopping about, showing me to a table and bringing me a photographic menu. He hopped back to his place. Immediately a woman came with another book of photos, which she proceeded to take me through.

'Fish ... meat ... veal – you know, baby cow.'

'No, thanks,' I said, 'I'll have fish.'

I chose stingray with ginger sauce. The woman took me to a chilled cabinet, where among other raw fish already cleaned and filleted were some prepared pieces of stingray. She shovelled some onto the scales.

'That'll be so many ringgits.'

'Okay,' I said, 'may I have rice?'

'Yes. Steamed rice?'

By then she had another photo album in her hand. This was the veggie album. I chose a mixture.

'And to drink?'

'Yes, I'd like some beer, please.'

'The beers are over there,' she said pointing to the other side of the restaurant.

'I'll have a "Tiger", please.'

'Would you like to find somewhere to sit?'

I found a table outside. It was all very quick and straightforward. There was a complimentary starter of pieces of garlic with a sauce so hot that you could hardly taste the garlic. In fact I gobbled up the garlic to soothe my mouth after it had been savaged by the sauce.

Stingray is not the easiest fish to eat in the dark as it has so many bones. I had to concentrate, but I did notice two monks in saffron robes go by and that next to me at a large round table a respectable-looking man was drinking Carlsberg on his own. A party of eight men with trim black hair, trim black moustaches and dark brown complexions arrived. The boss woman was with them immediately. She asked the respectable man to move onto my table. I made a welcoming gesture. He moved over, bringing with him his British-style glass tankard with the dimpled glass and stout handle. he gave me an encouraging smile.

'I've just arrived in Malaysia,' I said. 'I'm from England.'

'I know England,' he said. 'I've been to London many times – Bayswater.'

'Oh, yes, I know Bayswater.'

'Queen Mary's Hospital. I'm a doctor. I needed ... for my masters ... gastro-enterology ... Queen Mary's Hospital.'

Above the chatter of the eight trim Indians, I wasn't catching every word.

'You are going round the world and you are not flying at all!' he exclaimed.

'It's a challenge I've set myself.'

'Nearly everybody here has a connection with England,' he told me. 'We were ruled by Britain, you know, until 1957.'

'Yes,' I said, 'you are celebrating the 50th Anniversary of your independence.'

'Britain did a lot for Malaysia – gave us our legal system, our democracy, planted tea, brought us rubber from Brazil. Not like the Dutch in Indonesia. They left nothing. We look up to London. We are many different peoples – but we all get on.'

That should be the motto of the world.

Later I had a stomach pain and a feeling of queasiness, which lasted until 5am, although I slept off and on. I learned later that if you consume high-voltage chillies they keep you awake. The next day I came down the stairs on my way to breakfast. On the first floor landing I was met by a cuddly woman of Indian descent. She had an expression of indestructible serenity. She looked me in the eye and smiled.

'Good morning, sir!' she said.

'Good morning!'

'How are you, sir?'

'I'm very well, thank you.'

'Sir, are you a Christian?'

'No.'

'I am a member of the Kingdom of Jesus. If you pray to Jesus ...'

I'm afraid I missed the next bit, so I can't tell you what she said would happen if I prayed to Jesus. For breakfast I had 'toasts with kaya.' Kaya is Malaysian jam – sweet, tasting of coconut and a spice redolent, unsurprisingly, of the East. They gave me four tiny toast sandwiches with kaya as the filling and two perfect cups of tea.

I went to Kuala Lumpur Sentral to find out about trains to Bangkok. It should have been easy because every notice was in English as well as Malay. This was the main station of the capital of Malaysia. It was on the one line that went North to Thailand. Yet nowhere could I find, either as a notice or in leaflet form, any information about trains to Bangkok. I wanted to find out if I could travel on the Orient Express, as I'd read of this train and the journey sounded appealing. I asked at the inter-city enquiry desk for a timetable. They had none, but the woman gave me a telephone number of 'Orient Express Trains & Cruises'. I didn't believe this was all the information available on the station. Eventually I found the Tourist Information Office.

'Do you have any information on Eastern & Orient Services?'

'No,' a man said. 'Where do you want to go?'

'Bangkok.'

'What do you want to know?'

'When the trains go from this station. How long they take. What it costs. What the service consists of ...'

'Take a seat.'

He rang someone up and had a conversation in English, although I didn't catch much of it. Then he put the phone down.

'There's one train a month – one in August, one in September.

'When?' I asked.

'11.15.'

'I mean – what date?'

'I don't know.'

This was about 9.45am. There might have been a train that very morning. It was a one in 31 chance. He wrote three telephone numbers on a small square of green paper.

'That's the agent,' he said, 'but I don't know if he'll be there today.'

'Thank you.'

It was Sunday. This was officially a Muslim country, but many services, for instance two Internet cafés, were closed. I blamed the British – Sunday meant something when we were in power. I found a third Internet café, and this one was open. I blundered about in cyberspace and hit on a relevant website. I poked around in the website and found that the Orient Express, with its once-a-month train from Singapore to Bangkok, was described as a 'luxury cruise' – not something a railway station would sell although I still expected them to have leaflets to give out. They offered October and November – no mention of September, and I'd already missed the August train, which had travelled earlier in the month. So that was the end of that! I found information on trains going over the border into Thailand as far as Hat Yai. I clicked on 'Monday'. There was no sleeper. 'Tuesday?' Yes, there were six lower-bunk sleepers available on the basic class. How to order the seats? It didn't tell me, no matter where I probed and peeked. I'd just have to go back to the station.

At breakfast the next day the CD player in the Lemon Tree Café was playing 'Smoke Gets in your Eyes'. Then we had 'Hello, Dolly!' in an unpleasant version for strings. A man in his seventies was talking to the woman I took to be the manager.

'Then I get on the train,' he was saying, 'and that takes me where?'

The manager told him.

'This is all a bit confusing for me,' he said, chirpy as a chaffinch.

His Asian wife, half his age, looked content. When the manager went away to get something I went over to the septuagenarian. I thought he was a Londoner, because he had a quaint perkiness about him, but he turned out to be Australian.

'Have you just arrived?' I asked. 'There's always someone who speaks English. Almost everyone has some English. You can ask. They're very helpful.'

I went to the central market to buy presents and a male urine bottle. The presents were for some British people I hoped to meet in Bangkok. The urine bottle was for me. I thought I would be afraid to go to the toilet on the train leaving my luggage unattended. A Western woman with dyed blonde hair and a low-cut top, revealing a cleavage to rival that of the Ukrainian viola player on the QM2, paused with her man at the jewellery counter. She was served by a Muslim woman in hijab and jilbab (full-length dress with long sleeves). The Western woman leant forward over the counter revealing even more of her bosom. The assistant remained calm and professional throughout. I could only admire the self-assurance of both women in such a meeting of contrasting cultures.

In the market I had a lunch of fish in a sauce, with rice, two types of veggies and a beer mug of water. All this cost 3.50 ringgits (60p), the cheapest meal of the whole trip. The ringgit, I discovered, was a wonderful thing. You could get six of them for a pound but one ringgit bought as much as one pound back home. It was self service. I didn't know what I was choosing although I do know a dead fish when I see one. You learn to eat fish with a spoon and a fork. But when it comes to vegetables, what do you do with the long stringy bits of stalk? You push them to the side of your plate and try to think about something else.

On the television in my room there were continuous oriental pop songs, sung by young girls too pretty for their own good, with silk costumes in brilliant colours, make-up to match their expressions, which varied between deep contentment and unexpected ecstasy. The backing groups looked as though they had stepped out of a Bollywood movie, the lighting was atmospheric and the bass beat throbbed like a Derby winner's aorta. Anything was better than what I saw on the box another evening – a local version of the excruciating British programme 'Deal or no Deal', the only thing to be said in its favour was that they had a local presenter instead of the emetic Noel Edmonds.

Anticipating the 50th Anniversary of the country's independence, the Malaysian flag was everywhere. With its crescent and red-and-white horizontal stripes it looked like an Islamic American state – if such a thing were even thinkable. The municipal gardeners were going frantic with bedding plants. Merdeka (Independence) Square, a grassy rectangle the size of a football pitch and surrounded by important buildings, was being prepared as a centre piece for the celebrations and I watched workmen constructing a grandstand.

The National History Museum cost only two ringgits to enter. In the first room an illustration showed a dog, which had been pursued by Parameswara (a Malay prince), being 'kicked into the river by a mouse deer'. It was Parameswara who claimed the region, naming it Malacca. In the 15th Century the area was a crossroads on the trade routes between East and West. Some of the traders stayed behind, so even in the fifteenth century the place was cosmopolitan, with Arabs, Gujeratis, other Indians, Siamese, Chinese, Japanese, Cambodians, Persians and Malays. The museum followed the story from there, giving appropriate weight to the various invasions and changes of governance. The Japanese occupation from 1942 to 1945 was very harsh. The Japanese intention was to eliminate Western influence. This engendered an anti-Japanese feeling that fed Malaysian nationalism. I saw two Japanese visitors in short shorts posing on the stairs for photographs. They spent only 60 seconds in the Second World War Room and no time at all on the Japanese invasion.

The commentary was clear and the English translation good. I couldn't resist, however, noting the following rather pleasing usage:

'The Federation of Malaya Flag was flapped off in London signifying the Independence Day on 31ˢᵗ August 1957.'

And some of the text regarding the Malaysia Agreement in 1963 didn't marry up with the pictures. A caption reading, 'Mr Duncan Sandys *(then UK Secretary of State for Commonwealth Relations)* signed the Malaysian Agreement' had been placed under a photograph of the British Prime Minister Harold Macmillan looking at a document, pen in hand.

Presently a French family came into the room. I guessed they were French before I heard them speak for the mother had stylish well-cut hair, a white short-sleeved shirt and black ¾-length trousers and smart sandals, obviously bought as an ensemble, and the children were beautifully turned out too. They were accompanied by the curator or head of the museum, who spoke French to them. I understood quite a lot of this. I wanted to butt in to tell the curator about the Sandys/Macmillan mix-up but I sensed that it wasn't the moment. Once the French party had left I could find no one in authority to speak to. If you're ever in Kuala Lumpur you might just pop into the history museum for me if you've got the time and see if they've corrected the error by then – I don't know when I shall be that way again.

In a park I photographed two security guards sleeping on a bench. A helicopter flew overhead. The din woke both men. They stood up and tried to look lively. After a while one went away. The other finished his rest and then investigated a filled carrier bag, which someone had hung in the large formal shelter where the guards had been sleeping. As a trained security guard he knew what to do with a suspicious parcel. First he gave the bag a good squeeze. As it didn't immediately explode he bravely peered into it. Then he boldly poked the hand he could more easily spare into the bag. I moved away. There was no reason for us both to risk our lives.

On my last night in Kuala Lumpur I decided to go the Indian Quarter, which is known as 'Little India'. I thought I'd be able to enjoy a genuine Indian curry. It was difficult to find this district, even with a map, a compass, the help of the bus driver and the advice of people in the street. Even when I was near it, the quarter was difficult to detect. I don't think it was a quarter – more like a sixteenth! It had been raining since I'd got off the bus and the rain was getting heavier. Eventually I pulled out my waterproof and put it on. The best I could find in the way of an Indian restaurant was the Garden City Hotel Café.

At the table next to mine, there was an Indian man with three Indian women. Those staying in the hotel seemed entirely Muslim. The waiters, looked Indian. They brought me mutton rogan josh, vegetable curry and naan bread. A family with two children came in. The mother was wearing the niqab (she was in black from head to toe, everything covered except for a slit for the eyes). The father was wearing western dress with a shirt and tie. I felt uncomfortable seeing the woman almost completely covered while the man was required to make no concession at all. I wondered how she would eat a curry. I decided to order a dessert so that my meal would last long enough to allow me to complete my research. After a couple of minutes the mother changed places with her husband, presumably to avoid facing four lusty young Europeans (not me!). Imagine having to wear black in that climate! She turned to one of the little boys. All he could see of her was her eyes and her hands with their gold bracelets. I didn't see her take her gloves off. The boy must have thought the other women in the restaurant very odd! I saw the father and the two boys eating rice. The mother had no food in front of her.

There was no dessert so I asked for a black de-caffeinated coffee. A glass tumbler of something the colour of the river arrived with a light froth. It was sweet white coffee, but it would serve the purpose of allowing me to linger. I was careful not to be seen looking at the Muslim family – just an occasional glance, turning away before any of them looked in my direction. Suddenly the mother had some food in front of her. She unfastened that part of the hood that covered her mouth and began to eat. Once her face was uncovered she looked much the same as any other Muslim woman. I don't know what I expected. But how terrible to be covered up! When she finished eating she fastened the flap again. A while later I became aware that the father was walking towards my table.

'Why are you looking at my wife?' I guessed he'd say. 'You've no respect. You should respect other people!'

And I would have felt ashamed. He gave me a smile.

'Are you staying in Malaysia?' he asked me.

'I am tonight,' I said, 'then I'm going to Thailand.'

'Be careful! Don't carry much cash. Don't go in isolated places. Be careful!'

'Thank you for the warning.'

He shook my hand. Then the whole family went out. When I'd paid my bill I went out into the street. It was quiet and dark. After the warning I'd just been given I took a taxi back to the YMCA.

The next morning, as it was my last in Kuala Lumpur, I decided to try the equivalent of a full English breakfast – chicken frankfurter, fried egg sunny side up, 16 cold baked beans to stop you finding the sausage strange, two slices of cold toast put together as a sandwich with a pat of butter inserted but not spread, to keep your mind off the coldness of the baked beans, and tea that had been in the urn since Keats wrote his 'Ode on a Grecian Urn'.

I went to the Golden Triangle, a wooded hill in the city, the site of the Kuala Lumpur Tower. I was trying to find a way up to this landmark when a man dressed for the office saw me. He was swarthy and sported a black moustache.

'Can I help you?' he offered.

'Thank you,' I said. 'I'm looking for a way to get to the tower.'

'Wait. There are two ways. You can gooo that way there, thooo it's a bit steep.'

He was sounding more and more Scottish with every syllable.

'Your English is very good,' I said. 'Excuse my asking – did you learn it in Scotland?'

'Noo,' he said, 'right heeer in Kuala Lumpur.'

'Was your teacher a Scot?' I persisted. 'Was he Scottish?'

'Yes,' he said, 'as a matter of fact she was. Where are you from?'

'England.'

'Wheerabooots?'

'The south. Near to France.'

'Near Bath, are you?'

'Quite near.'

This sort of conversation always made me feel that the world was a smaller place. I walked up to the tower. At first-floor level there was a balcony all the way round. I took photographs in several directions. The tower was 421 metres high, nearly as tall as the Empire State Building. And you could go 300 metres up, but because the land fell away I felt I was high enough already. I ordered an iced lemon tea, which I sent back because it arrived full of sugar. They replaced it without question. I went back on the monorail, which gives you a wonderful view because there is no other traffic at that level. I saw bits of the city I'd never seen before and I saw the old bits from a new angle. Altogether I saw more bits than I should have done because I got on a train going the wrong way and had to go to the end of the line and come back. I felt guilty because it was the rush hour and I was taking up space in a crowded car. But I still got back in time to have a meal before I took the train to Thailand.

There was a big open-fronted restaurant on a corner, with considerable frontage on each street and tables inside and out. I went in from one of the two streets and saw someone selling beer while people were eating at tables inside. I tried to work out what the system was – waiter service, self-service or a combination of the two. I asked if I could eat there.

'Yes,' the man behind the bar said.

'Where do I go to order the food?'

He pointed across the room.

'Thank you.'

I chose a table, sat down and sipped my beer. I beckoned a woman to come over to me.

'What do you want?' she asked.

'Some dinner, please,' I said. 'Is there a menu?'

'No.'

'Well, how do I order?'

'Go over there.'

She pointed to a cooking stall outside the restaurant in the other street. A middle-aged couple were preparing food, facing out into the street. I went over. There was no queue so I didn't know where to stand. I say there was no queue but a young, rather thin woman was standing quite near me, doing nothing in a surly kind of way. I waited for a bit. As she seemed to be waiting and looked local I thought she would know the ropes. But still nothing happened. Then she suddenly stared at me.

'What do you want?' the surly girlie asked, as if I were pushing my luck.

'Excuse me,' I said, 'is this where you order the food?'

'Do – you – want – to – fuck – me?' she asked in the tone of a newsagent saying to a customer, 'If you don't want to buy that magazine put it down – we're not a library!'

Her voice was as clear as anything. The middle-aged couple must have heard her, but they didn't react. Maybe they were used to this particular chat-up line – or they didn't understand what she was saying. I looked at the surly girlie and as gently, politely and clearly as I could, said, 'I just want to know how you order food here.'

With a disdainful shrug she indicated the middle-aged couple. Well, I wasn't to know that this was her pitch and that I was queering it.

'Thank you very much,' I said.

'We've got a right one here!' she must have thought.

Once the middle-aged woman realised that I was her customer not the surly girlie's, she couldn't have been more helpful. And once I'd eaten, I had a cup of black coffee so that I wouldn't keep my fellow passengers on the train awake with my snoring. Then I collected my rucksack from the YMCA and walked to the railway station. I was relieved to find that I was not in a small compartment but in an upper bunk in a coach with a line of double bunks length-wise down both sides of a long corridor. The only privacy came from the thick grey-blue curtains in front of each berth.

From the bunk below me a very young man smiled up at me as if he was pleased to have me as a neighbour. He looked happy and excited. Then I saw he had a girl I took to be his fiancée in the lower bunk opposite. A tall young man in western clothes had the upper berth opposite mine.

'This is going to be fun!' I said.

'Yeah,' he said, 'it is!'

'It didn't look like this in the picture. They hadn't any first class left. Well, I could have gone the next day, but you want to get on, don't you? Where've you come from?'

'Well, ten days ago – from Australia.'

He had an Australian accent.

'So did I,' I said, 'came by ship from Fremantle.'

'I flew to Singapore. Arrived ten days ago. Going to meet my girlfriend in India. Ship, you say?'

'Well, I've got time. You young people have to work … how long are you taking?'

'Thirteen months.'

'Then what?'

'Then … something else.'

'… like working to pay for more travel?'

'No, just travelling cheaply.'

'Some countries are cheaper than others.'

'I'm Matt by the way.'

'I'm John.'

'It's good to travel at this time – before the world becomes all the same.'

'Yes. Culture is spread around by travel, television and the Internet. Genetically determined national differences are breaking down. There's more difference between rich and poor than between one country and another.'

The black coffee worked a treat, unfortunately. At 11.45 a man pushed a trolley along the corridor offering late night snacks. Out of boredom I peeped out from behind my blue-grey curtain. At midnight the young man was still sitting on his fiancée's bed, holding her hand. Then there was a bit of respectable kissing. I stopped peeping and lay quietly. I slept off and on. At least no one shook me for snoring. The train reversed at Butterworth. At 7am I looked out of my window, which was long and narrow, to see half-conquered jungle or jungly bits, palm trees and sweetcorn. We passed through dense woods with the vegetation almost touching the window. I saw a river smooth as brown glass. There were shacks with corrugated metal roofs. People on motorbikes were waiting at level crossings. We stopped often at stations. We stopped between stations as well. We passed a mosque, the giant onion-shaped roof a dull gold.

The fiancée hadn't yet put on her hijab. She had a sweet face with almond-shaped eyes. At 7.15 an old boy started pontificating in a way that made me think he would have been just as boring if I had understood what he was saying. He was sitting on one of the lower bunks waving a list up and down. After a while I heard he was speaking English with idiosyncratic emphasis.

' ... dri-ver ... conduc-tor ... If they didn't run the trains,' he was saying, ' the vegetation would cover the tracks in weeks. Nev-ar mind!'

He didn't shut up for ten seconds. A woman was drawing him on. The two youngsters below me made a sweet couple. He was sitting on her bunk beside her holding a mirror for her while she did her make-up.

Just before we reached the border with Thailand we stopped at a small station. Everyone had to get off. We were told we could leave our luggage on the train.

'Someone might open it,' a passenger said.

I took this to mean that someone other than the immigration officers might steal from us. Matt and I took all our luggage with us. I was glad of that when I later saw the train pull out of the station. I learned that this was for fuel and water. After we'd been seen by immigration we got back onto the train. In minutes we would be in Thailand.

19. Thailand

August 22 – 29

When we arrived at Hat Yai the train stopped a distance from any platform. Everyone, including a family with a pushchair, had to climb down to the ground and then cross four lines of track. I think I was the only person who looked both ways every time. I found the sort of restaurant I liked, where the food is on display and you just point to what you want. The woman who ran the place sat down at my table. She smiled when I drew a globe on a stand with arrows going right round it. She laughed when I followed this up with simple sketches of a steamer on the sea, a train on the track and a bus on the road. I didn't get as far as drawing a plane and crossing it out. I know all this because the drawings were in one of the notebooks I sent home.

I checked in at the Louis/Louise Guest House – the spelling varied (and therefore the gender). I was tired after a night on the train and felt dirty because I hadn't washed for 30 hours, so I had a shower and a little rest. I studied the train timetable to work out how to do the journey in two bites, both of them by day, and still be in Bangkok by the weekend, when I was to meet my nephew.

When I went out again I noticed that on the pavement in front of the shops were earthenware bowls of water with tiny water lilies and goldfish 3 cm long. I went to an Internet café that was part of a bookshop – that's a smart innovation! A guy who looked European and in his forties gave me a warm smile.

'How you doing?' he asked.

'Okay,' I said, 'I can't make up my mind what would be the best way to go to Bangkok – where to break the journey. I prefer to avoid travelling at night because you don't see much.'

'Avoid weekends. Talk to the girls on the information desk at the station. If you really want to see the country go third class, bump along.'

'How will I see more?'

'You go more slowly!'

I got my map out and he gave me a run down on the merits of various stopping-off places. He told me of a place to stay in Surat Thani. Then he pointed to an island.

'I lived there,' he said. 'That was my home for some years. I married a Thai woman but I fell out with her and her children.'

'Where did you come from originally?'

'England. I'm half English, a quarter Swedish and a quarter German. I've enough German to want to get things right first time – including invading Poland!'

I raised my eyebrows high.

'I like Hat Yai,' he said, 'but one of these days I'll have to find something to do, somewhere to go.'

'Will you go back to England?'

'I've been away from England for 16 years. I don't think I could go back.'

'What about Australia? The Australians are easy-going.'

'I don't know.'

Later I went back to the station but the ticket office was closed so I sat on a seat to wait. At 6pm a sharp whistle sounded. Everyone, including me, stood up and the jolliest, chirpiest song came over the loud speakers. Everyone kept still including a woman on the level crossing balancing a platter of prepared food on her head. The music must have been the Thai Royal Anthem.

The next day I had a breakfast of crumpled fried eggs, sweet-and-sour sausage, a hamburger, a few beans of a delightful green and some gravy. At ten past nine it was already very hot. I sat on a step in some deep shade. I saw a photograph of the King and Queen some five metres high, framed in a heavy gilt frame. I was to see numerous smaller portraits of the Royal couple in shop windows and numerous historical photographs inside hotels. My breakfast had challenged my digestion but I felt like buying some grapes for the journey. I changed my mind when I discovered that they'd come from the United States.

I went back to the Internet café in the bookshop, to see the guy who had left his Thai wife on an island. I wanted to give him my remaining credit for Internet access at the café. On the screen was a photograph of a hideous building.

'They've put up this monstrosity in Birmingham,' he said. 'You haven't been keeping an eye on things! So where are you off to?'

'Bangkok on two day-trains, stopping at Surat Thani so I'll have a night in a stationary bed.'

On the train I was lucky to have the first window seat on the shady side. The soil was brick red, the grass a healthy green. A man was cutting it with a scythe. The cows were an attractive shade of brown, a number tethered by the nose. Some had humps like the cattle I'd seen in Central America. We passed a plantation of deciduous trees. In a natural pond there were platforms for fishermen raised above the water on stilts and with roofs to keep the sun off.

Passengers were provided with a clean white blanket in a polythene bag to help us survive the rigours of air conditioning. Refreshments were included in the price of my ticket – a roll, a cake, a tumbler of orange squash and a nicely cooked dinner of fish, rice and vegetables.

At Surat Thani I got off the train and as I paused to marvel at the veritable street of shops and stalls inside the station I was besieged by taxi drivers wanting to whisk me away from all this. When I thought they'd forgotten about me I marched straight out of the station like a mad thing.

'Taxi! Taxi!' men cried again.

My room had a television set mounted high but the electrical plug was so heavy that whenever you plugged the television in it unplugged itself. I managed to rig up a device using a shoe to hold the plug in.

A bathroom had been created by adding an internal wall. There was no shower curtain and the tiled floor sloped down to the main floor so that the water didn't hang about under the shower but quickly spread over the bedroom floor. The drain pipe from the basin disappeared into the outer wall of the bathroom but came back into the room 40 cm lower. Thus when you let the water out and thought you would never see it again, blow me down if didn't come back at a lower level to give your feet an unexpected rinse. The toilet had no cistern but there were two bowls on the floor and a short hose with a spray nozzle like you'd use to wash a car. It was an unusual approach but hygienic. In this strange world it was not surprising that I dried myself on something I realised later was intended as a bedspread.

When I went back to the railway station I was beset by taxi-drivers as usual.

'Where are you going?' asked one.

I pointed to the information desk a few metres away. Even a Thai taxi-driver had to admit I could manage that distance without his help. I tried to find out if there would be food on the train. I thought the answer was 'yes' but to be on the safe side I bought some fresh cut pineapple, a packet of garibaldi biscuits and a small carton of orange juice. It was a two-car train but I managed to get into the wrong car. I didn't find out until we had got up speed. The ticket inspector had me move into the other car with my rucksack and hand luggage. I had to press a button to open the door of the coach I was to leave. Then I could see that I would have to step across overlapping metal plates and press a button to open the door of the other coach, at which point I would be between coaches, with the ground whizzing past underneath clearly visible through gaps big enough to fall through. At the moment of pressing the second button I would have had no hand free to steady myself, so I handed my hand luggage to the ticket inspector and stepped into the danger zone trusting him to follow. My trust was well placed. He followed so closely I could sense he was impatient with my nervousness. This did nothing to reassure me and it was only the thought that there was no going back and anything was better than being stuck with a strange ticket collector in this precarious no-man's-land between two cars that made me press on and press the second button.

Once settled in my seat, I could see through the window what I took to be paddy fields with the bright green shoots of young rice plants. I saw a rectangular pond divided into sections. There were water pumps and rows of little fountains so I guessed it was a fish farm. I moved for a while to the front of the car where I could enjoy more or less the same view as the driver – a single track with vegetation so close it was like speeding down an endless rabbit run.

When we got to Bangkok it was dark. I shot into the Station Hotel. I didn't want to be walking around in the dark choosing the ideal place to stay. I telephoned my nephew Chris and arranged that he would collect me from the hotel at 10 o'clock the next morning. I hadn't seen him since he was a boy. Now he was 21. He was reading sports sciences in England but staying during the summer vacation in Bangkok with his Thai girlfriend Jib (pronounced 'Jeep'). I slept well on a mattress of orthopaedic firmness.

In the morning Chris took me round the city, introducing me to Bangkok's wonderful and varied transport system, a useful training for me. On the underground for instance I learnt to pay for my ride by buying tokens in the form of metal discs, which I tended to lose among my small change.

We continued by ferry on the murky waters of the Mae Nam Ping river to the Temple of the Emerald Buddha. Large, complex and lavishly ornate it was too. We were allowed into the *ubosoth* of the Temple, a sacred edifice, where certain rituals were performed. I was shocked by the lack of respect shown by some of the tourists, who were taking flash photographs despite the ban on photography inside the building.

We travelled on the Skytrain (monorail) and in a taxi too. We entered Paragon Mall, which was as smart and up-to-date as the name implied – more Fifth Avenue than Bangkok High Street. The stationery department boasted a display of colour-blocked biros so extensive and arranged in so aesthetically appealing a fashion that I wanted to photograph it but they told me this was not allowed. Jib worked in a ladies fashion franchise in the Mall and we met her when she finished for the day. The two had accepted my offer to take them out for a meal.

'Where would you like to go?' Jib asked.

'A nice restaurant that you've wanted to go to,' I said, 'or one you haven't been to for a long time and would like to go to again.'

Jib knew just the place. Still in downtown Bangkok, it was upstairs, making it seem private and exclusive. We were met by charming staff with the gracious Thai greeting, palms together, nodding the head as if they were welcoming back important regulars. They gave us damp cloths for our hands. The menu was in both Thai and English with photographic illustration. Jib provided expert linguistic help. We settled for kingfish, deep fried in batter and served with a sweet and sour sauce. You added the sauce yourself so the batter had little time to get soggy. There were two dishes of vegetables – one spicy, the other bland – as well as a neat hemisphere of rice made by inverting a bowl of the stuff. We helped ourselves to these, which made the meal take longer and seem more of a shared experience. Meanwhile two musicians played with serenity and professionalism, wearing pink silk frocks and pearls. One played the sore duong, a stringed instrument the length of a violin but held vertically like a viol, the other the kim, a mellifluous Thai version of the dulcimer family. The nasal poignancy of the sore duong was offset by the bell-like sweetness of the kim.

Chris explained that he liked Thailand because 'you can get a meal any time in the night.' Jib said that medicine was good in Thailand. The doctors trained in the West. Arabs went to Bangkok for their operations because of the price.

'She's delightful,' I said to Chris when she was out of the room, 'very pretty, very sweet.'

Later, when he left the table, I asked her about her family. She'd two younger brothers, one studying architecture, the other engineering. As she seemed intelligent and capable of putting her mind to many different subjects I wondered why she wasn't heading for a professional career like her brothers. Perhaps her parents held a traditional view of the role of women. The young pair were good enough to walk me to a bus stop, Jib taking my arm to steer me in the right direction. They waited with me until the right bus came along. I asked the driver for the train station, loud enough for everyone to hear. Someone was good enough to translate. I sat in the front looking out for the station but it never appeared. I felt someone tapping my arm. For a moment I thought it was a pickpocket, but it was a woman signalling that I should get off there, and when I did, I found myself at the end of a subway that led to the station. I wouldn't have found it without that help.

The next day I discovered a new place for breakfast. When I arrived they were opening up for the day. A woman was going around the building lighting joss sticks. Beside each she knelt, put her hands together and prayed. The smell was exotic, heady and sensuous. Three small cats, a tortoiseshell, a black-and-white and a ginger, their build resembling the Siamese cats I'd seen in Britain, jumped up to investigate the joss sticks. They kept returning to sniff them. The menu included fried ducks' mouths, but I had rolls with spicy pork, a pleasant sauce and sliced fresh tomatoes. Around the world breakfast seems to be the meal with the most surprises.

Chris had told me about a spectacular show called 'Siam Niram' at the Siam Ratchada Theatre. I set off to go to the venue by train in order to buy a ticket for the evening. The station authorities recognised that people needed to wait so they provided seats for them – 552, in straight rows as if for a concert – United Kingdom rail companies, please note! Passengers were queuing at separate windows for specific needs such as 'postponement of journey' and 'refund of fare'. There were two windows for foreigners only, 16 for 'rapid & express' and three for 'commuter trains'. Employees wearing yellow shirts were there to help passengers, directing them to the appropriate queues. I asked one of these 'yellow shirts' where the tourist information was. She beckoned a roving advisor over, who told me I could go to Ratchada on the underground. There was only one underground line from the rail station and I took this to the only station with the word 'Ratchada' in the name, 'Ratchada Phisek'.

When I got there I found no sign of the theatre or the box office. I walked up and down the street in the heat. It was hopeless. I decided to look for lunch – problems never seem so bad when you've eaten. I spotted a small restaurant advertising 'vegetarian food for health'. Three women were sitting at a table having a jolly time. The eldest got up to serve me and then went back to sit with the others. There was no one else. One of the women, called Natkritta, spoke English, translated and invited me to join them. When I'd finished eating the food I'd ordered, they shared some of theirs with me. It was Natkritta's birthday and this little get-together was by way of a celebration. She was an air stewardess with Thai Airlines. You don't have to fly to meet an air stewardess. She had bought some blueberries in Tesco and they were now sitting on the table, there in Bangkok. Natkritta and the blueberries were looking very fresh.

I thought she'd just flown in from London and brought the blueberries with her. But I found out later that Tesco have branches in Thailand. The world, I realised, was definitely getting smaller. The woman who had served me ran the restaurant. She wanted to move to England and open a similar restaurant there. She asked me what I thought about this idea.

'Well,' I said, 'the British enjoy Thai food and more and more people are becoming vegetarian. But a Thai vegetarian restaurant is a bit unusual so I think it would be best to go to a city, not a small town, so that there would be enough people who would want to eat in your restaurant.'

The third woman was Natkritta's sister. She was in admin, for her sins. I really enjoyed being with these people, even though I could only talk to Natkritta – or through her to the other two. I was touched by their friendliness. By the time the little party was breaking up it was raining quite hard. Natkritta offered me a lift, with her sister, to the theatre.

'Be careful,' she warned, 'there are people who want to take your money – or kill you!'

She gave me her e-mail address and I agreed to let her know when I got home. I bought a ticket for the evening show, went back to my hotel and had a rest. I hid my camera in my room and set out again for the theatre. I was glad I'd done a recce because I'd learned that there was a courtesy bus from the appropriate station to the theatre. The venue had the biggest foyer I have ever tramped across, laid out like the forecourt of a palace with statuary and fountains. I walked past a big heap of cameras, which had been taken off the audience for the duration of the show, and I was glad I hadn't brought my camera with me. Losing a camera is one thing, but losing photographs of an unrepeatable round-the-world odyssey is another! The usherettes were the smartest I'd ever seen. The seating was raked. The seat numbers were illuminated. There was an audience of about 400 people. That sounds respectable until you realise that the theatre could seat 2,000.

'Ladies and gentlemen, please rise for the Royal Anthem!'

The stage was wide, deep and high. The players, not the tallest in the world, in that arena looked like miniatures. The show (presented by Chang Drinking Water) offered a 'Journey to the Enchanted Kingdom of Siam', with sections such as 'Journey Back to History' and 'Journey Through Joyous Festivals'. It was seamless and slick with stunning effect after stunning effect. No expense had been spared. There was a cast of 150, wearing 500 costumes. We were offered music, drumming, rain, thunder, lightning, incense burning on stage and some huge, solid-looking scenery. There were dancers on the platform and in the auditorium. There were shadow puppets, 'big heads' and mythical creatures. Statues came to life. There were real goats. An elephant came through the audience, a couple of metres from my nostrils. Somebody bathed in a river on stage – no, not a simple trough of water, but a moving river. I know that because later floating candles moved across the stage, all going one way. The flying ballet made 'Peter Pan' look like kids' stuff. The show was more pageant than drama. I was impressed rather than engaged, even though there was a good synopsis in the programme. I came away marvelling but not particularly stirred.

The Thai people, I learned, had great respect and fondness for their king, but Monday was a day when they particularly liked to show their feelings for him by wearing yellow shirts; and there were many in evidence at Bangkok railway station. On platform 10 someone was washing a train with a hose. My train on platform 11 was less well cared for. The seats were blue, in a slippery, artificial leather. The windows were more or less opaque. I found a hard seat on the shady side with a reasonably clean window. A man moved through the train sweeping the floor and came back later with a mop. A veteran athlete, wearing shorts, which showed off his wiry brown legs, was sitting holding a large gold-and-yellow presentation cup with a ribbon. The back of the man's shirt bore the legend 'London Mini Marathon. The cup said, 'Second prize, over sixties'.

The train kept stopping, sometimes at stations. Vendors came on the train, sold their wares and got off at the next station, like they did on the buses in Mexico, although their baskets were bigger and their selling style quieter.

I checked that we were going north by making sure the morning sun was on the right hand side of the train. I ate a sausage on a stick and some biscuits. I drank some of the water I'd brought with me. I took my usual pills plus a multi-vitamin pill as I didn't expect to be particularly well nourished that day, but at 10am they served breakfast. Maybe they couldn't afford smart new rolling stock but at least they believed in feeding their passengers. After eighty minutes we kept up a good speed and overtook another train.

Through the window I saw a game of football, all the players boys. Both sides wore yellow, presumably royalists to a lad. In a place that seemed very ordinary a Buddha appeared as if by magic, the size of a two-story house, gleaming in the sun. There were droopy-eared cattle with humps. A man was cooling off in a deep pond. More amazing, I saw a small hippo. I know that from a moving train you can't be too sure, but this must have been a hippo because it was a dirty grey colour, it was standing in water and it had a fat, rounded backside. What it was doing standing around in a field like a farm animal I didn't know. Then I saw some more and realised they weren't hippos at all – they were water buffalo. After the skinny and angular tropical cattle they did indeed look rounded, but I then saw they had horns.

At Khon Kaen I stayed at the 22-storey Hotel Sofitel. Towering above unpretentious buildings of ordinary size, it looked like a stork in a frog pond. Disgusting hotels exert a powerful fascination over me. Even indifferent hotels offer something of interest. Luxurious hotels make me smile, but when they do what they do well, you will find that I am not grudging in my praise. The Hotel Sofitel, Khon Kaen was an establishment of immense charm and comfort – not to mention size. The forecourt was elegantly dressed with greenery including palm trees, evergreens in pots and perfect hedges. Siamese lions glowered, fountains frolicked, clever lighting emphasised and lanterns smiled. A grand carriage drive directed your carriage to a porch that could house two double-decker buses. I entered to the beguiling sounds of a kim, placed on a giant coffee table with room for the player to sit on a cushion, her knees modestly to one side, her feet tucked away out of sight.

The hotel had been designed around a super-atrium lit by daylight through a vast sloping glass roof. Some elegant boutiques were incorporated into the grand scheme. Throughout the building, the structure and its fittings repeated a single motif, a square balancing on one corner, everything in a restrained palette of rust, black and beige with occasional highlights of gold, a conceit carried to its logical conclusion, even to the most stylish yet practical hotel suite I have ever collapsed in. As you entered, a light came on. There was marble on every surface except the ceiling, the toilet seat and a desk whose top was apparently made from a single piece of knotty rosewood or something similar from the forests of Thailand.

There was a terrifying view of the city (I was on the 15th floor) and an air-conditioning system of subtlety and discretion, but with hidden reserves of power. The subtle and flexible lighting was controlled by a panel of buttons. The minibar included a barbecue-flavoured taro fish snack, 'French fries', four Toblerone, a can of lemon-grass juice, chewing gum, 14g of mouth freshener and six fresh condoms.

The wardrobe, which stood between the entrance of the suite and the bathroom, could be attacked from both sides. The knobs on the bathroom door were gold on the outside and silver on the inside, to match the respective décors. A glass-walled shower was big enough to ablute the largest visitor. The vast vanity unit possessed a giant shaving mirror with an additional magnifying mirror mounted on it, which would have enabled me to count my face hairs before mowing them down if I had been so minded. A socket for electric shavers with a choice of voltage was accompanied by a separate voltage control next to it, presumably to allow fine tuning to the mini-volt. The maid not only re-made my bed, she organised the books and papers on the desk into aesthetically pleasing piles, rationalised the mess I'd left in the bathroom and threw out a toothpick I had thought would do 'one more time'. One night in this palace including breakfast cost 2,400 baht – a crippling £16!

The staff were graceful, gracious and charming. But when will hotels pack in this nonsense of the 'welcome drink'? It is said to be complimentary. Who pays for it? We, the guests do. Second, the welcome drink is hedged about with so many limiting clauses that you need to bring your own lawyer! At the Sofitel you were allowed to have 'a beverage, a soft drink or a Kronen beer'. I didn't want a soft drink. I didn't particularly want a Kronen beer. I prefer to try the local beer. Indeed I'd already discovered that Thai beer goes better with Thai food than European lagers, which probably cost more, being imported. Either hand me a glass of champagne or forget the whole thing! However, I'm prepared to play by the rules. Noting the word 'beverage' I thought I'd use my complimentary 'welcome drink' ticket to pay for a cup of lemon tea.

'I'm sorry, sir,' the waitress said, 'that doesn't count. You can have beer or a soft drink ...'

'Thank you. I would still like the tea. You'll just have to put it on my bill.'

The waitress brought me a silver pot of tea and poured me a cup. The 'lemon' tea, however, had been made with a slice of lime. The lime is a staple of Thai cuisine but tea is a subtle flavour that calls for subtle treatment. I had to fish out the offending fruit with a spoon to make the stuff drinkable.

I did have my welcome drink (Kronen beer) before dinner and sat in the vast lobby, where entertainment was being provided by an accomplished pianist, playing jazz with great smoothness and assurance while a female of a certain age played the bongos. Her hair, which had been dyed brown, went past her bosom. She had kept her dainty figure and wore a top with a pink ruched bodice and a salmon-pink bra portion. She had a sort of lacy pink doily wrapped around tiny black shorts, which clung to her neat little pins like something meant for cycling. She balanced on pencil-thin heels, which (despite the fact that you could have posted the whole of the performer airmail for very little cost) dug deep into the carpet. I could hardly keep a straight face.

She gave us (I should say 'me' – there was no one else around) 'Que sera, sera' and the two of them revived 'Dream, dream, dream, dream – dream', made famous in the fifties by the Everly Brothers. Culture is like a bottle with a message inside – you never know where it will wash up. I had been a wonderful audience, applauding eight or ten numbers. I got up, walked over to them, gave them both a Thai-style greeting and requested they sing a Thai song. They obliged. Then they announced an interval of 15 minutes and moved towards the bar. But I cut them off and offered to buy them drinks. This they accepted gracefully.

'It was wonderful for me,' I told them, 'from England, to hear those old songs – so far from where I learned them.'

'Do you play an instrument?' the man asked politely.

'No,' I said, 'but I played the flute at school. I was in the school orchestra.'

'You don't play now?'

'No, I'm a writer. Well, I'll let you have your break.'

I said a few words to the woman, shook the hands of both of them and went in to dinner.

The next day, after breakfast, I went to the station to buy my ticket for the last leg of my journey through Thailand.

'I want to go to Nong Khai.' I said, 'tomorrow morning.'

The ticket seller showed me the screen. There were a number of very early trains but not the 9.42, which I'd seen on some timetable. Maybe he thought I wouldn't want to travel third class. I pressed him for a train at nine something. He brought up the 9.42.

'May I have a seat by the window?'

He looked blank. I moved to the actual window of the ticket office and squatted beside it, grinning supposedly like someone enjoying the view from a train window. He smiled and said something.

'Air conditioning?' I asked.

He shook his head.

'Fan?'

I made a rotary movement with my hand.

'Yes.'

So he booked me third class. I smiled, gave him a Thai greeting and left. I decided that when the time came I would take cold water and ice, wrapped to stay cold. I would keep my rucksack and hand luggage with me at all times. Wilting fast, I was looking for a stationers, when I came to a restaurant with shade outside and a fan under it. A nice Thai woman let me join her and we had something like a conversation. I managed to convey that I was going to Laos and Vietnam, but I lost her when I got to China. I ordered what she was having. Why not? I hadn't a clue what it was but it had lots of brown juice and some noodles, which she was eating with chopsticks. When it came I found it was salty – it would replace the salt I'd lost through sweat. I looked for cutlery. My new friend pointed to a canister of chopsticks. I selected a pair and got stuck in. The stir-fried beef – if that was what it was – I could readily grasp. Some rubber balls the size of lychees, which I took to be mini-dumplings, I could carry to my lips at the first attempt. Much harder was to draw a mouthful of the slippery and elastic noodles, out of the general tangle without either picking up too many or dropping the lot. So I conveyed a single noodle to my lips and sucked, chasing the quivering end up with the chopsticks to show willing. It wouldn't fool a Thai – I doubt it would have fooled anyone – but it kept me happy. There was a short-handled spoon intended for the sauce. I could always bring that into play if desperate.

While I'd been travelling I'd invented 'The John Barclay Leapfrog-Currency Gambit'. The idea was to avoid the dodgy business of exchanging money at the border when the traveller is at his most fraught and the people available to help you invite the most suspicion. When leapfrogging, while you are in the middle of a country, you exchange all the currency you still have from the previous country, for the currency of the country you will enter next. This way you don't have to judge how much to keep of the current currency to get you to the border. And you don't have to deal with touts. You arrive at the border already stocked with the currency of the next country. It takes all the stress out of the business. While perfect in theory, I was about to learn that in practice there can be problems. Some countries refuse to handle the currency of one or more of their neighbours.

I went into a Western Union office to get some Lao kip, the currency for Laos. The process was most impressive. One person talked to the customer. Another took the customer's money. A third took a wad of the new currency from the company's reserves and placed it on the desk. Finally, a fourth put the customer's money away in a drawer. All four I asked for Lao kip. After I'd signed various documents, unintelligible because they were in Thai or too faint to read or both, one of the team laid out a quantity of Thai baht on the counter.

'But,' I complained, 'I asked for Lao kip and you are giving me Thai baht. Please may I have Lao kip?'

They looked at me as if I were asking if the King of Thailand would be available to address the Langton Matravers branch of the Women's Institute next Tuesday, tea and biscuits provided. But you don't get round the world by giving up at the first hurdle. I got out my map of SE Asia.

'Tomorrow,' I explained in a jaunty voice, walking my fingers cartologically in a northerly direction, 'I go to Laos.'

By now the four clerks were agog.

'We can't supply Lao kip,' one of them revealed in a tone of regret, 'but in Laos they like baht.'

'Thank you very much,' I said, smiling and Thai-greeting each one of them, as I gathered up the Thai baht and went on my way.

In the night I woke and started thinking about the journey I was to take in the morning. What would third class be like? I didn't mind a hard seat or lack of air conditioning. There would be fans and I hoped they'd be working. What scared me was the thought that I'd be the only European on a train full of poor people. I might be robbed. I found the ticket I'd bought. The cost was 35 baht (23p) – for a journey of 180 km (113 miles). What could I expect at that price? Certainly not security! Telling myself that if it seemed too scary I needn't go – or I could get off at an intervening station, I got up and poured myself some chilled water from the fridge. I decided I wouldn't leave my luggage unattended on the train while I went to the toilet. The other day I had gone eight hours without urinating – I did sweat, of course. I could easily go three hours without visiting the toilet. I would need to drink enough coffee at breakfast to keep me awake to thieves but not so much as to act as a diuretic. On the back of the ticket it said, 'animals or strong-smelling food/fruits are not allowed in air-conditioned coaches'. This implied that animals and smelly food would be allowed on coaches that were not air-conditioned. That meant that once the smells had entered the train there'd be nothing to take them away. But that was the least of my problems. Finally, I had a cold. I'd run out of paper tissues. Would I have time to buy some before the train left? I was now in such a tizzy that when I heard the noise of an aeroplane I thought it was going to crash into the hotel.

As I checked out, I bought some paper tissues at Reception. I was pleased to see that most of my fellow passengers on the train were women – decent street traders. One had a camera – they weren't desperately impoverished. Some had baskets of fruit but it didn't smell and there wasn't a whiff of livestock. I sat next to one of the street traders on a seat on the platform. She said something to me. I don't know what it was. I said, 'Nong Khai'. She gave my rucksack a squeeze, half affectionate, half curious. Perhaps she thought I was carrying some exotic produce, such as cauliflowers. Everyone had at least two seats. I sat with the woman who had squeezed my rucksack, and a friend of hers. On the other side of the aisle was a young woman in a smart shirt, decent jeans with a leather belt and black slippers with a silver satin trim. She had a little bag with zips and a personal stereo. She wore a gold band on a finger. I looked less respectable than her. On reflection I was safer with these people. If you were a thief, would you look for victims to rob on a train where the passengers had paid only 35 baht?

None of the fans was working. Most of the windows were open allowing a pleasant breeze. I didn't like to open mine too much in case someone took a dislike to me and threw my rucksack off the train. I had a lovely drink of water, still cold after an hour wrapped in a towel. We passed a man pushing a cylinder with a handle like a lightweight roller right through a big brown puddle. I think he must have been carrying out one of the stages in cultivating rice. It looked like a messy business. I later saw men wading in muddy water.

We stopped at a station. There was a pleasing smell of warm damp earth, but this quickly gave way to the smell of ammonia – presumably from the train's own toilets. It began to rain and the rain came in through the open window. I put my cap on sideways to keep my hearing aid dry. It was now too cool to sweat much. Two hours to go and already I felt the urge to pee. I couldn't push the window up to close it or bring the shutter down to cover the gap. When the guard came along I got him to try. He brought the shutter right down so I was dry but I lost the view. The door at the back of the coach, which had been difficult from the start, was swinging with a clanking sound as the train bounced along. The breeze was welcome. The train was as draughty, bumpy and noisy as a local bus in Guatemala. I found myself singing, to myself of course, 'I'm going round the world!'

Finally I stopped worrying about being robbed or assaulted and started worrying about entering Laos. I stopped worrying about Laos when a pain in one leg started me worrying about deep vein thrombosis. I think it was worrying that kept me going.

At Nong Khai I got off the train feeling much happier than when I got on. After a rushed visit to the toilet, I soon found myself in a tuk tuk with four other passengers going to the frontier. The old anxiety returned; I was stepping into the unknown. But I knew that every frontier I crossed would take me nearer to my goal of going round the world without burning a centilitre of aviation fuel and of course I pressed on towards Laos.

20. Laos

August 29 – 31

It took a long time to pass through Immigration. I was seen by five different officials. I gave in 4,000 baht and got back a wad of Lao kip as thick as my finger. The last official I saw was at the Passenger Ticket Desk.

'Tuk tuk, taxi or minibus?' he asked.

'Er, er, minibus,' I said.

I thought a minibus would take the largest number of people and therefore be the cheapest, so I bought a ticket.

'D'you want to share a tuk tuk? An English girl asked.

'I'd love to share with you,' I said, 'but I've already bought a ticket for a minibus.'

'Is that some terrible amount of money?' she asked.

'I've no idea.'

I was used to minibuses waiting till they were full. As it turned out I was the only passenger and I travelled in style to Vientianne. I found the Laongdao Hotel down a side street. Having checked in, I went for a wet walk through the town. In Malaysia and Thailand they drive on the left. In Laos they drive on the right. I had gone from countries where the main European influence had been British to a country where the French have unquestionably left their mark. I noted the *'Institut de Recherche en Urbanisme'* and the *'Desjoyaux Piscine'*. But there was also the 'B&T Alcohol Shop'. Two young girls were playing draughts on a chequered table using bottle tops as pieces.

I had my first Lao meal and made my first acquaintance with yard-long beans. They were like runner beans and because they'd been cut up diagonally I wasn't able to check whether they measured up to their name. With the beans I had stir-fried spicy pork and rice. There were five people on a round table next to mine. The oldest man was smoking between courses – I hadn't seen that for some time. Then with a magnifying glass he set about threading a needle. After the pork and beans I was still hungry so I asked to see the menu books again. I chose cashew nuts with mushrooms and orange. It arrived with spring onions but no orange as in the picture.

The next morning it was raining again – well, it was the rainy season. I walked along the street looking for breakfast. I found a place with a notice saying 'café'. I pointed to a bowl of broth a man was eating and asked the woman for coffee. I sat down at a table close to the motor mechanics' shop next door, where a man was repairing motorbikes – a good business to have in that part of the world. The woman brought me a small glass of warm tea. I was about to complain that I'd asked for coffee, when the broth arrived. The woman took a pair of chopsticks and wiped them on a sheet from a roll that wouldn't have looked out of place in a bathroom. The tea was drinkable. The broth was great, with tender lumps of pork falling off the bone, and noodles, all of it easy to lift with the chopsticks. It came with a separate dish of bean sprouts, some spring onions with a segment of lime to squeeze on them and a plastic pot of shredded ginger in some kind of liquor. Then the coffee arrived, hot in a glass with the Nescafé logo on the side. It wasn't Nescafé as we in the West know it but I managed to get it down with sugar, which I don't normally take. Almost at my elbow the mechanic next door started up the motorbike he was working on. It coughed and belched thick smoke. Mercifully the exhaust was pointing to the road. Then he tuned the engine, revving the throttle continually. A woman wearing a conical 'coolie' hat went by with two baskets hanging from the ends of a bendy staff over her shoulder. Another, wearing a similar hat, was pushing a vegetable stall on wheels with its own sunshade.

The Thais had struck me as elegant, charming and gracious. The Lao people seemed more subtle and rather more real. It was a shame I couldn't afford to spend longer in the country. I was not much more than 200 miles from the border with Vietnam, where I was heading, but I was running behind schedule. I was supposed to be averaging more than 1,000 miles a week – and goodness knows what difficulties lay ahead. Just because Laos was a separate country – and a beautiful one too by all accounts – I couldn't justify staying to explore.

I checked out of the hotel and took a tuk tuk to the International Bus Station. The only bus going to Vietnam was the night bus to Vinh, which would be leaving at 7pm. The distance was 250 miles. I didn't like the idea of arriving in the small hours and I didn't want to miss the countryside, but there seemed to be no choice. There wasn't a white person in sight. I had some lunch under one of the two fans in the building. A man came up to me.

'Where are you going?' he asked.

'Vietnam', I said.

He went away. I started studying my Lonely Planet Guide to S E Asia. Another man came and sat next to me. He started looking at the book with me. I felt exposed sitting there in the bus station. So I got up and went for a little walk in the sun. After three-quarters of an hour of serious dithering I went back to the bus station. I went up to the ticket window.

'This bus at 1900 hours to Vinh,' I asked, 'is it the only one?'

'Yes.'

'When does it get in?'

'12am.'

I needed to know whether this meant 12 noon or 12 midnight. So I drew a picture of the moon and wrote '5 hours' next to it, then a picture of the sun with '17 hours' next to it. The answer was '17 hours'. An average speed of 50 mph did seem a bit ambitious, while 15 mph was a snail's pace. But it looked like the only way to the coast, where I hoped to take the railway north to Ha Noi. So I bought a ticket. I asked the woman, mainly in sign language, whether I'd be able to put my rucksack on the luggage rack above my head or whether I'd have to put it in the hold. She nodded to both. She agreed to look after my rucksack in the meantime, but wouldn't give me a receipt. I didn't like this because the rucksack wasn't locked away, but sometimes you have to accept risks. My cold was better, so that was something to be cheerful about.

I went and had a drink in another restaurant under two big fans. A little boy from the next-door house came out in pyjamas and slippers to play. It was three o'clock. He must have just got up from his siesta. I went back to the bus station. I had a look to see if my rucksack was still there. It was, but the woman guarding it had fallen asleep. The bus station had an Internet café so I spent some time there.

At 5.30 I collected the rucksack and went to the toilet to wash. After a day in the heat I was in no state to sit all night close to a lot of fellow travellers. Natives of those parts don't suffer from BO – unless a European sits next to them! The floor of the washroom was wet all over – I couldn't put anything down. I needed to get my wash bag, a clean shirt and my medical bag out of my rucksack. By hanging bags on both handles of the door and using a small rail I managed to give my top half a good wash, spray myself with deodorant and put on the clean shirt. When I finally came out again the woman on the door gave me a funny look, presumably because I'd been so long. Then I realised I'd forgotten the medical bag. This was essential because I needed to get out my pills for the morning. So I chose a quiet spot in the bus station and started to unpack my rucksack. Immediately a guy spotted me and sat down a metre and a half away to watch. In England I would have said, 'Do you want something?' in an indignant voice. But there in Vientianne I just had to grin and bear it. I looked at him. He smiled. I never thought of trying French. Then I noticed, just outside the window, something that could have been a shrine. Maybe that was the problem.

'I need to get something out of my bag,' I said to the guy watching me, 'is it all right if I do it here?'

He nodded and continued to watch me. Perhaps he was just a nosey sod. With him breathing down my neck the job of unpacking and repacking took longer. Finally, I got up, swung my rucksack onto my back, picked up my two bags of hand luggage and started to move. The guy pointed outside.

'No,' I said, 'bus!'

'Don't you want tuk tuk?' he asked.

'No, I'm going on the bus.'

It was a bus station, not a tuk-tuk station so he shouldn't have been surprised. I walked away from him, just to make it clear. I then went to the other end of the bus station, where the café was situated, to have an early supper before my journey. I ordered soup. In these unglamorous surroundings I was very touched that they brought me a finger bowl. The bowl felt hot, so the water must have been. What a lovely gesture. I didn't need a finger bowl as I'd just had a good wash. I sat there waiting for my soup. When it didn't arrive I began slowly to accept the possibility that the finger bowl, which was cooling by the minute, might not be a finger bowl at all. It might be a soup bowl. And the once-hot water might be some very, very clear soup. They had after all put a little sprig of parsley on it. So I waited for the waitress to reappear.

'Soup?' I asked pointing to the water.

She nodded and smiled.

'We've got a right one here!' she must have been thinking.

The soup was lovely. It would have been fantastic while it was still hot. When I'd finished the rest of my meal it was time to board the bus. Outside, a line of shiny, colourful vehicles were waiting. None was going to 'Vinh'. By then I was an experienced bus traveller so I knew what to do. I showed my ticket to a man. He led me away to a corner of the bus park. There was a single bus with no light on. Women were sitting on stools so small they looked as though they'd been stolen from a primary school. Men were throwing filled sacks onto the roof of the bus. A man standing on the roof to stack this freight took his shirt off and his torso gleamed in the lamplight. Meanwhile what seemed in the darkness to be a boy came up to me.

'Where are you going?' he asked.

'Vinh,' I replied.

'Have you paid?'

'Yes.'

'Have you got a ticket?'

I showed it to him. He encouraged me to take my rucksack inside the bus – there wasn't room on the roof. That suited me and I wedged the rucksack between two seats. At five past seven we started off. At quarter past we pulled into a parking space next to a smaller bus. The driver and the conductor got out. It became very hot in the bus. The passengers started to get out as well. When the bus was almost empty I got out myself. I stood by 'my' window to keep an eye on my bags. I could see that we were parked at what looked like the back door of a restaurant. It seemed a bit soon for a meal break. Ten or more passengers joined the party. More goods were stowed on the roof of the bus. At 7.50 some men came aboard with heavy discs of wood. I was beginning to understand how a 250-mile journey could take 17 hours. We moved off.

With the extra people, some westernised oriental music and a Japanese film with the sound off but Lao subtitles, the atmosphere was jolly jolly. People smoked but the bus was draughty and the smoke didn't linger. I couldn't get comfortable enough to sleep for long. I kept my eyes on the window. I was eventually rewarded with the silhouettes of mountains and several glimpses of an almost-full moon. Its reflection in the Mekong River was a romantic sight, which lent an air of mystery to the trip and reminded me of a boat trip upstream that at one point I'd hoped to work into my itinerary. On the other side of the Mekong lay Thailand, because for many miles the boundary between Laos and Thailand follows the river.

At 1.15am we unloaded a lot of stuff. At 1.20 we stopped alongside another bus outside another café. I ran to the loo not knowing how long we would be there. When I got back I saw that some people had settled down to sleep in the bus. The driver, the conductor and some of the passengers had disappeared. It seemed to be a transport café. I didn't know what facilities were on offer. I'd heard no announcement – not that I could have understood it – but everyone seemed to know what was happening except me. The parking area was huge. I hung about outside to keep an eye on the bus in case my luggage walked. It was warm enough. Obviously, I thought, the driver needed a break. Maybe he was asleep in a bed paid for by the bus company. I heard someone having a shower.

'Do you want a room?' somebody asked me.

'No, thank you,' I said.

By that time I'd already lost at least an hour. In any case I was afraid to leave the parking area in case the bus went off without me. When eventually we did move on, it was getting light. I think I slept a bit in my seat.

We followed the Mekong or one of its tributaries, as it snaked through a wooded valley. At times it had sandy banks, spits and islands. In or beside the white water there were chunky rocks, their edges rounded by erosion. It reminded me of the upper stretches of the River Loire in France. I saw three women standing in the water washing clothes.

There was confusion at the Vietnamese border. I managed to get rid of all my Lao currency. The queue for passport inspection was chaotic. The locals respected a queue – as long as they were at the front of it. I stood in the throng while very little happened. There were two British couples from another bus. We exchanged sarcastic comments to keep our spirits up. Suddenly a woman in pink appeared, whom I'd not seen before.

'Passports, passports!' she called and started collecting them in.

She wore no badge of office and for all I knew she could have been a key player in a stolen-passport racket. What better place to steal them? Someone else collected up passports and handed them in as a job lot. For some reason I deduced from this that it would be a good idea to give my passport to the pink woman. After some anxious moments I saw Pinkie pass a pile of passports through a window. I don't know why her passing them through the window was any better than my handing my own passport in – except that people let her push to the front of the throng. Anyway she managed to get a pile of passports back and she handed them out again. The best of it was that the passport she handed me turned out to be mine and what's more it had been stamped. Sometimes you just have to go with the flow.

21. Vietnam

August 31 – September 6

On the Vietnamese side, things were much better organised. Here the delay was caused by a conscientious inspector with a microscope (really), poring over the European passports. He'd obviously heard about the passport racket on the Lao side. We also had to wait for a check on the bus. This was performed by an Alsatian dog, on a leash all the time. He was so eager to begin his inspection that he got an erection. Whether he was looking for explosives, drugs, illegal immigrants or a bitch on heat I never discovered.

The countryside was beautiful with deep, wooded valleys and dramatic with hairpin bends. We were stopped by a water buffalo standing in the road, causing the driver to do a lot of hooting. I saw more people wearing coolie hats. Everyone seemed to be engaged in different stages of harvesting rice – cutting it, bringing it home or spreading it out to dry. For the first time I saw a buffalo drawing a cart. As we came into Vinh we passed lots of children cycling home from school, many wearing peaked caps; some had anti-pollution masks. Adults were pushing bicycles laden too heavily to ride. Some were riding bikes piled so high that from behind all you could see was the luggage and the back wheel. One bike was loaded up with the contents of a stall – bright colourful plastic kitchen items carefully balanced and built out to the width of a tuk tuk. A woman was riding a bike with a big mesh basket of live piglets tied onto the rack behind her. The creatures were moving, but only just. The luckiest were the two put in last because they were on top of the heap. Pale lilac and mauve water lilies were growing in boats filled with water at the side of the road.

They threw me out on a busy street opposite the bus station, dumping my rucksack on the pavement. Immediately the usual suspects were round me.

'Ha Noi?' one tried.

I looked up and down the street hoping to find somewhere serving beer. A group of men were sitting on little plastic stools around a low table on the pavement, drinking the stuff. I had a look at the label on a beer bottle so that I could order it by name.

'Would you like a beer?' asked one.

Never accept a drink from a stranger. They found a stool for me and invited me to join them. We spoke a little English but mostly it was a matter of smiling and nodding. Every time someone felt like it we clinked glasses. We were outside the Nokia shop where these people worked. I asked if it was a special occasion.

'No,' one of them said, 'we just have drink.'

The next day I found that a bus went every 20 minutes to Ha Noi. It turned out to be a large minibus. The journey took six hours. Heads of sweetcorn had been spread out on a blue cloth in front of a house to ripen. Where there was vegetation it was thick and a bright green. I took Immodium as I had an unsettled 'tum' and couldn't afford to be caught out on a bus with no toilet. The door was kept open. I was careful not to let my bag slip forward because it could have been in the road in a second. If the driver had braked suddenly I would have been thrown forward myself to tumble out the open door, hitting the road at speed.

The driver meanwhile had a job to do – to get us all to Ha Noi in the time allotted – or earlier if possible. He tackled this with unwavering commitment, not to say spirit and aggression. By moving out onto the wrong side of the road, whenever there was a possibility of overtaking the vehicle in front, he maximised his chances of doing so, while greatly increasing the chances of causing a grisly accident.

He pulled in again whenever he came face to face with an oncoming bus or truck but, to make it more exciting, he left this until the last second. Many was the time that I grabbed hold of the rubber window seal, more for psychological comfort than out of any belief that this would save my life. Every time he tried to overtake, the driver emphasised the drama by sounding his horns. He had several and could produce a discord to make a European jump out of his skin. A fade effect added a little gratuitous eeriness. And all of the above he did just as much when we were whizzing through a built-up area as out on the open highway.

Once we nearly hit a police car. But to be fair to the driver, when an ambulance came up behind us, flashing its lights, our man did the decent thing and let the vehicle pass. But when the ambulance, then in front, didn't go fast enough for his liking he overtook it. This time the ambulance pursued us with its siren whining but it never caught us up. If we'd crashed we'd have needed a fleet of ambulances! To add a further frisson none of us enjoyed the benefit of a seat belt. If the driver (placed low down) had braked suddenly, the little girl standing on a seat directly behind him would have been thrown over his head against the windscreen blocking his view until he pushed the poor creature out of the way, dead or alive. The child's mother wouldn't have saved her. She was busy on her mobile phone! Throughout the journey, the conductor and many of the passengers, amazingly, were asleep. The Vietnamese live on the edge – it's the way they seem to like it.

Miraculously we arrived at Ha Noi bus station in one piece. I sneaked out the back way to avoid the taxi touts but they were waiting for me, in taxis, on motorbikes and on foot as I walked along a busy road beside what I took to be the Red River. The motorbikes may have been scooters. They weren't very big so I didn't make a distinction. From now on I will call all motorised two-wheel vehicles motorbikes, because I don't want to belittle them.

'Where are you going?' someone asked me.

I didn't know the answer to that.

'It's a long way!' said another without knowing where I was going either.

The more they importuned me, the more determined I became to find a hotel on my own. At 6pm it was still hot but there was plenty of shade. My determination to walk until I saw a hotel worked in small towns. In a large city the hotels were clustered. Between the clusters were large hotel-free areas. I must have said, 'No!' to 50 offers of lifts before I found a hotel. And that was full. I asked people who weren't taxi-drivers but they gave me vague instructions, which never bore fruit.

'Sit down!' said a good-looking woman on her own at a little table outside a café.

She patted the empty seat next to her, hoping perhaps for some international trade.

'I won't sit down,' I said, 'I'm looking for a hotel.'

From then on I suspected every establishment of being an immoral one. It was getting dark and there was no street light. By the time I did find a hotel I thought it wisest to ask to see the room. This exchange took some minutes as it was done in a sort of sign language. A tall handsome young man showed me a room on the third floor. There was no lift. It had air conditioning, two room fans, a large mirror alongside the bed and an entirely separate bathroom – more than adequate.

'Passport, please,' he said, 'and 200,000 dong.'

I didn't like parting with my passport – let alone so many dong. After my hair-raising journey and my search for accommodation I felt hot, tired and dirty. I took off my clothes and was just about to step into the shower when there was a knock at the door. I wrapped a towel around my waist. It was so small I had to take care that the 'split-skirt look' came at the side. It was Tall-and-handsome holding a bath plug. He fitted it and explained how to get it out with your finger nails.

When he'd gone I tried myself to get the plug out. You don't need a plug for a shower! My finger nails weren't up to it, but I managed it with the nail scissors. Why do hotels give you a dainty tea service, a jar of tea leaves and two boxes of matches when there is no way of heating water?

The next morning I realised I was very short of dong, so I went out looking for an ATM. As I walked along the street some people laughed at me, presumably because I was obviously a foreigner. I managed to find a machine.

'Your card will expire soon,' the machine said. 'Contact your bank … No money available … Thank you for banking with us.'

I didn't like the last bit – 'thank you for banking with us.' It sounded so final. I wasn't going to stand around on the street with my bank card in my hand, in full view of all the passing thieves and ne'er-do-wells, so I went back to my room. I put the air conditioning on and looked at my card. The ATM had got me worried. You don't need a shock like that when you're thousands of miles from home in a strange place where you don't speak the language. I had two other cards, but they were useless. One, you may remember, had expired and the replacement promised hadn't arrived before I left. The other was an American Express cheque-card, which I was unable to use because I couldn't find a record of my pin number. I was skating on very thin ice.

I went out to get some breakfast. Again people laughed at me, but that was the least of my worries. I bought two soft rolls and a carton of 'orange milk' to take back to my room. I'd seen orange milk many times and hoped it would be a special sort of orange juice, but it was sweetened milk, flavoured with orange flavouring and coloured, I was sure, with artificial colouring. It was not quite as disgusting as it should have been. I went out again to try the other ATM. This wouldn't pay up – 'problem with service'. I asked to stay another night, but I hadn't got enough dong. I had a few American dollars for such an emergency and offered to pay with them. Tall-and-handsome changed them into dong but wouldn't take any money before 12 noon. So I went up to my room to wait until then. Notice how I kept returning to my room. I think this was from insecurity. There was a knock on the door. It was Tall-and-handsome with a friend he'd brought to interpret. I managed to get across that I wanted to stay another night. I pulled out 200,000 dong.

'… Eleven o'clock tomorrow,' I think the interpreter said.

His English was limited and he had a strong Vietnamese accent. To make things worse he insisted on speaking with a toothpick in his mouth. I put the money away. He wrote something down. I couldn't read it. It didn't look like 200,000 dong. Eventually he got through to me that I had to pay 250,000 dong.

'But it was only 200,000 yesterday!' I protested.

'You come late.'

'What?'

'Yesterday, you come late.'

So I paid up. A little later I went out to look for lunch. Then I returned for a siesta – stress is tiring. I set out at 2.45 to find an ATM that worked. There were motorbikes everywhere. I nearly stepped in the path of one. I walked for about 40 minutes without seeing an ATM. At a big crossroads there was a level crossing. I saw four women closing the gates by hand. The motorbikes were held in a mass, like contestants waiting for the start of a race. The ATM at the Agribank wouldn't touch my card. The sky grew dark. There was forked lightning and it began to rain. I sheltered under a canopy but the wind was so strong that I still got wet, so I went inside. On the second floor there was a parade of high-class fashion franchises. I'd only 10,000 dong in my pocket but I went round all the menswear shops for something to do until the rain eased. I was also hoping to get into conversation with someone who'd cash a cheque for me. It was starting to get dark. The wind dropped. The rain became vertical again and not so hard. But everywhere was flooded. I was working out how to get to the other side of an extensive, deep puddle between me and the pavement, when I saw a woman backing her little motorbike towards me, as if to rescue me. I couldn't see her face properly because she was wearing a waterproof and one of the small green hats you see so many of in Vietnam.

'That's very kind of you!' I called out.

As the bike came near I saw she was in fact a small man with a horizontal black line on his upper lip by way of a moustache.

'Are you going that way?' I asked, pointing back the way I'd come.

'Get on!' he called.

He got off and, wading through a deep puddle in his shoes, pushed the bike towards me. I realised he was a 'taxi-driver.'

'How much?' I asked.

'That's okay!' he called back.

I knew it was not a free lift.

'How much?' I asked again.

'Ten!' he called, and held up ten fingers (ten thousand dong).

That was all the money I had. But I had to get back to my hotel. He had me get on the bike. There was nothing to hold onto except the edge of the seat in front. He got on himself, stepping through the gap between me and the handlebars. Despite the wet and the fact that we were standing in deep water, the engine started first time and we were off. Almost immediately we were weaving through the traffic. I looked over the little fellow's shoulder and tried not to do anything to make him swerve or tip up on that wet surface. He dropped me at my hotel. I got out my 10,000-dong note, the only dong I possessed in the world.

'Two!' the little fellow said.

I thought he meant that he was only charging 2,000 dong. But he gave me no change. Tall-and-handsome, who'd been warming his hands at a little bonfire he'd lit at the side of the hotel, came forward and talked to the little fellow. Tall-and-handsome produced a 5,000-dong note and offered it to the little fellow, who held out his hand to me for my 10,000 dong. Then I realised he wanted *more* than 10,000 not *less*. So I took the 5,000 dong and returned it to Tall-and-handsome.

'You told me it would be 10,000,' I brazenly argued. 'If I'd known it would be more, then I wouldn't have got on the bike! We can't take this man's money.' I said, indicating Tall-and-handsome. 'You asked for ten. Here's ten. It's all I've got!'

When he saw that he wouldn't get any more from me, he took it.

'Thank you very much!' I said.

I walked quickly into the hotel and up to my room. I locked myself in. But when I realised that I had given the poor fellow the equivalent of only 30 pence, I felt mean. And he had waded through the water to get me! I don't remember ever being so bloody-minded and stingy. I had 26 US dollars hidden somewhere, but I would need them the next day. I was finding reserves of self-preservation I didn't know about. It gave me an insight into the desperation of *really* poor people. The stupidest thing was that I had gone out with only 30p on me. But what else was I to do? I had to go out looking for money. And 30p in Ha Noi is not the same as 30p in England.

I was up against it. But this shameful incident had sharpened my blunt brain. I remembered that I still had more than 2,000 Thai baht (about £30). I decided I would go to Western Union in the morning and change my baht into dong. I would keep the dollars for an emergency worse than the one I was then in. Meanwhile I had run out of something even more important than dong – drinking water! I didn't think I could go into a shop and expect to buy a bottle of water with dollars. Nor did I want to ask Tall-and-handsome for help after I'd behaved so badly over the little fellow. But I had a way out. I used my water-purifying tablets to purify a litre of tap water. I didn't have a litre bottle. It was a fiddle to make two 500-ml bottles of purified water with a tablet intended for one litre, but I had plenty of time. After all I couldn't afford to go out to eat. I had no food – only 180 millilitres of orange milk, which I would consume before I went to sleep.

I used the time to sort out a few things. Then I put the television on. There was a programme in French on archeology, another on golf from the United States with commentary in American, a football match between Arsenal and Plymouth with English commentary, an American film with Vietnamese subtitles, European athletics in English dubbed in Vietnamese, a Vietnamese programme, the 'Disney' channel, the 'Discovery' channel in American with Vietnamese subtitles, a nature programme from Australia and a Chinese drama with English subtitles. What a wide and international choice!

In the morning I set out on foot to find the Western Union. I'd seen it on the first day but now it seemed to have disappeared. It started getting dark and I heard thunder. I hoped I wouldn't be caught in another downpour. I went into a Nokia shop. They told me that it was Independence Day and all the banks were closed. I spent two dollars getting back on the back of a motorbike. As I did so I spotted a sign for Western Union high above a shop with its shutters closed. Back at the hotel I collected my passport and checked out. I had made up my mind to head for the Sofitel Hotel in the Old Quarter. It was the right area for banks and I knew that there I could pay by credit card. A motorcyclist offered to take me but I refused and took a taxi. I didn't fancy holding onto two bags with a rucksack on my back threatening to unbalance me. The taxi cost $5 so, still feeling guilty about my behaviour the previous day I gave the driver $6 and he seemed very pleased. But how could I not when arriving at an expensive hotel? I was delighted to find next to the hotel a 24-hour ATM of HSBC, my own bank! I drew 500,000 dong without difficulty – no mention of my card running out.

Now that I'd found a place to draw money I no longer had to stay in the Sofitel. But I kept returning to it every time I wanted to draw a million dong because I didn't come across another ATM. In this smart area there were always beggars hanging around. A woman was standing, breast-feeding her baby, with one hand free to take what I had to offer.

I was in the Old Quarter. It had a down-market feel to it and was favoured by tourists. In five minutes I was in a café ordering scrambled egg, bacon and coffee. The coffee came with additional hot water. The egg and bacon were delicious. They came with tomato and a crisp warm roll. I was out of the gutter and back in the civilised world!

I walked round the main lake in the rain, keeping close to the water to avoid the taxi touts. A man approached me, urbane and charming.

'Why you walk with rucksack?' he asked.

'I like to walk,' I replied. 'When you walk you see the trees and the birds.'

'I have a bike,' he announced, 'If you used me it would be good for business,' he continued.

This seemed to be stating the obvious. I had to assume that the bike was hidden behind a tree. Then he produced from nowhere a portable cardboard bookcase stocked with paperbacks.

'I couldn't possibly take any books,' I said, 'I have to carry everything on my back.'

Immediately he produced a selection of postcards. Meanwhile another man, a little younger, appeared and stood watching the master at work. I knew then I should move on.

'I don't want to take any more of your time,' I said and walked away.

Now that I was in the tourist area, I suppose, I should have expected such approaches but at least now no one looked at me as if my willy were poking out of my trousers. And so I came to the place I should have been all along – Camellia Hotel 5, recommended in my Lonely Planet Guide. There was a lovely atmosphere. It was clean and well run. Everything worked. The staff spoke English.

'Where you going tomorrow?' the man at the desk asked.

'Maybe China,' I said.

He gave me a street map of Ha Noi, marking the hotel and the bus station.

'Buses leave three times a day,' he said, '7.30, 9.30 and 11.30.'

'How long does it take?' I asked.

'Ten hours. You have to book. I can do that for you.'

'Thank you. I need to decide when to go.'

Before I left Ha Noi I had to buy a strap that had gone missing from my rucksack, an extra body pouch to keep the fund of American dollars I was trying to build up, razor blades, toilet paper, paper tissues, food for the bus and water. I also had to draw dollars and exchange my Thai baht. I hung up my wet clothes, locked the door and lolled on my new bed, with the fan on to cool me and to dry my clothes. My waterproof jacket was wetter on the inside from sweat than on the outside from the rain. My room was on the ground floor near the dining area but I was pleased to see that for extra security it had been built without a window.

Ha Noi shops are packed tight, like bricks in a wall. And each shop is packed tight with goods. Outlets of one kind are grouped together – as they are in many cities, but more so. All the shoe shops have been shooed into the shoe-shop quarter. When I went looking for the toiletries street, I found Toy-shop Place, Spectacles Space, Key-cutters' Court and Smokers' Parade, where a trader would sit with a basketwork tray of 50 different brands of cigarette. Goodness knows how stale the less popular brands were! There was a hairdressers' street but the best salon was on its own. This was in the open air and consisted of a mirror hung on a wall with a shelf fixed to the bottom of it at right angles, to hold the hairdresser's paraphernalia. The client sat on a chair on the pavement.

In the travel-goods section, all the shops selling rucksacks seemed to be together. So I went down Rucksack Road looking for a rucksack strap, couldn't find one, so I made do with a suitcase strap, which I adapted. Once I understood the principle of retail groupings I had little difficulty buying razor blades and the pouch I needed for my dollars. The layout must make life easy for the suppliers. I imagine they drive their vans as near as they can and ring a bell for all the shopkeepers of the particular trade to come out and restock.

The traffic never stopped. If you wanted to cross a road you had to dodge between the vehicles. In fact you had to look out for yourself all the time. It was worse at night, because many of the bikes didn't have lights. Even when you thought there was a gap someone would come at you the wrong way down a one-way street. The pavements were not made for walking; they were made for parking motorbikes, riding bikes to their parking places, trading, cooking, serving and eating food. The road is not for walking either; it's for motorbikes, taxis and buses. Pedestrians had to keep out of the way! Nowhere was for walking. Walking was for getting you from your bed to your motorbike or to a taxi.

Although this was a tourist area I saw few Europeans. Some were very visible because they had chosen to see this part of the city on cycle-rickshaws, which solved the problem of getting through the traffic. Because you never saw a native travelling in one of these vehicles, they put me in mind of Britain's colonial past. A middle-aged couple – he was from South Africa, she from Melbourne, helped me to find my way back to my hotel.

'This network of narrow streets is very confusing,' I said.

'You wait till you get to India!' replied the man.

We Europeans did look as if we were out of our element. European females, for instance, with their long strong legs and sensible shoes, standing next to the local women teetering on their pencil heels, looked like mares beside does.

On a café by the lake I had coffee and a chocolate pancake. The lake, I learnt, was called Hohn Kiem. It was visually peaceful, with its calm green surface and its pleasing reflections. Sometimes a wind brought up ripples all over the lake, an effect even more soothing. Hohn Kiem was the still centre of a hectic world. While you were looking at it you couldn't be looking at the traffic, weaving, jostling, hooting, cutting in, cutting across and cutting up other traffic, the restless, never-stopping traffic of the one-way orbital road around the lake. If you were looking in towards the lake, you'd still hear the sounds of the traffic, mostly motorbikes, but merging to become a continuous hum punctuated with horns. If you looked out from the lake, it was as restful as a wasps' nest.

I went into an exhibition of paintings put on by the Association of Vietnam Fine Arts. The paintings were like the Vietnamese, vigorous and 'in your face' – not particularly sophisticated but highly effective, with an undeniable humanity. One was an aerial view of a flyover packed with buses, cars and motorbikes – like red blood corpuscles coursing through an artery. Another aerial view, this time of an artists' life class, unusually showed the individual work of the students better than the students themselves. There was a wonderful painting of eight female bathers, inspired, I guessed, by the French Impressionists – seven women and a little girl, some washing, some drying themselves – no unnecessary detail, the skin European in its pallor. Apart from that and a sandy bank it was all in tones of blue and navy, which unified the scene.

The exhibition continued upstairs. I realised then that there were fewer pure landscapes than I would expect in such an exhibition and rather more depictions of human figures in action, real people, pleasingly placed within the frame. Again, a restrained palette used to strong effect – a war picture was done in reds and blues, the figures in blue/grey uniforms in the foreground while a battle raged in the mountains in red. A painting almost 2m by 1m of two women mending a fishing net while the rest of the family looked on except for grandfather, who was smoking and thinking his own thoughts, was designed like an old European master, but executed like a Japanese print. The exhibition reminded me of European art in the first half of the twentieth century, but it had a vitality and an integrity all its own.

The next day I went to an Internet café. In Ha Noi I was alert to every touch or movement near me. A draught catching my trousers would make me jump. The Internet café was arranged to get as many people and computers into as small a place as possible. In Ha Noi this meant being touched, jostled, bumped and having your chair knocked. Personal space seemed to be in short supply. Next to me were two boys looking at a single screen. They kept knocking me or my chair, which I found disconcerting. When they saw me react they made cheery, presumably jokey remarks to each other. What, I thought, if one of them puts his hand in my back pocket?

I had lunch in a different café on the edge of the lake. I got talking to a tall young Californian man, who was a perpetual traveller.

'The States may not remain the wonder currency,' he said. 'Much of America has no quality of life. People spend two hours a day travelling to work. One suburb merges with the next. They watch television, get married, get divorced, … '

'You're in no hurry to go back?' I suggested.

'I like to take my time,' he said. 'I taught myself Thai.'

'Vietnamese seems a noisy language,' I put to him.

'It's a pitched language,' he explained, 'like Mandarin Chinese. If the meaning depends on pitch you can't use pitch for emphasis, so they use volume more. At the weekend there was a celebration for their Independence Day – a great gathering, in some open space. There were acrobats and other performers. I got in with a lot of children – well, my age …'

'… but half your height?' I suggested.

'Yes, they invited me back to their place and it was incredible. There were builders there. Everyone seemed to be wearing a hard hat, so they had about 30 sleeping in one space, but they were so sweet, so sweet.'

'All statesmen, or so-called statesmen, should travel like you do,' I said, 'staying a while in a spot and seeing how the people really live. Then they would see these were decent people. If you travel on the buses you see everyone helping each other, or strangers like me. If the politicians saw that, how could they order the bombing of … ?'

He didn't need me to continue. Later I helped a man who was struggling with an umbrella turned inside out by the wind. I held the handle for him while he pushed the spokes back into place. Then he held the handle while I fed the spikes back into the slots in the material. I went back to have another look at the art exhibition. It was being broken up and many of the pictures had been taken away, although I was able to have another look at the bathers. I saw one of the artists taking a painting away tied upside down on the roof of a tuk tuk. Another artist drove a motorbike while a woman I took to be his daughter sat behind him holding a big picture.

That evening I hid my camera under my bed and set out to eat. It was getting dark so I dived into a restaurant. The dining room was upstairs but before I reached it I was greeted by a welcome party of flunkeys and pretty girls in smart uniforms. I seemed to be the only customer.

'I see I've beaten the rush!' I would have quipped – if I'd been in Britain or Australia – but this place was too serious for such frivolity.

I was led into a room, where I took the only small table. A waiter brought the menu and stood over me while I pondered, chose and ordered. There is no pleasure in choosing under pressure so I tried to choose quickly, but I wasn't quick enough.

'A drink to start with?' he suggested.

'Yes, please, I'll have orange juice.'

'If I might suggest, ...' the waiter began.

'Yes, yes, please do.'

'Some steamed rice ...'

Well, thanks a lot! Trust him to do the easy bit. Anyone can recommend steamed rice! I looked up and down the menu, for something to go with the rice. Of the items I could understand, the only thing I thought I would like was chicken. But that wasn't very adventurous.

'I'll have the pigeon, please,' I said, 'and some beer.'

'But you've got the orange juice!' he argued.

'That's for a starter. I'll have the beer with my meal.'

What happened to 'The customer is always right'? Another waiter came in. He was junior to the joker who had taken my order. They stood apart and hovered. A member of the lower orders brought my orange juice up the stairs on a tray, from which my waiter collected the juice to bring to me while the other waiter continued to hover. The orange juice came with a segment of the fruit impaled on the rim of the glass. It was delicious. As soon as I finished, the junior waiter picked up a telephone and started to speak into it. He remained to hover until a member of the lower orders brought my main course up, as before, on a tray.

Inside a sealed packet I found an elegant pair of chopsticks made, I guessed, from a local hardwood and given a highly polished surface. By then I'd had quite a lot of experience with chopsticks but somehow that evening I was self-conscious and lacking in confidence; the chopsticks felt awkward in my hand. But the rice held together allowing me to get a couple of clumps of the stuff into my mouth. I was doing well enough, I thought – but not well enough for the waiter.

'You may like to …' he said placing a knife and fork on either side of my plate.

'Ah, thank you,' I said, 'I may need them – especially for the pigeon!'

I liked the idea of having a choice of weapon. Then I could cope with anything. But, in the same movement as the waiter put the knife and fork down, he silently confiscated the chopsticks. The rice and the vegetables were served in separate bowls. The pigeon lay on a flat plate the size of a dessert plate. Set in the prime position in front of me, where in a Western restaurant you'd expect to find a dinner plate, was another deep little vessel like a grapefruit bowl with nothing in it. It was the ideal shape for chopsticks, but totally wrong for a knife and fork. I helped myself from the serving bowls but I couldn't get the knife low enough to cut the vegetables or to dissect the pigeon pieces in their crispy coating. Also I couldn't push the rice onto the fork with a knife because the shape of the bowl meant that both implements had to be too steeply inclined. I did not want to make eye contact with the waiter, who must have been watching my struggle. With my eyes lowered I became aware that the waiter's legs were moving towards a sideboard. Oh, great, I thought – he's going to bring me a proper dinner plate! His legs bent at the knee. His hand came down to open a door in the sideboard. His legs became still. I guessed he was looking at the contents of the sideboard. He drew something from a pile with a clatter, closed the door, straightened up, turned round and came towards my table. In one move he withdrew the grapefruit bowl and replaced it with the item he had found in the sideboard, his considered solution to the problem – a tea plate!

The pigeon is a small bird. It has just as many bones as a large bird but you have to cope with the whole skeleton and the bones are fiddly. The pigeon I faced had been quartered, then cooked in a crispy coating. To manage bones, flesh and crispy coating on a dinner plate, along with stringy greens and rice, would have been challenge enough. On a tea plate it looked impossible. The servings were generous. I had a lot of work to do. I sensed I would get no more help. I longed to use the plate holding the pigeon pieces but I felt the waiter would disapprove. There was nothing left for me to do but to struggle, while the waiters hovered. I struggled some more. They hovered some more. They tried not to watch me. They looked at the floor. They looked round the room. They looked at each other. They probably only looked at me when I was looking at the mess on my plate and the tablecloth. Eventually the senior waiter could stand it no more and went out. I could stand it no more either but I wasn't going to let the waiters know that.

The remaining waiter hovered solo, at spitting distance from me. Suddenly he came right up to my table and without warning rearranged the dishes. He moved back to his previous position. He turned this way. He turned that. He adopted a professional pose by the sideboard. He had nothing to do and to his credit he did not pretend that he had. He answered the telephone, keeping an eye on me as if I were a patient in a psychiatric hospital, who might suddenly exhibit inappropriate behaviour, or an escaped convict, who in an instant might become violent.

He decided to risk moving to the doorway, where, like Janus, the Roman God of T-junctions, he looked out to where he wanted to be and back in to where he was supposed to be. He was probably as uncomfortable as I was, the only difference being that he would get paid for his discomfort while I would have to pay for mine and his.

Finally, perhaps because I refused to look at him and because he'd realised he was surplus to requirements, he summoned up courage to break the protocol. Yes, he went right out into the corridor, indeed he crossed the corridor and entered the other room, where his superior was lurking. I knew they were talking about me. What else was there to talk about? I saw them looking at me, silent laughter on their faces. But I was glad I'd been left to try and enjoy my meal on my own. Their attitude hardly hurt me. In fact I wanted them to know that I was happy to be on my own. For the first time I assumed a relaxed posture and a cheerful expression, just for their benefit. With a careless shake of my head I showed them that nothing could upset me now. The waiter reacted as if the mental patient were setting fire to a cushion or the convict were drawing a knife from its hiding place in the heel of his boot.

I laboured on until at last there was no food left on my plate, although there was plenty on the tablecloth. I finished my beer. Precisely as I did so the two waiters came in. They cleared my table of crockery and cutlery. The débris on the tablecloth was now plainly visible. The junior waiter swept it up. But I had regained my usual sang-froid.

'Sorry about the mess,' I said. 'Lovely food, but difficult to eat off a *small plate!*'

'Do you want some desserts?' the senior waiter asked coldly.

'May I see the menu, please?' I asked.

'The menu!' he exclaimed, as if I'd asked to see the accounts.

'Yes,' I said. 'I can't say whether I'd like a dessert until I know what they are.'

He said nothing.

'So, please may I see the menu?' I persisted.

Now the boot was on the other foot! Having offered me desserts, he was obliged to find some on the menu. He flipped through it, playing, I presumed, for time – which wasn't going to help him.

'We've orange juice, papaya juice, ...' he said, running through the list, every item of which contained the word 'juice'.

'But they're all juices!' I declared. 'I've already had orange juice. I think you'd better bring the bill!'

I paid it, adding a tip, deliberately on the mean side. The restaurant still appeared empty as I walked down the stairs, to be greeted again by all those who had greeted me on my way in. They opened doors for me. They smiled. One handed me a card so that I could recommend the restaurant to my enemies. It had not been an enjoyable experience, although I did leave with a sense of achievement.

When I got back to my hotel, the boss handed me my ticket for the bus to China and told me he had booked a taxi to take me to it. I got it into my head that the taxi would leave at 7.30am. The next morning at 7.00 he heard me ordering breakfast.

'It's too early for breakfast!' he said.

This gave me quite the wrong impression. I realised later that he had meant to say, 'too late for breakfast!'

I wasn't worried. The girl had taken my order, so it couldn't have been too early. I went back to my room to do some more packing while waiting for the breakfast to arrive. When it came I ate it. Then I went back to finish my preparations. The boss came into my room and started picking up luggage.

'Just a minute!' I said.

'Come on!' he urged.

'You said, "7.30"!'

'7.30 the *bus* leaves!'

He hurried me out. The taxi was waiting. I couldn't help noticing that it was a motorbike. The motorcyclist put my rucksack in the front between his arms. I held my two bags in one hand, leaving the other free to hold onto the edge of the seat. I thought there was nowhere to put my feet. Then I spotted two collapsible footrests. I managed to push these down just as we dived into the traffic. Halfway I remembered that I'd left my camera under the bed. It had all the pictures I had taken since Melbourne. The noise of the bike and all the other traffic was so loud I decided not to try to explain as we went along. We just got to the bus in time.

'Wait a minute!' I called out to the motorcyclist. 'Let me check I've got my camera!'

I knew I hadn't got it. I went through my pockets.

'We've got to go back. I left my camera in the hotel – with all my pictures! We have to let the bus go. I'm sorry.'

I told the bus conductor I wouldn't be taking up my place. I got onto the motorbike and we went back. The boss was amazed to see me.

'I'm terribly sorry!' I said. 'You had it all so well organised. I've messed everything up.'

He agreed to get a ticket for me for the same bus the following day – and another taxi! He was very good about it. My camera, I knew, was full. With a whole extra day ahead of me, I went out to see if I could get my digital images transferred onto CDs to send home. I'd already tried a couple of photographic shops. I tried two more. Then I spotted a man in one of the green tropical hats. Hanging from his neck was a Pentax camera with its focal lengths displayed for all to see. I asked him where I should go. He told me he could deal with it, pointing to somewhere near. I was afraid he would take my money and the memory stick with my images on it and I'd never see any of it again. He had a friend tagging along with him, who nodded enthusiastically and grinned, which did nothing to calm my anxieties. Then the photographer suddenly linked arms with me as if we were buddies and hurried me along.

'I'm not running away,' I cried, 'there's no need to hold onto me!'

With his free hand he did a mime of someone revving up a motorbike. I thought I'd have to endure another bike ride, but he was only indicating that we were linked for speed and it seemed to help as he pulled me through the chaos of the road around the lake. At this point his friend was on a motorbike, which he drove at right angles to the traffic, forcing it to get out of the way, while the photographer and I used his bike as a shield. What had always taken minutes before, we now achieved in seconds. Very soon we were in a camera shop. The photographer's friend had parked his bike and joined us. I bought four blank CDs from the woman at the counter. Then the two men went with me to the back of the shop, where some people of student age sat at screens. The photographer spoke to a young man. Then, with the young man's friend acting as interpreter, I explained what I wanted. Once the job was in hand, the photographer started getting restless. I heard him say the word, 'money'.

'Well, thank you very much for bringing me here,' I said. 'How much do you want?'

'A dollar?' he suggested.

'I've only got dong,' I lied. 'I'll give you 20,000.'

This was $1.20 – very little, you might think, but an improvement on what he'd asked for. He and his friend seemed to be shocked that I had accepted the price the photographer had quoted. They started to talk about 'a souvenir'.

'What is this "souvenir"?' I asked.

They couldn't tell me. I asked the interpreter. He couldn't – or wouldn't – tell me. Someone said, 'haggle'.

'You asked for a dollar,' I said. 'I'm giving you more than that.'

I couldn't get my head round this perverse, reverse bargaining, where the seller asks for a sum below the amount that he'll accept. Then it came to me what was going on, so I offered 40,000 dong. This was agreed – or so I believed. I had nothing on me between a 20,000-dong note and a 100,000-dong note. When I produced this, the photographer got excited.

'Have you got change?' I asked him.

No answer.

'Well, I'll ask in the shop,' I said.

He came with me and spoke to the woman.

'Give him two fifties,' he must have said, knowing that I would then be forced to give him one of them.

And that was what happened. So he got three dollars in the end. Then he and his friend left the shop. I offered 100,000 dong to the whizz kid who had done the work. This he accepted. Then I'd to pay 100,000 dong to the woman on the counter for the use of her facilities. It cost £9 in all on top of the cost of the CDs – more than it had cost in Melbourne but well worth it to be able to send one set of pictures home to Edward for safe keeping. And with this experience of Vietnamese-style haggling I could then see why the poor taxi-driver who'd rescued me from the rainstorm had been so indignant.

Ha Noi had been tiring. I kept returning to the peace of the lake, to sit in one of the cafés. A lot of people smoke in Hanoi – hardly surprising given its frenetic lifestyle. Smoking is allowed in public places. In cafés you get that smell I remember from the sixties. Not bad out of doors, certainly nostalgic. As all the tables were in the open air, beggars could easily approach those sitting there. I gave two of them money. Then a young woman and her mother (or grandmother) came in. The security guard appeared. By then the smallest note I had was 20,000 dong, which still seemed a lot of money, although it was worth only 65p, which I could easily have spared. I gestured 'no' and they moved on. The security guard gave me a grin and a thumbs-up signal. I don't know which made me more uncomfortable – my meanness or the security guard's attitude.

By the time I was familiar with the customs and the currency of a particular country it was time to move on. I apologised again to the boss of the Camellia Hotel for my performance the day before. I gave him my phrase book and my guidebook on S E Asia to add to the information he kept for guests. The Hanoi Touring Company provided a spanking new Chinese bus in a blue-and-white livery. It even had seat belts. The Chinese conductress looked smart in her tailored white blouse with little magenta flowers to match her well-pressed magenta uniform. She gave out complimentary bottles of water and laminated information cards, which meant nothing to me. A video played continuously giving us Vietnamese or Chinese songs – sadder, less sugary than Thai songs.

I was anxious about what lay ahead – finding my way across China, staying safe, keeping well. I believed my hearing aid had completely packed up. My teeth, repaired so drastically in Panama, were holding out bravely. My stomach was doing heroic work with whatever I sent down to it. It was good to be on the move again. The thought that I would be home in eight weeks was encouraging. I had a mental picture of me, the writer, back home in Dorset, sitting in my house beside an open fire. I'd been away so long that I'd forgotten that it was my previous home in England that had had the fireplace, not the current one.

From the bus window I had my last look at Vietnam. I saw four adults riding on a single motorbike. Beside the road were individual traders, each with a dozen loaves to sell to any driver who stopped. I noticed people picking through rubbish. For the first time I saw rice grown on an industrial scale. Individual workers were wading through the soggy pathways between strips of planting, which added up to a single field extending from the road we were on to the next one. I saw a couple working in the rice, watched by a water buffalo. In among the rice fields were trees planted on ridges to keep their trunks out of the water. I also saw numerous duck farms, often with more than 100 birds.

The conductress handed out 'mixed congees in syrup'. These were like beans, sweet corn and puffed wheat swimming in what looked like washing up water and tasted only marginally better. The whole concoction made my fingers sticky because the folding spoon secreted in the lid didn't reach the bottom of the carton. This was unfortunate as we were just coming to the border where we would have to handle passports and other official papers. Vietnam had been challenging. Would China be any easier?

22. China

September 6 – 25

As usual we had to get out of the bus with our luggage and go through Immigration on foot. I changed my remaining dong into Chinese renminbi (also referred to as yuan). I had foolishly left my food, water and waterproof on the bus. A courtesy minibus took us to the buses that were going on into China. Unfortunately these were not the same buses as had brought us from Vietnam. I found the bus for Nanning and told a group of conductresses, also very neat in magenta and white, that I'd left some items on the other bus. Immediately one of them got on the phone.

'It's all right,' she said, 'someone has found your things. She is bringing them.'

I was most impressed that, five minutes later, on the next courtesy bus a conductress arrived with a bag containing everything I'd left behind. The roads were good, some of them toll roads. The traffic was calmer than it had been in Vietnam. There was less of it – bicycles, motorbikes and tuk tuks, but no hooting. The buildings were less attractive. In contrast to evidence of substantial recent investment, we passed a herd of some 200 goats on the road. So far the people didn't look much different from the Vietnamese but they wore rather comical hats shaped like buckets.

In Nanning I checked in to the Yunzhao Hotel, where I had to pay a deposit of 100 yuan (about five pounds) on top of the 130 yuan room charge. In the room there was an assortment of condoms and related products – a sort of sexual mini-bar. I made myself a cup of green tea. Then, drawing my own map of the city as I went along so that I could find my way back, I went out to get some Chinese currency, but I couldn't find an HSBC bank. The other ATMs wouldn't accept my card.

In Nanning I quickly formed a view of China as a dynamic country with strong central control, a country flexing its economic muscles. It had embraced the obvious features of western economies – well-appointed roads, modern bridges, overpasses, dual carriageways with barriers to protect pedestrians, traffic control, good order, street lighting, attractive municipal planting, skyscrapers, some smart stores and advertising to European standards. As I travelled through China I had no reason to revise this picture although more traditional ways of life existed alongside this brave new world. For the time being, however, my preoccupation was with the problems of communication and the difficulty of obtaining cash.

I asked in places where I thought there might be English speakers, such as the enquiry desk of a department store. Almost no one spoke English. I saw no Internet café. I wanted a map of the city but I couldn't find a tourist office. After trudging fruitlessly and with an unsettled stomach, I urgently needed the loo. I saw no toilet although of course I didn't know what a Chinese toilet looked like or what the Chinese word was. The only thing to do was to go back to my hotel, which I did quickly, thanks to the map I'd drawn – but not quickly enough. I had a shower and did the necessary emergency laundry.

Then I managed to find among my papers the pin number for my American Express Travellers Cheque Card. I re-read the instructions for the card. I set out again and found a machine that would accept it. The only option offered was 'balance enquiry':

'Your balance is nil. You have no funds available.'

So I just had to find an ATM that took my HSBC debit card. It was dark now, a lovely warm night. The place was swarming with people. Some were playing cards or Chinese chess. I was scared to stop and watch as I didn't want to be robbed of the little I had. I found nowhere to draw money. I needed to eat. Macdonalds, I discovered, had laminated-picture menus with the prices clearly marked. I pointed to a hamburger, to a portion of chips and to a bottle of water. I held out some money and the person serving took what money they needed. I was down to my last 62 yuan (about £3!). I'd already changed all my dong into yuan and spent most of them. I had some US dollars for an emergency – and now I had the emergency!

I had imagined that the HSBC Bank (Hong Kong and Shanghai Bank) would have conquered China before it conquered the world, but I couldn't find an HSBC in Nanning. I wanted to get onto the Internet to find out what branches there were in the region but I hadn't managed to find an Internet café. Originally I'd planned to enter China via Hong Kong. There would have to be an HSBC there and some of the staff would speak English.

Meanwhile I decided it was too late to be wandering around in the dark in a strange city so I went back to my hotel. I fell asleep because I was tired. I was up in the night thinking over my next move but I woke refreshed. I breakfasted in my room on three biscuits, a muffin, a cup of green tea and my last orange. I went out and found a bank that would change dollars into yuan. The bank staff hadn't heard of HSBC. I found it very difficult to hear what they were saying through the grille and their accents, but we did some of our business by passing notes.

'Please may we see you ID?' the clerk wrote.

I passed my passport through the glass.

'The exchange rate is such and such,' the clerk told me.

'Thank you,' I replied. 'Do you know where the nearest Internet café is?'

She wrote down instructions and handed them to me. I followed the instructions but found no Internet café. I double-checked by walking up and down the street in question. The bank clerk had given me the Chinese characters for 'Internet'. When I showed it to someone he sent me off on another wild goose chase. The third person I asked was good enough to lead me along the road and point the Internet café out to me. In those early days in China I took instructions seriously, naively assuming that if someone didn't know the answer they would say so. The whole business took ages.

The Internet café was a large basement room, the darkest such café I had ever seen. There was a rumbling noise, like thunder – probably coming from a computer game. No doubt the games were more vivid and compelling in this atmosphere but I had to take my glasses off and put my face 10 centimetres from the keyboard before I could read the keys, which were black. When I complained they said I could move, but everywhere looked equally dark to me. When again I said I couldn't see, they gave me a torch, which I held in one hand while I typed with the other, but the light from the torch was so feeble it was useless. I complained again and they gave me a big light. Then I couldn't get onto MSN, my mail server. I called the expert over.

He got me MSN with the names of my contacts in English but everything else was in Chinese characters. I called for help a fifth time. They sent a message to Microsoft. One way and another it was 20 minutes before I got my e-mails. I sent short messages back to my contacts. I'd paid for an hour's computer time but I'd only half an hour left to find the branches in China of HSBC. 'The world's local bank' never felt more remote.

'The Hong Kong web-site,' the message came back, 'is temporarily unavailable due to a system upgrade.'

I went onto HSBC (UK). At least that had no Chinese characters.

'Find a branch near you,' it offered.

'Yes, please,' I pressed.

A map of the United Kingdom came up on the screen. If I had been in Huddersfield or St Just-in-Roseland they could have helped me. Unfortunately I was in the Chinese city of Nanning. Try as I would, I could get no further with HSBC. I called the manager over. He must have been getting fed up with me but he never showed it.

'Can you help me, please?' I asked. 'I've got no money. The HSBC bank is all over the world, but as far as I can see it's not in Nanning. I want to know whether I have to go to Hong Kong.'

He tried on the screen but got nowhere. I thanked him and went for some lunch. I asked for chicken (or so I thought), but I got something mammalian. I couldn't tell whether it was monkey, dog or hedgehog, but I ate it. I needed to keep my strength up. I went back to the hotel, had a shower, felt better, packed up and left my room, pulling the door closed behind me. Then I remembered to leave a tip for the chambermaid. I tried my key card in the door but it had obviously been cancelled and I couldn't get in again. Three chambermaids stood in the corridor looking at me.

'Who is going to clean my room?' I asked.

There was no answer.

'Well,' I tried again, 'I've got something small for whoever it is. Who is it?'

No answer.

'Well, I'll stick it here,' I said, poking a banknote into the key-card slot.

They must have thought I was mad. I went downstairs on the dot of checking-out time, two o'clock. But they wanted to levy a surcharge.

'Don't get angry,' the Lonely Planet book had warned.

But you can't help getting angry. You just have to hide your anger. I argued the toss. The woman kept pointing to the clock above her desk, labelled 'Beijing time'. It was a clever design with one of the hands in the shape of a hammer. This made it hard to read. Eventually I made out the time – three o'clock.

'So you're on Beijing time!' I exclaimed. 'I came in from Vietnam. Nobody told me the time was different. I'm sorry!'

I adjusted my watch. Just then a chambermaid appeared at Reception and handed in the banknote I'd left in the door.

'What's this? The receptionist asked.

'It was something for the woman who cleans my room,' I explained.

'Not here!' she said, giving it back to me.

I was finding China difficult at every level. I'd decided by then that drastic action was needed. I went to the bus station and bought a ticket to Guangzhou, a big city just inland of Hong Kong. I was on the 2100, which got in at 0600. I'd time to kill and I found a pleasant bar on the first floor of another hotel. I sat with a beer and wrote up my notes. Eventually I had some dinner of duck (chopped up with a cleaver), rice and an acerbic sauce, all washed down with much complimentary green tea.

I didn't like the idea of going east – it was quite the wrong direction. I wasn't looking forward to another night bus ride but when I saw the conveyance I cheered up. I'd never come across a 'sleep-over bus' before. It took some 32 people in three long lines of double bunks down the length of the vehicle, with two long aisles between them. I had an upper bunk next to a window. The floor was wood, or imitation wood. You took your shoes off and put them in a plastic bag provided. I needed two bags for my boots. I got a receipt for my rucksack. My reading light didn't work. I was in bed and ready for the night by 9.30 – something of a record. I had my valuables on me. I put my hand luggage inside a jumper and put this unlikely bundle under the bedclothes next to my feet. There was nothing to appeal to the casual thief and the bundle contained nothing of value to a professional. The beds were narrow but then so are the Chinese. A couple found a way to share a berth. He got in first with his head propped up on a pillow. She got in after him and sat between his open legs, leaning back on his stomach. Thus they could enjoy some togetherness and a light comedy on the TV screen.

I slept on and off. There were a few coaches on the road and a lot of lorries. I didn't see a car until 6.30am. I wondered if the poor visibility was due to morning mist or industrial pollution. I inclined to the latter as it seemed to get worse as we neared the city instead of better. We got into Guangzhou at 7.20. People were already sitting outside playing mah-jong. It was Saturday morning, very quiet. I went into a café and washed my hands in hot soapy water – very nice after a night on a bus. I had breakfast, ordering what another customer was having without knowing what it was. When it arrived I still didn't know what it was. It appeared to be a kind of soup containing unfamiliar solid bits – something that might once have been a sea creature, something that looked like a part of a pig and two shreds of lime rind. It was perfectly edible, possibly nutritious and rather unexciting.

In a little alley among a handful of vendors a man was quietly dispatching toads, presumably for a customer. I didn't see the instrument of death, just the man's left hand reaching into a container to bring one of the doomed creatures out, while his right arm came down immediately.

On an ordinary wall I saw a mural of the Great Wall of China. In a public park the planting softened the harshness of the concrete architecture all around. I wandered into the Metro. The station manager appeared in his shirtsleeves.

'Can we help you?' he offered.

'I'm looking for the HSBC (the Hong Kong and Shanghai Bank),' I said.

'Hold on a minute.'

He consulted colleagues. He made telephone calls.

'Wait here,' he said.

He went into his office. I could see him through a window, speaking to his team. A man came out to speak to me – presumably the one who spoke the best English. No one had heard of HSBC. I kept asking them to look in the telephone directory, which would have settled the matter. Eventually the manager came out with his jacket on.

'We can go from this station,' he said. 'I'll come with you. We go out Exit B.'

This sounded most encouraging. We emerged in a street I hadn't seen before and walked along it. We didn't talk much – we couldn't. We passed some banks. When we got to the Shanghai Bank we stopped.

'Give me your card,' the station master said.

'No,' I said, 'I'll come with you.'

I wasn't going to part with my one and only means of economic survival. So we went in to talk to someone in the Shanghai Bank. More and more members of the staff appeared. I could hardly have drawn more interest if I'd been a member of an unknown species presenting itself at a dinner in the Natural History Museum. I had to keep producing my card and handing it to the station manager, who passed it to each new arrival, who would look blank and shake his head in his own way. We came out into the street again. But the station manager would not give up. We came to an ATM.

'I've tried this one,' I said. 'Look it doesn't have "Maestro" or "Cirrhus" – I've tried it.'

We came to an imposing branch of the Royal Bank of China. It was no good. No one had heard of HSBC. I sensed we were getting nowhere. We were standing in the street in the tropical sun. I had my rucksack on my back. I was getting hotter and hotter while nothing was happening. He made a call on his mobile.

'... ring back,' he said to me.

He put the instrument away and stood there.

'Don't you need to get back?' I asked the station manager, tapping my watch. 'You've been very kind, but this is taking your time and it's taking my time. You go back.'

Still he stood there. This was an impasse to surpass all impasses – the zenith of the sun, the nadir of the expedition.

'Are you waiting to get a phone call back?' I asked him.

'Back?' he queried.

'From the man?'

'Man?'

'You told me you were expecting a man to ring you back.'

He looked blank. I didn't know how to get rid of him.

'Let's at least start walking back,' I suggested.

We stopped while the station manager made another phone call. Fortunately this was outside the China Minsheng Banking Corporation. This was a new name to me, although I'd noticed it on our way out. I now saw it had an ATM.

'I'm going to try this!' I signalled to the station master.

The ATM worked! I drew a wad of 100-yuan notes so fat I could hardly get it into my back pocket, although it was only worth £70. The station master finished his phone call.

'Look!' I cried. 'I've got the money! Thank you for all you've done. I can continue now. You go back.'

'Are you sure?'

'Yes. Thank you very much.'

Still he stood there. I shook him by the hand. I pressed his arm. Finally, he left me. What a relief! He had done me a great kindness in leaving his work to show me a street with so many banks. But when his idea of the Shanghai Bank failed, he couldn't bring himself to say, 'Sorry, I can't help you any further.' He didn't want to lose face. It was only when I solved the problem myself and thanked him for it, that I could get rid of him.

Meanwhile I had to restore my strength. I booked into a hotel and had a shower. After my night on the bus I needed it. I collapsed on the bed. At two o'clock I went looking for lunch. As usual I chose from laminated cards with small, fuzzy photos, something with meat, rice and veg. The meat was like steak but not steak. I'd no idea what it was – perhaps it was water buffalo. Then by way of pure indulgence I pointed to a picture of what looked like a tropical bird sitting in a sundae glass. When it came it looked even more like a tropical bird sitting in a sundae glass. It had a long green tail cut from melon rind with a bit of the flesh of the fruit left on it to be stuck into the glass to stop it tipping over.

The rest of the bird was made up of blobs of ice cream – pink, white and green, together with star fruit, orange, an apple cut with the skin on to look like more feathers, water melon, peach, items I didn't recognise and others I couldn't remember. It was impossible to eat without getting yourself and the table in a mess but I really enjoyed it.

I wanted to go to the railway station so I went again to the metro, hoping not to bump into the station manager and his crew. The ticket system was like Bangkok's so I knew what to do. The station names were given in English as well as Chinese – and very poetical they were too – 'Peasant Movement Institute', 'Martyrs Park' and 'Higher Education Megacentre North'. I managed to buy a disk with the help of two girls fed up with waiting behind me in the queue. They also told me which train to get on. Once I was on it, it seemed to be the wrong train. So I had to work out where I should be. Because I couldn't read the names of the stations all I could do was count them. After a few wrong journeys, guarding my valuables carefully on crowded trains, I arrived where a high proportion of the population of Guangzhou was – the main railway station. There were police everywhere.

I entered the station through an x-ray scanner. I walked all round the station looking for any words of English. There was a plan of both floors of the station, with symbols and a code. (This showed symbols for 'ticket office' and 'enquiries'.) However I could not see the ticket office symbol on the map. The enquiries symbol was on the map but the actual enquiry office was not where the map said it should be. I kept looking and going back to the map but I couldn't find either Enquiries or Ticket Office. For want of anything better to do I went upstairs. A Chinaman, who looked intelligent and experienced in life, travelled with me up the escalator. We exchanged smiles.

'Are you all right?' he asked.

I had learned always to be specific.

'I can't find the ticket office,' I said.

'You go back down again,' he said, 'out those doors there and you turn to the left.'

So it was outside the station – that's why they couldn't show it on the map. Of course, then I had to find out how to get out of the station. Outside there were more people than you could ever squeeze into the station – waiting for other people, waiting for trains, smoking in the smoking area or staring up at the open-air screens as if they'd heard that the end of the world was to be announced from there. Very few were stomping around in a frenzy of frustration like me. I asked someone if they knew where the enquiry office was but they had no idea. The ticket office, however, was obvious. A long hall, within the station building but approached only from outside, with some forty ticket bays along one long wall. Each bay had an in/out queuing system fenced with metal barriers. And each bay was labelled with Chinese characters so I was none the wiser. However, on the opposite wall was a desk manned by four cheerful people in blue uniforms. Here there was no queuing system, indeed there was no queue. People were seen straight away. I wondered if this could possibly be the enquiry desk. I thought I'd give it a go. A man in blue immediately stopped chatting and smiled at me.

'Can I help you?' he asked.

'Well, yes, please,' I said, 'I was wondering if there was anywhere I could get information.'

'Where do you want to go?'

'I don't know yet,' I said. 'I'm trying to find out where I can go.'

'But where would you like to go?'

'Well, I want to get across China to Urumqi (pronounced 'U-ruhm-chee'). I don't know whether to go by train or bus. I need to find out what is possible.'

'It might be easier to fly,' he said.

'Well, I'm going round the world. I've set myself the challenge of doing it without flying. I've gone three-quarters of the way and now I want to cross Asia to Europe.'

'You can't get a train to Europe.'

'Well, maybe several trains – on one ticket?'

'But where do you want to go?'

I got out my map. He helped me to hold it. He was charming and a good listener. It must have been about then that I read the label on his chest – 'Police'. This was a temporary police presence to manage the crowd.

'Well,' I said, 'I could go through Changsa, Wuhan, Xian, Lanzhou.'

'You can get a train to Lanzhou,' he said, 'but not to Europe.'

'That's very encouraging, but I need to know the details – how long it takes, how much it costs, is there a sleeper? You see, it might be quicker by bus.'

He looked surprised. I didn't tell him I'd already overtaken a train on a bus. 'I can't decide until I know what's possible.'

'You can get a train to Lanzhou,' he repeated.

'But are there any timetables, any leaflets?'

He said nothing.

'You've been very kind,' I said, 'very helpful.'

He helped me to fold up my map again.

'Could you tell me where the enquiry desk is?'

He looked at me blankly.

'You don't know? Well, thank you very much. Goodbye.'

And I shook his hand. I should mention that all the time I'd been in the station I hadn't seen a single employee of the railway moving about, whom I could have asked, only a woman with a short besom and a long-handled dustpan, who had a vast station to tidy. I looked up and down the ticket bays and chose the one with no queue. I asked for the enquiry office and was sent to number 18. Number 18 looked no different from the other windows.

'Where do you want to go?' the clerk asked.

'Lanzhou,' I said, pronouncing the name as accurately as I could.

She looked blank. I got out my map and pressed the relevant portion to the glass.

'Lanzhou!' she exclaimed, '15!'

By this method it was not too long before I found someone prepared to open up on the subject of Lanzhou. I must say that all the employees I spoke to were calm, friendly and, apart from occasional knowing glances to adjacent colleagues as if sharing a private joke about the ignorance of tourists, professional in manner.

'What do you need to know?'

'When the trains go? How long they take? Is there a sleeper? Do you have to change? How much does it cost? Is there a leaflet?'

Of course, there wasn't a leaflet – it was all on the computer. But you'd think that the country that invented the firework would have had a timetable of a major route! The ticket clerk herself was most helpful. I passed my notebook under the glass and she wrote in clearly:

hard berth	upper	494 yuan
	middle	510
	down	528
hard seat		293 yuan

It leaves at	20.45	10/9
and arrives at	6.39	12/9

I liked the idea of a journey that took a day and a half arriving at 0639 hours, not 0640! I tried to pin the clerk down on the sleeper accommodation – if you'll pardon the expression – by drawing pictures of stick men lying on rectangles but she looked mystified. She was patient with me and once I'd got all the information I could out of her I thanked her profusely.

There are so few non-Asian people in Guangzhou that even in the one queue for the window marked 'Booking Office' in English, I was the only Caucasian. While I was waiting a young Chinese man came up to me and showed me a small ticket with the word 'Lanzhou' printed on it.

'You can go to Lanzhou,' he said.

'How did you know I wanted to go to Lanzhou?' I asked.

His companion looked bewildered to see his friend talking to a white man. When I got back to my part of the city I slipped into a restaurant and bar, with a leafy forecourt boasting an artificial waterfall and an artificial frog spouting streams of real water. Although it was still hot, these surroundings calmed me down, helped by a bottle of Chinese beer – not as good as Vietnamese beer but better than French. I went to my room and dropped on the bed, where I slept until it was too late to go out for dinner. But I banished my hunger by eating a confection I had bought which had the texture – and for all I knew the nutritional value – of foam rubber.

I caught up with the sleep I had lost on the bus from Nanning and woke in the morning refreshed, having regained my sense of humour and my sense of purpose. I remembered that in the excitement of the day before I had failed to take my pills – for blood pressure and malaria, both to be taken regularly with food. I'd thrown away the rest of the foam rubber but I was able to make a breakfast of biscuits, some other cake and a drink made from the complimentary packet of Nescafé. It contained artificial sweetener and artificial milk powder, but it helped me to get the pills down. My washing was nearly dry. I knew how to get to Lanzhou. I even managed with a toothpick to get some gunge out of the battery housing of my hearing-aid. The poor thing squeaked with relief.

I checked in for a second night. The blighters charged me a second deposit without returning the first! I went back to the railway station and bought a ticket for the next day to Lanzhou. When I came out of the station I had to ask a European guy to let me pass him. We spoke English at first but when I learned that he had come from Germany, German tumbled out of me like French had when I'd met some French people in Mexico. Minutes later I was having difficulty finding my way back to the Metro. I asked a young white couple.

'Is that the sign?' one of them said. 'We usually take a taxi.'

'I'm afraid that they'll take me to the wrong place,' I said.

'We just show a business card.'

'Where are you from?'

'Bristol.'

'I'm from Dorset.'

'Oh, right!'

From such a distance the two places seemed very close.

'What are you doing in Guangzhou?' I asked them.

'We're working here for two years.'

Another young couple joined us, friends of the Bristol pair.

'Are you English too?'

'Scottish.'

'I beg your pardon. You're British then.'

Our conversation was unexciting, but somehow it gave me moral support. On the metro train a young man offered me his seat, which I accepted with gratitude. That had never happened to me in the UK. Either the Chinese are more polite to senior citizens or I had visibly aged during the journey.

In the afternoon I went back to a place I'd seen the day before offering free Internet use between two and six. It was some kind of health club and I guessed they wanted to increase their footfall. When I turned up that afternoon I was thinking only of the free access to the Internet. As I went in I was greeted by gracious young woman.

'Hullo,' I said, 'I'd like to use the Internet.'

I let my fingers play over an imaginary keyboard by way of illustration. The receptionist gave me a key. I'd never before needed a key when using a computer – a code sometimes but never a key. But this was China and I thought perhaps they did things differently. The receptionist then indicated I should go with a certain man. He took the key from me and led me up a flight of stairs. We passed a swimming pool full of water and nude men and boys, to arrive at an alcove with a table spread with a towel, as if for a massage. Other fresh towels lay about the place. Using my key the man opened a locker and held up a towelling dressing gown in the same corporate beige as the towels.

'No, no, no!' I exclaimed, 'I've come to use the computer.'

I repeated the keyboard mime. The man led me to another part of the building, where three male attendants confronted me. One offered me something that looked like a short-sleeved shirt but it might have been pyjamas. I pushed them away.

'No, no,' I protested, 'you misunderstand.'

They made to conduct me somewhere else.

'Wait a minute!' I cried.

Pulling out my notebook I quickly drew a computer screen, keyboard and mouse, then repeated my mime. The first guy led me back past the swimming pool towards yet another part of the building I hadn't seen before.

'No,' I insisted, my voice getting louder as I spoke, 'I want the way out. I want to go. I want to go to my hotel! *Which is the way to the street?*'

The clients in various states of undress, some completely naked, were staring at me as if they knew that under my clothes I had a penis shaped like a corkscrew. Now I am a fair-weather naturist and the thought of wearing nothing among these naked, health-loving types held no terror for me. I just didn't see the point of taking my clothes off to answer my e-mails.

'Can I help you?' asked a thin, intellectual, nude apart from his glasses.

'Yes, please,' I said, calming down a little. 'I came in to use the computer. They want me to undress. I want to leave the building but they won't show me the way out. Would you kindly explain to them?'

He did. I thanked him. The man who had brought me in pointed to the exit. But that wasn't good enough for me.

'I don't know the way,' I said. 'Will you please show me?'

He did.

'Thank you very much!' I said and stepped quickly into the street.

I walked around for an hour. I couldn't find anywhere with access to the Internet. I went back to the hotel. I wanted to ring my son, Edward, but I couldn't get an outside line from my room although I tried many times. The hotel had what they called a 'business centre' but it was hardly 'state of the art'. It offered 'fax, telegram and typing'. The door was locked. I looked through the window but could see no computer.

That evening I watched the news on the Guangzhou 'English Channel' or 'GZTV', an all-English programme designed to help viewers to learn English. The news reader was Chinese. She spoke clearly, making an effort to get her tongue round those English sounds the Chinese find difficult. The outside reporters also spoke English. I learned from the programme that the crowds at the railway station had been students arriving for the new term. After the news they showed a classic film, 'The Singing Mermaid', an ideal choice because the story was easy to follow, being straightforward and largely told in pictures. The English dialogue was supported by English subtitles.

I went to the Bank of China and drew 2,500 yuan, the maximum allowed. I wanted to exchange some of this into US dollars. While I was queuing I asked someone if I could change yuan to dollars. They said, 'yes' so I continued to wait. But when eventually I was seen the teller called a supervisor. He asked for my ID.

'Here is my passport,' I said.

'We can supply dollars,' he said, 'but as you are a foreigner ...'

'There's nothing wrong with these notes,' I protested. 'I just got them out of your machine.'

'You could get a friend to do it for you,' he said.

'You mean a Chinese friend?'

'Yes,' he said.

'I haven't been in China long,' I told him. 'I haven't got a friend.'

He looked dismayed.

'Could *you* do it?' I asked, keeping a straight face. 'Could you be my friend?'

'No,' he replied equally seriously.

Then he started to make some suggestions, but I wasn't going to wait while he ran through the face-saving routine.

'So I can't do it,' I said. 'Thank you very much.'

At the Western Union, a sign advertised foreign exchange, but as before they wouldn't let me have dollars because I was a foreigner. I tried other banks. I tried jewellers, because they attract dollars from the tourists. Eventually I was sent to a certain hotel where I managed to obtain $200, which was better than nothing.

Then I looked in earnest for an Internet café, but I couldn't find one. I did see a computer not in use in a shop doing design work such as signage. Desperate, I went in.

'Please may I use this computer?' I asked.

'Yes,' said a man, who was working on another screen.

I checked my messages and sent a paragraph to all my contacts. This ended abruptly, 'Sorry got to go – love, J.' The guy whose computer I was using had returned knowing nothing of the arrangement I'd made with his colleague. Not surprisingly he wanted to get back to work. I apologised and he was pleasant about it. I was grateful to both men.

The train left at 20.45. It was my first rail journey in China. I had the middle one of three bunks. The coach was split into a number of six-berth compartments completely open to the corridor. There was a table between the two bottom bunks providing a small dining area for those passengers. Seating was at a premium. For every six passengers there were two little tip-up seats in the corridor, either side of a little table. Otherwise the passengers with bottom bunks would let you sit with them. There was no reading light so I was glad of my torch. As I climbed the ladder to my bunk I banged my head on the luggage rack over the corridor. This had a length of carpet, which meant that people could move silently and sometimes they did.

I slept better than I had on the train in Malaysia. Through the mist I saw a long goods train and the outlines of mountains in the distance. There was a patchwork of small fields, each the size of a badminton court. I picked up the smell of instant pot noodles coming to life as someone added hot water from the urn. Two girls were sleeping on the bottom bunk under duvets. A foot protruded from one, magenta toenails shaking with the movement of the train. I saw a man sitting on a bunk reading a paper. A younger man was sitting at the head of the same bunk, asleep, flopped forward against a pillow on the table, which seemed to me a strange position.

A woman went down the train picking up rubbish with a short broom and a long-handle dustpan. Her hair had been dyed chestnut and she wore a uniform that included pin-striped navy trousers. The conductresses went up and down selling hot meals, fruit, drinks and books.

By day, in order to make the most of the view, I opted for the little tip-up seat in the corridor that faced forward. Sometimes I moved to my bunk to give someone else a turn on the seat. I was resting when I became aware of a big man with close-cropped hair and a goatee beard sitting cross-legged on the other middle bunk, his back bent to fit under the top bunk. It can't have been comfortable. Then I realised he was saying his prayers. I pretended to be asleep so that he wouldn't realise that I was studying him.

The visibility in Wuhan was poor. A man joined me on the other little seat. He worked in Guangzhou as an 'Araby'-Chinese translator.

'Is it usually as misty as this?' I asked.

'Yes,' he said, 'it's the car industry.'

My fellow passengers were kind and helpful. Anything I dropped from my bunk they passed up to me. The Chinese are great people to travel with because they are quiet and don't take up much room – imagine a party of Texans crossing China by train! The coach was always full. If someone left the train at a station invariably someone else would take their place. I saw the man who'd been flopped over the table being led out by two men with baggage as if to get off at the next station. The young man must have been a prisoner as he was handcuffed, which explained his unusual sleeping position earlier.

I realised that I had spent the first 23 hours without washing more than my hands. There was no shower and it didn't seem fair to keep people waiting for the toilet while I had a strip-wash. On the second evening I decided to beat the rush and at least wash above the waist.

That night my religious friend started talking to a woman who had recently joined the train. At half past midnight he was still talking at normal volume. I shone my torch on my watch and put it in front of his face. I mimed him talking and pointed to the woman's bunk. Then I mimed someone with sore ears, followed by someone sleeping. He got the message.

In the morning I was up early as I had to leave the train at 6.30. As we came into Lanzhou the orderly was trying to sweep around the feet of passengers standing in the corridor. I saw a river, brown as gravy, with rocky banks. We passed through tunnels, under arched bridges and by a very tall tapered chimney yielding sad grey smoke, which went straight up as there was no wind. There were satellite dishes on the roofs.

When I got off the train the first thing I needed was a toilet. Half the cubicles were closed for cleaning. I joined a queue of men. One in front of me got fed up and went away. I ended up in a cubicle with no lock. As usual there was a hole in the floor over which you were expected to squat. I managed to keep the door shut most of the time using my three bags, careful that none fell down the hole. I was in the process of trying to hit the target below me when there was a knock on the door. I expect I called out some phrase in English. Later someone actually tried to push the door open. While I was washing my hands a woman pushed a boy of three or four into the room. Not surprisingly the little fellow went out again. She pushed him in again. Still he went out. I didn't blame him. I put my rucksack in the left luggage and went for breakfast. A big mirror on the wall helped me to keep a watch out on all sides. I had a plate of noodles, bean shoots, vegetables and so on – fairly hot and very salty.

I told my supporters:

'Guangzhou was my last stop in the tropics … I have just arrived in cool and rainy Lanzhou, some 900 miles north and west of Guangzhou. The Internet café smells of burning coke.'

I checked into the New Century Hotel. The receptionist dealt with the formalities while the manager looked on.

'When is breakfast?' I asked the manager, more out of habit than anything else. In England it always seemed to round off that first encounter in a new hotel and once you know when breakfast is served you have all the information you need to make your plans.

'When do you want it?' she asked.

'I don't know yet,' I said, already beginning to realise that mentioning 'breakfast' had been a mistake.

'You want breakfast, but you don't know when?'

'That's right. I won't know until I've bought my train ticket. When do you serve breakfast – seven to nine?'

I don't know where I got 'seven to nine' from.

'You want breakfast but you don't know when?'

'Yes.'

She handed me a pen and paper. There was no escape.

'I would like breakfast tomorrow,' I wrote.

She took the pen from me and added, 'MORNING'.

I felt this was being pedantic. Despite China's efforts to launch itself as a big player in the modern world, I didn't believe that the *all-day* breakfast had already reached Lanzhou.

'Well, yes,' I said, 'you only serve breakfast between seven and nine.'

'You would like breakfast between seven and nine?'

'Yes.'

'Seven o'clock?'

'I don't know!'

'Eight o'clock?'

'I don't know yet! Surely you don't need to know at 12 noon when I want breakfast tomorrow!'

It was like a sea lion trying to have a conversation with a goat. I can't remember how I managed to withdraw from this interchange. We could perhaps have agreed that foreigners were impossible, but I expect I just said, 'Thank you, I'll let you know,' and walked away.

Chinese men, I noticed, wore shoes with pointed toes that reminded me of London in the early sixties. Lanzhou people appeared ethnically different from those I'd seen in Guangzhou. The men wore Chairman-Mao-style caps or white hats shaped like jelly moulds. Some women wore headdresses like loose Balaclavas. Among the street vendors were fur sellers and fortune tellers. You could play a game based on two rifles fixed at firing height to shoot balloons on stands. People offering shoe or bicycle repairs were there with all their gear, working on the street. Outside the post office I saw what I took to be a dead dog draped over a bicycle. I was right, it was a dead, shaggy, black-and-white sheepdog – but only the pelt. In a shop I saw 'Omo' and 'Tide', brands of washing powder I remembered from the fifties. With so much strangeness around it's easy to jump to wrong conclusions. I thought the marble-covered pillars of a building had been wound with barbed wire to deter people from stealing the marble. When I looked closer I saw that it was really grey plastic wire with white fairy lights not switched on. In front of another building I saw a mass of petunias. Even the familiar seemed strange.

I went to a simple café for lunch. The menu was all in Chinese, no pictures. I drew my own picture of rice, wrote, 'rice, vegetables and meat'. They produced a super meal in minutes.

From my bedroom on the ninth floor the atmosphere looked foul, largely because of the opacity of the double-glazed windows. The outer pane was tinted grey as well as being filthy. When I opened a window, the scene didn't look nearly so grim. In the distance was a murky mountain. I'd an uninterrupted view of the railway station – the platforms, the covered stairs, a bridge over the tracks, and ten level crossings, all unmanned except for a final gate. Local trains drew their power from overhead electric lines. With the window open I could hear the sound of diesel engines. But the horn of the diesel was so loud I could hear it with the double-glazed window closed and my hearing aid switched off. I went back to the station and bought a ticket to Urumqi, the only city in a remote north-western region of the country, a stepping-off point for Kazakhstan.

I put the 'Do not disturb' sign on the door while I washed some clothes. To get the drying process under way smartly I did my trick of squeezing as much water as I could out of the wet clothes, then sandwiching them between two towels, rolling them up, doubling or trebling the resulting sausage and squeezing it between my body and the wall. I then hung up the clothes and the towels to finish drying.

I found a pleasant restaurant for dinner. Some of the tables had three cloths. Mine had two under glass, which suited my level of proficiency with chopsticks. Some poor girls had to carry the dirty dishes upstairs and bring the clean ones down. The menu had no pictures.

'I can't read Chinese,' I said.

So they brought me a bilingual version. I didn't seem to be able to learn from my mistakes. I chose a chicken and mushroom stew with rice, because I thought it would be mild. When I'd ordered (by pointing), the two waitresses stood there like naughty schoolgirls not quite sure if the head teacher had finished telling them off. They smiled, looked at each other and shifted their tiny weights about. I smiled and nodded. What else could I do?

The stew was mild all right but I'd forgotten about the Chinese stick torture. The stew arrived in a dish shaped like a butterfly. As usual the fowl had been chopped by someone demonstrating how sharp his cleaver was without thought for the poor diner. The mushrooms were quartered and slippery from the gravy. Think about a quartered mushroom – it has no parallel surfaces. When you squeeze it with your chopsticks it always escapes. I developed two ways to capture the elusive buggers; one was to work it onto its base then stab it in the gills with a chopstick, the other was to nip the quarter stalk close to the bell and hope you could get it to your mouth in one go. The other vegetables – marrow, garlic, carrot and so on – were diced small, like you might find in minestrone soup, thus rather fiddly. The chicken pieces you had to lift from the broth as lumps to bite from before you dropped them. This was made harder because they'd left the skin on. I ended up using my fingers, which made them slippery for when I did want to use the dreaded chopsticks. Even so, one piece splintered in my mouth. It was like eating toothpicks.

After I'd bought my train ticket I went back to the hotel desk and spoke to a receptionist I hadn't seen before.

'I promised to let you know about breakfast. Is it in the dining room?'

'No,' she said.

This went some way to explaining the bizarre conversation I'd had earlier with her colleague.

'Well,' I said, 'I don't want breakfast in my room. So – thank you very much. I won't have breakfast after all.'

Breakfast in your room has no appeal for the lonely lone traveller. After a night on a train, unsurprisingly, I always sleep well in a hotel bed in a room of my own. At five to nine, the telephone rang.

'*Something, something,* breakfast,' a woman's voice said.

'Oh,' I replied, 'I told them I didn't want breakfast.'

She put the phone down. I quickly put on some clothes and hid my washing. There was a knock on the door. A petite body in a pale blue uniform stood there smiling and holding something, which at that hour could only be breakfast. I took it from her, smiled and nodded.

'Thank you!' I said.

I realise now that in my conversations about breakfast I had been concentrating too much on trying to get my own point of view across, rather than thinking about where the other person was coming from. This was a lesson I kept failing to learn. The breakfast consisted of a thick slice of bright pink sausage, discreetly hidden inside a small white roll, two terracotta eggs in a paper bag, a white bun the size of half a brick and a sealed plastic tumbler of white liquid. The shells of the eggs were so tough they were hard to break. The big bun was not the slightest bit stale, although it had no other virtue. The contents of the tumbler looked like watered down milk, smelled of cornflour and tasted of a milk substitute made from rice. The bun and the rice water as separate items were equally hard to get down; only by taking them together was it possible. Look, if I'd wanted coffee and croissants I would have gone to France! Meanwhile outside, the mountain was disappearing as the haze thickened.

Security at the railway station was rigorous. You could not enter without undergoing a baggage inspection. Inside, all tickets were checked. Then the stream of passengers was split into two – I'd no idea on what basis. An official of the railway stood between the two queues urging us on through a loudhailer. Anyone who broke away from one of the two streams got barked at. I don't mind being barked at, but I do mind catching the wrong train, so I deliberately walked into the middle. I showed my ticket to the official who indicated which stream I should be in.

On the train I found I'd an upper bunk in a four-berth compartment with three other men. The space was less cramped than last time. The bunks were wider and, being on two levels rather than three, I could sit upright. During the day the lower bunks became seats for the four of us, with lacy coverings over the backs. The window had a lace curtain. There was a carpet and we were offered padded coathangers. The compartment was all in a blue and white livery. I think I must have been travelling first class. I showed my fellow passengers my route on a map. One spoke English. He had something very noticeable inside his trousers, but whether it was a hernia, a colostomy bag or a packet of cocaine with a street value of 10,000 yuan I never discovered.

We went through a tunnel I estimated to be more than 10 miles long. I saw a walled garden whose walls seemed to be made of mud. Two women were speed walking; I think we were passing a barracks.

I find dining cars excellent places to sit and read, or look out of the window. The dining car on this train was lovely, but I was too early for dinner and they told me to come back at 6.30. I returned at 6.35 to find the place almost full. Everyone else had ordered and some had started eating. A girl came through the car trying to sell books. I sat with two men, one of whom took me under his wing, throwing his weight around on my behalf. He clinked glasses whenever he could – if clink is the right word with paper cups! When his mate left I was still waiting for my meal. My new friend encouraged me to tuck in to the food the other guy had left. Thus I must have eaten a metre of chopped spring onions. Then mine arrived – with more spring onions. When the chummy guy shook hands and left, I moved to a window seat to watch the sunset and make notes. Two men and a woman joined me. She remarked on the speed with which I wrote. To her, European handwriting must have looked as difficult as Chinese characters seemed to me.

I lingered to finish my beer. Then I went back to join the three men in my compartment. One of them turned up the background music – romantic, Chinese and orchestral. A mixed landscape (rural and urban) sped past – beautiful trees, little fields, smallholdings. There were circular mud buildings that looked like chocolate suet puddings with windows. As dusk fell the colours became muted and the silhouettes of the trees dominated the scene. The novelty for me was just travelling across this vast, unknown country.

The next morning I woke to harsh sounds of a radio presenter's voice. My three companions were asleep. I got more and more annoyed by the radio, which none of us were enjoying, so I got out of bed, located the switch on the lower level, turned the radio off and went to breakfast.

This included two balls of white dough, which might have become food if it had only been cooked, a sort of omelette flopped over strips of vegetable marrow and some round beans left over from dinner. I was also given fried lettuce, seaweed pickled in oven cleaner and a tepid watery mess with a little rice in it. When you're presented with something so unfamiliar, what you long for is hot coffee. But not a whiff was to be had. I had six sips of the watery mess and a tentative bite of one of the dough balls. I had never before developed a mild stomach ache so quickly. The locals on the other hand ate most of what they'd been given. And more people ate the dough balls than left them. They would no doubt find porridge or scrambled egg disgusting. I behaved myself, as I'd noticed a policeman was on the next table.

The new landscape was fascinating. First there were shapeless lumps of red sandstone and a general mess of red sand, with nothing else – a landscape so barren it made the Nullarbor Plain look like a vegetable garden. This was presumably where the Chinese tried out their secret weapons. The rocky desert gave way to a level playing field for giants, with a sparse, low weed that might appeal to a temperate variety of reindeer. After miles where the only sign of human or other life was the train-load of passengers including me, I noticed a road to the site of a bridge yet to be built, which would take it over the railway. In the distance was a ridge of bare mountains. Then we came to isolated white buildings where the lonely weapons experts toiled. A look-out door had been included just in case one day there might be something to look at. Then beyond the red-brown mountains I saw higher, snow-capped peaks. The sun was warm on my shoulders. Man-made ridges at an angle to the railway led to tunnels under it, perhaps to allow water from rain or melted snow to pass without disturbing the track. Dense white smoke from some industrial plant stretched out close to the ground in a long narrow cloud. We approached an industrial town, which surprisingly possessed trees. When we stopped at a station, I got out and stood on the platform just to savour the strangeness. Of course I was careful to board the train again smartly before it moved on.

We came to a plant with big cylinders and a tangle of pipework. I took this to be a power station or refinery. I was careful not to take photographs in case the policeman arrested me as a spy – or, worse, confiscated my camera with my precious images. A wide river bed was as dry as the rest of the land.

A little boy of about six in the dining car with his parents was looking at me. In fact all three were looking at me as if I were a Martian. They might never have had such a good chance to study a European before. The boy came over to my table. I was missing my grandchildren, two of whom were the same age as this child, and I found myself playing funny faces with him. I looked at the parents to check that they were comfortable with this. Then I went through my repertoire of games to keep children amused. The parents now regarded me as if I were human. I showed the boy a stunt with my fingers, which he very quickly cottoned onto and did himself. All this, you understand, was without a word of any language. With drawings – and a little help from the parents – I conveyed to the boy the information that I had two sons and four grandchildren, together with the ages of the children. I showed him my map of China. He ran his finger along the roads and quickly learnt how to fold the map up, a thing some adults never master. His trousers said, 'Peugeot', his T-shirt, 'Ultraman'. The boy's parents kindly bought me a bottle of iced tea.

The land became greener. I saw cows, poplar trees, water sitting in hollows, stooks of corn built around a tree. There was nothing between us and the snow-capped mountains but a barren featureless plain. The mountains looked majestic, the whole scene awesome.

We'd gone more than a thousand miles, much of it lifeless desert, and the last part in the huge but remote north-west province, Xinjiang. This borders on Mongolia and Russia in the north, Tibet and India in the south and five 'stans' in the west, including Pakistan and Kazakhstan, where I was headed.

Urumqi is the furthest city in the world from an ocean. As we came into it one of the first things I saw was a mosque. When I'd alighted I went for lunch. Fewer people here spoke English. They kept showing me a menu with no pictures. I failed to get through to them that I couldn't read a character of Chinese. I turned the menu upside down. I held my head as if it ached. I showed them my notebook to try to impress on them that the menu was as meaningless to me as my notes must have appeared to them. Finally, I drew a picture of a bowl of rice and got one. Don't go to China if you can't draw!

I walked until I came to a tree-lined road. It was the first Chinese city I'd come to where the atmosphere seemed clean. The sun was bright, the air was good to breathe and the sky was blue with small white clouds. I saw people with narrow faces.

In fact in the province of Xinjiang, apart from the Han (original) Chinese, there are a number of ethnic groupings, of which the largest is the Muslim Uighurs, who speak a Turkic language. These people, I was told, hate the Han Chinese, who, they say, have all the good jobs. They have their own language and they want independence.

I went through the revolving doors of the Vili Hotel, an experience in itself. The doors had a great sheet of glass across the diameter and two small sections walled off in glass – dead spaces, not accessible to anyone. In each of these was a big vase of artificial flowers. The doors turned automatically whenever someone approached them. The artificial flowers were doomed to go round and round until further notice. I managed to take a pleasing room with a big glass window that you could open between bathroom and bedroom. If I'd had a partner I could have talked to her through this window while she shaved her legs. As well as that, there was a stuffed toy elephant, which had a very short trunk so as not to make the male guests feel inadequate.

I had a shower and went down to Reception. I picked up a free plan of the City and asked the receptionist to show me where we were on it. She either didn't understand the question or didn't know the answer – or both. The street names were all in Chinese characters but I could recognise the railway station and some of the more distinctive road lay-outs such as a flyover. I asked the receptionist which bus station had buses going to Almaty (pronounced 'Allah-mah-too'). She said no bus went from Urumqi. I didn't believe this as Almaty was the nearest city and the former capital of Kazakhstan. According to the map the highest classification of road went there and there was no direct railway. Also my Thomas Cook guide said there was a bus.

I moved to the bar where I had a cup of coffee, because this was the only place on the ground floor with a window admitting daylight. I'd seen some people arrive who, I guessed, were British. When I went to the desk to ask another receptionist about bus stations, I was lucky enough to find myself behind the Brits in the queue. I got into conversation with one, a very tall youngish man, a public-school type. He was speaking Chinese with utter confidence and arguing with Reception. The woman with the tall Brit referred to him as 'my cousin'. She explained that he worked in Shanghai. She told me his name was David and that he was big in tomatoes. She was visiting Urumqi and he'd been helping her with some of the things I'd been finding so difficult. By the time my turn came, David and I had become acquainted and he'd offered to help me. He asked in Chinese about the bus to Almaty. Although it was a different receptionist the answer was the same as I'd received previously.

'But I've seen the buses!' he argued, raising his voice.

The receptionist took us to the hotel's business office. My new ally got the girl to make some telephone calls on my behalf. There was a bus on Sunday. (This was Friday.) The girl marked the stop on my map. David later apologised to me for losing his temper.

'No need to apologise,' I said, 'I fully understand your frustration.'

The Chinese stay calm so I found his temper refreshing. He told me the Chinese word for 'bus station' and wrote down the characters.

I went to the bus station.

'No, we don't go to Almaty,' they said.

The bus that the hotel receptionist had finally admitted existed was still proving hard to track down. I tried another bay. And another. Eventually someone told me to go out and walk round the bus station. I walked round three sides of it looking for another entrance or ticket booth. By this means I came to a separate small bus station. A man on a mobile phone, whose features looked totally un-Chinese, saw me and gave me knowing 'hold-on-a-minute' expressions and gestures, which I hadn't seen for a long time. When he'd finished his conversation he took me to the counter that dealt with buses to Almaty. The buses went only at night. I bought a ticket for Sunday evening. Whether I would have found this bus station without David's help I don't know.

The next morning I had breakfast with David, the woman cousin I had met and four other friends and relations. I couldn't find anything I wanted to eat and there was no decent coffee to be had, but it was the happiest breakfast I'd had for a long time. It was wonderful to be among my own kind, to talk about the things that matter to the British – our travel plans, the weather, the coffee and how to get a decent piece of toast from the toaster.

David had grown up in Australia. I particularly took to his cousin Miranda, not just because she had the same name as my granddaughter. I said 'goodbye' to them all and kept bumping into them around the hotel and saying 'goodbye' all over again. David gave me his e-mail address and told me if I had more problems to consult him.

I'd been thinking of getting my hair cut. I was walking along a side street hoping to buy batteries for my camera, when through the window of a shop I saw a boy having his hair cut. The hairdresser seemed to be doing a good job. Someone inside saw me looking in. I pointed to the boy's hair and then to my own. They beckoned me in. A male hairdresser made a snipping motion with his hand. I did the same. In no time I was in a chair.

A young woman who'd been watching the boy's cut progressing (presumably a trainee) came up to me and put a sheet around my neck. Then without discussion (which was impossible anyway) she took some liquid from a bottle, put it on my head and rubbed it into my hair. Then she took something from another bottle and rubbed that in. Adding no water, she worked the stuff on my hair into a lather. As it happened I'd washed my hair that morning but she didn't know that and I had no way of telling her! She massaged my scalp, hammered my skull with her clenched fists – gently, I am relieved to say. Then she did the same with the edges of her hands. She worked my scalp with her fingers, then with her thumbs. The best bit was when she massaged my temples with her fingers because then I could feel her palms brushing sensuously against my ears. She worked on my neck, which I'm sure had been tense. She did the same with my shoulders, massaging me through my jumper. I hoped she dried her hands first. I guessed that she had been bored silly just watching her teacher and had leapt at the chance to actually *do* something. Indeed I believe she would happily have worked her way down my tense body at least as far as the small of my tense back but her teacher made a clipping movement with his hands and I nodded. So the girl let him take over while she went back to watching. He did a good job – a much-needed tidy up. I got him to trim the hair that had been growing in my ears. This tickled him. It didn't tickle me – in fact I didn't feel a thing!

With a weight off my head, I returned to the business of battery hunting. I came to a row of electronics shops and went into one selling mobile phones. I spoke to a boy, who beckoned me into the shop next door. There I spoke to a man, who could have been the boy's father.

'How many?' he asked.

'Twenty,' I said.

'I get them. Wait here.'

He was gone for a quarter of an hour – probably on a motorbike. He came back with 30 batteries. I bought the 20 we'd agreed. It was a question of weight as much as anything.

Back in the Vili Hotel I was really happy sitting in the window of the bar, writing my notes or watching the world go by, while I sipped rice wine – a bit low on flavour but a clean, refreshing feel in the mouth. A man went by pedalling a tricycle cart, probably on his way home from a day's trading. On the back was a vast, flat-topped bundle and on top of that, like someone riding an elephant, was the man's wife. I often returned to my seat in the window

The folk of Urumqi seemed happy. They liked to laugh, to lark about, to tease each other. I saw a man banging a woman's bottom with his fist as they walked cheerfully along. I thought laughter must be an important release for a people who tried to stay calm all the time. Several times I saw parents playing with a single child. A mother and her son, for instance, holding hands to chase the father. I've never seen parents talk so much to their children, except possibly in Mexico. The parents were happy to carry them. Children must be particularly precious in a country where the state provides economic support for the first child only. If the parents don't play with their small child they know there are no brothers or sisters to do it.

One of my most rewarding discoveries in Urumqi was the People's Park. It was marked on my street plan of the City and I deliberately sought it out. I have never seen a public park so well used. It was a Sunday afternoon and the place was full of people who had come for all manner of recreation.

Before I entered the park I passed a line of tables where people were playing Chinese chess, watched by an equal number of spectators. Once inside there were the usual footpaths, bright flower beds and people lolling on the grass, but it was the range of activities that impressed me. There were food stalls and a café. A play was in progress, in an exaggerated style that reminded me of British pantomime. There were playgrounds for children including a high-level track for pedal cars as well as a boating lake. On another small lake children could play inside great see-through beach balls, which floated like bubbles on the water. The child was zipped in and presumably unzipped before the oxygen ran out. While inside, the child could propel the sphere by walking on the inside surface of its skin. No doubt fun to do and fascinating, if a little bizarre, to watch. At that time I hadn't seen the invention in Europe, but I shouldn't be surprised to do so as so many of our toys come from China.

There was also social dancing of a mysterious kind. I found it strangely touching. It was like a less earnest version of Tai Chi. People danced as individuals, moving gently rather than energetically, with the steady pace of the music, but not to pre-arranged steps, indeed expressing whatever they were moved to express – with their faces, with hand and arm gestures and in the way they held themselves. Dancers did not touch but they could relate to each other – or not, as they chose. It had a graceful, organic feel that was lovely to watch. But the best thing was to see the happiness on the people's faces. Three dancers beckoned me to join in, which I could have done. All you needed was nerve – but for some reason I had a bag with me that I didn't want to put down.

Fifty metres away a group of singers and instrumentalists (two violins, flute and something like a balalaika), were making music just for the joy of it. A small audience had formed sitting on the edge of a dry culvert. Some members of this informal audience beckoned me to join them and I did. Meanwhile the group continually re-formed as individuals came forward to sing a solo or left when they'd finished. When there was a break in the music some people who'd been listening got up and stepped forward to drop something into a bright orange bin. I assumed this was for donations so I too got up, reached in my pocket for some coins and went to drop them in the bin, only to find (just in time) that no one had put anything but rubbish into it. There were other musicians spaced out through the park so closely that in places you could hear two performances at once. In a pavilion-style covered area, a man with a two-stringed instrument like the sore duong I'd seen in Thailand and a singer were performing to a rapt audience. Other musicians were playing for the love of it; some were just having a go.

I was having coffee in the hotel, when David and two of his party joined me. He was about to take them to the airport to fly home to England.

'Are you going to come back to China?' he asked me.

'I don't know,' I said. 'It's certainly a fascinating place, but this trip may change my life. I don't know what's going to happen.'

When I checked out I tried to tell the receptionists that I'd lost my cap. They immediately grasped that what I was trying to say concerned headwear and they took me to the hotel shop and showed me the display of hats. I shook my head. I went up to my room. There I met the manager and a chambermaid. We looked round the room. Suddenly the chambermaid lifted up the end of the king-size bed and held it while the manager and I looked under. The chambermaid was a tiny thing so she couldn't lift the bed very high. That meant she had to wait while we got right down to look. Then the chambermaid lowered the bed to the floor, looked surprised at her own strength and even more surprised that she had survived. I tried not to feel guilty. We found no cap, but I noticed a pair of my underpants hanging on the back of the bathroom door. I stuffed them in my pocket before either of the women saw. The hotel looked after my luggage while I went off to look for my cap. I thought I might have left it in the shop where I'd waited for the batteries. But I couldn't find it. I couldn't even find the row of electronics shops. Not only had I lost my cap – I'd lost an entire parade of shops as well! I thought of trying the hairdressers but I'd no idea where that was. Luckily I remembered the Internet café, where the cap was waiting for me on top of one of the screens.

Before I boarded the bus for darkest Kazakhstan I needed to get some nourishing food inside me. In Mr Lee's restaurant there was a menu in pictorial form on the wall. The camera cannot lie and I chose a dish that contained cubes of succulent brown meat – just the thing to keep me going on a 600 mile bus journey. When my order arrived, however, the braised steak in onion gravy I'd been expecting had transmogrified into pale suet dumplings coated in a dark brown sauce. Luckily it came with a cup of hot water, which helped me to get it down.

There was chaos at the bus station – a traffic jam in a small space, vehicles parked in the way, luggage and parcels heaped in the path of a bus due to leave. One bus took five minutes to travel its own length. I had been told to report at 7.20pm, so to be on the safe side I arrived at 7.10. At 8.30 boarding began. At 8.45 they were rounding up late-comers. At 8.50 the driver started the engine. At 9.10 the bus began to move. I'd had to wait two hours but the clock in the bus showed it was only 7.10 anyway. The Lonely Planet Guide to China explained that Urumqi is supposed to be on Beijing time but the locals often use a local time two hours behind the official.

I had an upper berth. The design of the bus maximised the number of berths by overlapping the ends of them. They did this by tucking a covered space for the feet of one berth under the curved headrest for the next berth. I discovered that it was impossible to sit up, unless you dangled your feet over the side. I didn't like to do this because my feet were too smelly to put so near the passenger below. It had been a warm day and as heat rises the temperature on the upper bunk meant it was more than cosy. I hadn't showered for 12 hours, so I was probably pretty high by then. All I could do was to lie on my bunk and try to relax. The two drivers shared a bed. I don't mean they got into bed together, but one would rest while the other drove.

At 8.07 (bus time) we stopped and people got out. I asked someone how long the break was. Ten minutes I was told. It took me nine to get my boots on, find and walk to the toilet, wash my hands and get back. There was no time to go to the café although others had. I couldn't see the driver and conductor

– nor any other passenger – but I dared not risk it. In the end the break lasted nearly an hour. Luckily I'd got cubic dumplings and hot water inside me. I topped this up with some small soft rolls I'd kept from the train and an apple.

Half way through the night the road became rough, bumpy and very winding. It was too dark to see what the scenery was like, but I made out road works. When we stopped I saw that the stars were wonderfully clear. When it was light I noticed mountains. We passed people on horseback. Cattle and sheep were being driven along the road. One of the women on the bus turned to me.

'You … old?' she asked.

'Yes,' I said, 'I'm sixty-four.'

After one stop I got into the wrong coach. The passengers were very friendly. Luckily they started laughing and I realised my mistake. I hated these breaks on buses because I could never find out how long they lasted. When we stopped early in the morning I asked the driver.

'It's only for the traders,' he said.

As before, by the time I'd been to the loo the driver had disappeared. We were in a large bus park, where traders had set up stalls to sell fruit, toys, clothes and mobile phones. Currency touts were touting currency. The traders certainly didn't look Chinese. Their faces were angular and rugged. I'd been unable to obtain Kazakh currency in Urumqi so I changed 500 yuan for 800 of the new things. I'd no idea whether that was right. I wasn't so uptight about these things as I'd been in Central America. One of the men on my bus bought a doll with long wavy blond hair. He said, 'Mama!' to it and the doll said, 'Mama!' back – in his deep voice. I went round all the stalls and bought nothing but a banana. Eventually everyone had had enough and hung around waiting by the bus for the driver to come back. He did – only to disappear again! I thought we'd stop for ten minutes. It must have been more than an hour and a half. I couldn't see the point in having two drivers if we didn't get a move on. You didn't have that nonsense on the trains.

When we finally got going we went for five minutes, then stopped in a place called Korgas, very close to the border. This was to wait our turn at the border crossing. Here I learned that the long break in the bus park had been for breakfast, which of course I'd missed.

'China is very interesting,' one of the passengers said, 'but it's not clean. Kazakhstan is clean.'

After 20 minutes we moved on to Immigration. The struggle to get into the building was epic. We all had to go up steps which led to a much narrower entrance. On these steps were people with normal luggage and many with parcels, some bigger than hay bales. They were a competitive mob. You had to press forward, otherwise you were forced back. We were all trying to get through the same narrow doorway at the top of the steps. Meanwhile a lot of people, also with huge parcels, thought they could push in by approaching from two flights of steps at the side, all leading to the same entrance. Naturally this jammed the queue completely and forced some of us in the main body down a step or more. Most of the parcels were soft bundles. This was lucky as people were falling over. I did so twice. Tough old women were heaving luggage up the steps. One, overweight and using a stick, was manhandling a large parcel. No one helped her. We all had our own problems. The doorway got jammed and for a while nothing moved. An official shouted at us to go back. No one did. If someone had we would have collapsed en masse. Eventually there was some movement through the doors. I went with the flow – such as it was – and found myself inside the building filling in forms. Several fellow travellers came forward to help me.

'Thank you,' I said, 'but look – the form is in English. It's easy for me.'

I only hesitated on questions that didn't have an obvious answer, like, 'address in China'.

It had been a tedious journey but I believed that in minutes I would be in Kazakhstan. I showed my passport as I had at so many border crossings, expecting to be waved through. This time the clerk called an official over.

'Why haven't you got a visa?' he demanded.

This threw me. I came out with the first excuse that entered my head.

'I was told I could get one on the other side,' I said.

'Who told you this?'

'The agent who obtained the other visas for me that I needed.'

This wasn't true, but my memory was confused.

'Hold on a minute!' he said, and went off with my passport. He came back with a more senior official, a tall Chinese, and handed him the passport. I could see the other members of our party being let through.

'Why haven't you got a visa?' he asked.

'I'm sorry. I made a mistake. I thought I didn't need a visa. Can I get one here?'

'You have to go to Beijing.'

'I'll have to tell my bus that I can't go on.'

'I'll come with you.'

We caught up with one of the passengers. I told him.

'We need to tell the driver,' I said.

'He is the driver!' the tall official insisted.

He left me on a seat in the middle of the hall. A young man was looking dejected. They had his passport too.

'My group are waiting for me!' he said hopelessly.

The tall official came back.

'Where is my passport?' I demanded.

'A friend is doing some research. He has your passport. It'll only take ten minutes – two minutes!'

I breathed deeply. I like to think that the Kazakh took courage from my fearless attitude.

'Why have you got my passport?' he demanded.

'You had too many bags.'

'Too many!'

'Yes, you had five, instead of two!'

I thought the Chinese would have been glad that foreigners were buying their goods. 'You said "two minutes"!' I remonstrated. 'I need to have my passport.'

My own nerve surprised me, but what had I got to lose? I'd already lost my passport.

'Just a minute,' the senior official said, and walked off.

He came back with an A4 sheet of paper.

'There,' he said, 'will you sign that?'

'I'm not signing that,' I declared, 'I can't read it!'

'It's just a report of what happened.'

I had only his word for that. For all I knew it could have said, 'I, John Philip Barclay, hereby confess that I am a drug trafficker, a sex trafficker and a spy in the pay of Tibetan separatists, and throw myself at the mercy of the mighty Republic of China.' I made a quick decision.

'I'm not signing this,' I declared, 'if I haven't got my passport.'

'Look,' he said, 'It's perfectly safe. It's just sitting on a table. I'll show you.'

He led me to an open door. I looked through and saw another official, but there was no sign of a passport. The other official came out.

'What is it?' he asked me.

'I was asking to have my passport back,' I explained calmly.

Without further discussion he handed it to me.

'Thank you,' I said.

I checked the passport was mine and immediately put it away in my high-security money belt. I had got my passport back but I was stuck in China. Then the tall official handed me the sheet of Chinese characters, so I signed it.

'Thank you,' he said. 'Now can we help you any more?'

I suppose I should have been grateful that the Chinese authorities hadn't let me out of their country without a visa. Otherwise the Kazakhs would have forbidden me entry and I might have been compelled to languish in no-man's-land until I died of thirst.

'No, thank you,' I said, 'I've got my passport. I think I can manage on my own now.'

So near and yet so far! I came out of the building the way I'd come in. As usual I refused all offers of taxis. I was hot, tired and fed up, while at the same time being thrilled that at my lowest moment, immediately after showing myself to be an incompetent fool, I had found reserves of nerve and spirit, no doubt drawing on a long British tradition of throwing our British weight around in far-flung places, but always in a dignified British manner.

It was the middle of the afternoon and very hot. I had some lunch at a makeshift al-fresco café under a sunshade. It was good to be out of the immigration building. I'd made a costly mistake. Because for all the other countries I'd either had visas or hadn't needed them, I'd carelessly assumed I'd be all right for Kazakhstan. I had forgotten that to save time Simon Corcoran, the visa agent in Melbourne, had agreed with me that I would get a visa for Kazakhstan myself when I came to Urumqi. And I'd crossed so many frontiers on my travels that I'd become blasé.

I hoped I wouldn't really have to travel the 2,000 miles to Beijing, but I knew I had to go the 400 miles back to Urumqi. I set off on foot to find a bus, pursued by taxis. I walked beside lorries parked on a road awaiting their turn at Immigration. No one could see me except the lorry drivers. The gaps between the lorries were so narrow in places that I couldn't squeeze through. The vehicles afforded good shade. The thought occurred to me that if I went to the nearest airport on the Chinese side I might be able to obtain a visa there – although possibly I would have to buy a plane ticket, which would destroy my chance of meeting my challenge.

While the bus I had been on continued to Almaty I managed to find a smaller bus with no bed, which was going to Urumqi. I got told off for walking on the carpet in my boots so I stopped where I was and started to take my boots off. They pointed to the front of the bus. I knew that to go back I'd have to walk on the carpet but by then I'd got one boot off so I hopped on my stockinged foot to the front of the bus. I thought this would get a laugh and it did.

Going back in daylight I was able to see the scenery I had missed on the way out – and very dramatic it was too. This went some way towards compensating for the set-back. As the view got more interesting I moved to a seat near the front, where I could see through the windscreen. I had to ask if I could squeeze in between two men. One of them handed me a bottle of something he said was from Moldova. I thought it was beer so I took a gulp. Wow! I soon realised it was spirits. Then I heard the women behind us whispering. We had the bumpy, winding road with the rough surface again but this time I could see the context – a climb to more than 3,000 metres, with hairpin bends, steep drops and ever-changing views, until we reached a plateau, where for miles we ran beside a lake so big you couldn't see the other side, like Lake Nicaragua. There were seagulls – although we were hundreds of miles from open sea. Between us and the lake lay a long narrow strip of land with horses and sheep.

Once we'd left the lake behind, we stopped for a comfort break. The air was beautiful, probably the sweetest to be sniffed in China. 'Sweet' would not be the adjective to choose for the outside toilet. Three walls screened it from the road. The fourth was missing leaving the facility open to a field where the land and all contributions from members of the public fell away. The floor was a slab of concrete with three irregular holes. The concrete had begun to crumble and one hole was bigger and more irregular than the other two. A small boy came in to use this. It was probably just as well that I didn't know the Chinese for, 'Steady young man, or you'll fall right through that hole, then you'll really be in the shit!'

It was calm and quiet now – a long straight road with a good surface. It was very late when we came into Urumqi. The bus dropped a few passengers off early but the bulk of us were deposited in a part of the city I had never seen before. Everything was strange. I first thought all the signs were in Russian, because I saw the Cyrillic alphabet and for a moment I wondered if I'd got on the wrong bus and ended up in Russia. But the Cyrillic alphabet is sometimes used by the Uighurs so I realised later that I must have landed up in the Uighur Quarter of Urumqi.

The other passengers disappeared into a big building that looked like a hotel but didn't say 'hotel' so I looked for a building that did. I couldn't find one. Meanwhile I'd gathered a group of young men around me like a horse gathers flies. The men seemed to have nothing better to do than to hang about the streets waiting for confused foreigners to befriend. One of them helped me to find a hotel. The others came along for the hell of it. Between them they had more English than the receptionist. I was trying to have a conversation with her, while they kept chipping in. It was difficult to distinguish between single and double rooms on the one hand and single and double occupation on the other. Once I got across the fact that I didn't want to share, the receptionist said 'no room'. So my new friends took me across the road to another building. I handed in my precious passport, was given the key to a room, went up in the lift with my friends, opened the door and saw a man in a bed. I shut the door and shot down again. As soon as one of the gang explained this the receptionist handed back my passport and said, 'no rooms'.

As we continued the hunt, the gang began to lose interest and faded away – all except one guy who was much keener than the rest and a little manic. I'll call him 'Mukhtar'. Soon it was just the two of us. He had already nominated himself as my spokesman – amazingly as it turned out. I'd noticed that he did a lot of gesturing. Mukhtar and I should have got on well. Once I had him on his own I realised that he didn't speak at all – or even grunt. He was probably deaf, because that's the usual reason for not speaking. But to give him credit he did know where the hotels were. In one they asked me to wait a minute. I sat on a sofa. Mukhtar immediately sat next to me and started finding advertisements in the newspaper to show me. I couldn't read them, of course. I don't know if Mukhtar could. So I never found out whether they were for accommodation or for prostitutes. When I was called back to the desk Mukhtar came over too and tried to interpret my words and gestures with his gestures. When I was given the key to a room, he was for carrying my bags up in the lift with me.

'You've found me a lovely hotel,' I said loudly, so the receptionist could hear even if Mukhtar couldn't. 'Thank you very much. I don't need your help up to the room. I'm not a baby.'

The receptionist grasped the situation and very quickly came forward to go up with me in the lift. This helped to exclude Mukhtar and he disappeared. How pathetic! I should have given him a few coins. But if I hadn't got rid of him he might have got into the shower with me and started to wash my back. The receptionist showed me my room. I opened the bathroom door and once again there was a person already there. Luckily this time it was the chambermaid, poor thing, cleaning the bathroom. It was well after midnight. After my long and pointless journeys I was glad finally to be alone.

I slept well for six hours. At 7.40am I went out looking for breakfast. All I could find was a supermarket. I bought rolls and orange juice, which I brought back and ate in my room. Then I packed up and checked out. Three taxi-drivers didn't know the Kazakhstan Consulate so I got the third to take me to the bus station where I'd left for Almaty. The clerks recognised me and wondered what I was doing still in Urumqi. I explained but it took me ages to get them to see that I was there to ask about getting a visa. Some bus stations, for instance in Central America, are authorised to issue entry permits, so it was possible that these people would know something. After all, their buses crossed the border all the time.

'I'll buy a ticket,' I said, 'if I can be sure I can get through immigration.'

I did a mime of the scene at the barrier, much simplified, playing the parts of myself and the immigration official not letting me pass. Everyone in the room laughed.

'You don't have to buy another ticket,' said the English-speaking manager who had helped me before. 'You have to pay some money – that's all.'

'But the same thing will happen again!' I argued. 'If I don't have the authority …'

'Authority?'

'If *you* can't give me a visa, how can I get one?'

No answer.

'Do you have a telephone directory?'

'You want to telephone?'

'No, I want to find the address of the Kazakhstan Embassy. Have you got a telephone directory?'

The manager looked blank. I drew a picture of one.

'Come! Come!' he said

I started picking up my bags.

'Leave that, leave that!' the manager ordered.

So the girls on the desk looked after my luggage.

'We go upstairs,' said the manager.

He knocked on a door and opened it cautiously. I could see a meeting in progress. He went in leaving me to wait in the corridor.

'The lady says your government and Kazakhstan have an agreement,' he told me when he came out. 'No visa necessary.'

I knew from painful experience that this was not true.

'Thank you for your help,' I said.

'Well, if you come back,' he said, 'I may be able to help you – I work here!'

'Would you look in the telephone directory for me? I can't read Chinese characters. Do you have an office?'

'No telephone directory. So you don't want to buy a ticket today?'

'No, because the visa might be delayed. Thank you very much.'

Now at least I was back in the part of Urumqi I knew. I went looking for a hotel. The first three were full. The fourth, 'Ramada' had a room and I took it. I shouldn't have been surprised that, with a name like that, the hotel had a Muslim restaurant and no bar. So I went back to the Vili Hotel and sat in my old favourite spot, the bar overlooking the street. Some men were noisily playing cards. I had a beer and relaxed a little.

Perhaps my new hotel could give me some pointers for getting a visa. The Ramada Hotel 'business services' put me onto the hotel management. They got an address of the Kazakhstan Consulate over the telephone – well a trainee did, writing it down in Chinese characters. After a 25-minute ride in a taxi I was in the road I'd been told to go to. I walked up and down looking for something remotely resembling an embassy. I asked people, but got nowhere. I had no option but to take a taxi back again. When I checked my e-mails I found I'd one from David, the tomato man. So I had an excuse to e-mail him asking again for help. I also e-mailed Simon Corcoran in Melbourne for advice for both Kazakhstan and Ukraine. I fell asleep over my dinner.

I woke in the night and began to take stock. I saw that my visa for Russia expired on the 9th October. It was then the 19th of September. This meant that I had exactly three weeks to get out of China, travel the length of Kazakhstan and be in and out of that bit of Russia I had to cross to reach Ukraine. I would have to move quickly, but first I had to get that visa. After breakfast I went to reception and asked to stay on.

'Sorry,' the clerk said, 'today the hotel is full.'

I went across the road to another hotel.

'Please may I reserve a single room tonight,' I asked, 'for one person?'

No reply. I wrote something on a piece of paper. I did a mime of someone entering my name in a big imaginary book. They showed me the rules about checking in and out.

'The hotels are full,' I said. 'I have to move out of the Ramada Hotel. If I wait until 12, this hotel may be full.'

'Please wait,' they said, indicating a seat.

I guessed that meant 'nothing doing'. Eventually I found a room in the Gong Xiao Hotel. A notice in the window of the hotel business centre bravely offered to help guests with communications in the wider world.

BUSINESS□□□CENTRE
Offers□secretarial□and□transltion□sericves. □thping□and□photo□□□copy ing ... woud□□pyocessing□□ayts□and□crafts ...

If you are dissatisfied with our servics□, please dial litigation number.

Despite this effort to reach out to the world of business, they didn't accept credit cards. As usual I was short of cash and I went hunting for ATMs. The China Construction Bank ATM accepted 'Cirrus' but it held my card. Losing my card was the thing I dreaded most. The machine 'timed out' and I got no money. Mercifully, after anxious seconds, it did return my card.

I thought of breaking off the trip, flying home to get my bank cards sorted out, flying back and continuing where I'd left off – not very green! Meanwhile Simon Corcoran e-mailed to say I didn't need a visa for Ukraine and David sent me details of the Kazakhstan Consulate in Urumqi and put me in touch with a friend called Michael, a New Yorker who worked not far from the city. I e-mailed him and he filled me in with the other details I needed. I had been desperate and these people's kindness and quick responses touched me.

So then the only problem was money. I had the money in my account – all I had to do was to access it. I was heading for a less developed country, where obtaining cash might be even more difficult. I was worried that I might be stranded in a remote place with no money to move on. I wrote a list of what I might have to spend money on to get out of such a situation – taxi to the airport, final night in a hotel, phone calls, bus fares, food and water. I decided that if I dropped below a minimum of $200 I should cut my losses and fly home. $200 seems very little but life is cheap in 'second world' countries. Meanwhile I thought I should investigate the possibility of getting one of my sons to wire some money to me. I was tired. I had a cold coming. I still hoped to be home in six weeks – could I keep going that long?

I discovered the reason why the hotels were full – it was the first day of Ramadan. But where were the Muslim women in their headscarves like I'd seen in Malaysia? I never discovered.

The next morning I packed and checked out, because I couldn't spare the cash to check in for another night. I found a photography shop and had some passport photos taken. The photographer put some unglazed spectacles on me to give the look of someone who wore glasses, but without lenses which would have reflected the light.

I tried again to get to the Kazakhstan Consulate. A woman taxi-driver with a note of assurance in her voice dropped me close – or so I thought, but I had to take a second taxi to the actual road. I knew the consulate was at number 31. This was a small building with a pair of locked double doors, part of a terrace of ordinary shops. Some locals assured me that what I had found was not the Consulate. I had to wander, wonder, ask and explore before I found what I believed to be the correct road but still I couldn't find number 31. David had told me to look out for a crowd of Kazakhs. And outside number 216 there was a throng of people milling and muttering. Some had papers in their hands. It was chaos. An official was failing to keep order. Another official guarded a gate in the railings. Two people told me that they had been there three days.

'How do you get a form?' I asked someone.

'Try to capture *his* attention!' he said, indicating the man on the gate.

As I was the only European it was easy to catch his eye. When he saw my British passport he spoke to me in excellent English with an American accent. I was through the gate in three minutes from arriving – not three days! Inside the building there was chaos on a smaller scale and I found myself in a crowded lobby. There was no indication of where you were supposed to go, but a number of people were trying to get into an inner room. I went in but was sent out straight away. I waited a minute, then tried again. This time somebody gave me a form before sending me back into the lobby. I filled in my form. Two presentable young men of student age and unknown nationality, also with forms, borrowed my map of China.

'What did you put for which town you are going to be visiting?' one asked.

'Almaty and Kandyagash,' I told them. 'I'm going through by train and I'll probably stop there.'

It was like comparing notes after an exam – 'What did you put for the causes of the Peasants' Revolt?'

One question was, 'Have you ever been refused entry into Kazakhstan?'

This got me worried for a moment, then I realised I'd only been refused exit from China – not entry into Kazakhstan.

'When are you going into Kazakhstan?' my new friends asked me.

'As soon as I've got my visa,' I replied.

Once I'd filled in the form I went back into the inner room. The official asked me some questions I didn't understand, so I handed him the Kazakh version of the sheet of personal information I'd had the foresight to prepare before I left England. He smiled.

'What are you going to do in Kandyagash?'

Was this a catch question?

'Stay in a hotel,' I said, 'and have a look around.'

He passed my papers on to the cashier, who took $30 off me, bringing my secret store down to $420. They told me the visa would be ready on Monday. This was Thursday. Back in the familiar part of Urumqi I went to the Internet café. I tried to get into my American Express account via the Wonderful Wonderful Web, but I couldn't remember my security word.

'Helpful hint – it could be your mother's maiden name.'

I keyed this in.

'Due to a technical problem,' the machine said, 'the service has to be discontinued.'

Meanwhile I had to find another hotel room and pay for it. I went back to the Construction Bank and put my card in the ATM hoping it wouldn't 'time out' again. The sun was shining on the screen and the English words were tiny. Suddenly I heard a man's voice speaking Chinese in my ear and I nearly jumped out of my European skin. It was the next customer, standing behind me. I always felt vulnerable when my card was out in the open and I didn't want to mess up the transaction – it was too critical. The last thing I wanted was someone calling out instructions in Chinese. That's not true – the *last* thing I wanted was someone to hold a knife to my throat. But to my relief the machine gave me 2,000 yuan. I stepped quickly into the bank to put my card and cash away safely before going back onto the street.

With my new-found wealth I went back to the Gong Xiao Hotel and checked in to a different room for another four days. I was rather pleased with my passport photos so I went back to the shop and asked for an enlargement. There was the usual display of photographs. There were lots of shots of babies – all nude boys with their penises clearly featured. Not a single photograph of a girl baby could be seen, confirming the general preference for boys. I wondered who all these boys were going to marry!

The next day I saw workmen packing up the summer tables in a little park. In a long raised bed in my street municipal gardeners were replacing the summer bedding with chrysanthemums and Michaelmas daisies. It was September 21st. In six weeks I would either be home or dead. I drew a picture of a woman's face with earrings and a necklace. Using this I was able to locate an area of jewellers, where I hoped to top up my dollar reserve. None of the jewellers would let me have so much as a dime. They all recommended the Bank of China. But as before the bank refused me as I was still a foreigner and still hadn't acquired a Chinese friend.

I had another of those 'I'll have what she's having' dinners. Luckily they asked me if I wanted chilli paste. That was a near one! It was a deep bowl of broth with bits in it. The bowl was very hot. The waitress carried it with a horse-shoe-shaped broken ring of iron fixed to a wooden handle. The iron could be withdrawn once the table took the weight of the bowl – ingenious. The other surprise was that the broth smelled of bonemeal. If it did for me what bonemeal did for floribunda roses, I might be in for a late flowering. I wasn't surprised it smelled like that. There were lumps of dead cow lying in the bottom of the broth – bits of hoof, perhaps. Further nutritious benefit lay in noodles, vegetables, a big flat scone with herbs in it and something like sauerkraut made with cabbage and a delicate shade of pink. To wash all this down, they'd provided some cool green tea. Green tea is a marvellous beverage. It's comforting when hot, refreshing when cold, but drinkable at any temperature and it will go with just about any food.

In the Ramada Hotel I had caught a waitress, in full view of the guests, spooning instant coffee into a kettle before adding tepid water from a thermos that had been on the go for a couple of hours. So when I came to an establishment called 'Good Coffee' I felt compelled to investigate. There I had a proper cup of real Bolivian coffee. This satisfied my craving and showed me that there is hope for China after all.

The next day in the Guang Xiao Hotel I brought my own rolls to breakfast because I knew that in their restricted buffet there'd only be tasteless unleavened white lumps. I collected my hard-boiled egg and helped myself to the vegetable matter on offer. The two teapots on the side table were both cold. I took an empty beaker and went up to the waiter.

'Please may I have some hot tea?' I asked.

He lifted one of the tall thermoses from the floor and proceeded to pour into the beaker.

'That's water!' I exclaimed. 'Don't you have any tea?'

'No.'

'Do you have any coffee?' I asked, knowing full well that he had nothing of the sort.

He smirked as if I'd asked for panda sperm. Fortunately another guest gave me tea from his pot.

If I have given the impression that Chinese catering left a lot to be desired this would be unfair. Without the language I found I always got on better in communication terms if I stuck to the more basic outlets. I would like to go back with an interpreter and enjoy the better restaurants. I have seen enough to know that the Chinese restaurants in other countries give an inadequate picture of the creativity and abundant variety available across the regions of this vast country.

I managed to get 2,000 yuan out of one of the ATMs I knew but gave up hope of converting yuan to dollars. By e-mail I asked my son Rupert to be prepared to wire money to me through Western Union and to check his e-mails every day in case there was an urgent plea from me.

On the day I was due to make my second attempt to get out of China, I rationalised and reorganised my entire kit. The weather was overcast and much cooler. I wore my jacket for the first time since the Melbourne winter. It was good to be moving on.

I collected my visa. Once I had found the consulate, the process had been speedy and more or less painless. It wasn't like that for the locals. In a group of tough-looking Kazakhs I saw a woman with her eyes watering after an official had shouted fiercely at her.

In the evening I left to travel the bumpy road between Urumqi and the Kazakhstan border for the third, and I hoped final, time. At the bus station I knew so well people were heaving giant parcels sealed with sticky tape. This time I was more relaxed. At the border hours later, when I was in the immigration building for the second time, I saw a tall man looking at me.

'Do you remember me?' he asked.

It was the senior official who had confiscated my passport – how could I forget? This time he didn't hold me up. As the woman behind the window was looking at my passport, the guard guarding the queue kept telling me what to do. The woman handed me a form.

'Do I have to fill it in now?' I asked.

'Yes,' she said.

The guard tried to take it off me.

'You can't fill it in for me,' I said, 'you don't know my name.'

'Passport number!' he snapped.

'I can do that – when I get my passport back.'

The woman handed it to me. I filled in the form and returned it to her. Then I looked round to see where I was supposed to go.

'Go, go, go!' the guard shouted.

I think he was in the wrong profession. He would have made an effective terrorist. But I was through Immigration. Having lost a week I was now back on track. It was the same chaos as before and there was a lot of waiting. Four buses, one of them ours, were parked so that no vehicle could get past them. The drivers walked away. Nothing could happen until they came back, which turned out to be an hour and a half later. There seemed to be an unspoken agreement between the drivers that they would all stop work, no one would lose their turn and we'd all get a long siesta. I wished I'd brought my own giant parcel to sit on. The air was cool but the sunshine was hot. A group of Kazakhs gave me some food and one of the women, called 'Svetlana', flirted mildly with me, which helped to pass the time for both of us. Another woman, almost hysterical, was standing on a truck refusing a parcel that officials were trying to load onto the truck. She pushed it off. They loaded it back on. I couldn't work out what was going on. It would have been farcical if it hadn't been for the desperate screams of the woman.

Having wasted a couple hours, most of it sitting in the sun, we repacked our luggage on the bus and squeezed into what space was left. It was with a feeling of profound relief that we headed for the actual border. I'd always known that China would be challenging. Kazakhstan, on the other hand, was a country I knew very little about.

23. Kazakhstan

September 25 – October 2

Kazakhstan had a pleasant autumnal feel to it, the trees turning gold and the sun setting behind the mountains. The bus stopped at a restaurant and for once it was clear that this was a meal break. I sat at a big round table with some Kazakh women passengers and it was good to feel one of the group. We had something like tea, which came out of the pot already white with milk. The women drank it with sugar. At least it was hot. I had borscht for the first time and that was marvellous. I also had **балтикд** (I think that was how it was spelled), which I thought was a fortified beer. After the watery beers I'd been having it was amazing. I didn't know whether the written language I was seeing was Kazakh or Russian but, unlike Chinese, it was not impenetrable. The word for 'café' for instance was **'сафе'**.

We arrived at Almaty about 11pm. By the time I'd found a hotel and got into my room it was after midnight. I had to share a toilet and washbasin with a woman in the next room. We had no bathroom. After 26 hours on a bus, I asked the receptionist if I might have a shower. Each time I spoke to her she looked dejected. She sent me to a communal loo with three holes in the floor, but no shower. I went back to her. This time she gave me a key to a communal shower room on the floor above mine, with instructions to bring the key straight back. As I emerged after my shower a man with one leg and crutches hopped in and demanded the keys.

'I'm sorry,' I said, 'I can't give them to you. I have to take them back to the woman.'

Most of this was in hand gestures on both sides.

'No,' I think he said, 'I've spoken to her. You should give the keys to me!'

He was vehement. So I handed over the keys. He might have been the owner of the hotel. Then I went straight downstairs and told the woman in gestures, incorporating a telling mime of a one-legged man who was hopping mad.

There was no café near the hotel so in the morning I bought food for breakfast and took it back to my room to eat. I checked out of the hotel and took a taxi to the railway station to investigate trains. I sat in a café re-planning my route. I bought a ticket for the next day with the help of a man in the queue who spoke English. Then I set out to look for another hotel. There was one near the station, but a woman said there was no room for me, so I made a thorough trawl of the area. Not a single hotel! I decided to go back to the station. I asked a taxi-driver.

'You want hotel at station?' he asked.

'Yes,' I said.

'There – hotel!'

He indicated the hotel I'd tried before. I went into the station and asked again. People sent me out of the station by various routes. By asking and failing I eventually found the 'Hotel Transit'. When I got near I realised that it was the hotel I'd been turned away from two hours earlier, approached from a different angle. I thought I might as well try again. This time I was offered a double room with bath and toilet but no wash basin or curtain, for 5,500 *tenge* – whatever that was worth. I took it – but what a waste of time!

I did some washing. Then I went looking for ATMs. Almaty was an attractive city, mostly re-built at the beginning of the 20th century after an earthquake. There were wide roads and lots of trees, many of them gold or brown. I had the agreeable experience of walking on crisp fallen leaves. I found one ATM, but it wouldn't take my card.

The next morning I got cross because I was the first into the dining room for breakfast. I'd a long wait before anyone took my order. I ordered an egg, which shouldn't have taken long to prepare. A woman came in after me, ordered an egg. She got hers first and had eaten it before I got one – in other words she must have eaten my egg! Maybe she was the boss. I couldn't complain because I didn't have the language, so I channelled my anger, a useful source of energy, into packing up.

I went into the station forecourt and 'chatted' to some locals and taxi-drivers, trying to find out where the big banks and the big shops were. One suggested I ask the woman who ran a kiosk. She wrote some words on paper. There was a trolleybus waiting. The driver was sitting in his cab trimming his finger nails. He gestured to me to get inside. I liked the idea of taking a trolleybus. I hadn't ridden on one since I was a child. I had no idea where the centre of the city was but the bus took me to a part where there were some banks. Unfortunately none would take my card. I was thrilled, however, to recognise the Kazakh's word for Internet outside an Internet café. I e-mailed my son Rupert asking him to wire money to me at Kandyagash, my next destination. Then I took a taxi back to the station. I'd had the sense earlier to copy the name of the station in the local script so I had something to show the driver.

After a quick lunch at the station café, I boarded the train. I'd asked for 'soft sleeping' but the train had none. Also, my timetable had said there was a dining car but there was no food on the train. A young woman in my compartment, called Anastasiya, told me that we'd stop at certain stations for five minutes when I could buy food. But I was so nervous about being left behind that I didn't make a very good job of it. Half an hour after my hastily bought supper, hunger gave way to stomach ache.

Anastasiya was a 24-year-old living in Kazakhstan. She taught English privately to all ages. Her mother was Kazakh, her father half German, half Ukrainian. She had never travelled to an English-speaking country so she leapt at the chance to practise her English on me. She told me she was going to stay with a friend for two weeks.

'Is it true,' she asked, 'that in England a person can live on his own when he's 16?'

'Yes,' I replied, 'but most of them don't want to, because they are either in further education or they are working and want to spend any money they earn on themselves, not on food and accommodation.'

'I'm 24. I'm living with my parents. They say I can't live on my own.'

'If you can't win them round, you just have to do it – leave. Are you an only child?'

'Yes.'

'If they don't speak to you, that will be very hurtful, but they'll soon realise that they've lost their daughter, so they're hurting themselves. I think it's good you are going away for two weeks. Talk to your friend about it.'

'I'm looking for another language to learn,' she said, 'given that I've got English and German, I want to learn French.'

'English sits between German and French,' I argued. 'Your English will help you with French, but there aren't many places outside France where you can speak the language. When I was in Central America I wished I'd learned Spanish.'

We exchanged e-mail addresses and I promised to send her my book of poems, when I got home.

Kazakh trains are designed to make the most use of the space. The whole coach was open apart from the divisions made by three-tier bunks fitted in as shown in my drawing. There were solid luggage racks, like shelves, above all the berths. I was on a top berth. It was so cramped I couldn't get onto my berth the first time I tried. It was like sleeping in a giant larder without the benefit of food.

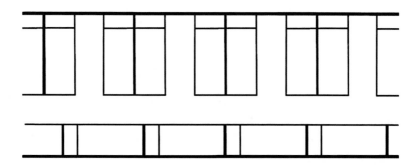

At midnight I realised that we had stopped at a station. People were going up and down the train, talking at full volume, while they looked for places to park their luggage. I felt someone tapping my knee. It was a woman who wanted me to move my rucksack from the luggage shelf above me so she could put a parcel, bigger than a trunk, in its place. I moved the rucksack and, taking care not to tread on somebody's melons, tried to help the woman lift the parcel. I hurt my back raising one end a mere 40cm. Somehow someone had loaded it onto the train. The challenge now was to get it (and others lying in the corridor) onto the shelf.

The train started moving. I decided to return to my bunk and keep out of the way. A young man sat on one of the parcels and watched me. He'd probably never seen a feeble European writer up close before. He was waiting for the help of two other men, who with him would make a threesome of different sizes, like the team of a removal van – there's always a little wiry one who ends up under the double wardrobe. I was no help. I could hardly lift my own modest weight onto my berth. Sure enough, the little wiry guy ended up under a parcel so heavy that the three of them couldn't get it onto the shelf. The lighter of the other two climbed up onto the shelf above me. Through sheer determination and bloody-mindedness, helped by grunts, which sounded professional for being in a language alien to me, the three heaved the parcel up to an angle where they could slide it tilted onto the shelf. I reached out from my bed and pathetically pushed at the parcel with one hand to show willing. The biggest parcel of all they got almost to the height of the shelf, again with the little wiry guy underneath. A bigger man replaced him to push the parcel higher. Then two men lay on the bunks and pushed with their feet. One got onto my bunk with me. Luckily our combined weight was not enough to bring the bunk crashing down onto the passenger below. Finally, at 1am, after trying various other moves, they got one end onto the shelf and forced the rest of it up to the same level. Then they slewed it round to make a bridge over the corridor – a brilliant use of space.

At 1.20 people were sliding more parcels along the corridor, blocking it, but only one-parcel high so you could still squeeze through. The parcels were giant, plastic zip-bags reinforced with sticky tape, which amazingly kept them from bursting despite all the manhandling. I imagined that they contained goods to sell in the markets. The packages were so big that, once hoisted into position, they overhung the berths, blocking the one central light and making my little space darker.

I woke to see frost-covered roofs and a field of corn stubble in the early light. I wanted to take a photograph but, with all the luggage, I couldn't get to the window. None of the luggage shelves had collapsed in the night and no one had got crushed. While the train was moving smoothly on straight rails, its shadow bumped jerkily over the rough ground beside the track. Clothing vendors managed to move up and down the train, showing their wares, although it was too dark to see the colours of the fabrics. At one point the compartment, already acting as guard's van, also became a fitting room. Other vendors came on at stations with toys, magazines, videos and food.

Two men began to crowd Anastasiya, sitting on her berth and drinking beer. When one of them got up she asked me to take his place in an attempt to get rid of him. So I did. But when she got up to help an old woman who was trying to untie a string bag containing a melon, he slipped into her place and sat next to me. I dared not get up myself in case the two men took over. So I studiously looked out of the window and refused his offer of beer. He must have thought me unfriendly but I knew where my loyalty lay. The moment I got out my camera, the train's policeman happened to come along. He took my camera out of my hand without asking. He offered to take me with the view – a bad idea because the sun would have been on the lens. I took my camera back, closed it down, thanking the policeman but indicating that the photographic session was over. As we approached a station I saw camels, and men riding donkeys.

A man, slightly drunk, squeezed in next to me, his body warm against mine. He claimed to be a poet. He wrote out a poem of his in my notebook and later shouted it out across the compartment at me.

'There's no need to shout,' I said, 'I can't understand what you're saying anyway!'

Of course he couldn't understand what I was saying either. Later, a woman said something to Anastasiya.

'This lady wants to be your guest in England,' Anastasiya translated.

'You'd be very welcome,' I said.

'She can't afford to travel.'

'Too bad!'

I thought she could have managed it by selling her gold teeth. At 4pm I had a wash and changed my shirt, keeping a woman waiting as there was only one toilet and wash basin in the whole coach. I couldn't look out of the window in one of the doors because it was completely blocked with luggage. I couldn't get to the other door because of a little woman asleep on two bags. In the passage connecting us to the next coach were a trolley and a form (bench) loosely tied together to rattle and act as a death trap. Another form half blocked the corridor. I was pleased to find that I wasn't the only person to pong, proving that I was now among people genetically closer to my kind. We were passing through what looked like salty grasslands. Perhaps what I'd thought was frost had actually been salt.

I helped Anastasiya to leave the train, carrying her bag to the door and down the steps to the final drop. Because of some problem with her leg she couldn't make the final jump. Another man appeared and two of his friends helped her down. A woman assisted her on the platform – I hoped it was the friend she was going to stay with. These places don't have raised platforms so it's hard for anyone to get on or off. I wondered if this slight infirmity of Anastasiya's was the reason her parents were overprotective. The idea had got around that she was my interpreter. The irony was that without her there to interpret for me I couldn't explain that she was just someone I'd met on the train. The men in the compartment decided I'd be more comfortable in her former place and helped me to move. Although it was nice to be on a low bunk, I now felt I was in the corridor and more exposed to disturbance but I tried not to be paranoid about it.

The second night, when I was in bed a man came and sat on my bed for ages, his buttocks against my shins. I imagined he was waiting for me to fall asleep so that he could strip me of my valuables. I closed my eyes and lay still.

When he went to the loo, I seized the chance to move my money belt under my trousers. I closed my eyes again and waited for him to come back. This he did and sat in the same place. After what seemed like half the night he suddenly got up and climbed to a high bunk and bothered me no more. The next morning I was able to watch the sunrise from my new bed. In time it lit the rough carpet of grasses, bringing out the glorious mix of colours.

After this strange journey it was a relief to get off the train at Kandyagash. I'd chosen to break my journey there because a branch line ran from there to Atyrau, which was the most direct route to Volgograd in Russia. On my railway map it looked a moderately important place. I stepped out to see a rough road, some houses and little else. I didn't know which way to walk. I tried going to the left and found nothing of significance so I went to the right and came across a bank with a sign saying 'Western Union'. Great! I thought I'd be able to collect the money Rupert would have sent me. I went in.

'Western Union?' I asked.

The man behind the counter crossed his forearms, which I took to mean 'closed'. I continued to explore until I came to a large area of what looked like common land. On the far side there were some bigger, taller buildings so I guessed the town, such as it was, must be there. I walked across the common to a traditional collection of market stalls. The bigger buildings I'd seen turned out to be blocks of flats. In a little supermarket I bought some long-life rolls and a bottle of water. I found somewhere that looked like a café. Four men were drinking beer. I asked someone serving if they did food. Once he understood he had me sit down. When I went to wash my hands, I found there was no water in the tap but they supplied a kettle of warm water. I had minced meat in pancake rolls with some very pleasant bread, which I guessed was home-made. I asked the men for an Internet café. There was none. Was there a hotel? Yes, they said, but I couldn't find it.

I took a taxi back to the station. I asked at the ticket office about trains to Atyrau. Two very smiley women behind the counter found my request amusing. There was a train at 12.00. I was just querying whether this was midday or midnight, when a man in a grey sports jacket appeared behind me and drew me away from the ticket office.

'Passport?' he said.

I showed him.

'Wait here!' he commanded, indicating the seats in the middle of the station.

He went out in the direction of the trains. When he didn't come back I went to the ticket office, only to find that the women had gone for a break. It was after 2.30pm. The other railway personnel wore uniforms, so the guy who'd told me to wait was either very important or very unimportant. Meanwhile I found an ATM at the station, out of which I managed to get 10,000 *tenge*, which went some way to solve one problem. The women came back sooner than I expected.

'Who was that man asking to see my passport? He told me to wait. It's nearly an hour. He hasn't come back. Nothing's happened.'

Three minutes later two men arrived in brown uniforms, one tall and thin, the other short and fat – like a comedy double act. Mr Tall took my passport.

'This is ridiculous,' I protested, like some latter-day Phileas Fogg. 'I'm going round the world. I'm three-quarters of the way and I've never been stopped like this – for no reason! All I'm trying to do is buy a ticket. There's nothing wrong with my passport. I have a visa for Kazakhstan, a visa for Russia.'

By then I had an audience of the two men in brown, the two smiling ticket clerks and a number of passengers, who must have been amused by my bellicose tone.

'John?' the tall guy exclaimed. '*My* name is John!'

'That's very nice,' I said, unimpressed.

From then on I treated them as respected allies, complaining to them about how I'd been dealt with and trying to get them on my side. But they were determined to have their moment of importance. Why, it might be months before another crazy foreigner came their way. They kept moving me about. For my part I made a big thing of putting all my items of luggage down one at a time in a pile each time we stopped and picking them up just as slowly when they wanted me to move on. As they marched me around I acted relaxed but irritated, raising my eyebrows, shrugging my shoulder, throwing my hands out as much for my own entertainment as that of the other passengers. The officers took me to a telephone. One of them rang for an interpreter, a woman in a navy uniform, who came and interviewed me, translating my answers for the men in brown. I couldn't make out which were railway officials and which police.

'Please speak more s l o w l y!' she begged me. 'My Name is Such-and-such. What is your name?'

It was like English as a Foreign Language, the beginners' class.

'John Barclay.'

'Where are you go ... ing?'

'To Atyrau.'

'Have ... you ... got ... a ticket?'

'No. I was trying to buy a ticket when I was interrupted.'

When the interview was finished, she stayed with me to act as my minder. She helped me to buy my ticket. When I went to the Left Luggage to see if I could leave my rucksack there, she came with me to interpret. The other two tagged along because they'd got nothing better to do. As I'd got this woman sitting on my tail I thought I might as well get something out of her so I asked her if there was a café on the station. She led me there, sat down with me and 'helped' me to order. I asked for beer. They didn't understand. I asked to look in the fridge. There was no drink in the fridge. So I opted for 'tea – no milk'. It was very hot. I sat and waited. Then I put it to my lips.

'It's got sugar in it!' I cried in a loud voice.

The woman brought me another cup empty except some brown powder in the bottom.

'Oh, I see!' I said, 'it's all mixed in.'

She said something about 'coffee'.

'Yes, please,' I said, 'no milk.'

It arrived black with a full bowl of sugar. I sent the sugar away to make my point. I produced the money to pay and the navy woman took it to the counter and handed it in.

'Have you been told to stay with me?' I asked.

No answer.

'You're very nice,' I went on, 'but there's nothing wrong with my passport. I've got my train ticket. It's four hours until the train goes. I'd like to move about on my own.'

I led the way to the toilets. As I did so she got on her mobile. I went into the gent's, wondering if she would follow to pull my zip down for me, but she stayed and chatted to the lavatory attendants. When I came out I walked past them all and kept going fast, straight out of the station, turned smartly into a supermarket. I took my time to buy two pencils – I'd lost one during my ridiculous interrogation. I also bought myself an ice cream and casually licked it. I thought this would make me look more like a tourist and less like a spy – if I ever had looked like a spy.

I wandered on looking for an Internet café. I found three park benches in front of a block of flats and sat in the sun, which was very warming at 5pm. The caretaker joined me and two of the residents. I peeled and cut up an apple, offering them pieces. They were very interested in my route. One man showed me the time on his mobile. It was only four o'clock.

'Is your time different from Almaty?' I asked.

I'd gained an hour without realising. I might have been able to catch an earlier train – if those clowns hadn't held me up! When the two residents moved on, the caretaker invited me into his office for tea. He told me he was from Uzbekistan, a country directly to the south, which (I found out later) had a small border with Afghanistan. He accepted the fact that I didn't want sugar in my tea and offered me a little cake. The conversation was slow but socially easy. It took a long time to get a single point across but this made up for the fact that we couldn't take any subject very far.

'I see you have lots of keys,' I said, trying to keep things simple. 'Do you lock up the whole building?'

And we tried to compare notes on our respective children. As I left I shook his hand.

'We couldn't talk very much,' I said, 'because of the language, but I really appreciated you inviting me in. It's been a lovely afternoon. Thank you!'

I went back to the station café and had steak, kidney, raw onions and bread with a beer. I saw the navy woman again. She seemed to have come to terms with my giving her the slip, but I was glad she saw me get on the train. The young man on the berth above me was very quiet. I slept for some hours but got up early and packed ready to leave as I wasn't sure with the confusion over the time differences exactly when we'd reach Atyrau. I didn't seem to have disturbed the young man. When I saw the train manager I said, 'Atyrau?' She held up three fingers. To check that she meant hours rather than minutes I pointed to my watch and circled it three times. She nodded.

'This is Makat,' she said.

Makat was marked on my map, a distance from Atyrau that could well take three hours. I took off my boots, pushed my rucksack under my bed, hung my bags up and went back to sleep. I woke in time to watch the sunrise. At 7.45 I got up and breakfasted on a hard-boiled egg, a raw tomato (peeled), two soft rolls and some fizzy water. I noticed for the first time a black jacket with red collar and cuffs on the post above the young man's bed. He must be in the services, I thought. Then I noticed a satin headscarf of a distinctly feminine character. There was a side to my travelling companion I hadn't suspected. Also his hair was more auburn and bushier than it had appeared the night before. The rest of him was covered with bedclothes, except for a black-trousered leg poking out the end. I was just thinking how pleasant and peaceful life was when he got up, giving me a shock. In the night he had turned into a well-upholstered, middle-aged, woman.

'Oh!' I exclaimed.

My first thought was that I was in the wrong compartment. But there was my rucksack under my bed. The woman smiled and apologised. It was one of the train's guards, who had seized the opportunity to get some horizontal rest.

'Where's the man?' I asked.

'Oh, he's down there,' she said, pointing towards the rear of the train.

'Well, I'm getting out at Atyrau,' I said, in something of a non-sequitur.

The more people who knew I was getting off there, the more likely it was to happen. I wondered if I'd driven the young man out with my snoring. The guard and I sat in companionable silence for a while. Then she took a hairbrush from a small holdall and brushed her auburn hair in the mirror on the door.

On my little train-route map Atyrau looked as if it was on the coast of the Caspian Sea, which was one of the reasons I'd decided to stop there. I'd never seen an inland lake big enough to be called a 'sea' and the Caspian Sea was one of the features we were expected at my prep school to be able to identify on an unlabelled map of the world. When I left the school the Caspian Sea and I went our separate ways but I never forgot that the Caspian was the big one a bit to the right of the Black Sea. Now over 50 years later I believed I had the chance to actually see it. But when I came out of the Station there was no evidence that I was in either a port or a seaside resort. I went back into the station and found it had an enquiry kiosk. Under the window of the kiosk was a notice with some popular information I couldn't read. In order to hear the woman in the kiosk I stuck my head through the window. This annoyed some of the other passengers because then they couldn't see the notice. They tried to push me out of the way, banging my head against the side of the window. I soon got fed up with this and asked to speak to the woman through the door. I could hear her much better that way. Soon I was inside in the kiosk sitting on a chair talking to the woman as an equal, to the annoyance of those in the queue. I had one question, 'How far is it to the Caspian Sea?' We spent minutes on this tricky matter. Then the woman telephoned a friend and put her on to speak English to me.

'How do you want to go?' the friend asked.

'That depends how far it is,' I replied. 'If it's four kilometres, I'll go by taxi. If it's 20, I'll go by bus.

'Would you go by train?'

'I might.'

'Well, it's 20 km by train.'

'Thank you.'

I handed the receiver back to the information woman. Then the friend asked to speak to me again.

'I made a mistake,' she said. 'It's 800 km to the sea. You could go by boat.'

'Is there a river?'

'Yes.'

'I think it would take too long. Just a minute – my map makes it look very near. This *is* Atyrau?'

No answer.

'Are we in Atyrau?'

This question, even simpler than my first, caused more difficulty. I suppose with two alphabets and the problem of pronunciation, there could be two places of similar name, which were not close together – like confusing Lake Victoria in East Africa with the Australian state of Victoria or Victoria Station in London. Eventually the three of us agreed we were in Atyrau, however it was spelled.

'Well,' I said, 'my map must be wrong. I'm so grateful. You have saved me from ordering a taxi for a 1,600 km round trip. Thank you.'

When later I was back in England and looked at some more accurate and detailed maps, the distance seemed to be about 25km as the crow flies, 30km by road. The boat trip would have been interesting but it was probably just as well I didn't take it as I was short of time. I deposited my rucksack in the left luggage and had a coffee. Then I went looking for an Internet café. The roads were made up but the 'pavements' (at that, the driest, time of year) were irregular surfaces of baked mud, sometimes with a smooth path set in the mud. There were very fat pipes laid above ground between the road and the path. It's a good system because unlike in Britain they don't have to dig up the road every time they do repairs. To enable you to get from the road to the path or to the buildings beside it, at intervals there were steps up and down over the pipes, with handrails for added safety. Over the six months I'd been away I'd developed the habit of moving quickly to keep out of danger. I ran up and down some steps, making good use, as I thought, of the safety rail. Unfortunately the safety rail was broken and I cut my hand on a jagged rusty bit of iron – irony in both senses. I was glad I'd brought a small first-aid kit.

Someone directed me to an Internet café, but when I got there I saw it had been closed down and the computers had been removed. In a café, while I was having lunch and a beer, I got into 'conversation' with three young men on the next table. I was relaxed and they were a bit merry on beer. We had some harmless fun. When I'd finished my lunch I said, 'goodbye' to the others and set off for the station to telephone Rupert to tell him that the Western Union place in Kandyagash was not operating and that I'd had to move on. I was walking beside a busy road when a young man starting joshing me. I didn't think he was one of the three in the café, but he might have been. He put his arm round me, pushed me, patted me, poked me, nudged me, buffeted me, held onto me, squeezed me, danced around me and cajoled me. He was like someone drunk or mentally unstable. I didn't know where this would lead – perhaps to a mugging. I had two bags with me. I was smaller and much older than him. He could easily have got the better of me. I acted relaxed, as if I didn't mind the game, but I worked my way towards the road.

'Nice to talk to you,' I said. 'Good-bye!'

Then I stepped quickly into the traffic and started to pick my way between the vehicles, which were going at about 25 miles an hour. I could tell he didn't like this. I now had the better of him. For him to continue pestering me he would have had to stop looking at the traffic and look at me, whereas all I had to do was to dodge the traffic. Thus I managed to put some distance between us. I got to the other side before him and immediately went up to two middle-aged men standing beside a van. I acted as if we were having a conversation in gestures, pointing to my attacker and holding their attention. The lad could hardly come up to me with them standing beside me and continue where he'd left off, so he gave up and disappeared. I thanked the men and went on to the railway station. It was a scary experience but I felt good that I'd handled it so well.

In the station I discovered that telephone lines to the UK were closed. I set off again and found a hotel. The girl on the desk had dyed blond hair and strong dark eyebrows. She checked me in with the help of an English textbook, looking up such phrases as 'a single room'. From my window I could see a line of storage containers, like those I'd gone to sea with, all opened at one end and used like sheds or garages. I went back to the station to buy my train ticket and collect my rucksack.

'So there's no train in the morning?' I asked.

'No train in the daytime,' the clerk replied.

'Can you offer me a train in the evening?'

'Yes.'

'What time does it get in at Aksaraskaya?'

'One in the morning.'

'Well, if it gets in at one in the morning, I'd rather stay on to go further. I don't want to be arriving in a strange place in the middle of the night and have to find a hotel. Would you tell me when the train gets in to Baskunchak?'

'Do you want some help with translating?' asked a small young woman behind me.

'Yes, please,' I said, 'it's difficult to plan my journey. I can't read the timetable – if one exists.'

The young woman took over. I could now find out the options and discuss them. She got me a ticket for a journey involving changing trains, with the times printed on the ticket. I don't think I'd managed that since Australia. She was the best person to help me because she'd worked as a translator for an international company, often making travel arrangements for people. She was very sweet and helpful. I added her to my list of people to contact when I got home.

I decided that if I couldn't go to the Caspian Sea I would at least go to the river. In my hotel there was a map of the city in Reception on the wall facing my young friend with the English textbook.

'Could you please tell me, where we are on this map?'

She shook her head. I took a taxi to the main post office, where with a lot of help I sent a telegram to Rupert, asking him to cancel the money transfer and let me know what that cost. I found another Internet café but it too was gutted – so was I! I went on to the River Ural. I took a photograph of it – the nearest I was going to get to the Caspian Sea! On the way back – third time lucky – I found an Internet café. At last – the real thing! It said 'ИНТЕРНЕТ' outside plain as anything. And it was operating. There were lots of kids staring at screens and a pretty girl at a desk.

'Internet?' I asked.

'No, no!' she said, 'only games!'

So three out of three Internet cafés offered no access to the Internet. I went back to my hotel, gave my washing in to be washed by the hotel during the afternoon and checked out. I went once again to the station to buy a notebook and a pencil. I noticed that despite the condition of the pavements the Kazakh boys and girls wore shoes with long pointed toes and high heels (stilettos in the case of the girls).

Inside the station, like stalls in an indoor market, were a series of lock-ups, operating as tiny shops. I was thrilled to notice for the first time the smallest Internet café I had ever seen – three screens in a space for four people. In Atyrau you can't be choosy! I opened the door. All three screens were taken.

'Internet?' I asked.

'Ten minutes,' said the man in charge.

I found a seat within sight of this mini-Internet-café. Within two minutes the man in charge called me back. It was cramped inside. I had to put my rucksack directly behind me. This meant that every time the door opened I swung round to see whether someone was stealing my luggage. I had little time before my train left, but the man in charge, who didn't have enough to do and had no screen of his own to play on, was bored. He wanted to chat, and practise his English.

'You American?' he asked, and so on.

I tried to keep typing. Then I noticed he was reading what I was typing. It was hard to concentrate. There was a small window in the door. This opened very quietly and caught me like a karate chop to my neck. The first time I jumped. After that it was just annoying. In time the man in charge got so bored he went out. A woman knocked on the window. I recognised her as someone who ran one of the other outlets. I opened the window.

'May I come in?' she asked.

'I'm sorry,' I said, 'I can't let you in.'

It wasn't for me to open the door. It was distraction after distraction. I looked round to see next to me a naked woman kneeling on the floor, fellating a naked man – on a screen, of course. Then the man in charge came back and said it was time to finish. I'd just managed to e-mail Rupert and answer a few messages.

In the station café I had *shashlik*, some pleasing bread, raw onions and a big glass of beer. At nine o'clock I saw a train on the platform nearest to the station. I didn't know whether this was my train or not. There was no one to ask except one of the train guards. I showed him my ticket.

'No,' he said, 'not this train.'

'Where is my train?' I asked.

He made a strange gesture, which I interpreted as, 'Go back and wait in the waiting area.'

But there was no announcement. There was no railway employee to ask. At 9.10pm I went out to try to find out where I should board my train. The train I'd seen before was still there and very long it was too. It hid the other trains, if there were any, and blocked the way to the other tracks. It was very dark on the platform but I had my torch. I couldn't find a guard. Some passengers saw me looking panicky. Some tried to send me one way, some the other. A man grabbed my arm and ran with me towards the back of the long train. I didn't like him holding onto me and managed to break away but he caught up with me, because I was carrying a rucksack and two small bags – and was twice his age. He led me across the nearest line. Then apparently sensing some new problem, he grabbed me again and tugged me over the line to the long train. Then he pushed me up onto it. I felt I'd lost what little control I'd had over the situation. Luckily the door on the other side of the long train was open. I could now see the train I hoped would be mine. At some point I thanked the guy who had helped me and I continued on my own, dropping down to the ground – there was no platform. If you're confused, imagine what it was like for me in the dark.

I crossed the empty track between the two trains and ran to a guard I could see at the back of the second train. I pushed my ticket into his hand and shone my torch on it. He sent me further up the train. I showed my ticket to another guard. No – further up! Quick! Get on now! (All done by gestures, of course.) The second guard got on after me. Then, as the train started moving, he hurried me forward along the corridor. He got impatient with me when I shone my light before stepping into the precarious passage where the coaches joined. We went through the 'hard sleepers' to the 'soft sleepers'. He introduced me to some sort of steward. We went past my seat and had to go back. More impatience through the joins. I refuse to step if I can't see where to put my feet. If I'd lost my left leg I would have looked a right fool.

'It's all very well for you,' I said to the steward, 'you do this all the time!'

Once in my compartment I acted stupid to get the maximum information out of my companions, two men and one woman, sophisticated people – Russians, I thought. Mine was an odd existence – wandering around strange cities looking for ATMs and Internet cafés, struggling in railway stations to find out what trains there were and fighting to get on them, then sleeping, not very well, in compartments with strange people.

At 4.15am I heard a woman walking along the corridor quietly chanting what sounded like, *'Rush-iss-key'*. I took this to be the Kazakh for Russia. Soldiers in battledress came aboard. One entered our compartment and checked that no one was hiding in the luggage space over the corridor. The lights were on but we stayed in bed. A man in a brown uniform checked our passports. He took mine away. Once again my information sheets came in useful – not just for the immigration people but to explain to my companions what I was doing. We would soon be in Russia, but I couldn't afford any delays – I had just a week to be in and out of that country before my visa ran out.

24. Russia

October 2 – 7

On the Russian side passengers were checked on the train once more. I went back to sleep. When I woke up, I looked out of the window to see a magnificent river, wide, blue and sparkling in the sun.

'It's the Volga,' said a man.

He was a writer who lived in St Petersburg. He had studied German for 30 years. Two stories he'd written in German, he told me, had been published in a St Petersburg newspaper. Then he went to his compartment to fetch a copy of one of the stories for me to take home. It was called *'Der alte Kesselwärter'* (the high water tank). That sort of thing doesn't happen on a package tour.

I alighted at Aksaraskaya. At the station I went straight to the toilet. A railway official told me I couldn't take my rucksack into the wash basin area. I had to leave it with two women who sat at the entrance, one to take the money and the other to hand out the toilet-paper rations. When I'd had a badly-needed wash, I came back naked from the waist up in full view of those queuing for the loo to half empty the rucksack and find a clean shirt. When I'd finally finished and packed everything away I saw that I could have had a shower.

On the next train I was in a compartment with a big relaxed man, who smoked cigarettes called 'E & M' and let me face the oncoming view. He showed me his mobile, which indicated that London time was three hours behind Moscow time, which applied to us. When I pathetically pulled out Kazakh money, he even paid for five tea bags for me. And if he'd used earphones to listen to his music I would have pronounced him an all-round good egg, if eggs can be round. One of the railway staff produced a mug and Mr E & M went for hot water, which is on tap in Russian and Kazakh trains. He showed me pictures of his girlfriend, including one of her looking moderately abandoned on a billiard table. Not to be outdone I produced my personal information sheet (Russian version). He kept fiddling with his mobile and bringing up yet another picture of his beloved Anna and one of her five-year old daughter.

'Anna is younger than me,' he told me. 'She's 28. I am 41. We are going to Paris – and London.'

'London's an expensive place to stay,' I warned him.

We were following the Volga (upstream) to Volgograd so I shouldn't have been surprised when a vendor came through the train with fresh fish threaded on a single wire, far too many for the passengers on the train. The guard wore a uniform of a light-blue shirt, a navy skirt, short blue socks and black bootees. She looked strict and old-fashioned like a traditional nanny. She took my watch and pointed to the five. I took this to mean that we would get into Baskunchak at five.

Out of the window I saw two horses grazing. They had been hobbled (two diagonally opposite legs tied loosely). A very large flock of black goats were huddled together despite the fact that they had a vast space to spread out. Apart from the railway and the telephone wires it looked like a natural treeless plain with only the most occasional dwelling. The expression 'in the middle of nowhere' would be the one to spring to mind. It was not an ugly landscape to pass through, not even boring, despite the fact that there was little variation. Suddenly, for no apparent reason, a crater appeared in the red earth.

It was early evening when we reached Baskunchak. I got off the train, stepping down to ground level. I walked across a track and up onto a platform, to get the lie of the land. I went up the steps of a footbridge to get an overall view of the station, came down again onto the same platform – and there was my companion, Mr E & M, the guy with the girl on the billiard table, but without his luggage! Meanwhile another train had come in and parked between the platform and the train we'd both arrived on.

'What are you doing?' I cried, 'Your bags are still on the train!'

'Volgograd!' he declared. 'Get the train.'

'Look, don't worry about me! I'm going to a hotel to sleep,' I mimed.

'Wait there!' he mimed.

He went along the platform. As in many stations in Asia there was only one. He spoke to a guy in a big hat. I waited. I'd nothing to lose. He stood to lose his train and his luggage with it. He came back.

'There is no hotel in Baskunchak!' he announced. 'But there is a train in one hour to Volgograd.'

'Thank you! Okay – I'll get it. You go back to your train – and your bags.'

What a kind fellow! Presumably he'd checked how long the train would be stopping. He'd certainly gone out of his way for me. I went into the station. I wrote the word 'Volgograd' on a piece of paper and handed it to the ticket seller. This woman had the benefit of a powerful amplification system. She told me, in no uncertain terms and at a volume audible to everyone in the station, whatever it was she told me. I handed her another piece of paper and invited her to put down the gist of what she'd said for me to study. She did. I studied it and was none the wiser. Backwards and forwards we went. I'd say something in English. She'd reply in Russian. Parallel lines never connect. A young girl, who had more English than I had Spanish, tried to help but soon gave up. Eventually somehow the ticket seller convinced me that, despite what Mr E & M had told me, the earliest train was 3.18am, but confirmed that there was no hotel. She indicated some alternative accommodation on the station behind her booth. Meanwhile a woman appeared with dyed blond hair, dressed and built like a hospital matron in a 'Carry-on film'. She led me away and showed me some premises – three beds in one room (one bed already taken), a shower, loo and washbasin, a room containing a kitchen table with a pot plant on it. It was all clean and wholesome. So I booked a bed, bought my ticket for 3.18am and went out to the shop opposite to buy water and some pastries for the next day's journey. I came back, put the food away and asked someone where a café was. He asked the station master. The station master asked the ticket seller – no, there was no café.

'I'll go back to the shop,' I said. 'Thank you!'

But the station master came with me. I know they mean well, but I don't take kindly to these authority figures trailing around with me and guiding me at every step. It stifles me and stops me making contact with the staff in the shop. Meanwhile I couldn't get the door of the fridge open.

'You have to get the woman to press a button,' the station master told me.

I ought to have been grateful for that useful tip. I got a bottle of water from the fridge and went off to choose bread.

'Pay! Pay!' someone said.

I looked around for a shopping basket. I put the bottle on the counter, chose the bread.

'Pay! Pay!'

'This is ridiculous!' I exclaimed.

I treated them to a hectic mime of placing something on the counter, getting out imaginary money, paying it, moving three inches along the counter, repeating the sequence, more and more frenetically. This had them all laughing, including the station master. But a customer who'd got the gist of my antics indicated an imaginary barrier between the two parts of what had looked to me like an undivided shop. Then I got it. I should pay for the bread and then the rest separately. Meanwhile the station master, trying to be helpful, suggested tins. I didn't know whether there was a tin opener in the room I've so far avoided calling the kitchen. I'd seen no equipment of any kind apart from a kettle.

'Look,' I wanted to yell, 'I know how to shop. I just can't speak Russian!'

Apart from some sausages of questionable provenance, the only cooked meat was some ham, three-quarters fat, so I asked for that, some yoghurt, two oranges and a beer.

'Stella Artois?' the assistant queried.

'Stella Artois!' I protested, 'I can get that at home. Ruskie!'

The women in the shop thought that a great joke. I paid. I thanked the assistant. I thanked the station master. I went back to the station accommodation and made myself at home. By the time I'd removed the fat from the ham there wasn't much left to eat and I'd finished it before I'd finished the bread. I had no butter so I tried spreading yoghurt on the bread. It looked, and for all I know tasted, like non-drip magnolia emulsion paint, but it helped to use up both the bread and the yoghurt without serious damage to either or indeed to me. At 7.50pm a short stout man, wearing the uniform of an employee of the railway, came in to have his meal just as I finished mine. He accepted my offer of an orange and put the kettle on for 'cha'. I felt clean after a warm shower. I set my alarm clock and the two of us were tucked up in bed by 8.45pm.

When the alarm sounded I didn't feel I'd had much sleep. It was 2.45am. The train wasn't to leave until 3.18, which seemed a long time away so I carelessly went back to bed. My clock hadn't woken the other guy and all was quiet. I went back to sleep. I was woken by a hammering on the outside door of the accommodation. I decided not to answer it as I didn't have the Russian to deal with whoever it was so I walked round the flat wondering what to do. My little fat friend got up wearing nothing but a pair of briefs under his paunch. He answered the door. A uniformed guard with a truncheon dangling at his side came in. I went back into the bedroom. My little fat friend didn't follow me so I assumed that the uniformed guard's business was with him. I put the dim light on and quietly dressed and started packing. The guard burst in impatient and imperious. With his voice raised he urgently threw some Russian at me. With one finger I drew the figures '3.18' on the wall. He pointed to his chest.

'It's for *me!*' he seemed to be saying.

So I had to finish getting ready with the armed guard standing over me. I'd no idea I was getting an armed escort. I didn't know whether I was being treated like a high-ranking officer or a dangerous criminal. But I was very glad of him to help me find the train and the coach in the dark. I thanked him and was very sorry I'd kept him waiting. The station had looked after me really well. I was lucky to have had nearly six hours sleep in a bed and to have caught the train.

As we approached Volgograd (formerly Stalingrad) we were welcomed by a huge statue of 'The Motherland'. We arrived at 8.45am. The station was calm and quiet. It was like a cathedral in scale, and with its wealth of marble. I put my rucksack in the left-luggage department for three hours. I found a café with a bright, agreeable atmosphere. There were pot plants around the room and fresh flowers on the tables. Next to the salt and pepper was a little pot of mint-flavoured toothpicks. I had a warm slice of apple cake with some sweet white coffee from a Nescafé sachet.

As usual I went on foot in search of a hotel. I came to a building with flags of many nations, which appeared to be an International Language School. I thought that there I'd be able to find someone who spoke English. Sure enough the woman at the reception desk told me where to get a trolley-bus to an area with hotels, and wrote down what stop to ask for. I showed this to the driver but it was some young girls who told me when we got there. I tried to pay the driver as I got off.

'You don't pay the driver as well,' one of the girls, who was getting off at the same time, told me.

'Who should I pay?' I asked.

'A person in blue.'

'And where will I find this blue person?'

'The blue person is on the bus.'

'Well, I never saw her. Is that her?' I asked looking at someone in a blue overall.

'No.'

The bus moved on.

'Too late!' I said, 'but thank you very much.'

Thus I found the Hotel Yuzhnaya. As I like to take the stairs for exercise rather than the lift, I noticed that the décor was different on every landing. On the sixth floor, the low height of the ceiling had been disguised by a blue-tinted mirror on it, which made the reflected carpet look like the sky. I sat on a long yellow sofa looking up at myself looking down on myself. After a while I was rewarded (if I continued to look up) with the illusion of an undeniably solid chambermaid walking upside down on that glass ceiling we hear so much about and disappearing upside-down into an extra lift that been installed for an apparent mezzanine floor above.

When I'd moved in, I went out to find the River Volga. I knew it was to the East of the City so I set off in that direction. I had lunch outside – soup with small meatballs. It was after two o'clock and the staff were having theirs. A man came out of the kitchen and flirted with the girls, and they with him. Eventually I could see the river and found a way down to the water. The Volga was very wide and had sandy beaches. Black-headed gulls were massing around an effluent pipe into the river. Boat excursions were advertised and pleasure steamers were moored on jetties beside a big building, which I discovered was a complex of restaurants, bars, a night club, a shop selling furniture and a concert hall. I was cheered by the prospect of some culture, but there was nothing on that evening. I walked back along the central Avenue of Heroes.

I'd had a lovely day and taken photographs. I'd noticed that the Russians in Volgograd were much more cheerful than the sailors I'd encountered on the container ships. The girls were attractive in an earthy sort of way, with striking looks, long beautifully shaped noses, womanly hips and the longest legs I'd seen since I'd left Australia. And unlike some of the people in the Far East, they looked as if they were made of flesh, rather than porcelain.

Back at the hotel I had a shower and washed my clothes. I ate in as I was tired. On the next table two men, who smoked between courses, were sitting with two girls younger than them. One, a redhead with a bare midriff, was with a paunchy bloke, who paid the singer on stage for two requests. The redhead got up with Paunchy to do a soppy dance. With them out of the way I could see the other girl, slim and sexy in a short black leather sleeveless waistcoat. Then the waitress, who always had one hand behind her back, using the other, brought in a peeled and prepared pineapple with ice cream on top and the stem of a lighted sparkler stuck through it. She stood there holding this sensational dessert in her one hand until the sparkler had burnt out. I myself had ordered ice cream with chocolate and nuts, which came without pyrotechnics.

I wanted to photograph a pretty receptionist, whose name, as spelled out on her lapel badge, looked like your average hand in Scrabble except that the 'R' was back to front. But I didn't want to favour her in front of her two (almost as appealing) colleagues on the desk. I lost my chance, however, because the next day it was her day off. I may have found the Russian women attractive because they were sufficiently different from their British counterparts to appear exotic but not so different as to seem alien.

Near the station were some public gardens where I enjoyed the blue sky, cool breeze, warm sunshine and autumn colours. I had lunch outside at a café. A man left his companion and staggered over to my table to try to interpret for me as I ordered, but he had got too much alcohol inside him and not enough English.

'What ... you ... want?' he drawled.

The waiter took my order for food.

'What ... you ... drink?' the drunk drawled.

I wasn't falling for that one. I could have ended up drinking with him, which wouldn't have done either of us any good.

I found a wonderful bookshop. It was organised in sections on all the categories you could wish for. Some of the books had English titles but none had English text. I went all round the shop one way and then all round again the other way to make sure. I sat down tired from looking so long at so much bewildering print. I would have needed to find an English-speaking guide to explore the City properly. I felt ashamed afterwards that I hadn't paid attention to the memorials there were of the terrible battle of Stalingrad in the winter I was born, a battle that turned the City to rubble and cost over a million Soviet lives and the lives of 800,000 Axis troops. It was a turning point in the Second World War, marking the beginning of the end for Nazi Germany. When I got home I read that 65 years later the people of Volgograd were still finding human bones.

I caught a train that evening to Rostov na Donu, my stepping-off point for Ukraine. There were four of us in the compartment including a woman. A guy was busy on his laptop. The other man offered me something from a bottle of clear liquid. I guessed it was vodka.

'It's very good with sausages,' he said, breaking open a pack of the things and releasing an unpleasant odour.

I indicated that I'd already eaten and settled down to sleep. When I woke, the train had stopped. It was dark. I could hear a noise I was sure was gunfire. It sounded like an army exercise right outside our window. There were voices. Some of the words sounded like English coming over a walkie-talkie. It seemed terribly close.

'It's not safe to get so far away from the other tanks, sir!' a man's voice shouted. 'We should stick with the others.'

I reminded myself that I was in Russia. It was the 21st Century, not the 1940s. I looked across to the guy with the laptop to see what he was making of it, but he wasn't taking any notice. He was too engrossed in whatever was happening on his little screen.

'It's not safe to get so far away from the other tanks, sir! We should stick with the others,' I heard again.

Then I realised that the war I was hearing was merely my companion's computer game!

As we came into Rostov I saw another great river, the Don, from which the full name 'Rostov na Danu' comes. After coffee and a cake in the morning sunshine, with my rucksack on my back I set off on foot towards the river. At first I was walking through a grubby industrial area but this gave way to a smart residential neighbourhood with big blocks of flats facing the river. I needed a poo so I went into a café and ordered another coffee. Oh, the joy of a smart, spotless toilet with proper washing facilities! I sat sipping my coffee in the forecourt, with a view of the sparkling river.

The waiter told me where I'd find a hotel but I wandered round without success. Some of the old streets were very attractive. I felt more at home in Russia than I had since I'd left Fremantle. I was back in the European culture I'd grown up with. In a busy square I spotted a group I took to be middle-class intellectuals. I knew they would speak English. One of them, a tall, kindly man told me that they were from St Petersburg (1,000 miles away), but they made enquiries on my behalf and then gave me excellent directions, which took me to a hotel. I had to wait to get into my room so I left my luggage and returned to the river, where at another café I had a single piece of pork on a skewer cooked to order in a portable oven and served with raw onion, tomato and bread. I had a glass of Russian draught beer. The café was run by a couple from Armenia. He operated the oven while she served the drinks and wiped the tables. Sitting there in the sun by the river made me feel as if I was on holiday. On the next table was the tall, kindly man who had helped me to find a hotel. He told me he was a professor from St Petersburg who'd come to Rostov for an academic conference. We talked about my travels.

'May I ask,' he said, 'how old are you?'

'I'm 64.' I replied.

'I'm 62.'

'I wish you well.'

When I did get into my room I found out that it was a suite – a large twin-bedded bedroom, a small sitting room, a bathroom and a lobby. I took off all my clothes and before I took a shower helped myself to a bottle of orange juice from the minibar. Naked I stood sipping and beginning to unwind before I realised that with so many doors in the suite I'd carelessly left open the only one that mattered, the door to the corridor.

The hotel restaurant reflected a curious mix of influences. While the staff were without doubt Russian, the décor was dominated by a mural depicting Big Ben and the British Houses of Parliament. On a wide screen restless, optically distorted videos accompanied continuous Western-style pop songs. One cheer for globalisation!

My boots, which had gone round the world with me, were falling to bits so I went into a shoe shop and bought some strange, two-tone sports shoes 'made in Europa' to get me home. I put them on and surprised the assistant by asking her to dispose of the boots.

I dined in a restaurant in which a bucolic theme had been carried about as far as it would go. There were pitchforks, pelts, a scarecrow, traditional rustic kitchenware and on the wall some apparently real stags' heads. A farm cart supported a display of food embellished with life-size plastic chickens, sunflowers, real straw and logs. Above us was an artificial blue sky with white clouds and among the tables grew three full-size artificial oak trees.

I went back to the hotel to collect my luggage. My train didn't leave until 10.40pm so I'd plenty of time. I asked if I might sit down for a moment. The sofa was so comfortable that I was soon dozing.

On my travels I spent a lot of time tracking down the necessities – like information, accommodation, cash or Internet access. But, if I arrived by train, I usually had no problem finding the station again. In Rostov na Donu this principle proved to have limitations. I'd gone back to the station that morning to buy my ticket. At the ticket office they sent me to another building more or less next door, where I bought my ticket to Kiev.

'The train doesn't go from here,' the woman said.

Well, that didn't surprise me because I hadn't arrived there – I'd arrived at the station next door. That evening I set off again for the station in plenty of time. It was dark and there was a busy road to cross so I used the subway. When I emerged I saw a familiar landmark so I assumed I was going the right way, but I didn't arrive at the station. I arrived at a supermarket. It was an unlit area so for safety I dived into the supermarket. I put my rucksack in a trolley and had a look at my street map. I couldn't figure out how I'd lost the station except that I must have come out of the subway by the wrong exit. I was still in good time so while I was in the supermarket I bought some tangerines. I went out and found a taxi. I knew the Russian word for 'station' so there shouldn't have been a problem. We came to the first station.

'Here!' I cried, 'this one.'

But he wouldn't stop.

'No, no! This station,' I tried again, 'the one we just passed.'

I made him go back. I expect this annoyed him. He annoyed me by putting his hand out to be paid before I'd got my luggage out of the car. It all helped to get me keyed up for the journey ahead. I went into the station and showed my ticket. But it wasn't this station either. The clerk spoke Russian at me. I can't blame her for that but I can't pretend it helped – except I did hear the words 'bus' and 'taxi'. I made her write something down on a piece of paper. I could see words and a number. She pointed to a small fleet of minibuses. I was fed up with taxis by then and hurried over to the buses. I was in luck – one of them had the same number as on the paper. I tried to show this to the driver but the bus was so crowded I couldn't get near him. He was on the other side of the bus so he couldn't see. I showed it to a man I assumed was the conductor, but he took little interest.

The driver started up the engine so I decided to get in, but every time I tried to put a foot in the bus the top of my rucksack hit the top of the doorway. The passengers stared patiently until I managed it. When I could, I showed the driver the piece of paper but he said he hadn't got his reading glasses on. I tried to interest the passengers in my problem. One guy spoke English. Meanwhile the bus was speeding along through parts of the city I'd never seen before. I showed the paper to the English speaker, lending him my torch so that he could read it in the dark, but it seemed to mean nothing to him. I had no confidence that we were going to a railway station. For all I knew we were shooting off in the wrong direction. I persuaded the driver to stop and let me off.

'I'll have to get at taxi,' I said.

'Taxi!' exclaimed the driver.

'You can't read what's on the note. Nobody understands it. And I can't speak Russian!'

Having made this pithy speech, I got off. It was dark. I'd no idea where I was, except that I was in a strange country, where I didn't speak the language. Anyone could have stepped out of the shadows, which were many and extensive, and quickly murdered me, without anyone being any the wiser. On top of that, now I *was* running out of time. The road was a dual carriageway. I stood by the side, waving at taxis but none stopped. I had the feeling that I should be going the other way so I started to walk to some traffic lights in order to cross to the other side. A tall guy appeared.

'I want to help you,' he said.

'Were you the man on the bus?' I asked.

'Yes.'

'The only way now is to get a taxi.'

'Just a minute!'

He dialled a number on his mobile and spoke to someone. He put a woman on to me. It was a disconcerting experience. Everything I said was repeated; and with the woman's accent, my hearing difficulties and the noise of the traffic, everything she said had also to be repeated.

'Where do you want to go?' the woman asked.

'To the station that has trains to Kiev ... *that has trains to Kiev.*'

'Where are you?'

'I'm on a ... a ... a road ... *a ... a road.*'

'Calm down!'

'Just a minute ... *Just a minute ...*'

'Look,' I said to the tall man, handing him back his mobile. 'This is getting nowhere. I need to get a taxi!'

'I understand what you are saying,' the tall man reassured me, 'I'll come with you. We cross the dual carriageway.'

He managed to hail a taxi. I got in the back with my luggage so that he could be in the front to talk to the driver. The two of them spoke to each other in Russian.

'I'll give you some money to pay for the taxi and for you to get back,' I told the tall man.

'No – no money,' he said.

'It's the least I can do.'

'No, definitely not!'

'Well, that's <u>very</u> kind of you.'

He asked to see my ticket. Between them the men worked out which station to take me to. My contribution was to pass my torch forward. The driver got into the mood and drove fast. The tall man handed him two banknotes. We came off the main road. I saw a lot of buses.

'Oh, no!' I thought, 'they're taking me to a bus station!'

The car stopped suddenly. The tall man got out, saying something. I thought it was, 'Hold on – won't be a minute!' So I stayed put.

But he yelled, 'Go, go, go!'

I scrambled out with my luggage. He grabbed the rucksack. Then he thought better of it and grabbed the two small bags. I put the rucksack on one shoulder. We ran up the steep steps of a bridge over some railway tracks. I overbalanced and came down on one knee. The rucksack fell off. Tall man helped me up. I put the rucksack on properly. We ran over the bridge onto a platform. He helped me find the right part of the train. I got my ticket checked. I got onto the train. He stood on the platform. I reached down and shook him by the hand.

'I've got something for you,' I said. 'As you won't take any money, … This will tell you something about me and what I'm doing. If you e-mail me I will e-mail you.'

It sounded pathetic. I pulled out the Russian version of my information sheet and handed it to him.

'Goodbye!' I said. 'You've been very generous.'

I realised afterwards that the sheet I'd given him didn't have my e-mail address, only those of my sons. Meanwhile I was in a whirl. I was relieved to check that I had my three items of luggage, my passport, my bank card, my currency and my camera.

I'd been very grateful for the all the help I'd had in getting to the train, but once on it assistance of an unwanted kind was pressed on me. I was in a two-person sleeper. I threw my bags in and collapsed on the bunk. I found I was sharing with a woman. For once I had the bottom bunk.

'Hullo,' I said, 'my name's John.'

'I'm Irina,' she said.

She started fussing about immigration documents. She kept taking mine from me and muttering things like, 'Russia and Ukraine'. She would start speaking in English, then switch to Russian. When the guard came she behaved like my nanny.

'Look,' I said, taking the documents back. 'Thanks for your help, but I can do it.'

A bit later she picked them up again. She saw me looking at her.

'It's for me,' she said.

'Oh,' I replied, 'if it helps you, do look at them.'

Next time I looked up I saw she'd filled in the first two lines of my immigration form, copying the information from my passport.

'I can do it,' I protested, 'I've been round the world. I'm not a baby. It's kind of you to help,' I said, touching her arm, 'but isn't it better if I fill it in myself? And if I have a problem I can ask you to help me.'

'Sorry, sorry!' she said, adding nervously, 'We'll be at the frontier in an hour.'

'That's all right.'

I began to understand how disabled people must feel when patronised. I was amazed at my own patience. But it was good to find someone more neurotic than me. At the border with Ukraine, the Russian officials came into the compartment. I thought Irina would poke her nose in again but in the event she was too sleepy. It was the morning of the 7th of October. I had done it – and with two days to spare. I had crossed Russia before my visa had run out. I could relax. I had completed the hardest part of the challenge – crossing Asia. When the Ukrainian official looked at my passport I produced the Ukrainian version of my information sheet at just the right psychological moment.

'Good luck!' he said, smiling.

HEADING HOME

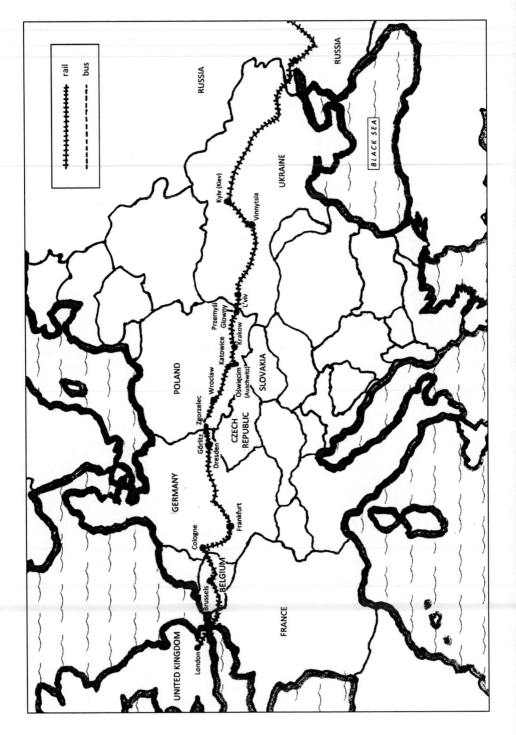

Map 4
Europe

25. Ukraine

October 7 – 11

We came to a station that had been taken over by soft-toy sellers. Along the platform was a line of big stuffed animals, some still in their Cellophane wrappers. As the train came in the vendors stopped playing cards and held up their toys in the hope of making sales. At Kyiv (Kiev) I got off the train. It was early evening and raining. I put my waterproof on. I took a while to escape from the station complex. By the time I came to a pleasant looking place with the air of a *gasthaus* it was raining heavily, so I went in.

Once I'd got some food inside me I felt better. It was dark but the rain had eased and I managed to find the Hotel Lybid, a smart establishment aimed at a business clientèle. The English-language Kyiv Post had extensive coverage of the results of the general election in Ukraine, which had shifted the power back to Yulia Tymonshenko's Orange party without removing the Country's political instability. Meanwhile the gas supplier Gazprom, which was directly influenced by the Russian Federation government, had raised the question of a debt of $1.3 billion owed by Ukraine and threatened to reduce supplies of natural gas. By this means, it was suggested, Russia sought to influence the make-up of the governing coalition that would have to be put together. It was not surprising therefore that I found in my bedroom this warning:

Hot water may not be available due to external circumstances.

I couldn't judge whether this notice was a straightforward practical warning to guests or a careful message to any in the outside world, who didn't know that President Putin was putting the boot in. While I was there the water was good and hot.

I slept well and in the morning went to the dining room for the first time. There was a shoal of spectacular ornamental fish in a smoked-glass tank, a live pianist and some half-alive guests.

The day was grey and uninspiring. After the excitement of my escape from Russia I was feeling low and listless. I decided to buy some things from the souvenir shop in the hotel, to take back to the family. I took an hour to choose sets of Russian dolls and other painted wooden items. Then I went back to the station to investigate my next train. I tried to work the information machine, a free-standing box with a screen and buttons to press. By the time I'd acquired a general understanding of its workings I was feeling weak. I went to the station cafeteria and had a big lunch. With this inside me I felt I had the strength to return to the problem of trains. I wanted to head in the direction of L'viv. The train got in at 23.25, which was very late, so I decided to go only as far as Vinnytsia. I found out the Russian version of the name by going back to the information machine, calling up the map and then identifying a station on a certain kink in the line. At the same time I was able to find on the machine the Russian word for 'information'. I went to the window marked with this word.

'Would you tell me the times of the next two trains to Vinnytsia, please?' I asked, pushing through the opening a home-made pro forma I'd drawn up.

Someone in the queue behind me corrected my pronunciation. This was an encouraging sign that the crowd were taking an interest. They would do anything to help someone ahead of them so that they would get served quicker themselves. Even the woman behind the glass half completed the pro forma. After some false starts I got served by cashier number 29, with help from a woman wanting to push in from the side, as they do. She asked me a question in Russian.

'I'm afraid I don't speak any Russian,' I said. 'I'm here to buy a ticket.'

This told her I was no pushover but it informed everyone I was English and needed help. As a result, from then on, she translated for me including (after my recent experience) the all-important question, 'Does the train go from this station?' I bought a ticket and had 28 minutes to go to my hotel for my luggage, get back to the station, find the platform and get on the train. There's nothing like a deadline to concentrate the mind. I even managed to find my hotel by a shorter route than the one I'd previously taken. And I just caught the train.

As we moved south-west, the woods looked pretty in the late afternoon sun. The journey was a little over three hours. My companion, a small man from Bulgaria, was on his way home. He was listening to Abba and Boney M. Meanwhile I felt I was losing my touch. The alertness, sharpness and sense of purpose that had helped me to get as far as Ukraine had been replaced by droopiness, vagueness and apathy. I seemed to make an effort only when I was under pressure. But then on the train, enjoying the countryside, I thought, 'So what? I am tired but I am moving in the right direction.'

At Vinnytsia I stayed at the Savoy Hotel. I was told that breakfast would be served in the bar, so that evening I did a recce. The bar was a miserable room on my floor (the third). There was no music, no atmosphere, no guest, and no barman. The bar opened for breakfast at 8am, rather late, I thought. The waitress looked flummoxed when I asked for breakfast so I ordered what someone else was having, although I didn't fancy it – slices of sausage on bread with melted cheese on top and coffee. When I was halfway through these delights she brought a bowl of shredded cabbage that seemed to have been sprinkled with a mix of vegetable oil and salt water. But she also brought some dense dry brown bread. I struggled with all these items and had nearly finished the cheese and sausage when two fried eggs came winging my way. I hope you're proud of me – I got it all down except for one quarter of the cabbage and three-quarters of the coffee dregs.

I took a taxi to Vinnytsia station, where I bought a ticket for the 1300 train to L'viv. I went to the left luggage room, where I showed my bags to the woman behind the window. She pointed behind me. I didn't know I was supposed to go first to the lockers. I became a bit silly, trying to open closed doors instead of looking for one already open. The woman had to come out of her office and shout at me in Russian. This didn't make me any more sensible. I got my bags into one of the lockers. Then using four knobs I had to set a code made up of one letter and a three-digit number. I then tried repeatedly to shut the door. The woman beckoned me over and shouted at me in Russian all over again. She put her hand out. After a few bank notes had passed backwards and forwards between us she settled for one she felt she could work with and gave me a handful of coins, which I dropped into one of my pockets ready to give to any beggars who might cross my path. I walked back to the locker but she caught me up.

'*Minoushka! Minoushka!*' (phonetic) she demanded, holding out her hand again.

Well, I wouldn't have known a *minoushka* if it had flown down from a tree and started to peck at my Adam's apple. She was cross with me because she'd had to abandon two business visitors, who'd just arrived from Odessa to demonstrate a new kind of pre-stressed-aluminium upper-locker-door flange – or something of the sort. What could I do but go through my five pockets hoping that miraculously a *minoushka* had materialised in one of them while my attention had been distracted elsewhere? Two other men, experienced *minoushka* handlers by the look of them, were watching me.

'Do you know what a *minoushka* is?' I asked them.

They looked blank. I brought out bank notes, my pencil, my penknife attached to my compass, bits of screwed up paper, an un-screwed-up piece bearing the code I'd just chosen (E197) and some tired bits of lint.

'Minoushka! Minoushka!' She was getting desperate. And I didn't feel particularly contented myself. She couldn't possibly be demanding to have her change back, or could she? I pulled out a handful of coins. I didn't want her to think I was deliberately being obstructive.

'Minoushka!' she yelled, as if it were the name of a greyhound coming in first at a hundred to one with her entire week's pay packet riding on it.

She pointed to one of the coins. It wasn't a coin at all. It was a plain metal disc the same size, thickness, weight and colour as a coin – a *minoushka* in fact. Had I learned nothing in the Bangkok Metro? She took the aforementioned *minoushka* and fed it into the locker mechanism. I'm afraid I was rather pleased that the mechanism refused to co-operate. Somehow she got the locker closed and, shouting some final instructions in Russian at me, she handed the *minoushka* back to me. None the wiser I put it in my train-ticket pocket so I wouldn't give it to a beggar.

'Thank you!' I said and walked out ten minutes older, if no wiser.

Foreigners are stupid. I should know – I'd been one for months. It was 10.30am. Feeling that I had earned a coffee (a questionable assumption) I went to a nearby café. There were two women standing at the bar. Another was already sitting at a table with a beer. A man came in and put his hand on the bottom of one of the standing women, who was wearing tight jeans, and he slid a finger into her bum cleft. She took this in good part. In fact she seemed tickled pink, if you'll pardon the expression, for she turned to the woman at the table and smiled. The man held a finger from his other hand to his lips as if to say, 'Don't tell Masha!' (or whatever his partner, the other woman at the bar, was called). So if you like bold unsubtle flirting, Vinnytsia could be the place for you.

The train I boarded was on its way from Moscow to Budapest. I had a narrow two-berth sleeper to myself. There was a washbasin with a lid that served as a table, a tip-up seat so I could sit at the table, a hanging area behind a curtain and a small wall cabinet fitted with grips to hold large bottles. At the end of the coach was a toilet with a carpet! I deduced that I was travelling first class.

The scenery was some of the most appealing of the whole trip – old-fashioned bucolic scenes like the world from which the old masters selected the green hills, the five cows, the cart, the clump of trees, the tiny cliff and the winding stream to build their romantic landscapes. I saw large numbers of ducks, a field of geese and various tethered livestock. There were farmsteads with very small fields, each in different use from the next. Little wells had tiny roofs. And everywhere there were trees in all shades of autumn colours, but I saw no forest. After a while the terrain became hillier. The fields became narrow strips. I saw horses pulling a wagon. As dusk fell I saw churches with turrets that made them look like fairy castles.

When we arrived at L'viv I was pleased to find it full of attractive buildings, a little cluttered for easy photography, but I guessed it could be the next popular destination for that long weekend away. I had dinner at the Grand Hotel. The décor was dignified and the ambience sophisticated. A small upright piano and a harp stood waiting to be played but it was after 9pm so I assumed that any musician would have packed up for the night. Three men in dark jackets on the next table were speaking English – businessmen, I guessed. At 9.25 a man came in and sat down at the piano. He had a delicate touch and I could hardly hear him above the conversation of the three men, although he was just loud enough for me to recognise one of Schubert's *'Moments Musicaux'*. There were three types of bread and pats of three different butters. I had a large glass of Georgian white wine.

One of the businessmen told a golfing joke, which made all three of them laugh.

'I heard every word,' I said, when I realised that they'd noticed me watching them. 'Nice to hear my nation's tongue.'

'Would you like to join us?' the man who had told the joke asked. He was a Scot called Ian, who had opened a factory in the area. The other two were German – Michael, an international business consultant from near Cologne, the other guy a potential customer for whatever Ian's factory produced. The Germans spoke excellent English. Indeed all four of us did.

'I might still fit in a river trip,' I told them once we got onto the subject of my odyssey.

'If you stop in Cologne,' said Michael, 'you can go all the way to the Netherlands on the Rhine.'

'I'll think about that. I expect I shall be in Cologne.'

'Ring me when you get there and if I'm free I'll take an hour off to show you the City,' he said, handing me his card.

It was a very good meal. I was delighted to have company and to enjoy conversation unrestricted by language.

The hotel, where I was staying, offered no breakfast. I hunted and hunted for a café. My feet were getting tired on the cobbles in my thin Russian shoes. The good thing was that my wanderings brought me to an old street I liked enough to photograph. There were plenty of bars but nowhere did I see people eating or food for sale to eat off the premises. By ten o'clock – yes, ten – I was so desperate I went into Macdonalds, which had an upstairs room, with what must have been one of the most splendid views from a fast food outlet in the world, overlooking as it did a charming busy square. I found an Internet café and started making arrangements to see my two sons and their families when I reached England.

I stayed a second night in L'viv. I needed an early start to get my train. The hotel organised a taxi and a picnic breakfast. I reached the station in plenty of time. Once the train had started I looked out to mist and ground frost, which imparted a mysterious appearance to the landscape. It made me glad that I'd decided to get home by November.

I knew we were at the border when a dog came into the compartment, did a quick inspection and went out. I'd liked what I'd seen of Ukraine. I felt it a pity that I'd rushed through it. Although I was keen to get home, I was also looking forward to Poland.

26. Poland

October 11 – 15

When we got to Przemyśl Glowny there was a high fence made even higher with wire mesh and spikes to stop anyone from getting further than the immediate platform. A Polish dog came into the compartment and did its business – I mean its business of checking for drugs, firearms and stowaways. When the immigration team had finished with us the train shunted into a siding, carefully aligned with a giant jack, which lifted one end of our coach, with passengers still aboard, off the rails while some repair was done underneath. Maybe someone was changing a wheel or Fungus the Bogeyman was re-aligning a bogey. Then we were lowered back onto the line and off we went. The whole operation took only half an hour.

Krakow is one of Europe's great tourist attractions. I found the old centre charming and full of interesting buildings. I stayed at the Hotel Warsawski. And joy, oh joy – it was more or less next to the tourist information office. I hadn't seen one of those for weeks! Thus I learned of a Chopin recital by a young Chopin specialist called Mariusz Adamczak. Where better to hear Chopin than in his native Poland? I know he spent half his time in France but he never abandoned Poland and the Poles are intensely proud of their son. I got a seat in the front row, well positioned to watch the pianist's hands. The programme was introduced by one of the organisers, who spoke first in Polish and then in English. We heard the B-flat minor sonata opus 35 with its 'Marche Funèbre', rendered so poignantly that I bought the disc and got the pianist to sign it.

The sky was grey and by lunchtime it was raining but I still took pleasure in being in the main market square, one of the largest in Europe. There was always something going on. Traditional carriages, each drawn by a pair of horses, were available to take tourists around the old city. These fine animals stood patiently for hours. They wore special over-shoes, twice the size of their horseshoes, to cope with the cobbled streets. Three accordionists played arrangements of popular classics, specialising in those pieces that required them to run up and down the keys at impressive speed. There was also someone dressed up as an ape. I'm sorry I can't tell you more about this attractive city. I had a nasty cold and was feeling too dull to make many notes. But I do remember that a young woman bounced up to me, full of zeal, laughing a little to cover the embarrassment of accosting a stranger.

'You speak English?' she asked.

'Yes,' I said.

I could see she had a supply of narrow cards bearing an image of His Holiness Pope John Paul II, the Polish pope.

'Well, we are concerned about people leaving the Church.'

I wondered why she was telling me this.

'You're a Catholic?' she checked.

'No,' I said, 'I'm an atheist.'

'I'm sorry,' she said, 'I didn't know. Have a good day!'

And she went off to try and find somebody who was a Catholic. She had treated me with more respect than she would have accorded a Protestant, a lapsed Catholic or even a fully paid-up, card-carrying member of the Vatican football team.

I had for a long time decided that I couldn't pass through Poland without visiting the Auschwitz Museum, which was very little out of my way. In the afternoon I went to the station to buy a ticket to Oświęcim, internationally known by the name the Nazis gave it –'Auschwitz'. A local came up to me and tried to sell me his taxi-based tour.

'I don't want a round trip,' I tried to explain. 'I want to incorporate Auschwitz into my journey.

The taxi-driver argued that his tour represented excellent value for money.

'Everything you say to me concerns money,' I said. 'I'm sure your tour is very good but I'd rather do my own thing.'

I took a train that went a long way round to Oświęcim. When we got near, it went very slowly as if out of respect for the millions murdered more than sixty years ago. I had a feeling of foreboding. The first hotel I came to had been closed down. I was rather pleased because I carried on to the International Youth Meeting Centre. I decided there would be no harm in asking if they had accommodation. They did, and it turned out to be the most appropriate place to stay. I had a single room with a shower, the only accommodation in use in one of a number of separate blocks. I was given keys to both the block and the room. It was all very clean and wholesome.

The building as a whole had a virtuous air like a religious place, or indeed what it was – an institution with a high-minded purpose, in this case to foster understanding and reconciliation in a place of the most appalling racial persecution. I'd hoped to enjoy the company of like-minded people. There were a lot of teenagers, mostly German girls. Like other such places dinner was served early but although I arrived late in the dining room they were expecting me and hadn't thrown my portion away. By the time I reached my main course I was eating on my own. At breakfast I was ahead of everyone else, the first to arrive as a matter of fact so again I ate on my own. Nevertheless I was heartened by my visit. I'd known about the museum but not this institution dedicated to relating the museum to today's citizens of Poland, Germany and the world.

'The International Youth Meeting Centre is a place where barriers and prejudices are overcome,' said the brochure. 'It is a place of reflection and dialogue, but at the same time a place of rest and fun.'

The 'fun' notion seemed strange. On reflection I felt it must be right. There was a good library, almost entirely Polish and German books, covering Auschwitz and closely related subjects. Parties of young people came there to visit the museum, learn about the holocaust and develop understanding of racism and international relationships. The world could do with more such initiatives.

The next morning, leaving my luggage at the Centre, I walked to the museum. I didn't know where the entrance was so I made the mistake of walking three-quarters of the way round it. I thus had acquired some idea of how extensive it was before I went in. It was a good day to go, sunny enough to take photographs but cold enough to help me to imagine the part that exposure to bitter weather played in the ill-treatment of the prisoners, for vast numbers died before having to face the gas chambers.

The Museum consisted of the buildings of the death camp almost perfectly preserved and exhibitions within those buildings, which bore witness to what went on there. The tours were very well organised. They had to be, to cope with the large numbers of visitors. On arrival everyone got to see a film to set the scene, grim but dignified and borne along on the funeral march from Beethoven's *'Eroica'* Symphony. The cinema was almost full.

I'd seen some excellent television programmes about the Holocaust. I knew what happened at Auschwitz but I hadn't fully appreciated the overall programme of consistent and deliberate ill-treatment, which hastened death for so many. The scale of the operation is hard to comprehend. It helped that we filed past a long glass-fronted chamber containing nothing but human hair.

Other chambers held heaps of artificial limbs and crutches, spectacles, toothbrushes, shaving brushes, shoes, small children's clothing and suitcases bearing the names of individuals.

We were taken by bus to Auschwitz II also known as Birkenhau. This held three key elements of the complex. First, the railway line that stopped dead at the camp. Second, the remains of the gas chambers and crematoria, blown up by retreating SS men at the end of the War in an attempt to conceal their crimes. Third, the Holocaust Memorial, awesome in its size, stark yet somehow conveying a sense of a humanity utterly denied. It made a fitting end to the tour, which had taken four hours.

Our guide had been an attractive young Polish woman.

'How many of these tours do you do?' I'd asked her.

'Pretty well one every day,' she'd said. 'It's hard.'

I can't remember whether she said she was committed to one year or two of this. It is gruelling work, which must wear these people down. But thank goodness there are those prepared to do it. The purpose of the Museum is to keep alive the memory of the Holocaust and thus to help prevent similar events. As you know, atrocities did not cease with World War II. All the more reason that as many people as possible learn about this particular vast-scale and highly organised horror from the evidence so carefully preserved and so well presented.

After the tour I had a very late lunch, collected my luggage from the Youth Centre and walked to the station. I caught a train to Katowice, where feeling weary I stayed the night.

'I'm tired. I'm losing it,' I wrote in my notebook.

I was certainly losing property. I was missing a comb, a face cloth, a nail brush, a tube of ointment, pencils, biros and a single sock. I'd also lost a pair of gloves, which I'd just bought in Russia against the colder weather I'd been expecting. And then I lost a notebook I'd just started. That's why I can't tell you anything about Katowice, except my efforts to get out of it, as well as a feeling of somehow being separate from the world and the situation I found myself in.

I had a ticket for the 3.25pm to Wraclow and a long time to wait for the train, but I couldn't find out from which platform it was expected to leave. I went to the information desk but there was no one on duty. The train wasn't listed on the timetable. Someone told me to go to Platform 2. I waited there until a passenger told me I should be on Platform 3, where a train was already standing. I showed the driver my ticket. He called an official over who sent me back to Platform 2, where I waited again. No train came except one going the wrong way. There was no announcement. I didn't dare go back to the Information Desk in case I missed the train. The other passengers seemed to know by experience what to do. Bit by bit people quietly left the platform. After half an hour I was the only person left on it. There was no one to ask, so I went back to the Information Desk. I was told the next train to Wraclow was at 5.20. I couldn't find out what had happened to the 3.25. This was the last straw. I threw my rucksack down. I jumped in the air. I stamped my foot. I suppressed screams that would have been terrible. I made the motion of banging my head with my hands. I went back to the Information Desk and with the help of a new, sweet girl, who spoke perfect English, I was able to find out that the 3.25 had either left from platform 1 (while I'd been waiting on platform 2 or 3) or it had been cancelled and hadn't left from anywhere.

'When is the next train?' I double-checked.

'7.20,' she replied.

'Do you mean 19.20?'

'Yes – 7.20.'

'Which platform?'

'Two.'

'Thank you.'

So the 5.20 had vanished too. It was like a bad dream. I walked a few paces away from the desk. Then I went berserk. Up and down the concourse I stamped. I was so totally absorbed in my own desperate rage and feelings of hopelessness that I didn't notice how people were reacting to me.

'Aaaaaaaaaaaah!' I howled, out loud this time.

Then I thought I'd better control myself. I didn't want people coming up to me and asking me if I was all right. But I'd wasted a whole day. All I'd achieved was to lose a notebook, send some e-mails and let trains slip through my hands like blobs of mercury. I decided to get out of the station. In a few minutes I felt that I'd calmed down but even then someone gave me a funny look. I thought I should go straight home – at least as quickly as possible. I'd only got 750 miles to go – I could cancel my *rendez-vous* in Cologne with Michael, the international business consultant. I decided I must keep a cool head.

I went into a pleasant restaurant and had a beer. I was tired. Auschwitz had affected me more than I'd admitted. I breathed deeply, sat down and sipped my beer. Eventually, I got myself together and felt strong enough to go back to the station.

There was an air of chaos, which made me think that my problems weren't all of my own making. It was a Sunday. Maybe there were engineering works at Lidzbark Warminski. Platform 2 was crowded. I made an effort to behave myself. My train wasn't shown on the indicator. It arrived half an hour late. A young man on the platform told me what was happening as he learned it. Thanks to him I got on the train, which was full, although I managed to get a corner seat. The luggage rack was crammed, but I was able to sit down by propping my rucksack up on the window ledge and letting it lean against my shoulder.

Despite the crush I managed to open my map out and a kind woman pointed out which station we'd reached. So I was able to see that I was (literally) on the right track. The guy who'd helped me to take the correct train alerted me when we arrived at Wroclaw and helped me find a hostel, where I had a room to myself. By the time I went out to eat, my spirits were up. In an oriental restaurant I had some fish soup, which was even better than I'd had in China.

The place I was staying in was called the '*Avant Garde* Hostel' and at 6.40 the following morning I discovered why. Personal privacy was under greater threat in the *Avant Garde* than it had been in the All-nations Backpackers' Hotel in Melbourne. Although it was early, I could hear people talking at normal volume so I thought I wouldn't disturb anyone if I had a shower. I opened the door of the bathroom. There were two toilet cubicles and a glass shower cubicle, in which a teenage girl was having a shower. The glass was clear except for the water running down the inside. I shot out before she saw me. I went into the kitchen. Two other teenage girls, dressed of course, were sitting there.

'Excuse me,' I said, 'is that the only bathroom?'

'Yes,' said one of the girls.

'Does that mean that I have to wait until she's finished in the shower?'

'No.'

The girls laughed. I went back to the bathroom. The girl, who'd moved quickly, was out of the shower and into her bra and pants. She looked about fourteen.

'Excuse me,' I said.

'That's all right,' she said sweetly.

I didn't want to be branded a paedophile. When I'd finished in the toilet, she had gone. I seized the chance for a shower. I'd no dressing gown and no towel was supplied so I put my own skimpy towel around me very carefully and got back to my room without anyone seeing me. There were one or two slightly older boys but the hostel was crawling with girls. When I went looking for breakfast I found a wonderful fun atmosphere in the kitchen. When a lot of young girls are doing something new together almost anything strikes them as funny.

'Excuse me is this your bread?' I asked, 'Or is it anybody's?'

'I think that's ours,' said a girl and they all laughed.

'Thank you.'

There was no room in the kitchen so I made myself a cup of tea and took it back to my room. After the disastrous time I'd had on Katowice Station, where I had made such heavy weather of catching a train, I was heartened by a very different experience at Wroclaw. The information displayed was excellent. The notices related clearly to what was happening on the ground. I asked at the Information Desk about travelling to Dresden. I took out my notebook to write down what the woman said but in seconds she handed me a computer print-out giving all the details including the fact that bicycle conveyance was limited on certain trains. I awarded Wroclaw the John Barclay prize for the station easiest to get out of.

I didn't have much time for breakfast so I went to the Kentucky Fried Chicken fast-food outlet, where I had a *burrito* and chips with tea. There was a man with one empty sleeve of his long-sleeve sweatshirt swinging about as he walked around the restaurant, begging with his other hand. His chest was mis-shapen and his eyes looked as if he'd seen something nasty. Most people refused him but because I was about to leave the country I gave him a handful of small coins. I saw him later queuing for food. In full view of anyone who was interested, he found his missing arm inside his shirt and worked it down the empty sleeve ready to pick up the meal he was going to buy with my money.

'Look – he's got two arms!' I felt like shouting, but if you'd seen the trick before, you really didn't want to be reminded of it.

The train left on time. As we went along I stood by the door and when it opened at a stop I would take a photograph, for some of the stations were pretty. At a little place called Węgliniec at the end of the line I had to transfer to a bus to take me to the border town of Zgorzelec. It was a beautiful ride in bright sunshine, which made the autumn colours even more splendid. The sky was an unbroken blue. Up and down we went, twisting and turning, past farms, a wind farm, a river, a lake (or reservoir), delightful woods, attractive villages, pleasant towns. By the time we got to Zgorzelec I was the only passenger. A two-coach train was waiting to take me on. It was very comfortable and quiet, as I made a peaceful, almost dreamlike progress towards the actual border with Germany.

27. Germany

October 15 – 18

The train took me a mile or two over the border to Görlitz, where I was the only person seen by the immigration authorities before they let new passengers on. Two officials visited me. One of them looked at my passport.

'*Danke schön!*' he said.

'*Danke schön!*' I replied with feeling.

The whole thing lasted 40 seconds. It was the quickest, most painless border crossing I'd encountered anywhere in the world. Then we continued to Dresden. I'd been to Germany before but I'd never seen the east of the country. It struck me as very pleasant – prosperous and orderly. Even the allotments were tidy, and laid out as gardens rather than vegetable patches. And each had a shed almost big enough to be somebody's main dwelling.

In Dresden I cried when I saw Saturday's Times on sale. (This was Monday.) I bought it of course. And when I found I could draw euros from an ATM, I felt I was almost home. The City was warmer than anywhere I'd been in Poland. People were sitting out at 5pm. I was glad of the sun because my cold was bad. The water in my hotel was hot enough straight from the tap for inhalations and after several of these I could breathe through my nose again. I decided to take a day's sick leave in Dresden. In the morning after breakfast I booked in for a second night. I'd been given a 'Do not disturb' notice in three languages. I put this on the outside handle of my door and closed it. I lay on my bed and fell asleep. A while later I heard a tapping on the door, like someone trying to knock without disturbing the person inside – virtually impossible and of course pointless. I ignored it, assuming that with the notice in place no one would be knocking at my door. It must have been someone else's. Some time later the timid knock came again. I got off the bed and moved towards the door. As I did so it opened and a chambermaid stood there. She pointed to the 'Do not disturb' sign, which had swung round to show the 'Please clean my room' side. I took the sign off and demonstrated to her that because there were two bends in the door handle it was an easy matter for any 'Do not disturb' sign worth its salt to turn completely round without once falling to the floor.

'I'm ill,' I said. 'I need to rest.'

She pointed to twelve on her watch.

'You have to be out by twelve,' she seemed to be saying.

'*Morgen* (tomorrow),' I said.

The news that I was staying another day had not reached the poor girl, who went away. I meanwhile waited till she'd gone to clean another room. I opened the door and found that the card had again swung round. So I took some sticky tape from my emergency repair kit and stuck the notice in position. This problem must arise all the time. Such cards have been around for half a century or more. Handles with bends in them ditto. The action of closing the door reverses the notice. Do the people who make the cards and the people who run the hotels never stay in hotels? Do they never talk to the chambermaids? *Mein Gott!* Do I have to go round the world and write a book about it before the hotel industry wakes up? I'm not having a go specifically at the German hotel industry. It's a world-wide problem, except in expensive hotels which have a sign that lights up at the touch of a button. The solution is easy – and it doesn't cost a cent! You don't need a card that says, 'Please clean my room'. The staff will clean it if the guest doesn't indicate he doesn't want to be disturbed. All you need is the 'Do not disturb' card. This should be printed on both sides. When it swings round the message doesn't change. End of problem. I'm just a writer! If I can work it out why can't the industry?

I went out to explore the city. The Dresden air-raid in February 1945 was one of the heaviest by the Allies against Germany in World War II – controversial or outright shameful according to your point of view. Many believe it was out of revenge for what the Nazis had done to Coventry. The night of the bombing, the city was overcrowded with some 200,000 refugees. The numbers killed in the bombing and the subsequent fires have been estimated as between 50,000 and 150,000. More than 30,000 buildings were flattened. Sixty-two years later the beautiful, mainly baroque, centre had largely been painstakingly restored. The magnificent Frauenkirche was completed as recently as 2005. Now, a visitor who did not know the history would not be able to guess it. In the middle of this amazing place of renaissance I saw a big deep hole, but this turned out to be an archaeological dig – for the remains of far older structures.

The next day, in Frankfurt, I went to an Italian restaurant called Vapiano, based on pasta and pizza. The novelty was the card system, which was explained briefly when I arrived. I was told you could sit where you liked. I did so and studied the menu. Nothing happened. Bit by bit I worked out what I was supposed to do. Basically you do your own waiting.

'Are you ready to order, sir?' you ask yourself.

'Yes, please' you reply.

'What would you like?'

'I'd like the *spaghetti bolognese*, please.'

'Well, go and get it yourself!' you tell yourself.

And you find the right counter, hand in your card, ask for what you want and somebody swipes your card – in the nice sense of the word, of course. It's a smart card. Not that smart. If it were it would keep you right.

'Are you mad, feller,' it would say, 'ordering your *spaghetti bolognese* first? By the time you've queued up at the other counters for your salad and your wine, the spaghetti will be stone cold. Get those first and *then* your main course. The human beings won't tell you these things. You should ask me next time – I'm *smart*!'

The next morning I checked out of the hotel. I started speaking German, but the receptionist spoke such good English we soon switched.

'Is that all?' I asked.

'Sat is all,' he replied.

I picked up my bags.

'Vere are you go-ink?' he demanded.

'To the station,' I said.

'Don't you vant se taxi?'

'No, I want to walk. I like to walk. I'm going to be on the train for five hours. I got here by walking. It's only 300 metres.'

'But se cab driver is he-ah!'

I hadn't ordered a cab.

'Look, don't you understand? If I prefer to walk, it doesn't matter how wonderful the service is.'

I turned to the driver.

'Danke schön,' I said.

I picked up my bags and walked out. The air seemed wonderfully fresh. Most of the way was pedestrianised. I could go more directly than the taxi. I would get there just as quickly and more healthily.

The train was fast, smooth and quiet as a Rolls Royce. I didn't have a reserved seat so had to dodge about. Then I hit on the idea of moving to the dining car, which was nearly empty. Here I could get to the big clean windows to take photographs. This was difficult because, although it didn't feel like it, we were going extremely fast. The landscape was beautiful and very tidy. This was the first time I'd seen plenty of big signs clearly showing the names of the stations. The German railways are even better than the French.

In every country I'd been in I'd had good opportunities for people watching and it had become a habit. In the restaurant car of this German train, on the next table were a couple of women, one about 25, striking if not beautiful, the other ten years older, plainer and somewhat butch. 'Butch' did most of the talking, the younger woman hanging on every word. The young woman was facing me. I observed her expressions and body language. The pair seemed to be in a world of their own. For some reason I felt a mild antipathy towards them.

Then a significant and alarming thing happened. It occurred to me that they were speaking German very strangely. Then I realised it wasn't German at all – it was Spanish! Immediately – but immediately – my attitude changed. Suddenly these were fascinating women. The younger woman was expressive. The other was a kind, sensitive person. They were good friends.

I started to try to justify my prejudice. I like Spanish people, I said to myself, because they're warm, earthy, direct, passionate and fun, which happens to be to my taste. I just don't feel so comfortable with German people – nothing wrong with that, I argued. *But these were the same people!* Nothing had changed except the label. I had caught myself out. Deep down I was a racist! I had fallen into the trap. The observation becomes a generalisation. The generalisation becomes the label. The label becomes the starting point. It was a shocking if salutary experience.

I can't tell you much about Frankfurt, except that within spitting distance of the hostel where I stayed there were enough sex shops to sadden the chirpiest visitor. And if you could get past them there was a fine Indian restaurant run by real Indian people who did a first-class mulligatawny soup and a garlic naan bread to die for.

The next day I went by train to Cologne. I rang Michael, the international business consultant I'd met in L'viv. Someone in his office told me he was out of Germany – not surprising with his line of work. I walked out of the station. It was grey and damp. It would have been nice, I thought, to have a look at Cologne, but even nicer to press on for home. I went back into the station and took a train to Brussels.

28. Belgium, France, the Channel Tunnel, the United Kingdom

October 18

Announcements on the train were made in four languages – German, Flemish, French and English. The names of the stations had begun to look Flemish or French rather than German so I guessed that by then we were in Belgium. As soon as I got to Brussels, I went to investigate the Eurostar trains to London. A big notice said that due to a strike in France some trains were cancelled and others would terminate at Lille. In the ticket office they weren't taking bookings for the next morning as they didn't know which trains would be running. I decided not to stay in Brussels in case I got stuck there. It was after 5.30pm. The first train to London left at 5.59pm. I managed to get on this. I was amused to hear the voices of British people speaking English on their mobile phones.

'Hullo, darling, it's me – I'm on the train.'

The sun was setting in the west – as it does. I could see it through the window on the left-hand side. That meant we were going north, which didn't seem right. Sitting near me was a gorgeous blonde business woman with big arms.

'This is the Eurostar to London?' I asked her.

'I hope so,' she replied, 'otherwise we're all on the wrong train.'

When she got up later I saw she was a giantess. She could see over the top of the luggage shelf. No wonder she had big arms – if she hadn't, she have been out of proportion. I bet her sons would be tall! Through the gap between the seats I could see the screen of the laptop of the guy in front of me. He'd have had no idea I could read his work. He was lucky I wasn't an industrial spy!

This one train would take me through a bit of Belgium, the northernmost tip of France, the Channel Tunnel and Kent, to London. I was virtually home. After Dresden the journey had gone very quickly. I had made a full circle of the earth taking in the antipodes. I had tasted the artificial delights of a luxury cruise. I had encountered evangelical Christians in Florida, ridden on Greyhound Buses through the Southern States, warmed to the affectionate people of Mexico, squeezed in with the locals on noisy buses through Central America, been mugged in Panama, marvelled at its Canal, experienced a peaceful and civilised life aboard a very British freight ship across the Pacific, taken in Tahiti, been enchanted by the Coromandel Peninsula of New Zealand, relaxed and laughed with Australians, taken a container ship across the Indian Ocean, found my way up South East Asia, struggled across China, hurried the length of Kazakhstan, nipped across a bit of Russia, in Europe touched some key sites of the Second World War and confronted some of my own prejudices.

I'd been away for 206 days. I'd travelled some 30,000 miles, as much as possible by land. I'd traversed three oceans, 23 countries, two deserts, some jungly bits and numerous cities. I'd crossed the International Date Line once, the Equator twice and myself 1,724 times. I'd spoken English, French and a tiny bit of German; I'd struggled with Spanish, and I'd been totally baffled by nine other languages. To do what I did, all you need is plenty of time, a touch of madness, not to say bloody-mindedness, flexibility, alertness, a cast-iron stomach, a dollop of luck and a flat wallet under your shirt to keep your passport and bank cards safe.

I took satisfaction in being a traveller not a tourist, mingling with the locals and using their infrastructures. I concluded that the main differences between peoples are between rich and poor, rather than between west and east or north and south, or the way people look. The difficulties I had were over details. The misunderstandings were due to language and differences of approach, not fundamentals. Every place has its own traditions but diluting them is a world-wide culture, a vast pot in which many spoons are dipped.

Not a drop of aviation fuel was combusted in the course of my odyssey. Even someone better organised than me would find it a slow and tricky business to visit so many places without flying. The world is geared up for air travel. But there are many people who do not wish to fly for reasons of health or comfort. There are many retired people who have the time for more leisurely modes of travel. I experienced much that would normally be beyond the reach of the traveller relying on aeroplanes. There are a large number of people like me who recognise that air travel is the fastest-growing contributor to greenhouse gases and who would use surface transport to a greater extent if it were more readily available. What we need is a network of passenger transport that does not rely on the aeroplane. We already have fast, comfortable trains across Western Europe and memorable one-off rail journeys further afield. There are some excellent long-distance bus services. We have fast-craft ferries across the English Channel. Some cruise liners offer part-cruises. If, as I believe, the demand is there, enterprising operators will develop the business and travel agents specialising in surface travel will spring up to arrange the bookings and help passengers make the connections.

Travellers who speak English have a wonderful advantage. English is spoken to a degree almost everywhere – millions have it as their second or third language. It is the language of the Internet, of marketing, of finance and of popular culture. The number of English speakers is growing because people everywhere know that, to get on in the world, English is the language they will need. Having said that, I wish I had learnt Spanish. While I proved that you can manage with some help and just English, if you want to get to know the people you meet, you need to speak their language.

Travelling by Eurostar and the Channel Tunnel I glided to England with little fuss and no fanfare. I arrived at Waterloo at 7.30pm British Summer Time. The first thing I did was to walk over to Platform 11 of the South-west Trains service, where on March 26th I'd caught the train to Southampton at the start of my travels. Thus at 7.35pm on October 18th I completed the loop. I was tired, but relieved and very happy to be home.

In these times when we all have to be aware of the world's problems, I feel I have become more of a global citizen. Everywhere I went, people were kind and friendly. Some generous individuals put themselves out considerably to help me on my way. Why, oh why, if the world is full of decent people, who are so helpful to complete strangers like me, why is it blighted by hunger, exploitation, hatred, intolerance, persecution, organised cruelty and war? I had come back with much to think about.

About the Author

JOHN BARCLAY studied medicine in London before embarking on a long career with Marks & Spencer, culminating in 15 years as Company Speechwriter. In his spare time he developed as an entertainer and wrote comedy material for himself and others. In 1998 he took early retirement and moved to Dorset to concentrate on creative writing.

For six years he contributed a light-hearted column *'Diary of an Incomer'* to the Frome Valley & Isle of Purbeck Gazette. He became a performance poet and brought out his first book of poems *'The Blood of Others'* in 2005. He has recently developed a way of presenting poetry he calls *'Poetry à la Carte'*, in which members of the audience choose pieces from a menu, for him to perform.

John is a widower. He has two sons, two daughters-in-law and four grandchildren. He is a member of Dorset Humanists. His interests include walking, most of the arts and world peace.

www.johnbarclayink.com